Preface

Craft and Design in Metal is a companion volume to 'Craft and Design in Wood' (formerly 'Woodwork for You'). A basic text is linked to a generous number of drawings and **photographs in a combination ideal for fourth and fifth form pupils of all abilities.**

The book begins with a detailed account of all common metals and alloys and a subsidiary section on their possible use incorporating wood and plastics. Basic benchwork processes, essential tools and finishes follow in a logical sequence and separate sections are given to tinplate work and beaten forms. Casting and the traditional craft of forgework are described in sufficient detail to satisfy non-specialist needs and the likely combination of metals with wood and plastics is covered.

In the machine tool section the use of power to saw, drill, mill and shape precede lathework operations. The emphasis is on safety throughout especially where the use of portable electric tools is concerned.

Techniques allied to basic metalwork processes include sculpture, enamelling, jewellery and upholstery and each is described in a stimulating manner.

A section on technical drawing describes traditional methods and extends into more relevant methods of graphical communication. Sketch techniques lead into examples of how design planning and principles can be related in a practical way.

Any student needing to write a project on craftwork will find the final section an invaluable guide.

The author uses his experience as a Chief Examiner in craft subjects to explain to students how they can best approach a craft examination. Each type of question is explained and there are copious examples of practice questions based on past papers.

Contents

Materials – Properties of Metals

There are three main types of metal:

1. **Ferrous** metals which contain mainly iron
2. **Non-ferrous** metals which rarely contain any iron
3. **Alloys** which are mixtures of different metals.

Pure metals are not often used because they do not have the qualities or properties of carefully mixed alloys.

Metals are described by their physical, mechanical and chemical properties. Thus aluminium may be described as a lightweight metal, bluish-white in colour, malleable, ductile, and a good conductor of electricity. It has good fluidity but a low tensile strength.

The following terms are often used to describe metals.

Brittleness is an undesirable characteristic. Metal which will break without bending can be dangerous. Brittleness is the opposite of toughness.

Colour helps us to identify metals. We can learn to tell the difference between yellow metals such as gold, gilding metal and brass.

Conductivity describes the ease with which heat or electricity travels through the material. The best conductors are silver, copper and aluminium. That is why copper and aluminium are used for cooking pans and electricity cables.

Ductility describes the property of metals which can be stretched cold without breaking — essential for making wire. Do not confuse ductility with malleability.

Elasticity is the ability of a metal to return to its original size or shape. Springs have a high elasticity.

Fusibility describes the ease with which a metal melts. Metals melt at different temperatures and in a molten state are used in casting and for soldering and welding.

Hardness describes how easy or difficult it is to mark or scratch a surface. Surfaces are tested either with a hard steel ball or a diamond point and given a number which describes their hardness. Hard metals are difficult to cut.

Magnetism is a property usually found in iron and steel.

Malleability allows metals to withstand being bent, hammered and rolled without breaking. Some metals such as gold and aluminium can be rolled until they are paper-thin. Do not confuse malleability with ductility.

Tenacity describes the tensile strength of a metal — how strong it is resisting a direct pull. For example, mild steel has ten times the tensile strength of aluminium, and chrome steel has about four times the tensile strength of mild steel.
Compression strength and sheer strength are two other ways of measuring the 'strength' of a metal.

Toughness allows a metal to be bent or twisted and to resist impact without breaking. Metals with a high tensile strength are usually rather brittle.

Specific gravity is the weight of metal compared with the weight of *an equal volume* of water.
Iron is three times the weight of aluminium — lead is heavier still.

Ferrous Metals

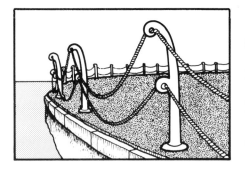

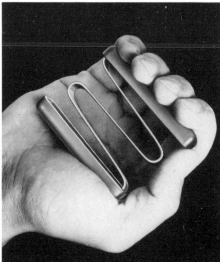

Ferrous metals combine iron and carbon in varying amounts and all of them are likely to rust when exposed to the weather.

Grey cast iron is an alloy of iron and about 3.5 per cent carbon. It is a brittle material which cannot be forged, but the high carbon content makes it melt and pour easily. It will absorb vibrations better than other ferrous metals so it is used for the large castings on machines, such as drill-stand bases and lathe beds. Unfortunately, it is brittle and may break when struck.

Malleable cast iron has a less brittle surface. Grey cast iron is heat-treated to remove some of the carbon from the surfaces to be machined.

The uprights which support seaside railings are made in grey cast iron. The body of a woodworker's smoothing plane, with its accurately machined sole, is made in malleable cast iron.

Dead-mild steel has only 0.15 per cent carbon and is the basis of tin plate – the thin layer of tin preventing rust.

Mild steel contains 0.15 to 0.35 per cent carbon and is three times more ductile than high carbon steel. It is used for nuts, bolts and tubes.

Black mild steel is coated with a grey scale from oxidation during the process of hot rolling. This is chemically cleaned and cold rolled to an accurate size and is then referred to as *bright drawn mild steel* (BDMS).

Medium carbon steel contains 0.35 to 0.65 per cent carbon and is relatively hard and tough.

Wrought-iron is almost pure iron and is both malleable and ductile. The lack of carbon means that it cannot be melted into a liquid state for casting, but it is excellent for forging. Wrought iron develops an iron-oxide surface which gives it self-protection against rust. It is expensive and has been replaced by dead-mild steel. The elegant wrought iron railings and balconies of the Georgian town of Bath have withstood two centuries of weathering.

The Qualcast 'Turfglider' lawnmower uses a wide variety of steels treated in different ways.

High carbon steel, often referred to as tool steel, contains 0.65 to 1.15 per cent carbon. It is at least twice as hard as mild steel.
Above 0.9 per cent carbon the grain contains a substance called cementite which makes the steel brittle and unsuitable for anything structural. Its most important property is the way in which it is increased in hardness at the end of the hardening process.

Cold chisels (0.8 per cent carbon) are hard but not brittle. A metal file (1.0 per cent carbon) is much harder but is relatively brittle.

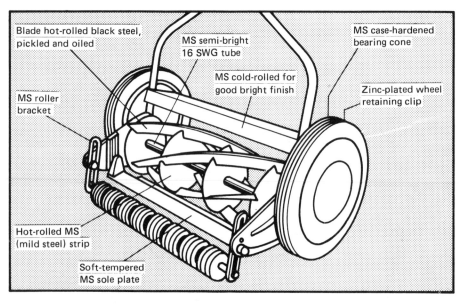

Blade hot-rolled black steel, pickled and oiled

MS semi-bright 16 SWG tube

MS case-hardened bearing cone

MS cold-rolled for good bright finish

Zinc-plated wheel retaining clip

MS roller bracket

Hot-rolled MS (mild steel) strip

Soft-tempered MS sole plate

Non-ferrous Metals

Non-ferrous metals *do not* contain either iron or carbon and *do not* rust.

Copper is a reddish-brown metal which is malleable and ductile. We use copper in the home for water pipes, electric wiring and high-quality cookware, as it is an excellent conductor of heat and electricity. Half the world's copper production is used in this way. A large part of the remainder is used in making alloys such as brass. Copper hardens as it is worked.

The photograph shows the London Central Mosque designed by Sir Frederick Gibberd. It has a dome covered in copper sheeting.

Zinc is a bluish-grey metal which is used mainly as the corrosion-resisting coating of galvanized steel. It is mixed with copper to produce both brass and gilding metal.
Zinc has a fairly low melting point (420°C) which means it is ideal for the pressure die-casting techniques used in industry. Zinc, with small amounts of aluminium, magnesium and copper added, produces an alloy used for casting carburettors and washing machine components.

Lead is a bluish-grey, heavy and extremely malleable metal. Because water and acids will not corrode it, it used to be the traditional material for household plumbing.
As it can cause lead poisoning its use in the home is now limited to waterproof flashings for slate and tile roofs.

Tin is a silvery, malleable and ductile metal used mainly as the thin rust-resistant coating of tinplate. The photograph shows a model of an Irish Guards drummer and mascot cast in bright pewter alloy, which is 90 per cent tin.

Aluminium is a bluish-white metal which is malleable and ductile. In its pure form it is weak so it is usually alloyed with other metals. The alloys combine strength with lightness so they are ideal for working castings such as engines. Aluminium is used as a cheaper alternative to copper in some electrical work. It is also a good conductor of heat. The photograph shows a range of seamless aluminium cookware which has been stamped and given a non-stick silicone surface.

Chimney stack

Roof tiles

Steel Alloys

We have seen how steel is affected by the quantity of carbon in it and that high carbon steel can be given heat treatment to change its working properties.

The quality of steel can also be changed by adding to it small quantities of pure metals to produce *alloy steels*. Common additives are nickel, tungsten, chromium and manganese. Molybdenum, vanadium and titanium are used for specialist steels in the manufacture of crankshafts and parts of aero-engines which need to be hard at high working temperatures.

Nickel makes a steel which is tough and which resists impact and corrosion — ideal for rails, points and parts of railway engines.

Nickel and chromium are both used in the manufacture of gears like the Sturmey Archer AW 3-speed hub.

Tungsten is used to tip cutting tools such as drills and the woodworker's circular saw. At high speed the tips become hot, but the tungsten steel keeps its cutting edge.

Chromium is present in large quantities in good-quality cutlery and is about 13 per cent of stainless steel. Chromium and molybdenum allow Reynolds 501 cromalloy-M bicycle tubing to be made thin, light and strong.

Manganese is present in most steels and its presence in different parts of the Raleigh sports bicycle is carefully controlled to help produce different wearing qualities. For example, the steering column and the main frame are both made from mild steel. The column has about three times more manganese (1.20 per cent) than the frame so that it will resist the wear of a lifetime of use.

Iron

Iron is the most commonly used metal. It is easily cast and made into a wide range of alloy steels. It is also easily available in large quantities.

Rocks which contain more than 20 per cent iron can be referred to as iron ores. The richest black ores (65 per cent iron), called 'magnetite', are mined in Sweden, the USA, the USSR and Canada.

Blast furnaces

The iron is produced by melting the ore in a blast furnace, using coke as a fuel and limestone as a flux. The process is a continuous one over a number of years until the brick-lined heavy steel furnace needs relining.

A continuous feed of washed and ground ore, coke and limestone is tipped into a revolving hopper. A double bell system prevents the gases from the furnace escaping. These carbon dioxide gases are fed through a dust extractor into a 'cowper' stove. Here they are mixed with air and burnt. When the temperature is above 500°C, hot air is blasted through a bustle pipe and through a dozen evenly spaced tuyères into the heart of the furnace.

The blast of hot air causes the coke to burn fiercely, producing carbon monoxide (CO) gas. This combines with the iron oxides to become carbon dioxide (CO_2) gas.

This 'reduction' process turns the iron into a mass which sinks into the hotter part of the furnace. It melts into the hearth. The limestone mixes with many of the impurities to form a liquid slag which floats on top of the molten iron. This liquid slag is run off through the slag notch. It becomes solid as it cools and is used as a filler for road building, or ground down and remade into building blocks.

The molten iron is run out of the iron notch (taphole) into *pigs*. These are castings of a convenient size for use in making cast iron or steel.

Cupola furnaces

This furnace is designed to melt and refine pig iron to make grey cast iron. The inclusion of steel scrap with the pig iron regulates the carbon content of the cast iron produced. Alternate layers of iron, coke and limestone are put on top of a bed of coke through which the molten metal flows into a hearth. The liquid slag and molten metal are run off in the same manner as with the blast furnace.

The furnace is also used to melt scrap iron for use in steel furnaces.

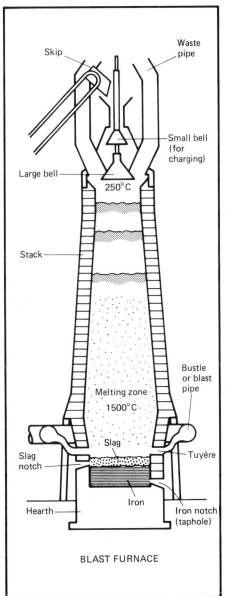

BLAST FURNACE

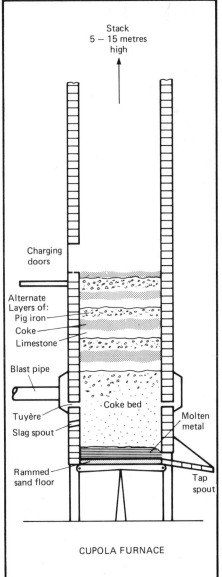

CUPOLA FURNACE

Chemical Processes

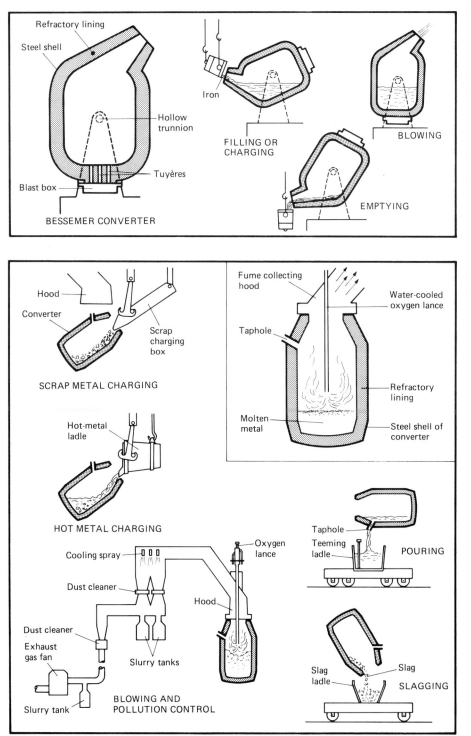

SCRAP METAL CHARGING

HOT METAL CHARGING

BLOWING AND POLLUTION CONTROL

POURING

SLAGGING

There are hundreds of different steels each made to a slightly different recipe but each having the common iron base. The iron which is produced in a blast furnace contains varying amounts of carbon, manganese, silicon, phosphorus and sulphur. The change that takes place when making pig iron into steel involves reducing the amounts of these elements.

There are two chemical processes — the *acid* process and the *basic* process. Most steels are made using the basic process. Lime is added to allow the phosphorus and sulphur to be removed in the slag.

The refining of molten pig iron to make steel is by the process of oxidation. Oxygen is put into the metal and this combines with unwanted materials to produce oxides. These oxides are either absorbed in the slag or passed out in a gas. This **Bessemer process** was a major breakthrough. Sir Henry Bessemer discovered that air blasted through hot metal would reduce the elements in the metal.

The basic oxygen process (LDAC)

This is most common method in use today. Pure oxygen has replaced air, and the oxygen is blown on to the hot metal from above. A modern furnace may have a capacity of nearly 400 tonnes and yet the process takes less than an hour! A typical melt will consist of 30 per cent selected scrap metal and 70 per cent pig iron. In the newest furnaces this will be delivered in its molten state directly from the blast furnace. A hood is placed over the furnace to draw off the unwanted gas, the water-cooled oxygen lance inserted and fluxes added as soon as the 'blow' takes place.
The furnace is tilted to tap the steel from underneath the slag. It is poured into a ladle where the alloying elements can be added. The furnace is then tilted in the opposite direction to remove the slag.

Electric arc furnaces

These are smaller and are used for producing the highest quality steels. The roof of the furnace is removed to insert the cold metal (often selected steel scrap) and the fluxes, and is then closed up again.
The three graphite electrodes are lowered and the powerful electric current switched on. This creates an arc across the gap between electrode and metal which produces enough heat to melt the metal. As the clean arc does not produce any impurities, close control over the finished product is possible.

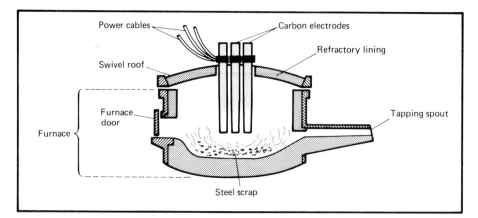

Heat Treatment

Tools made from plain carbon steel need to be heat-treated to give them the special characteristics which make them work well.

There are four basic treatments — two for stock materials and two for tools.

Annealing is done to make low carbon steel as soft as possible and to soften steels hardened by cold-working. The heated steel is allowed to cool slowly in the furnace.

Normalizing is done to low carbon steel to return it to its original condition. It is heated to a bright cherry red and allowed to cool in the air.

Hardening is done to higher carbon steels by heating them to between 700 and 900°C depending on the percentage of carbon in the steel. (The higher the carbon, the lower the temperature.) The temperature of the steel is quickly reduced by quenching it in water or a suitable oil.

Tempering is done to higher carbon steels to remove the brittleness caused by the hardening process. The steel is heated to between 100 and 400°C, depending on use. (A range of 230–300°C covers most objects.)

The photographs show high carbon steel files and screwdrivers which have been hardened to 820°C. The files are tempered to 125°C to give a hard cutting edge (67 HRC). The screwdrivers are tempered to 270°C to make them softer (about 56 HRC).
Alloy steels are hardened at much higher temperatures. For example, Sandvik drill burrs containing cobalt, chromium, vanadium and molybdenum are hardened at 1200°C and tempered at 550°C.

In industry, hardening and tempering are accurately controlled by electronics. In workshops, the *colour* of the metal is the only guide. It is essential to work out of sunlight and to have clean metal surfaces — surface oil or dust will affect the oxide colours.
Hardening takes place in the 'cherry red' range of temperatures. The heat from a torch should allow the metal to heat through and should always be directed away from a cutting edge.
Quenching must take place immediately. To avoid distortion, plunge the bar end-on. Plunge thin strips edge-first, and plunge thick parts before thin ones.

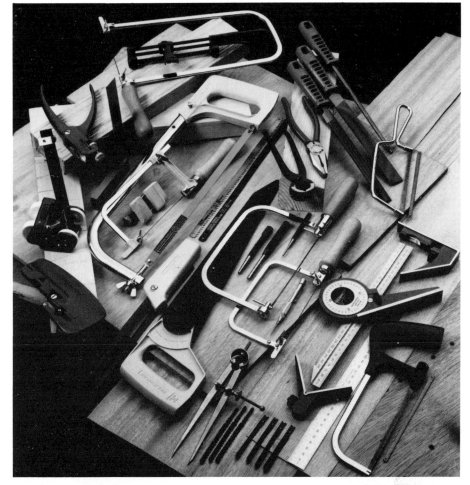

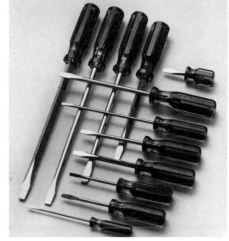

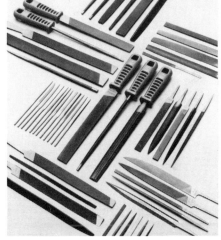

Tempering chart						
Temp.(°C)	230	240	250	260	270	300
Colour	Pale straw	Dark straw	Brown	Brownish purple	Purple	Blue
	Scrapers Hammers Scribers Lathe tools for brass	Lathe tools for mild steel Drills and reamers Milling cutters	Punches Taps and dies	Rivet snaps Plane irons Cold chisels Wood drills	Screwdriver axes Forging sets Wood chisels	Steel rules Springs Spanners

Hardening chart						
Temp.(°C)	500 — 550	550 — 600	700 — 800	800 — 850	850 — 900	900 — 1000
Colour	Dull red	Red	Dark Cherry red	Cherry red	Light cherry red	Orange

Aluminium

There is more aluminium in the world than any other metal, but it is only worth getting from Bauxite ore. Up to a century ago the chemical process needed to produce aluminium was so expensive that the metal was considered precious.

A hundred years ago reduction by electrolysis was invented. A decade later Karl Bayer developed a method of mixing crushed ore with caustic soda to separate the metallic elements from all the impurities. Crystals made from the solution are washed and heated to make pure alumina, which is used in the Hall-Herault reduction process.
In this process the alumina is mixed with molten cryolite which dissolves it. The massive electric charge used to heat the cryolite decomposes it and separates the aluminium from waste oxygen. The oxygen is released and the heavier, 99 per cent pure aluminium is tapped from the bottom of the tank to make ingots.

The common properties of aluminium are described on page 7.

Duralumin is one of the oldest alloys with the strength of steel and the weight of aluminium. It is made up of 92 per cent aluminium and about 4 per cent copper, with less than 1 per cent each of silicon, manganese, magnesium ferrite and a small quantity of titanium which improves strength at high temperatures.

There is a remarkable range of modern alloys each made to a British Standard number. Two common types suitable for casting in the workshop are known as LM4, a general-purpose metal (92 per cent Al, 5 per cent Si, 3 per cent Cu), and LM6 which is best for detailed work where its silicon content (12 per cent) allows it to flow more freely.

Uses

Aluminium is extremely *ductile* and ideal for extruding and spinning. One photograph shows a Brook Motor where the extruded casing keeps the motor clean and dissipates heat. The cooling fan is housed in a die-cast aluminium casing.

Much smaller extrusions can be used to protect the edges of wood and to join together sheets of fibreboard.

The chip pan and lid are common items of aluminium cookware. The body of the pan is produced by the spinning process. Aluminium is extremely *malleable* and is ideal for stamping. The pan's lid is formed by a die in a heavy press.

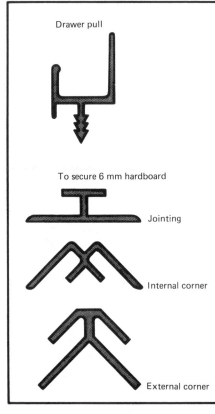

Drawer pull

To secure 6 mm hardboard

Jointing

Internal corner

External corner

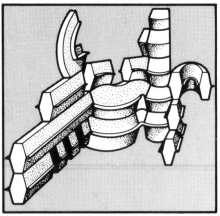

Eduardo Paolozzi is a sculptor who uses aluminium creatively. His outdoor sculpture 'A7 1972' is made from aluminium castings which have been welded together.

Aluminium is so ductile that it can be rolled very thinly. It is used for food cartons and kitchen foil.

Copper

Only copper, gold and silver are discovered in pure metal form, but most of our copper is obtained from ores. A process of smelting was used five thousand years ago, and cutting edges were obtained simply by hammering the copper. Early metalworkers had discovered that *copper work-hardens*.

There are a vast number of copper minerals and over half the world production comes from the USSR, the USA, Zambia and Chile. To produce copper the ore is first crushed, washed and filtered. Then, with the addition of lime flux, it is roasted to remove excess sulphur. This produces a 'matte' containing 70 per cent copper which is blown in a similar manner to the Bessemer process (see page 10) to oxidize the impurities to form a slag. The 'blister' copper poured at this stage is porous and brittle and has to be further refined by an electrolytic process.

Apart from some applications where high conductivity is needed, pure copper is rarely used — alloyed copper is most common.

Brasses, copper alloyed with up to 50 per cent zinc, are yellow in appearance but have varying characteristics.

Gilding metal (10–20 per cent zinc) is used for architectural metalwork and is easily enamelled. The goblet shown will appear to be made from gold because the metal has a golden colour.

Cartridge brass (30 per cent zinc) is ideal for pressings, and *Muntz brass* (40 per cent zinc) works easily when it is hot.

In the eighteenth century ships' hulls were protected by copper sheeting. This is a modern yacht hull made from a **copper-nickel** alloy which has a high resistance to sea-water.

Gun metal is brass alloyed with tin. The most common is UK 'copper' coinage (3 per cent tin and 1.5 per cent zinc).

Phospor bronze (10 per cent tin and 0.5 per cent phosphorus) is used for bearings and gears when strength and corrosion resistance are needed.

Aluminium bronze has the strength of mild steel and its aluminium content (5–10 per cent) allows the surface to oxidize and prevent further corrosion. In thin sheet form this can be cold-worked to cover roof constructions and is used as a lightning conductor.

Copper provides an even cooking heat when welded to the base of a stainless steel pan. In powdered form it can be *sintered* to make bearings, or held in suspension to create metallic paints. It is a most adaptable and valuable metal.

Summary of Ferrous Metals

Material	Melting point (°C)	Constituents	Appearance	Workshop tests for identification						Working Characteristics	Uses
				Drop on stone floor	Drill	Grind at high speed	Hand file	Heat to red heat and quench	Heat to red heat and hammer		
Grey cast iron	1200–1400	Carbon content varies: A basic iron may contain 3.5% carbon 1.5% phosphorus 1.0% manganese 1.0% silicon A trace of undesirable sulphur Remainder iron	Grey colour Granular texture on a fracture Black specks are evidence of free carbon	Dull note, no ring	Small chips which crumble easily	A few dull red sparks Some bright bursts	Files cleanly Fine black powder and small grey chips	No change but may crack	Crumbles	A brittle metal which has a softer core under harder skin Strong in compression but will not bend Casts well Absorbs vibrations Cannot be forged	Large machine castings including slideways (the free carbon helps lubrication) Cylinder blocks and piston rings
Wrought iron	1600–1800	At least 99% iron Remainder impurities	Scaley, developing a fine protective rust. On a fracture it is coarse and grey	Dull note with metallic ring	Curly shavings with cracks	Some bright yellow sparks	Drags and eventually clogs with white grains-pining	No change	Works easily	Soft malleable and ductile so that it bends, forges and welds easily. Cannot be cast	Hooks and chains Transformers
Mild steel	1300–1500	0.15–0.35% carbon Remainder iron with traces of impurities	Black mild steel covered with grey oxide scale Bright drawn mild steel (BDMS) is white	Ringing note	Long, grey shavings which curl into a spiral	Shower of long white sparks	Even texture and solid smooth finish	Little change	Works easily	Tough and ductile. Bends easily but will break when it becomes fatigued. Forges and welds easily	General metalworking Structural work Nuts, bolts and tube
Carbon steels	1200–1400 varies	Medium carbon 0.35–0.65% carbon High carbon 0.65–0.90% carbon Tool steel (HSS) 0.9–1.15% carbon	Smooth black oxide surface	High ringing note	Very difficult because of hardness Small broken swarf	Long bright yellow sparks Smaller red sparks with highest carbon steels	Very difficult because of hardness	Becomes hard and brittle — more so with higher carbon content	Works well but harder than mild steel	Brittle when hardened but tempering makes them more ductile and tougher. Forges well.	Most tools for mechanical and cutting jobs

Summary of Non-ferrous Metals

Material	Melting Point (°C)	Constituents	Appearance	Working characteristics	Uses
Aluminium	660	100% is an element	Light grey Brighter when machined	Light in weight. Machines easily, producing long curly shavings when drilled or turned. Oxides resist corrosion and make welding difficult. Polishes well	Car bodies. Cookware. Food wrapping
Aluminium alloys Duralumin		92% aluminium, 4% copper 1% silicon, ferrite manganese and magnesium 0.3% titanium		Harder to work than normal aluminium. The small magnesium content makes the metal harder and the titanium keeps the strength at high temperatures. Age hardens	Strength when hot allows use for engine castings
Typical casting alloys		88% aluminium 10% silicon and 2% others		The higher silicon content makes the metal run freely	Ideal for general casting
Copper	1080		Brownish pink	Malleable and ductile. Good heat conductor. Works easily hot or cold but work hardens and must be annealed. Easily joined by soldering	Tube for plumbing. Wire for electrical work and rivets
Copper alloys Brass 60/40 Brass Muntzbrass Common brass Naval brass	950 1000	Alloys of copper and zinc 60% copper — 40% zinc 63% copper — 37% zinc 62% copper — 37% zinc — 1% tin	Yellow	Works well when hot. Tin produces increased resistance to corrosion, but is less ductile	Casting and forged work — hot stamping. General purpose — simple forming. Boat fittings. Turned spindles and pinions and engraving
Clock brass		62% copper — 36% zinc — 2% lead		Lead allows sheet metal to be punched and turned more easily	Architectural fittings
Gilding metal		80-90% copper — 20-10% zinc	Golden yellow	Malleable and ductile. Solders and enamels easily and polishes well	'Imitation' gold jewellery
Bronzes Phosphor bronze		89·5% copper — 10% tin — 0.5% phosphorus	Reddish yellow	Small variations in phosphorus content alter working qualities and uses. All alloys are tough and resist corrosion. Casts well	Standard metal for bearings and gears
Aluminium bronze		92-95% copper — 8·2% aluminium. 80% copper — 5% aluminium 5% nickel — 1% manganese	Gold	Chips when machined. Malleable hot or cold — easy to roll, draw, spin or forge. Solders and brazes easily. Resists corrosion. Is a casting quality aluminium bronze	Architectural work. Sand casting
Zinc	400 420	100% is an element	Bluish-white	Castings are brittle. Resists corrosion	Coating of mild steel in galvanising. An alloying element of brass and bronze
Lead	330	100% is an element	Blue-grey	Extremely malleable. High resistance to atmospheric corrosion. Sheet lead folds and solders easily	Roof flashings. Car batteries. An alloying element — used with tin to make soft solder
Tin	230	100% is an element	Silver-white	Extremely ductile and malleable	Coating of mild steel to make tinplate. An alloying element and the major part of pewter
Pewter	240 280	92% tin — 2% antimony — 6% copper		Relatively soft and malleable. Buffed and polished to a bright finish it will not tarnish. Perfect for casting, turning, spinning and easy joining using a low melt solder	Decorative tableware, tankards and cast figures

15

Stock Sizes

It would be impossible to remember all the types, sizes and shapes of metal that can be bought. Fortunately, the suppliers of metal produce catalogues which list each item complete with its British Standard number and a description of its working properties.

I have two catalogues — one for ferrous metals and one for non-ferrous metals. Each lists more than five thousand items! Just imagine, when you begin to design in metal you have, in theory, a choice of over ten thousand different materials! Some of these materials will be too large, too heavy or too expensive for you even to consider, and your workshop stock will be relatively small.
Use the sizes given on this page to guide you in your choice of material. Then you can obtain the nearest size from your stock.

The three Tables are compiled from my catalogues showing the available metric sizes of general-purpose Bright Drawn Mild Steel (BDMS). It has a carbon content of 0.16, ensuring good machining and welding properties.
Table 1 includes Hexagonal rod which is made to imperial measurements — the nearest metric measurement is given.

Table 2 shows some of the flats available. Widths rise to 200 mm and thicknesses to 50 mm in 5 m lengths. You are unlikely to need the maximum dimensions of round (200 mm), square (100 mm) and hexagonal (90 mm).

Table 3 gives thicknesses of mild steel and three commonly used non-ferrous metals.
Much of the non-ferrous stock is still quoted in imperial measurements.

An example

Machining-quality free-turning brass rod is available in over a hundred diameters from 0.048 inches to 8.0 inches (about 1 to 208 mm). 60/40 brass is restricted to sixteen diameters between 0.71 inches (3.2mm) and 1.5 inches (38 mm) in 10 foot (3 m) lengths.
The machining quality brass rod is also available as:

Square section   2.5 to 100 mm in 33 widths
Hexagonal section 4 to 50 mm in 21 widths

Copper tube is available in 6 m lengths with the metric outside diameters (OD) of:

6, 8, 10, 12, 15, 18, 22, 28, 35, 42, 54, 76, 108 mm

There is a choice of 21 sizes of coiled soft copper wire, measured by the standard wire gauge (SWG) numbers 3 to 26.

Table 1

Size (mm)

	3 4 5 6 6.5 7 8 9 10 11 12 13 14 15 16 17 18 19 20 22 24 25 26 27 28 30 32 33 35 36 38 39 40 42 45 48 50 52 55 56 60	
Bright Round	X X X X X X X X X X X X X X X X X X X X X X X X X X X X X X X X X X X X X X X X X	max 200
Square	X X X X X X X X X X X X X X X X X X X X X X X	max 100
Hexagonal (A/F)*	X X X X X X X X X X X X X X X X X X X X X X X X X	max 90

Length 5 metres
*to nearest metric size

Table 2 Bright flats

Thickness	Widths 10	12	15	16	20	25	30	32	35	40	45	50
3	X	X	X	X	X	X	X	X		X		X
4		X			X	X	X					
5	X	X	X	X	X	X	X	X			X	X
6	X	X	X	X	X	X	X	X	X	X	X	X
8		X			X	X	X	X	X	X	X	X
10		X	X	X	X	X	X	X	X	X	X	X
12			X	X	X	X	X			X	X	X
16				X	X	X	X	X		X	X	X
20					X	X	X	X	X	X	X	X
25						X	X	X	X	X	X	X
30							X	X	X	X		
35										X		X
40										X		X

Max. width 200 mm
Max. thickness 50 mm
Length 5 metres

Table 3 Sheet metal

Thickness (mm)	3.0	2.5	2.0	1.6	1.42	1.2	1.0	0.9	0.8	0.7	0.6	0.55	0.5	0.45	0.4	0.35	0.3
Thickness (SWG)	10	12	14	16	17	18	19	20	21	22	23	24	25	26	27	29	30
Brass	X	X	X	X		X		X		X		X		X		X	
Copper	X	X	X	X		X	X	X	X	X		X		X		X	
Steel	X	X	X	X		X	X		X		X		X		X		
Aluminium	X	X	X	X		X		X		X		X		X			

Aluminium / Steel } 1830 × 915

Brass / Copper } 1200 × 600

Hand Tools – Steel Rules

Engineers' rules are precision measuring tools made from bright spring steel with a hard-wearing rust-resisting finish.

The photograph shows a typical range. The metric rules have lengths 150 and 300 mm.

The graduations are precisely etched into the metal for permanence. Two contrasting styles of metric graduations are illustrated. Some rules are graduated on both sides. Some rules have a curved end and a hole for safe hanging when not in use – others are usable from both ends. These 'zero' ends must be protected from damage and never misused.

Using a steel rule

For the best possible accuracy, measure from the zero end set against a datum surface and hold the rule on edge so that the graduations are in contact with the surface.

If a less exact measurement is needed, reverse the rule and measure to the zero end as shown.

Flexible rules

Flexible or pocket rules are made from thin flexible steel. The measurements are printed and protected by a crackproof finish and the blade is spring-loaded into a case. The case label indicates the total blade length (usually 2 m or 3 m) and the width of the case itself. (This information is needed when an internal measurement is being taken.)

Pocket rules are not as accurate as a steel rule, but they are ideal for measurements over a metre and flexible enough for measuring circumferences by subtraction.

The photograph shows plastic pipe being measured. The readings are 28 and 11 – therefore the external circumference of the pipe is 17 mm.

Dividers

Spring dividers are adjusted by a nut on a fine screw thread so that fine settings can be made. The points are hardened and ground so that circles and arcs may be marked on most other metals.

Dividers are often used to transfer measurements from a template to the new work. When using a rule, set the dividers from two graduations and not from the zero end.

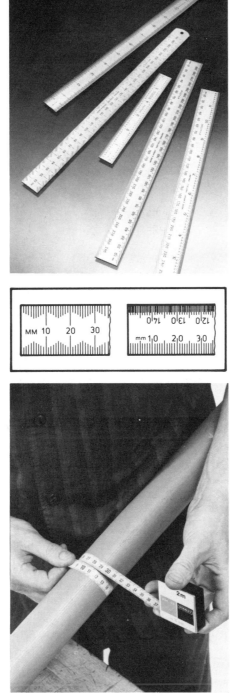

Quick method of measuring in from an edge

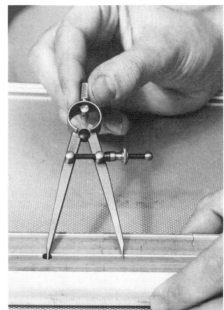

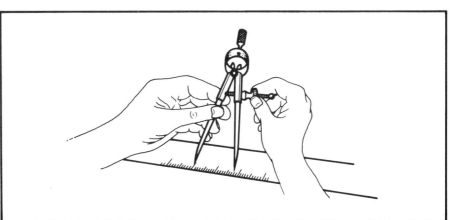

Micrometers

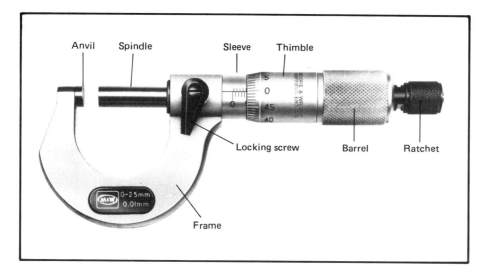

Anvil　Spindle　　　Sleeve　Thimble

Locking screw　　　Barrel　Ratchet

Frame

The external metric micrometer shown is designed to measure up to 25 mm with great accuracy. It is most often used on small-diameter turned work.

The outer casing protects a carefully machined screw mechanism which moves the hardened alloy spindle in relation to the fixed anvil.

The measurements are taken or read from the numbers etched into the sleeve and thimble.

Hold the micrometer lightly in one hand — excessive hand heat will expand the metal and make the reading inaccurate! The measuring faces should be kept square with the object being measured.

Use the ratchet drive to ensure a uniform pressure and consistent reading. Do *not* use force.

Anvil and spindle surfaces must be kept absolutely clean. Clean by closing the faces on to a sheet of paper and pulling the paper out.

When not in use, *always* store in a lidded box.

Reading an external micrometer

The spindle shows the one millimetre (1 mm) and half-millimetre (0.5 mm) graduations — every 5 mm being labelled. The graduations on the thimble show one hundredth of a millimetre (0.01 mm).

Thus the reading in figure 1 is:

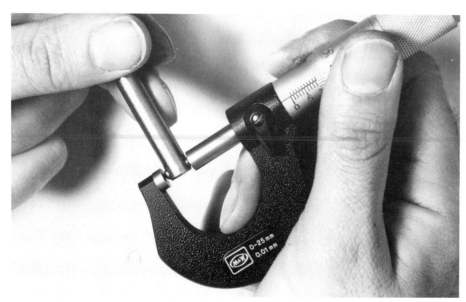

METRIC MICROMETERS

1 mm

0.5 mm

0.01 mm

Figure 1　　　　　Figure 2

On spindle
(highest whole number)　　17.00
(+ 1 subdivision)　　　　　0.50
On thimble
(+ 25 hundredths)　　　　 0.25

total: 17.75

You can now work out the measurement indicated in figure 2.

Digital Micrometers

The electronic digital micrometer has solid-state electronics protected by a stainless steel and tough plastic casing. It is powered by its own rechargeable power pack and is accurate to two-thousandths of a millimetre (0.002 mm) shown on a five-figure readout.

Micrometers (continued)

Micrometers are expensive to replace so some imperial versions may still be in use. Use these in exactly the same way as the metric version and convert using a table.

The spindle shows graduations in 0.025, 0.050, 0.075 and 0.1 (one-tenth) of an inch, every tenth being labelled. The graduations on the thimble show 0.001 (one-thousandth) of an inch.

Thus the reading in figure 1 is:

On spindle
    (highest whole number)   0.400
    (+ 1 subdivision)   0.050
On thimble
    (+ 1 thousandth)   0.001
               total: 0.451

You can now work out the measurement indicated in figure 2.

Internal micrometers

Each boxed set has a set of rods which can only be used with the one micrometer. The smallest set has a range of 25–55 mm using up to three rods with a range of 10 mm.

The set illustrated has eight rods with a capacity of 50–210 mm.

Depth-gauge micrometer

The ratchet on a depth gauge micrometer must be removed to insert one of the 3.17 mm diameter rods. The largest set has a depth capacity of 300 mm. The set shown has three labelled rods (0–25/25–50 and 50–75 mm).

Large-frame micrometers

These are available up to 450 mm long. The one shown will measure 250 to 275 mm accurately between the tungsten-carbide tipped faces.

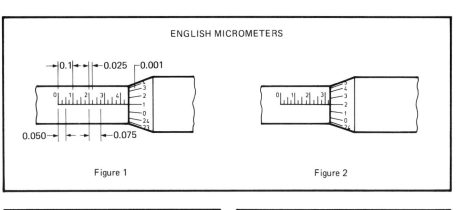

ENGLISH MICROMETERS

Figure 1

Figure 2

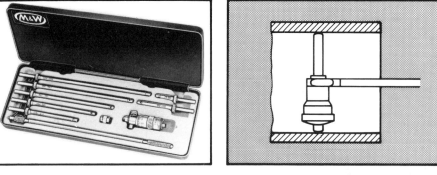

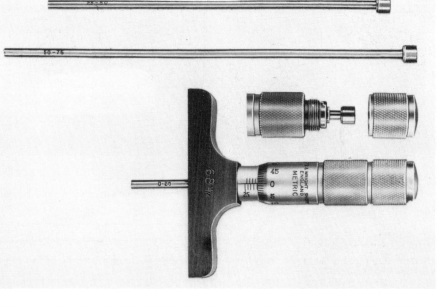

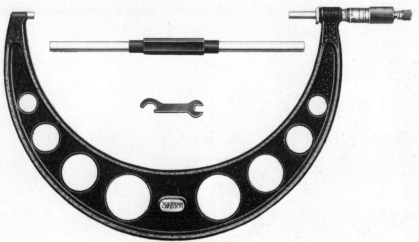

Marking and Testing Tools

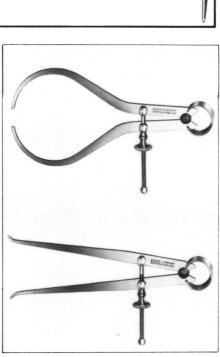

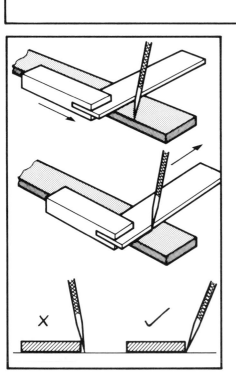

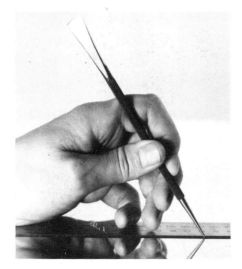

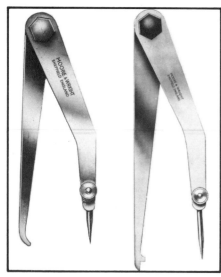

Scribers

The engineer's scriber is hardened and ground to a sharp point for marking out. It is usually used, together with a try square, to mark lines at right angles to a finished edge.

For accuracy, the point of the scriber must be into the corner made by the square and the surface of the material. Ensure this by first placing the scriber in position and moving the try square up to it.

The Handy Scriber in the photograph has an alternative knife edge ideal for use on wood and plastic laminates.

Calipers

The photograph shows some spring type calipers.

Use *outside* calipers to
1. transfer measurements
2. make comparisons of measurements
3. test surfaces for parallelism

When taking measurements from a steel rule use the zero end to locate one arm of the calipers. More precise measurements can be taken from an internal micrometer.

Important note: Do not force the tool over the material when testing.

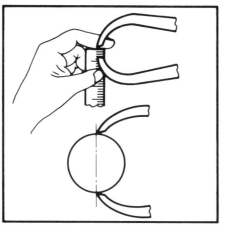

Use *inside* calipers in a similar manner to outside calipers.

When taking measurements from a steel rule use a datum surface as shown. More precise measurements can be taken from an external micrometer.

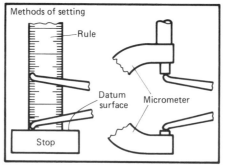

Methods of setting — Rule — Datum surface — Micrometer — Stop

Odd-leg calipers

Often called 'Jenny' calipers, the type shown has a firm joint instead of a spring. A fibre washer between the two legs ensures an efficient friction joint and the point is adjustable.

Use odd-leg calipers to scribe lines parallel to a machined edge.

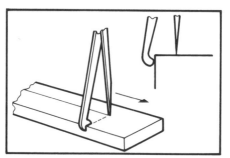

Marking and Testing Tools (continued)

Surface plates

The plate is an accurately machined surface which can be used as a 'plane of reference' for checking other flat surfaces. Its main use is for setting up work for marking out with the surface gauge.

The plate can be inverted and used on its edge. Keep the cast iron clean and protect the surface with light oil.

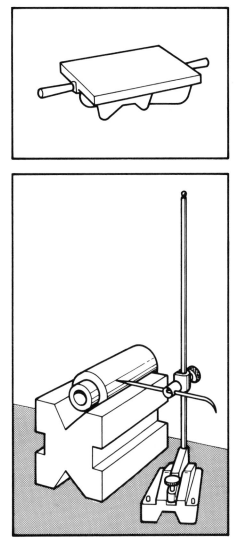

Surface gauges (scribing blocks)

The gauge has an accurately ground base for use on the surface plate. Move the collar on the pillar to make coarse adjustments to the height of the scriber. Make fine adjustments using the fine-pitched thumbscrew on the base. This pivots the pillar.

Use for marking parallel lines, finding centres of cylindrical stock and checking for parallelism. Hold work either against an angle plate or on a vee block.

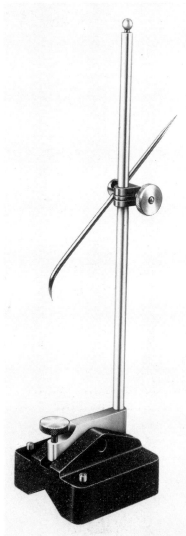

Angle plates

Open-ended or webbed angle plates are made from high-quality castings.

Both types are used to support work being marked out which cannot be held flat on the surface plate. The work is clamped to the plates through the slots provided.

Vee blocks

Vee blocks are supplied as matched and numbered pairs, each with a centred 90° vee. A block is used with a clamp to hold cylindrical stock to be drilled. Longer work would require the support of a matching pair.

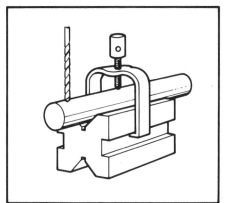

Finding Centres

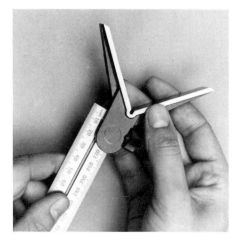

There are three common bench methods for finding the centre of a bar.

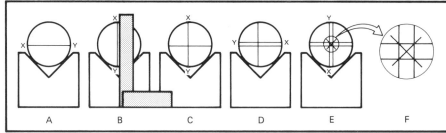

The *first method* involves the use of a centre square. The blade bisects the right angle formed by the stock at its centre. Two diameters are marked and their intersection locates the centre of the bar. Alternatively, use a combination set of rule and centre head.

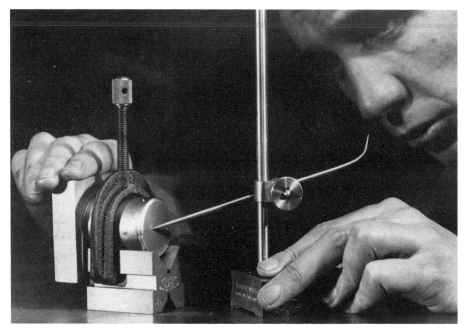

The *second method* involves the use of a surface gauge on a surface plate. Clamp the bar on to a vee block and scribe a line near to its centre with a surface gauge (A). Turn the bar at right angles and check with an engineer's square (B). Scribe a second line and repeat the process a third and fourth time (C and D). The centre of the bar can then be located by diagonals (E).
Note that the setting of the surface gauge is not changed.

The *third method* involves the use of a bell punch. This is a hardened centre punch spring loaded into a mild steel conical body which is self centring. It is limited in use to bars which are smaller than the diameter of the bell.

Punches

When located, centres are permanently marked with a punch. The two punches shown are made and hardened in the same way. They look similar but have a different grinding angle.

The *dot punch* is ground at an angle of 60° and is used to mark lightly before drilling.
The *centre punch* is ground at an angle of 90° and is used to make a heavier mark. It is often used on top of the dot punch mark.

Where a punch is needed to make a series of marks on a scribed line to make it clear, use either a dot punch or a spring-loaded automatic punch.

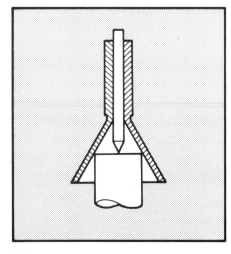

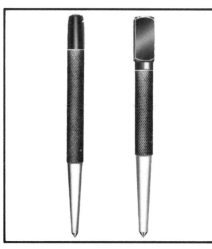

Squares and Bevels

Engineer's square

The square has a hardened and tempered blade set at 90° into a bright-steel stock. The stock has a slot cut across its inside face to prevent filings and dirt from giving an inaccurate reading. Use the square to check for squareness, holding the stock tight against a prepared face, and for marking lines at right angles to a prepared edge. Lengths vary from 75 to 1050 mm, with 100 mm being a popular size.

Adjustable squares have a blade which is interchangeable with a rule, and a blade with the ends ground at 45° and 60°.

Adjustable bevel

The parallel ground blade of the adjustable bevel can be locked in any position.
Use it to mark out at a given angle or for checking the accuracy of sloping faces.

Combination set

The set has three interchangeable heads which slide on to a precision rule and can be fixed in any position with a knurled nut.

Use the centre head to find the centre of round bars as shown on page 22.

Use the square head for a variety of marking and testing jobs. It is versatile because it has preset angles of 45° and 90° to the rule and is fitted with a spirit level.

Use the protractor to set any desired angle with extreme accuracy.

The drawings show the protractor measuring a closed angle of a machine slide, and checking an open angle.

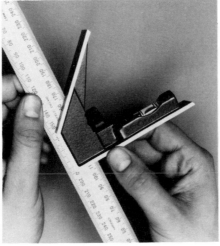

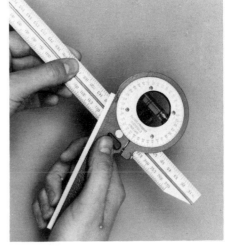

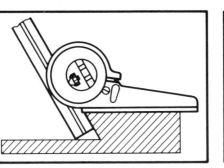

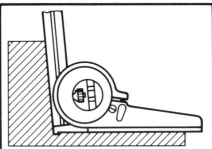

Templates and Jigs

Templates are full-size patterns which enable work to be set out quickly and accurately.

Use a paper template, which can be taken from a full-size working drawing, when a shape is to be drawn only once.
A template to be used more often is cut from card, and large templates to be frequently used are often made from hardboard.
Metal templates are essential when repetitive marking out has to be more accurate.

The heaviest type of template is probably the scroll iron around which the heated material is bent to make a forged decorative scroll.

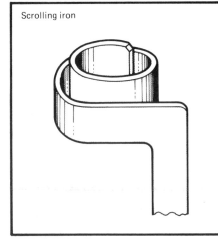

Scrolling iron

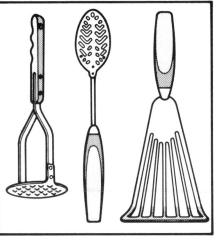

The simplest type of template shape is probably that used for marking out copper blanks that are to be used for enamelling. Often these are repeated shapes such as on a necklace. Another template may be used to mask off part of the surface when applying the powdered enamel.

A *jig* is a form of template with measurements of length rather than shapes being marked, cut or bent. A simple adjustable length guide is fitted to a machine used for bending, and on many metal guillotines.

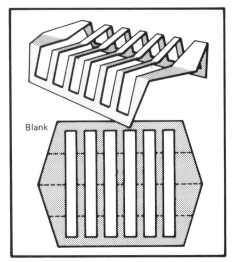

Blank

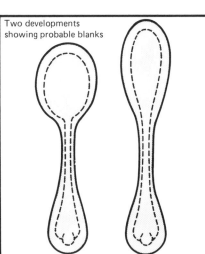

Two developments showing probable blanks

Many kitchen tools are pierced to allow liquids to drain away. Making tools of a similar design will require the accuracy of a metal template.

Where pierced sheet will be bent, such as in a toast rack, the template will be made the same size and shape as the drawing — this drawing is known as a *development*.

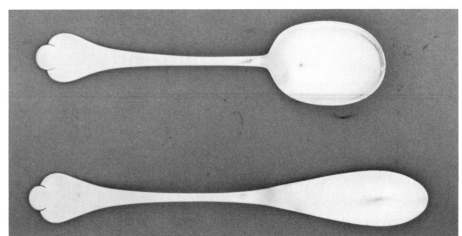

The spoons were designed by C.R. Mackintosh almost a century ago. The templates for marking and cutting out the blanks have to take into account the amount of curvature in the spoon bowls after the flat blank has been stamped.

Vernier Scales

The Vernier scale is named after its inventor. The most common use of the scale is on a caliper gauge which is made in a range of sizes to measure up to two metres with extreme accuracy. The calibrations are made precisely on the hardened steel rule.

Use caliper gauge for measuring most machine parts. The range shown is calibrated with metric and imperial scales. Some gauges are fitted with jaws for taking both internal and external measurements.
Both scales work on the same principle.

Metric scale

The main scale is graduated in millimetres.

The Vernier scale is 49 mm in length and is divided into fifty equal parts. Therefore, each division on the Vernier scale is 0.02 mm shorter than a division on the main scale. This difference is shown on the slide (e.g. VER.02 mm).

Use the Vernier scale in the following way. The number of the millimetre division below the Vernier zero could be '43'. Now locate the line on the Vernier scale which is *exactly* opposite a line on the main scale — this could be '26'. Next do the sum:

$$43 + (0.02 \times 26)$$

So the total dimension would be 43.52.

The imperial scale

The main scale is graduated in inches and twentieths of inches.

The Vernier scale is 2.5 in long and divided into fifty equal parts. Each division on the Vernier scale is therefore 0.001 inches shorter than a division on the main scale. This is the difference shown on the slide (VER.001 in).

Use the Vernier scale in the following way. The number of whole large divisions (inches) below the Vernier zero could be '2'. The number of whole small divisions (tenths) below the Vernier zero might be '3'. The number of half small divisions (twentieths) below the Vernier zero could be '1'. Now locate the line on the Vernier scale which is exactly opposite a line on the main scale (say '47'). Next do the sum:

$$2 + (0.1 \times 3) + (0.05 \times 1) + (0.001 \times 47)$$

So the total dimension would be 2.397.

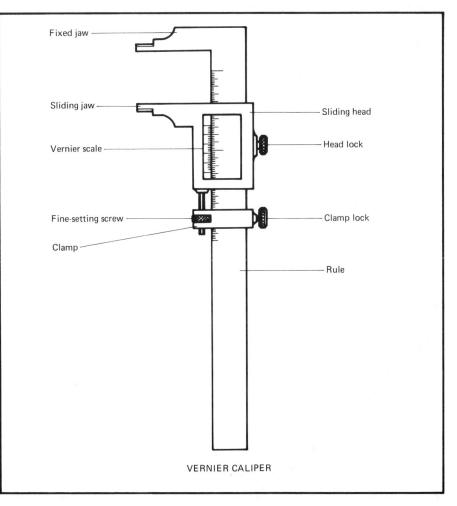

VERNIER CALIPER

Fixed jaw

Sliding jaw

Vernier scale

Fine-setting screw

Clamp

Sliding head

Head lock

Clamp lock

Rule

The Vernier Caliper in Use

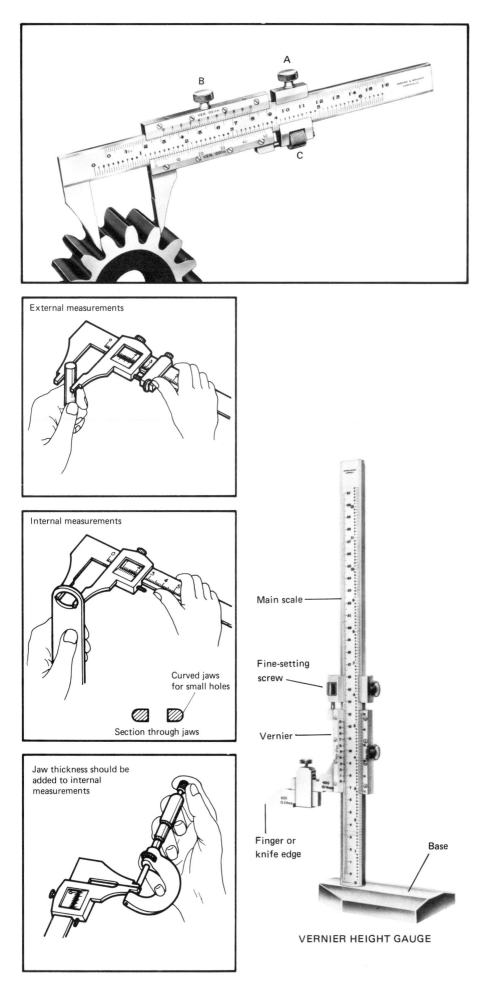

External measurements

Internal measurements

Curved jaws
for small holes

Section through jaws

Jaw thickness should be
added to internal
measurements

Main scale

Fine-setting
screw

Vernier

Finger or
knife edge

Base

VERNIER HEIGHT GAUGE

The illustration shows an external Vernier caliper gauge being used to measure a gear wheel.
To make the measurement:

1. slacken the screws A and B
2. slide the jaws up to the work
3. lock screw A
4. turn the fine setting screw C to close
5. lock screw B and remove the gauge from the work to take the reading.

In the photograph this reading on the metric scale is 32.00 mm.
The reading on the imperial scale is:

1 inch	1.00
2 tenths	0.20
1 twentieth	0.05
Number of divisions on Vernier scale = 6 × 0.001	0.006
	1.256 in

To read these on the photograph a magnifying glass is needed. Use a hand magnifier if you have difficulty in reading the fine markings on the Vernier scale.

When the internal Vernier caliper gauge is being used the combined width of the two jaws must be allowed for. This width is usually stated on the gauge. If the gauge shows signs of damage or wear, it would be wise to check this dimension using a micrometer.

Vernier height gauge

The gauge has a precision-ground base which supports a heavy Vernier rule — graduated in the same way as the calipers. Adjustments are made in exactly the same way.

Use the gauge on a surface plate as a form of surface gauge needing to be very accurate. Use for marking and testing for parallelism by holding the work against an angle plate or on a vee block.

Gauges

Most gauges are made from a high-quality tool steel which has been hardened and tempered. The best gauges are machined to fine tolerances and given a high surface finish.

Depth gauges

The 150 mm long gauge is graduated like an Engineer's rule. The gauge is adjustable, with a body ground so that the rule can be used either way. It is then suitable for use in confined spaces. In one type the blade can be used in alternative positions.

Screw-pitch gauges

These accurately milled gauges are protected by a holder labelled with the type of thread. Each gauge is marked with its pitch. The illustration shows a set of 22 blades with ISO threads in the thread range of 0.35 to 6.0 mm.

Use to measure internal or external screw threads by selecting a blade which fits the existing thread. Matching nuts and screws can then be supplied.

Feeler gauges

These thin steel blades are ground to precision limits and each is marked with its thickness.
The sets are produced in a variety of lengths and thicknesses. The illustration shows a set fitted with ten metric blades with a range of 0.05 to 0.80 mm.

Use for gauging, by feel or touch, the gap between components such as bearings or electrical contacts.

Wire gauges

This two-part gauge contains forty slots ranging from 0.2 to 10.0 mm in diameter. An imperial standard wire gauge numbered 1−36 is available.

Use for testing the gauge of wire.

Radius gauges

The set illustrated has sixteen blades with a radius range of 5.5 to 13 mm.

Use for checking both internal and external radii.

Care of gauges

1. Handle with care to avoid damaging precision surfaces.
2. Store carefully.
3. If used infrequently, lightly oil the surface.
4. Never misuse a gauge − each has one specific use.

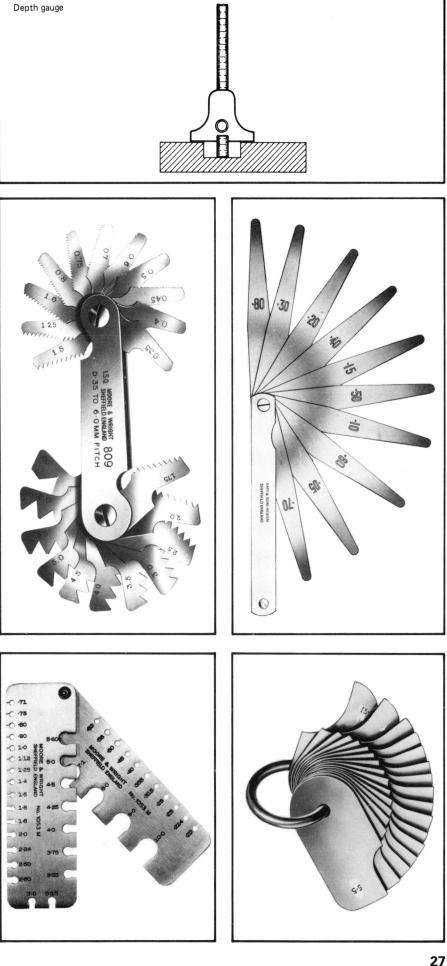

Depth gauge

Vices

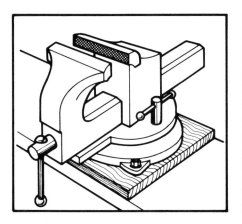

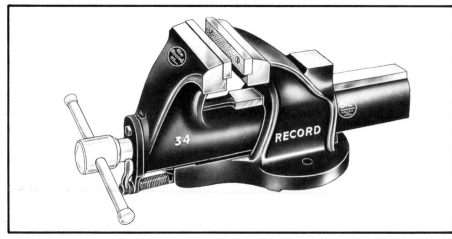

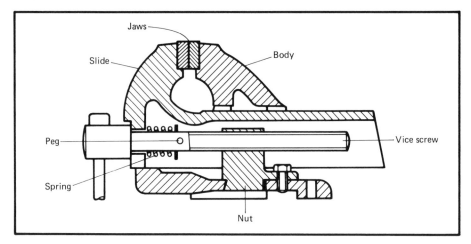

Jaws — Body
Slide —
Peg — — Vice screw
Spring
Nut

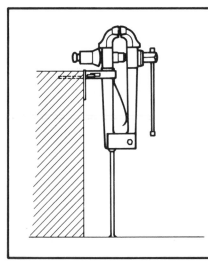

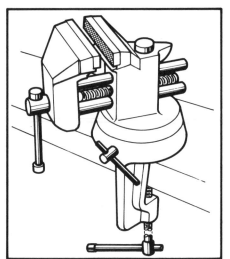

A variety of bench vices will be available in most workshops, each able to do a special type of holding job.

The mechanic's vice

This is a cast iron vice usually with a plain screw adjustment. The screw has a buttress thread (see page 50) to allow great pressure to be exerted in one direction.
The serrated parallel jaws vary in length from 65 to 200 mm.
Use the vice for holding most work to be filed or sawn.

The illustrations shows a vice with a swivel base which allows the vice to be rotated and fixed throughout 360°.

The fitter's vice

This is a heavier vice with a similar capacity but often fitted with a quick-release lever. In this vice the screw is located in a half nut. Disengage this by depressing the lever. Make the adjustment, then release the lever to engage the screw thread.
The vice is then tightened in the usual way.

The engineer's vice

This is available in either plain or quick-release forms and is often fitted with an anvil. The best type is extremely tough and guaranteed against breakage even when struck heavily with a hammer.

DO NOT strike the fitter's and mechanic's vices with a hammer.

Jaw clamps

The cast iron jaws of bench vices will mark many steels and all soft metals. Use jaw clamps to protect work of this kind. These are of lead, aluminium, copper or fibre and are clipped on to the jaws.

Leg vice

This is a wrought iron vice which is fitted so that the energy from blows struck on the material being held is transferred to the floor. It works on the lever principle so the jaws are not parallel.

Use this type to hold large material and hot metal being forged.

Portable vice

A new generation of portable vices has been designed for home use, made from light alloy and fitted with hardened jaws and an anvil big enough for riveting. The base can be attached to a table.

Vices (continued)

Hand vice

This vice works on the same lever principle as the leg vice. The jaws are held in tension by a spring and adjusted by a wing nut.

Use to hold small pieces of work to be drilled on the drilling machine.

Machine vice

The cast iron body has slots through which it can be bolted to the drilling table. The parallel hardened-steel jaws have vee grooves so that round material can be held both horizontally and vertically. The jaw is adjusted with a knurled handle.

Drill press vice

This is similar to the machine vice but is fitted with a front jaw which swivels to allow non-parallel work to be securely held.
The jaw is adjusted with a turning bar.

Use the machine and drill press vices to hold material to be drilled up to the jaw opening of about 75 mm.

Extendable machine vice

The Carver vice is a two-piece tool. One piece is fixed as a reference point and the other is positioned to hold the work.
The maximum jaw width is only limited by the size of the drill table.
Each part of the vice can be fixed at any angle through 360°, and the jaws (serrated or soft) can be changed. Tighten with a spanner.

The photograph shows the adaptability of the vice. Three parts are being used to hold triangular work that is being milled. These vices are a low-profile version, only 30 mm thick, shown with covers which prevent them being covered with cutting fluid and swarf.

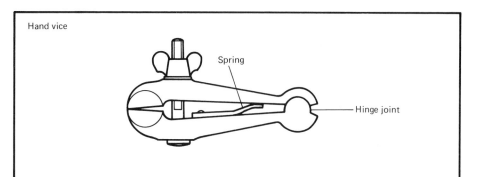

Hand vice

Spring

Hinge joint

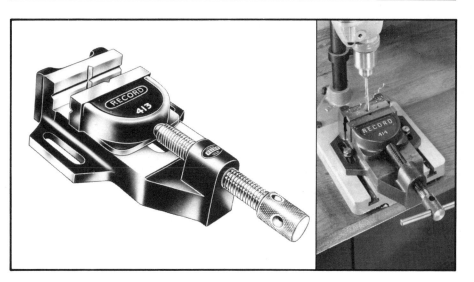

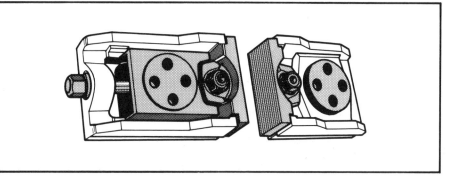

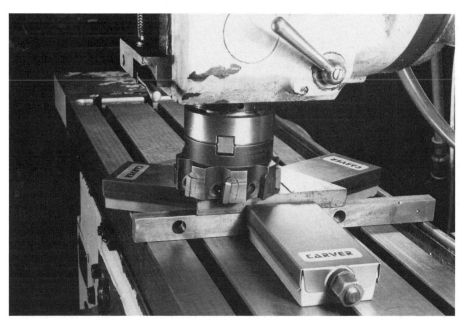

G-Cramps

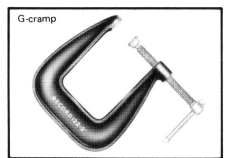
G-cramp

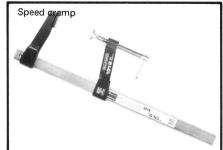
Speed cramp

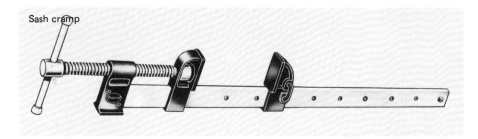
Sash cramp

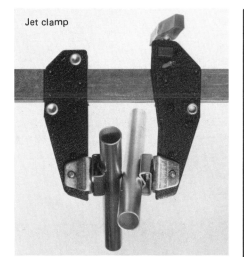
Jet clamp

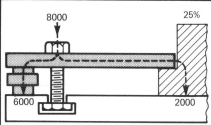

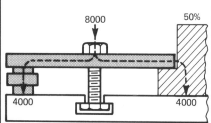

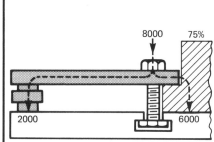

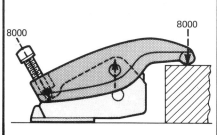

The malleable-iron frames are ribbed to give extra strength by resisting the pressures exerted from the square acme thread of the adjusting screw (see page 50). The swivel shoe allows it to be fixed on to non-parallel surfaces.

The throat size of a G-cramp is the depth of the inside of the frame and this restricts its use. The 'Deep Throat' cramp shown has a larger reach than normal G-cramps of its size. A mouth size from 100 to 300 mm is available in different weights of cramps.

Use them for holding work to be braced or welded and for holding awkward work to the bench.

Speed cramps

These have a high capacity (from 200 to 1220 mm). The swivel shoe is on an adjustable bar — the fixed bar contains the anvil.

They are quicker to use than the G-cramp, without its restriction on sizes.

Sash cramps

The plain-bar type has a tail slide which is adjusted parallel to the head.

The head is tightened on an acme screw thread with a toggle bar. Lengths from 460 to 1370 mm are common.

Use in fabricating frame works.

Jet clamps

These are versatile clamps, both arms of which can be adjusted along the bar. Interchangeable heads include flat, serrated, right angle and rubber to avoid damage to previously finished surfaces. The photograph shows jaws designed to secure round sectional material. These jaws will pivot in any direction.

Use for holding material to be welded — the zinc-plated parts resist splatter.

Tee-slot cramp

The drawings show how traditional methods of screwing work to a table with steel plates and bolts are not as efficient as the Carver cramps. The fulcrum arrangement ensures that all the pressure is directly transferred to the work. This leads to higher safety.

To adjust, slacken the screw, release the safety catch and move the arm along the column.

Note that two heads, fixed opposite each other, can be used on one column.

The cramps are shown in use on an industrial horizontal borer.

Hacksaws

The general-purpose hacksaw shown is adjustable so that blades of 250 or 300 mm can be fitted. The guarded handle is screwed to an oval tubular bow or frame and the blade is held in tension between them. Adjust the tension of the blade with a wing nut.

The reach of the saw is limited to the depth of the frame — usually about 120 mm. The blades of all the saws shown can be turned through 90° by swivelling the tension pieces at each end of the frame. Another photograph shows the blade turned at right angles to the frame so that a strip from the edge of a sheet can be cut.

Using a hacksaw

1. Ensure that the work being cut is firmly held.
2. Use your thumb to guide the saw at the start of the cut.
3. Apply light pressure to begin with, then transfer both hands to the frame as shown.
4. Saw slowly.
5. Keep the blade straight.
6. Remember that the blade cuts on the forward stroke — release the pressure on the backward stroke.

Blades

To enable the correct type of blade and size of teeth to be chosen the information is usually printed on the blade. The three main types are:

1. **Low alloy** — a cheap blade for nothing harder than mild steel.
2. **All-hard High Speed Steel (HSS)** — a rigid, inflexible saw for accurate cutting but liable to break or chip.
3. **Bi-metal** — a flexible blade unbreakable in normal use, with only the cutting edge hardened.

Teeth sizes on handsaw blades are 14, 18, 24 or 32 per 25 mm. On the first two types of blade the teeth are set alternately, as on a wood-cutting saw. On the last two types the teeth are 'wavy' set.

A general guide to choosing the size of teeth:

1. For thin material use a fine blade and have at least three teeth in contact with the material.
2. In soft metals a coarser blade than usual may be needed to prevent 'clogging'.

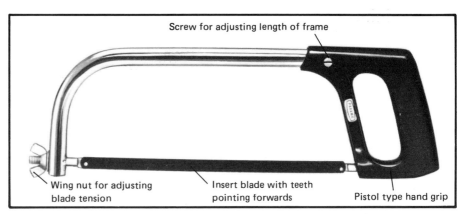

Screw for adjusting length of frame

Wing nut for adjusting blade tension

Insert blade with teeth pointing forwards

Pistol type hand grip

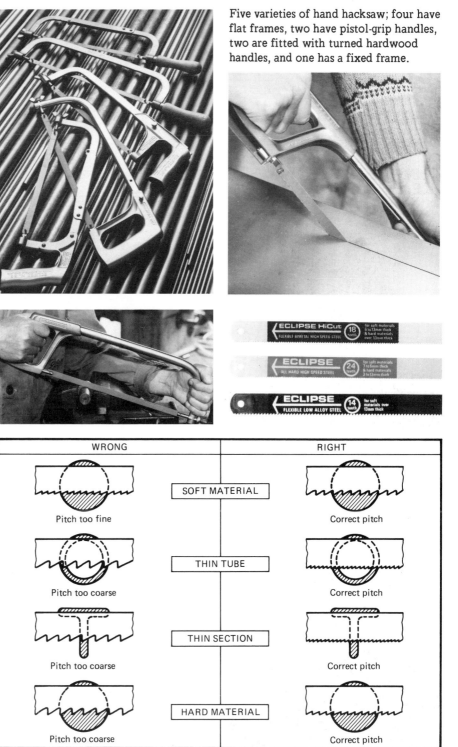

Five varieties of hand hacksaw; four have flat frames, two have pistol-grip handles, two are fitted with turned hardwood handles, and one has a fixed frame.

ECLIPSE HiCut — FLEXIBLE BIMETAL HIGH SPEED STEEL — 18 teeth — for soft materials 6 to 13mm thick & hard materials over 13mm thick

ECLIPSE — ALL HARD HIGH SPEED STEEL — 24 teeth — for soft materials 3 to 6mm thick & hard materials 3 to 13mm thick

ECLIPSE — FLEXIBLE LOW ALLOY STEEL — 14 teeth — for soft materials over 13mm thick

WRONG		RIGHT
Pitch too fine	SOFT MATERIAL	Correct pitch
Pitch too coarse	THIN TUBE	Correct pitch
Pitch too coarse	THIN SECTION	Correct pitch
Pitch too coarse	HARD MATERIAL	Correct pitch

Saws

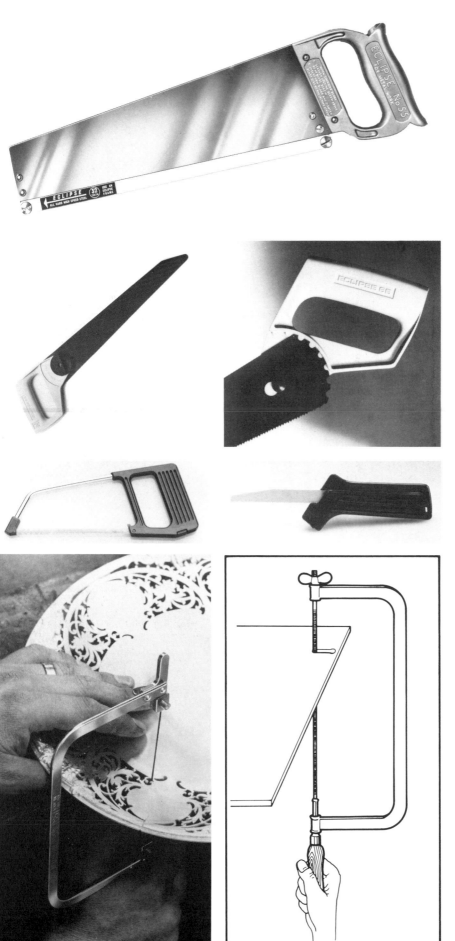

Sheet saws

Standard 300 mm hacksaw blades are screwed to a steel sheet to make a rigid saw that will cut accurately.
There is a large version of the saw needing 405 mm blades – these have large teeth: 6, 10 and 14 per 25 mm.

Use on plain or corrugated metal sheet and on materials such as thermoplastic brick or plastic laminate where hardened teeth are needed.

Vari-saws

The tapered blade will reach confined spaces, especially as it can be adjusted to nine different positions on the handle. The teeth will cut wood, plastics, soft metals and mild steel in light sections.

Use where wood structures may have embedded nails.

Mini-hacksaws

The traditional mini-hacksaw has a springy, all-steel frame which holds the 150 mm blade in tension.

The saw shown has a stainless steel frame set in a plastic handle with a blade tensioned by a lever. Use blades with 14 or 32 teeth per 25 mm to suit the material being cut.

Multi-purpose saw

The bi-metal padsaw blade can be fitted into the plastic handle, as shown, or set at 45° so that the handle forms a pistol grip. The handle can be used with broken hacksaw blades. It is used to cut in awkward places where a hacksaw cannot reach.

Piercing saw

Two types of saws are available. One has a fixed frame, 85 mm deep, and the other has an adjustable frame only 70 mm deep. The adjustable frame can make use of broken blades.
The largest teeth on the thin blades are 32 per 25 mm and on the smallest 80 per 25 mm.
Use for cutting shapes in all soft and precious metals – a Jeweller's saw.

The Abrafile

The file is a flexible wire with non-clogging teeth cut into it so that it will cut in any direction.
A choice of coarse, medium and fine wires makes it possible to cut irregular holes or intricate shapes in a variety of materials.

Snips

Snips are often referred to as Tinman's Snips as they are designed solely for cutting sheet metal. *Do not* use them for cutting wire.

The three types of hand-held snips shown are used in the same way. Work at right angles to the surface.
Do not close the points on to the metal.

Small snips (200 mm long) can be hand-held. Each handle has a small anvil which prevents nipping.
Large snips which are longer (up to 350 mm) and heavier may have one handle held in a vice and the sheet metal moved into position. This method is also advised when the sheet being cut is thick and considerable leverage is required.

Straight snips

These are general-purpose snips which can be fitted with a leaf-spring which opens up the handles after each cut.

Curved snips

Especially to cut curves which are smaller in radius than can be cut with universal snips.

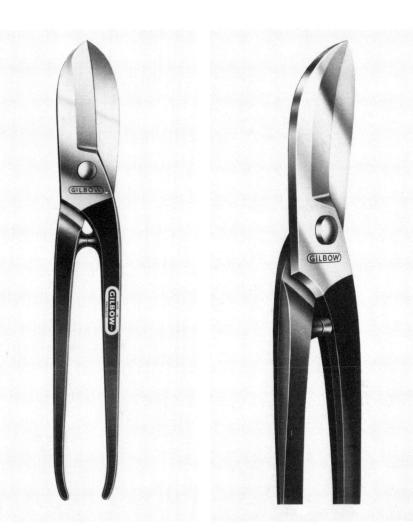

Universal snips

A heavy-duty tool usually with long handles to gain extra leverage.

The right-hand cranked snips shown are used to cut curves in an anticlockwise direction.
Left-hand cranked snips are used to cut curves in a clockwise direction.

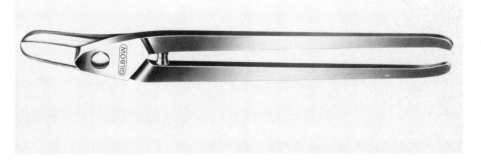

The section shows the cutting action of the snips. The inside surface of the blades are in close contact. The top edges are angled at 5° and it is these surfaces which are sharpened.

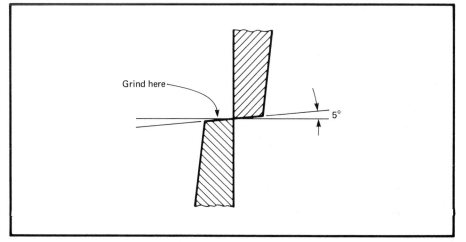

Grind here

5°

Chisels

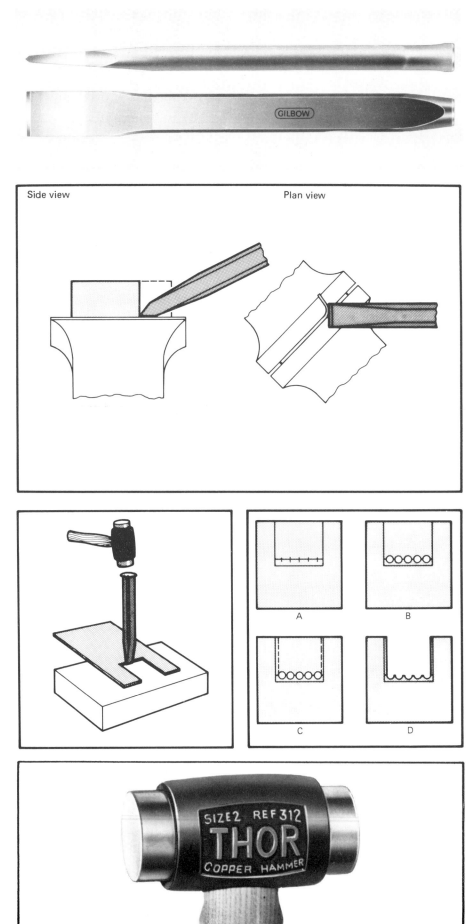

Cold chisels

Cold chisels are so called because they are designed to cut metal in its cold state. The quality of a chisel can only be discovered in its use, and only the best are worth having.

A good chisel is made from high-grade steel which has been structured to withstand heavy blows from a hammer. The cutting edge must be hardened with carefully controlled heat treatment and the striking end softened.
The blade may be ground straight or slightly curved and the striking end is often chamfered to resist 'mushrooming'. The angle at which the blade is ground varies on the work to be done. Choose a narrow angle (about 35°) for hard steel.

Flat chisels

The chisel shown is made from a chrome-alloy steel. A common length is 200 mm (the range is 100 to 450 mm) and blade widths are 6–25 mm. The chrome-alloy will keep its cutting edge a long time. It should be sharpened with a smooth file.

Shearing

Sheet metal or metal plate is held firmly in a vice and the flat chisel held at about 45° to the jaws. Strike the chisel with a heavy hammer.
Cut in waste material and file to size. Watch the cutting edge, *not* the striking end.

Vertical chiseling

Prevent distortion of the metal by supporting it on a soft steel cutting block and strike the chisel vertically. Alternatively, drill a series of holes in the waste metal to reduce the amount of material to be cut.

Hammers

Copper-headed hammers do less damage to the chisel than steel hammers. The one shown has two copper faces set in a heavy malleable-iron head on a hickory shaft. The size of the head increases with the weight of the hammer. The head of this one is 38 mm in diameter and weighs 3 lb (1.36 kg).

Chisels (continued)

Cross-cut chisel

This is a deep, narrow chisel for cutting slots. The blade is reduced in thickness behind the cutting edge so that it clears the sides of the cut. Widths are from 3 to 9 mm.

Half-round chisel

This is another deep, narrow chisel with a curved cutting edge which can be used to 'pull-over' a large offset hole.

Diamond chisel

The square, tapered blade is ground at an angle to produce a diamond-shaped bevel. Use this tool to clean out corners of cuts or to pull-over offset holes.

Maintenance

The high-carbon steel chisels can be re-ground on a small-diameter abrasive wheel. Coolant must be used and care taken to prevent the temper of the cutting edge being drawn and the edge softened.

Although a soft hammer will protect the softer striking end, heavy steel hammers will eventually put a dangerous burr on the edge. Remove this on the grinding wheel.

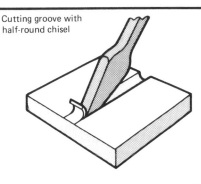

Cutting groove with half-round chisel

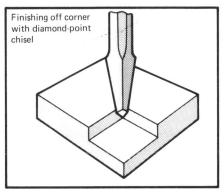

Finishing off corner with diamond-point chisel

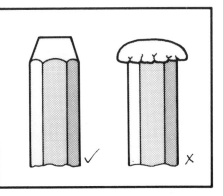

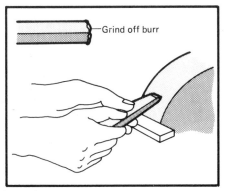

Grind off burr

Files

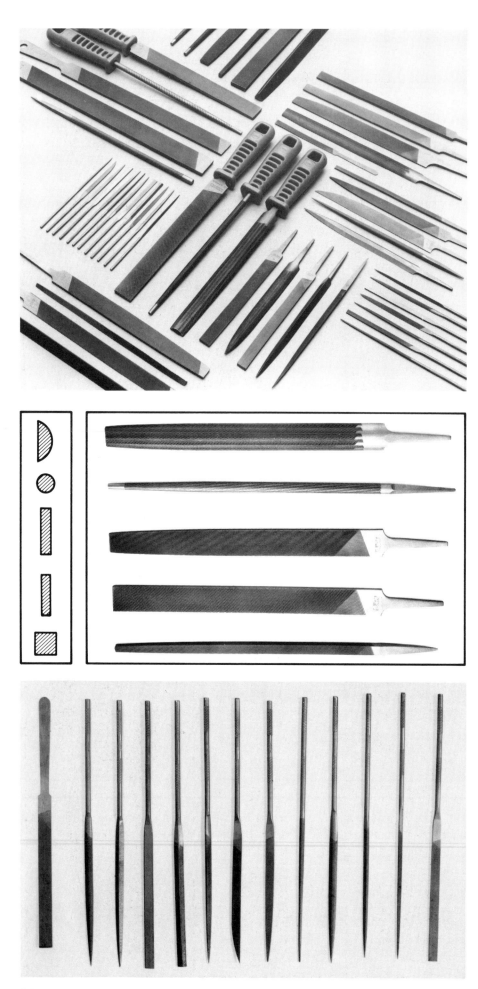

Files are made from high-carbon steel which has been hardened and tempered so that a cutting edge can be made on it. The tang, which fits into the handle, is left relatively soft.

Files have traditionally been supplied to be fitted into wood handles — a worn file being discarded and the handle re-used. Some popular files are now available fitted with moulded plastics handles.

The photograph shows a wide range of files differing in size, shape and tooth cut. The small precision files are about 150 mm long. Other files are 200–250 mm long (20–25 mm wide) but even larger files are available.

Half-round

The round face (double-cut) is used on concave surfaces.

Round

Common tapered files are often called 'rat tails'. Parallel rounds (6–8 mm diameter) are also available (double- or single-cut).

Flat

A long file (double-cut) which tapers throughout the last third of its length. Use for general bench work. A warding file is similar in shape but both smaller and thinner.

Hand

A parallel-sided file (double-cut) which tapers in its thickness and has one 'safe' or smooth edge. Use this to work into corners when only one face has to be cut. A *pillar* file is a smaller version of it.

Square

A square-sectioned blade (double-cut) which usually tapers but is available as a 'parallel square' 6–8 mm wide. Use for slotting and grooving.

Other files

A triangular or 'three square' tapered file is use for getting into corners.

A wedge-sectioned knife file (double-cut side and single-cut edge) is used for filing angles of less than 60°.

Needle files are precision files. They are available in a wide choice of sections and are stored in a protective wallet.

Files (continued)

The Aven 'Filemaster' is one make of file which has curved teeth, sometimes called a 'Dreadnought' file. The fast-cutting teeth do not clog and can be used on wood, some plastics and soft metal alloys. The reverse side of this useful tool has straight teeth for finishing soft metal surfaces, trimming plastics laminates and smoothing synthetic resin fillers. It does not clog or pin.

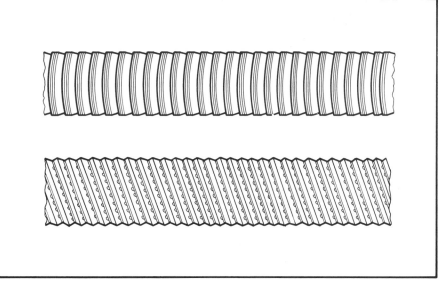

Stanley 'Surform' tools are fitted with hardened steel blades with curved raised teeth. Waste material passes through the holes in the thin blade to avoid clogging. The largest planes and files can be fitted with a strong blade with flat teeth especially for use on plastics and metals softer than mild steel.

Wood handles are fitted with a metal ferrule to prevent splitting when the file tang is driven in. To make fitting easier, drill a straight hole in the handle corresponding to the size of the tang.

The photograph shows three popular files fitted with injection moulded plastics handles which are thrown away with the file when it has become unusable.

Note

Keep new sharp files for use on fine metals such as brass. When they become slightly blunt and less effective they are still sharp enough to cut steel.
Do not try to use files on hardened high-speed steel.

Grades of cut

Single cuts are made across the file and double cuts at a steeper angle. The coarseness of these cuts is described by the terms Bastard (B), Second-cut (S) and Smooth (SM). The size of the cut varies on each file – the largest files having the heaviest cut.

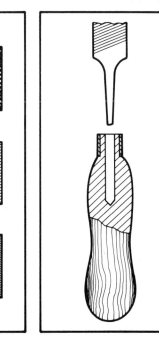

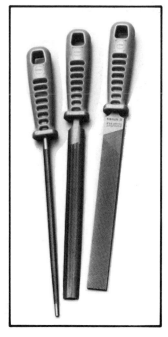

Using Files

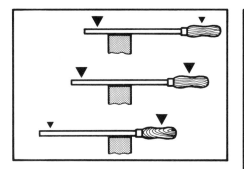

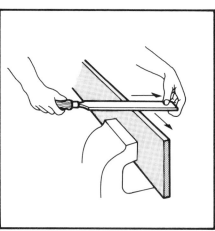

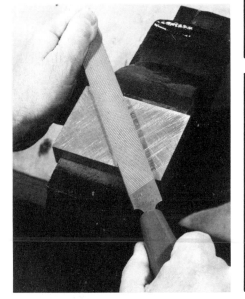

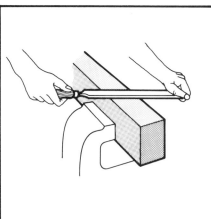

Ensure that the work is held firmly. It will not vibrate if only a small amount of metal projects from the clamping jaws. Make sure that straight edges to be filed in a vice are horizontal.

The drawing shows how the pressure supplied to the file changes during the forward cutting stroke. It begins at the tip of the file, balances out and ends at the handle. At the same time the weight of the craftsman is transferred from the back to the front foot.
Maintain a comfortable stance with feet well apart to form a firm base.

For light filing, hold the front of the file between thumb and forefinger to keep it horizontal. Cut on the forward stroke, taking the pressure off on the return. The drawing shows filing from left to right. Note the angle of the file to the work.

For coarse filing such as removing metal from a surface, change the angle of filing frequently to keep the surface flat. Check for flatness with the back edge of an Engineer's square.

For heavy filing apply pressure to the file using the palm of the front hand.

Draw-filing is the technique used to make a finishing cut to an edge, removing the marks of heavy filing. Use a smooth file held at right angles to the edge and push the file with both thumbs. A finer finish is then obtained by wrapping abrasive cloth around the file and finishing in the same way.

Remove the bulk of waste outside a convex curve with a saw. Make a series of flats nearer the guide line with a bastard-cut file. Remove the final corners with a second-cut file, and finish with a smooth file using a rocking movement. Remove the bulk of waste inside a concave curve with a saw and shape to the line using a half-round file. It can be finished by draw-filing with a smooth half-round file, reversed.

Files used to remove waste from soft metal can become clogged or 'pinned'. Avoid this by carefully selecting the correct file and rubbing the teeth with chalk before using it.

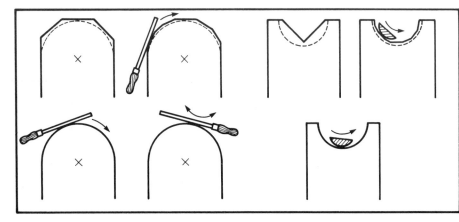

Scrapers

Scrapers are made of hardened alloy steel which is only slightly tempered. The tools keep a cutting edge a long time. Some scrapers are made from tungsten steel and most are between 100 and 200 mm in length.

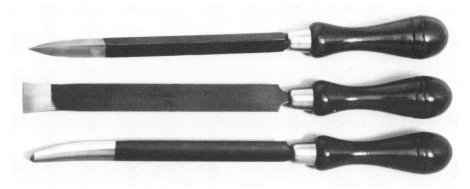

Much of the work previously done by scrapers on surfaces is now done by precision grinding, but they can still be useful. Use a flat scraper to remove the high spots from a flat surface. Test the surface on a surface plate. Cover the surface plate with a thin layer of Engineer's Blue and rub the 'flat' surface over it. The high spots that are marked are then removed. Work across the high spot — first along one diagonal, then along the other. The cutting edge of the flat scraper may be slightly rounded so that small high spots may be easily removed.

Use both the three-square or triangular scraper and the half-round scraper on internal surfaces, especially bearings.

Prepare the cutting edge of a scraper by careful grinding and finish smooth with an oil-stone.

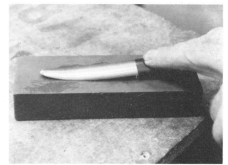

Engineer's Blue

Traditional Engineer's Blue is a liquid which is brushed on to a surface. The modern method of applying colour is by aerosol. The fast-drying solvent-based lacquer leaves a coloured film which will make marking out much clearer. Blue, red and green colours are available so that each operation or material can be colour-coded.
The colour is removed with an appropriate solvent.

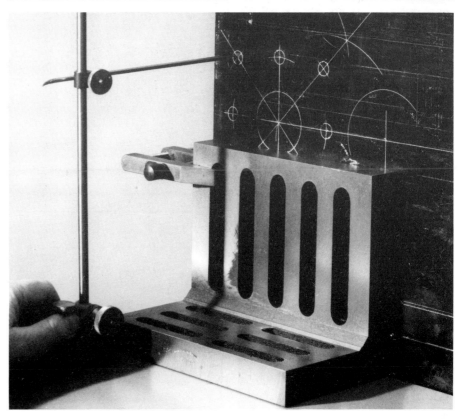

Drills

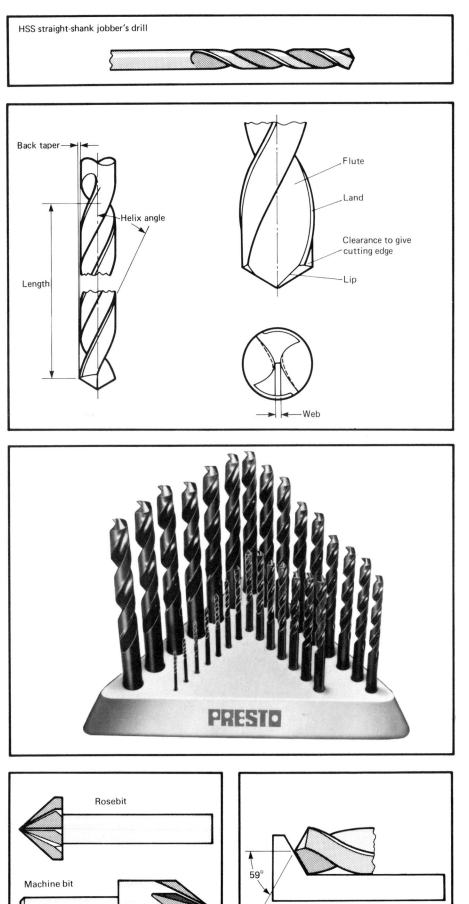

HSS straight-shank jobber's drill

Back taper

Helix angle

Length

Flute

Land

Clearance to give cutting edge

Lip

Web

Rosebit

Machine bit

59°

Checking drill bit on drill gauge

Straight-shanked drills are made from high-speed steel and are labelled on the shank (HSS). The shorter type of drill is often called a jobber's drill.

A drill is a complex cutting instrument and the enlarged drawing clearly shows each part.

The **web** is the central core of the drill which begins as the fine chisel edge.
The **lip** is the actual cutting edge, the drill being ground back from this to give clearance during cutting.
The **land** is the side cutting edge which is slightly raised so that the body of the drill clears the hole sides.
The **flute** allows swarf to clear itself from the cutting area.

The included angle of a jobbing drill is 118°. This is checked on a drill gauge during sharpening.

Drill grinding attachments for use with an abrasive wheel can be set at the desired angle. Note that some drills may be given a steeper point for cutting some plastic materials.

It is important that the cutting lips of a drill are equal or an enlarged inaccurate hole will be made.

Jobbing drills are available in 108 different sizes from 0.35 to 13 mm. Most often they are in sets. Sets from 1–6 mm and 6–13 mm are usually cased for protection.

Store drills with care to prevent damage.

Countersink drills

Jobber's drills are often used in conjunction with a countersink drill, and have an included angle of either 60° or 90°. Use the carbon steel rose bit on soft materials, such as wood. Use the HSS machine bit on metals. The bits cannot normally be sharpened.

Countersink drills are used for recessing screw heads.

Drilling

The common hand-drill has an iron frame and visible gearwheel and pinions. Another type has a similar mechanism but the gearwheel and pinions are lubricated and enclosed inside an alloy casing. They are free from dirt and swarf.

Hand-drills have self-centring three-jaw chucks which will accept straight-shanked drills up to 8 mm in diameter. Larger diameter drills, such as countersinks, are made with small shanks to fit these chucks.

The breast drill is a larger version of the hand-drill. It has a larger gearwheel and a chuck which will hold drill shanks up to 13 mm in diameter. It is fitted with a thrust ball-race for smooth operation. The breast pad is adjustable.

Both drills can be used for vertical and horizontal drilling.

Mark the position of the hole to be drilled with a punch. (For small drills a dot punch is sufficient.) Larger drills with a larger chisel edge need a centre-punch hole to stop the drill from drifting.

Hand-drilling is less accurate than using a pillar drill. Use a hand-drill only when the work cannot be taken to a pillar drill. Use a hand-drill with small-diameter drills.

Portable power-drills are often used instead of hand-drills, but they are often too fast and liable to be inaccurate. Slow drilling may be an advantage when the depth of drilling needs careful control.

To ensure reasonable accuracy when drilling vertically, hold the material horizontally in a vice and align with an Engineer's square.

Horizontal drilling is more difficult. Hold the material vertically in a vice and place a loose washer on the drill bit. If the washer runs towards the chuck, raise the hand-drill handle. If the washer does not move sideways the drilling is reasonably horizontal.

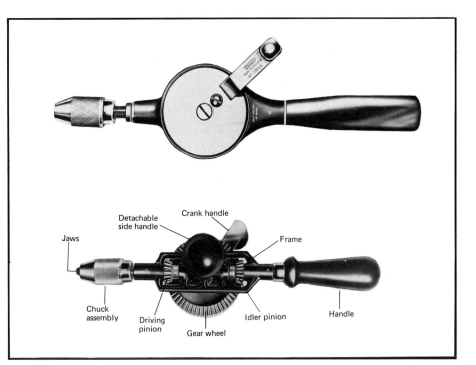

Jaws · Detachable side handle · Crank handle · Frame · Chuck assembly · Driving pinion · Gear wheel · Idler pinion · Handle

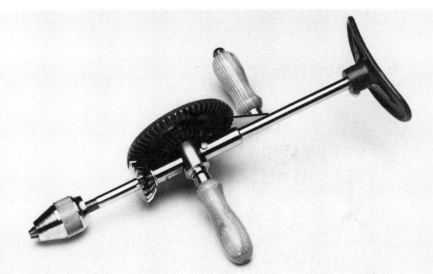

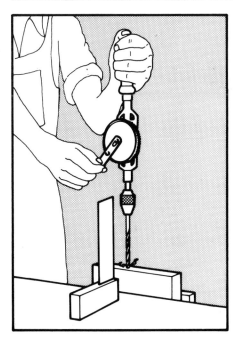

Washer

Pliers

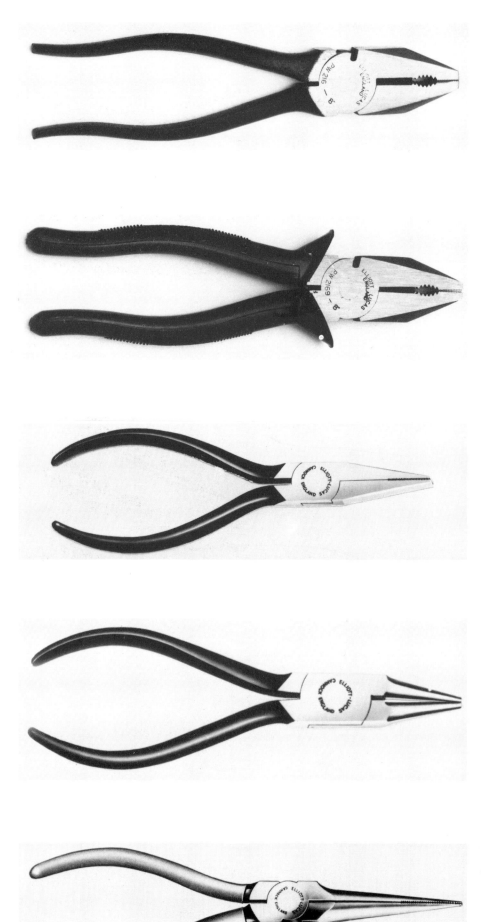

Pliers are useful holding and cutting tools. My tool catalogue lists more than a hundred different patterns, sizes and finishes. This suggests that most pliers have been designed with a particular job in mind.

The best quality pliers have been forged from high-quality steel alloys, often containing silicon and manganese. They have hardened cutting edges. Common lengths are from 150 to 200 mm.

Engineer's pliers

These are often called 'combination pliers' because they are designed to do several jobs. Serrations across the faces of the jaws will grip flat material tightly. Concave surfaces provide an excellent grip on small-diameter round material such as tubing. The side cutters are for wire cutting.

The pliers shown are stamped with a reference number. The PW mark guarantees that the cutters are sufficiently hard to cut hard wire.

Electrician's pliers

These are identical to Engineer's pliers but have PVC handles. The reference has a number 9 added — the manufacturer's catalogue shows that the handles are guaranteed to be insulated against 10 000 volts.

Flat-nose pliers

These have serrated jaws.

Round-nose pliers

These have smooth jaws. Use them for holding round material such as tubing and in simple jewellery work where soft metals may mark.

Taper-nose pliers

These allow access to awkward places such as radio work. The type shown does not have side cutters.

Pliers (continued)

The illustrations on this page indicate some of the range of holding and cutting applications of hand pliers for working metal.

End cutters

Although Engineer's combination pliers are used for cutting wire they are not suitable for accurate work. Jewellers and electronics engineers will have a selection of side, diagonal and end cutters for use on fine wire work.

Cable cutters

The heavy jaws are able to slice through copper and aluminium cable – the long handles give the necessary leverage.

Slip joint

The **water pump pliers** shown have four notches for adjusting the point of leverage.

Gas pliers work in a similar way but have reamers on the handle for taking burrs off the inside edges of sawn tube.

Locking pliers

These are made with less precision than the pliers already described, but they are effective clamping devices. A micro-adjusting screw ensures that the jaws will clamp on the material. This leaves both hands free to work. A release trigger loosens the pliers.

The serrated jaws of the standard 'vise-grip' are ideal for holding small pieces of work to be drilled or polished and for twisting wire.

The **long nose** pliers have jaws which taper to 3 mm. Use them for holding screws or nuts in narrow spaces where access is difficult.

The **sheet pliers** have 80 mm wide jaws with a throat depth of 48 mm. Use them for sheet-metal working and for stretching upholstery webbing.

The **welding pliers** have twin jaws which will hold together two pieces of bar, pipe or sheet to be joined. They may also be used for holding sheet to be riveted.

The **chain pliers** are commonly used in car maintenance, particularly for removing oil filters. Use them for holding odd-shaped pieces of metal together when welding.

End cutters

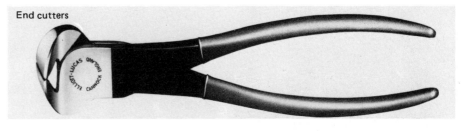

Cable cutters

Water pump pliers

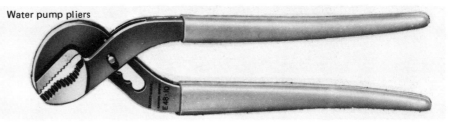

Locking pliers

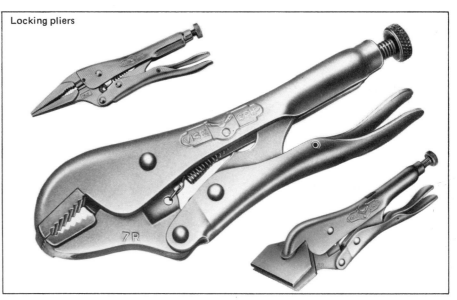

Welding pliers

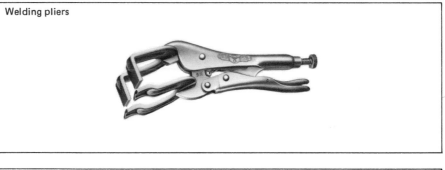

Chain pliers

Spanners

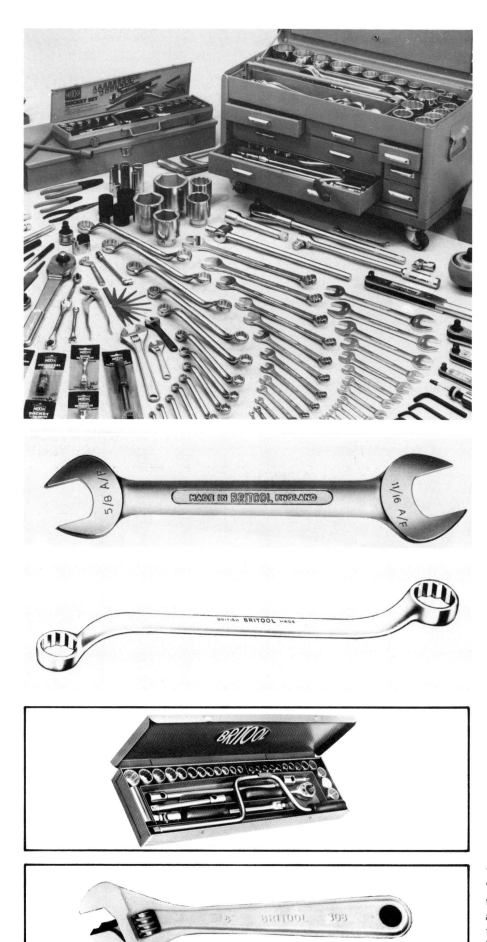

Spanners are made from a hard chrome-alloy steel which is nickel or chrome plated for protection. Open, ring and socket types are bought in sets to fit the various nut sizes — British, Unified & American, metric etc.

A major use of spanners is in auto engineering. Sets of spanners are often available cheaply, but the chrome-plating hides their poor quality which only becomes obvious in use.

Do not attempt to use spanners when they do not fit exactly — the spanner will slip and damage the corners of the nut. Damage may also be caused by using open-ended or adjustable spanners of poor quality.

Open-ended spanners

The jaws are set at an angle of $15°$ to the shank. Sizes are measured across the flats of the jaw. A range of 6–60 mm is available, with corresponding lengths from 120 to 500 mm to provide leverage. The best-quality spanners have relatively thin jaws for easy access to nuts. The cheapest will also have thin jaws, but they will lack strength so that they tend to open out and slip.

Ring spanners

These are designed to solve the problem of slip. The internal diameter of the ring is grooved to fit the corners of an hexagonal nut. The ring is cranked away from the shank to give access to confined spaces.

Socket sets

Circular heads are grooved at one end to fit the nut. There is a square recess at the other end into which a drive shaft is fitted.
The square drive may be of the fixed screwdriver type, or it may be a fixed bar fitted with a universal joint. A third type has a ratchet handle which gives good leverage and can be reversed without removing the drive from the socket.

Adjustable spanners

The best adjustable spanners are especially useful if nuts are not too tight and are accessible. In a confined space they are too thick.
If misused they damage nuts so badly that ring or socket spanners will not then fit the nuts.

Screwdrivers

The Engineer's screwdriver is made from a fully hardened chrome-alloy steel on to which a split-proof plastic handle has been moulded.
A common range would have tip widths of 6, 8 and 9.5 mm and several blade lengths to allow access into confined spaces.

Choose the correct screwdriver to match the slot in the head of the screw. Three common faults and effects are shown.

1. blade too narrow – damaged screw
2. blade too thin – damaged screw and blade
3. blade too wide – damaged work

The blade should be the same width as the head, and a firm fit in the slot.

'Cross' slots

These are commonly used on screws which have countersunk or raised heads and for fixing metal components, such as handles, to wood. They have the advantage of being exactly matched to a screwdriver so that the blade does not 'cam-out' and damage the surface or the head when force is applied.
Do not paint the recess in the screw.
Three types are in use. The first of these was the 'Phillips', the most common is the 'Posidriv', and the latest is the 'Superdriv' – each an improvement on the other.
The blades are numbered so that the correct tip size can be selected. The most common screw gauges – from 5 to 10 – have the same size of slot. A number two (no. 2) screwdriver fits all of them.

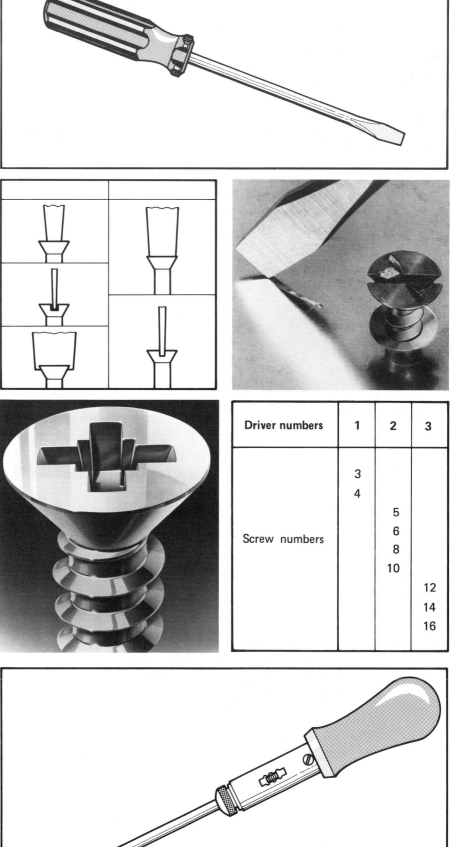

Driver numbers	1	2	3
	3		
	4		
		5	
Screw numbers		6	
		8	
		10	
			12
			14
			16

Ratchet screwdrivers

These can be used in either direction or as a fixed-blade driver. A wood handle is fitted into the metal ferrule.

Use a ratchet screwdriver where lack of space does not allow a convenient full turn on a fixed-blade screwdriver.

45

Screwdrivers (continued)

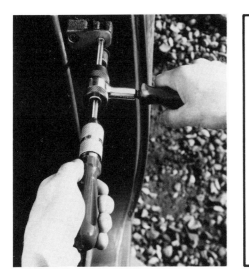

A **heavy duty** screwdriver will be up to 305 mm long with a maximum tip width of 9.5 mm or more (cross slot sizes 3 or 4).

A **square bar** driver can be given extra leverage by means of an adjustable spanner or locking pliers. The 'Paramo' screwdriver shown has an X-sectioned blade which can be turned either way using a detachable ratchet handle.

In spaces where a long-bladed screwdriver will not reach, the very short driver has its use. The 'Stubby' or 'Chubby' type will have a blade no longer than 40 mm and an overall length of 90 mm.

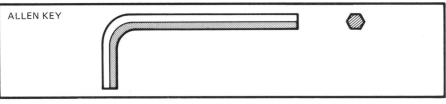

ALLEN KEY

Socket-head screws are turned with **socket wrenches** often referred to as 'Allen keys'.
Imperial and metric sets are available. A typical set stored in a wallet would contain nine or ten keys from 1.5 to 10 mm, measured across the flats.

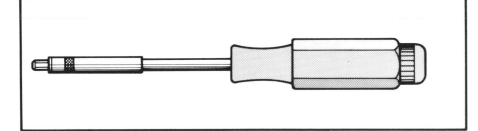

Magnetic screwdrivers are invaluable when a screw has to be inserted where it cannot be held in place to be turned.

The driver shown uses a range of hexagonal insert bits — those not in use are stored in the hollow handle.

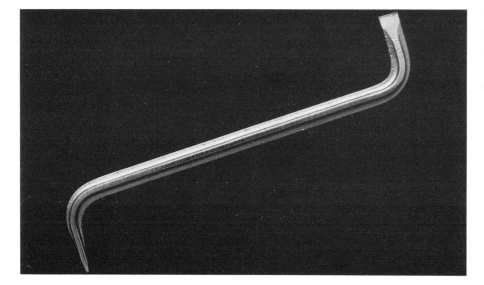

In even more inaccessible places the **double offset** driver has its uses. For slot-head screws, one tip of the driver is set at 90° to the other. For cross-slot screws, each end is a different number (e.g. nos. 1 and 2 or nos. 2 and 3).

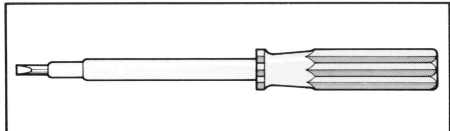

Electrician's screwdrivers are made in the same way as the Engineer's drivers described on the previous page. The blade is insulated by a PVC sleeve.

Jointing – Rivets

Rivets are permanent fastenings made from soft malleable materials such as aluminium, copper, brass and mild steel. They are annealed when made but work-harden as they are hammered into place.

Spot welding techniques have taken the place of many traditional uses of rivets, but they are still an effective way of joining sheet material to a framework.

Use **snap** or **roundheads** for all general riveting where a countersunk head would weaken the material.

Use **panheads** for general work and as a decorative feature.

Use the **countersunk mushroom** for decoration.

The **mushroom** or **universal** head has a large diameter which will give some support to thinner materials.

Use the **flathead rivet,** which is often made from galvanized iron, for tin-plate work. It gives support to the plate and does not rust.

Use **conical head rivets** as decoration, especially in copperwork, for fixing handles and fabricating fireplace canopies.

Use **bifurcated rivets** on soft materials such as leather upholstery and canvas webbing.

The 90° **countersunk rivet** is most commonly used. A 60° countersunk rivet can be used in thick material, and the 140° countersunk head in very thin material where a normal countersunk rivet would seriously weaken it.

The rivet '**set**' and '**snap**' are designed to do two jobs. They have a hole drilled to fit over the rivet shank for 'setting' and a domed recess to complete the process by 'snapping' the rivet head.
The set and snap are used together with a supporting '**dolly**'.

Heavy rivets may be used in erecting steelwork for a building. Much smaller ones are used for attaching a cycle mudguard to its stay. The principle is just the same.

Rivets are measured by length, to the shoulder, and by diameter. They are named according to the type of head – snap, countersunk, pan and round heads being most common.

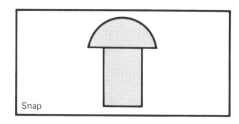
Snap

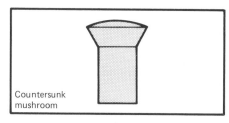
Pan

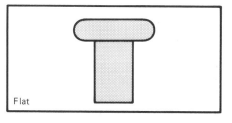
Countersunk mushroom

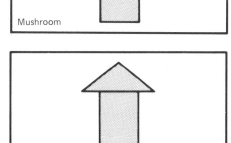
Mushroom

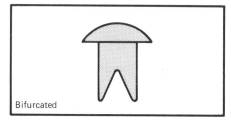
Flat

Conical

Bifurcated

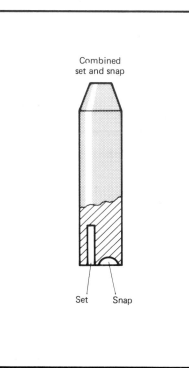
Combined set and snap

Set   Snap

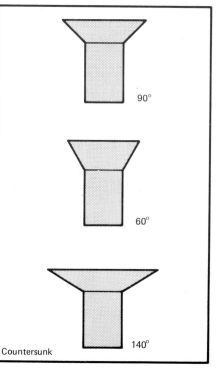
90°

60°

140°

Countersunk

Riveting

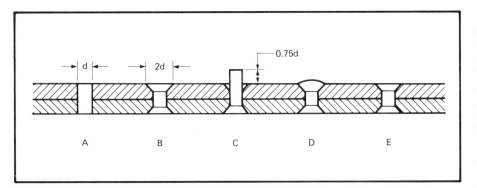

A   B   C   D   E

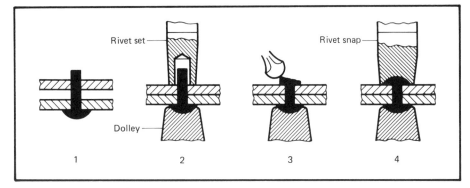

Rivet set

Rivet snap

Dolley

1   2   3   4

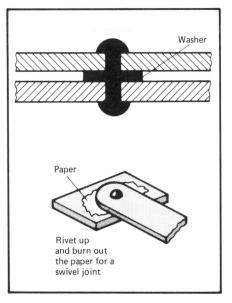

Washer

Paper

Rivet up
and burn out
the paper for a
swivel joint

Where a single riveted joint is needed to *swivel*, either: (a) insert a washer between the materials, or (b) insert paper between the material which can be burned away.

Faults

Holes too large	Rivet will bend
Too much rivet projecting	Rivet will bend, or head will be badly shaped
Too little rivet projecting	Countersink will not be filled
Gap between material	Failure to use rivet set, or drill burrs not removed.

Ensure that rivets have a diameter which is not less than the thickness of the metal being riveted and not more than three times its thickness.

Where several rivets are to be used, drill clearance holes in the top material and only one in the bottom piece. Remove the burrs and fix one rivet as described below. Locate and drill a second hole and rivet it. The two pieces are now fixed and the remaining rivets may be fitted.

Snap or roundhead rivets

1. Cut the rivet to length leaving a projection of 1.5 diameters.
2. Locate the rivet in its hole and place the head in the dolly. Use the set to close the material together.
3. Strike a *square* blow on the rivet to fix it, and then dome it using the ballpein hammer.
4. Use the snap to make a neat finish.

Countersunk rivets

Check that the countersinks are prepared to the correct size. Cut the rivets to length leaving a projection of 0.75 diameter. Locate the rivets in the holes and place the work on a hard flat anvil. Use the set to close the material together, then strike the rivet to fill in the countersink. File away surplus material.

Pop riveting

A pop riveter is the ideal tool for permanently joining thin sheet and plastics to each other and to wood using aluminium or steel rivets.

The riveter shown has interchangeable nose bushes for 3, 4 and 5 mm diameter rivets of lengths from 5 to 36 mm. The size of the hole is less critical than with traditional rivets.
The drawing shows how one rivet will adapt to a range of thicknesses.

Open the pliers and insert a pin. Insert the rivet into the aligned holes and squeeze the handles until the pin breaks. More than one squeeze may be necessary. Open the handles to release the broken pin.
Note that work proceeds from one side so that access to the reverse side is not necessary.

Use a large flange rivet for securing brittle materials such as plastics, glassware and hardboard sheet.

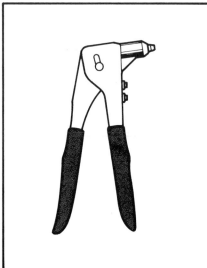

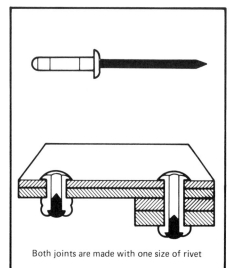

Both joints are made with one size of rivet

Nuts and Bolts

Bolts are temporarily fastened by nuts to make strong mechanical joints between components. The high-tensile-steel bolt shown has a length (measured to the head) from 12 to 150 mm, in diameters from 6 to 25 mm.

They generally have an hexagonal (six-sided) head. The head is measured in two ways: across the flats for the size of spanner needed to turn it, and across the corners to measure the greatest diameter to be allowed for so that the bolt can be turned.

Carriage bolts get their name from the original use for which they were designed – to produce strong temporary fixings between a wood-framed carriage and its metal chassis. They are used on agricultural vehicles and for fixing heavy vices to bench tops.
The domed head gives a neat finish and the square neck stops the bolt from rotating in the wood.

Nuts

Nuts are commonly made to match the bolt thread and head size, but they vary in thickness. **Half-nuts** can be used where there is limited space.

To prevent a full nut working loose because of vibrations, a half-nut may be used to lock it. Two spanners are used, one on each nut, to lock the first nut on to the component and then to tighten it back on to a second nut.

Slotted nuts are used with split or cotter pins fixed through a hole drilled in the bolt.

Where fixings need only be hand-tight or need to be frequently removed, use a hand-turned **wing nut** instead of a bolt.

When access to the protruding end of a bolt is restricted, use a **socket stud.** This has two thread lengths and is inserted into one component using a socket wrench to turn it. A nut is threaded on from the top to bring the components together and secure them.

Washers

Flat washers are used to increase the bearing surface of a nut or bolt head and prevent damage to a surface.

Use single- or double-coil washers where vibration may cause the nut to slacken. The coil presses against the nut and holds it in position.

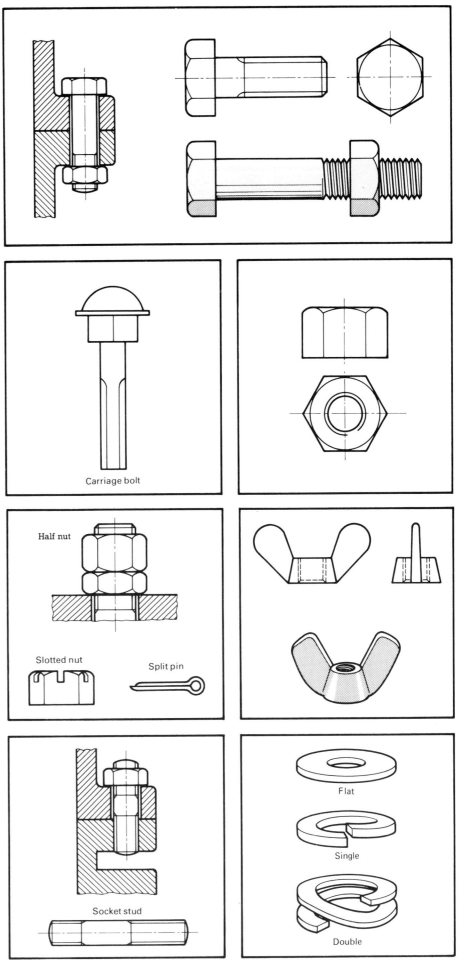

Carriage bolt

Half nut

Slotted nut

Split pin

Socket stud

Flat

Single

Double

Bolting

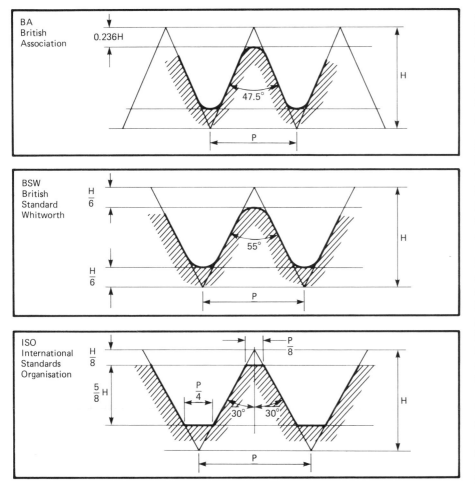

Common bolt sizes (mm)			
Nominal diameter	Pitch	Recommended tapping drill size	Clearance drill size
2	0.4	1.6	2.05
2.5	0.45	2.05	2.6
3	0.5	2.5	3.1
4	0.7	3.3	4.1
5	0.8	4.2	5.1
6	1.0	5.0	6.1
8	1.25	6.8	8.2
10	1.5	8.5	10.2
12	1.75	10.2	12.2
14	2.0	12.0	14.25
16	2.0	14.0	16.25
18	2.5	15.5	18.25
20	2.5	17.5	20.25

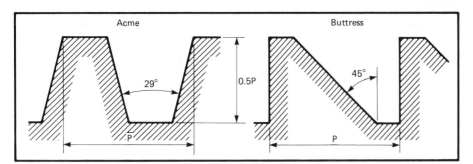

Although it is many years since the ISO Screw Thread Standards were introduced you will probably come across a variety of screw threads in everyday life for years to come. The needs of some special trades and the need to replace non-metric parts in repair work will guarantee that.

Items imported from the USA may still have UNF (Unified) threads, and bicycles may have BSC (British Standard Cycle) threads. Small-diameter screws with a fine pitch will often be found in electrical components and have BA (British Association) threads.

BSF (British Standard Fine) threads have a medium-fine pitch and, because they are less likely to work loose in use, have been used for the construction of parts of machinery. By contrast, BSW (British Standard Whitworth) threads are coarse and have been used for heavier construction work or with metals softer than steel.

The ISO threads are made in both a fine series (to replace BSF) and a coarse series (to replace BSW). They are described according to their nominal diameter and the pitch (prefixed with the letter M), both in millimetres (e.g. M10 × 1.5).

To order bolts you must be able to specify the following:

	Example
Nominal thread diameter	8 mm
Thread pitch	1.25 mm
Thread length	30 mm
Type of head	hexagonal
Length	50 mm
Material	steel
Finish (if any)	Bright zinc-plated

The Table on this page shows common sizes, along with recommended tapping drill sizes which will give clearance for the screw thread. This Table applies *only* to ISO threads.

Special threads

There are two threads which are used when motion between parts is required or power has to be exerted, and these have driving faces.

The **acme** thread is used on lathe lead-screws and on various hand cramps. The square face of the **buttress** thread will exert pressure in a bench vice, and the 45° rake will allow a quick-release mechanism to slide over it.

Taps and Dies

Hand taps are used to cut internal threads into which bolts and screws may be fitted. A master thread is made on hardened steel, and the flutes reveal a cutting edge which will cut a thread and remove waste material.

Hand taps are in sets of three, and are used in the order taper, second and plug. Each has a square shank to fit the wrench used to turn it.

To cut an internal thread, first drill a hole with the appropriate tapping drill. Insert the taper tap into the wrench and, using a cutting lubricant, insert it carefully along the axis of the hole. This is ensured if the tap is fitted into a pillar drill and the chuck turned by hand.

Turn the taper tap until it binds. Then turn the taper tap back to release cut material. Apply lubrication, and continue the cut.

The taper tap only cuts a full size thread along a small part of its length but this will be enough for thin material. Where it is not, proceed in the same manner with the second tap and, if necessary, the plug tap.

For **blind** holes the second and plug tap only will be used.

Blind holes cannot be tapped to the bottom as the tap will break. Drill the tapping size hole slightly deeper than required, then fit a nut on to the tap to act as a depth stop.

Tighten taps into a bar-type wrench and lock with the knurled locking nut. Three sizes of bar wrench will hold the following ISO sized tap sets:

M1 – 6   M5 – 12   M8 – 16

Hold firmly in the manner shown in the photograph.

Use a chuck-type wrench in places where there is not enough space for the tap wrench to be turned, such as on the girder section shown in the photograph. This is an extremely useful tool with lengths up to 250 mm.

Care

Hand taps are easily broken in use and care must be taken not to exert too much pressure nor to bend the tap. If you do it will snap.

If the thread becomes clogged with waste during cutting, remove the tap, clean and lubricate it.

After use, clean the tap thoroughly before replacing it in its storage box.

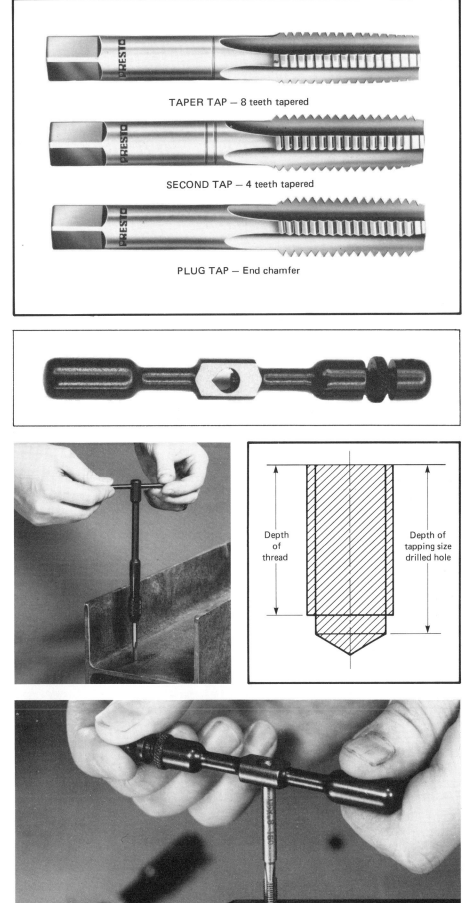

TAPER TAP — 8 teeth tapered

SECOND TAP — 4 teeth tapered

PLUG TAP — End chamfer

Depth of thread

Depth of tapping size drilled hole

Taps and Dies (continued)

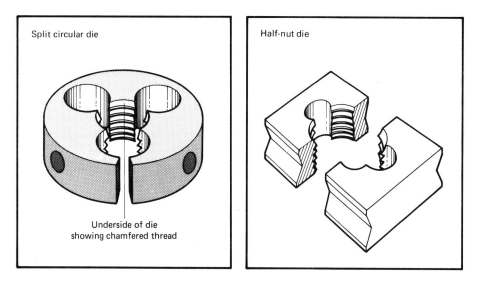

Split circular die

Underside of die
showing chamfered thread

Half-nut die

Dies are used to cut external threads on to which nuts may be fitted, or screw threads for inserting into tapped holes of matching size.

The hardened steel dies are of two main types: the **split-circular** (held in a circular die stock), and the **half-nut** (held in an angular die stock). They are both fluted to form cutting edges and allow cut waste to be released.

The half-nut is finely adjusted by means of a single screw, the split-circular by three screws. To 'open' the die, slacken the two outer screws and tighten the centre screw. To 'close' the die slacken the centre screw and tighten the two outer screws.

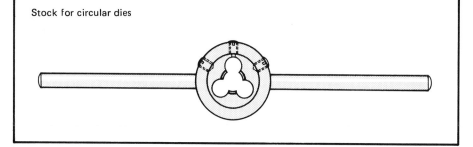

Stock for circular dies

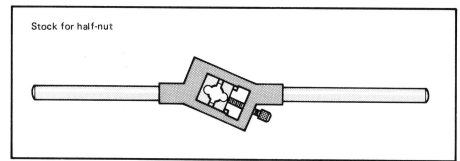

Stock for half-nut

To cut an external thread the rod or bar must be carefully prepared – squared at the end, given a chamfer or slight taper and lubricated.

Set the die open in the holder and place it firmly with the chamfered side down, on to the tapered bar. Rotate it half a turn. Check for squareness and make careful adjustments as necessary. Failure to do this may result in a distorted or 'drunken' thread as shown.

The thread is then cut in much the same way as for tapping. Turn the die about two-thirds of a revolution and then turn it back a third to release cut material. Continue to lubricate as necessary.

This method will produce a thread cut to half depth. Remove the die holder, 'close' the die and repeat the above procedures.

The final thread can be 'run over' with an appropriate die nut to ensure that it is clean and smooth. The hexagonal die nuts can also be used with a spanner to clean up threads which have been damaged or rusted.

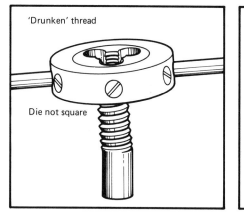

'Drunken' thread

Die not square

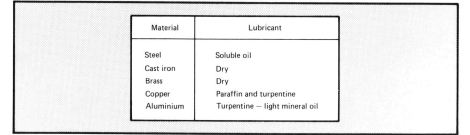

Material	Lubricant
Steel	Soluble oil
Cast iron	Dry
Brass	Dry
Copper	Paraffin and turpentine
Aluminium	Turpentine – light mineral oil

Lubricants

Cutting solutions act as lubricants for both taps and dies. They reduce wear on the cutting tool, help to release waste and improve the surface finish of the threads.

Screws

A large variety of screws, made from materials according to their use, are available. They may be threaded either for part of or for their full length.

The different types of head are shown opposite.

The **hexagonal head** is smaller than on standard bolts, the **cheese head** also protrudes from the surface, and the **socket head** is often recessed in a counterbore. Note that this is driven with an hexagonal wrench (Allen key) and is often referred to as an Allen screw.

Roundhead, raised countersunk and **countersunk** heads may be slotted for a conventional screwdriver or be fitted with a cross slot such as the GKN Supadriv. The photograph shows a stainless steel countersunk screw neatly securing a door handle to an internal metal plate.

Grub screws are slotted but do not have a head. Use them beneath a surface to locate components, both of which must be threaded.

Straight-slotted screws may need to be hidden to appear neat. Some screws are tapped to receive brass or chrome-plated **cover caps** which are simply screwed into place by hand.

Self-tapping screws

These are made from hardened steel and are used on sheet-metal work such as washing machines, cars and caravans for fixing trim or sheets together. They are suitable for use in steel, soft metals and hard plastics.
Like the tap described on page 51 they are fluted to give a cutting edge and the thread is always a perfect match.
The first material is often a trim or fitting which has pre-bored clearance holes. If the top material is comparatively soft, such as plywood, the screw will cut its way through it.

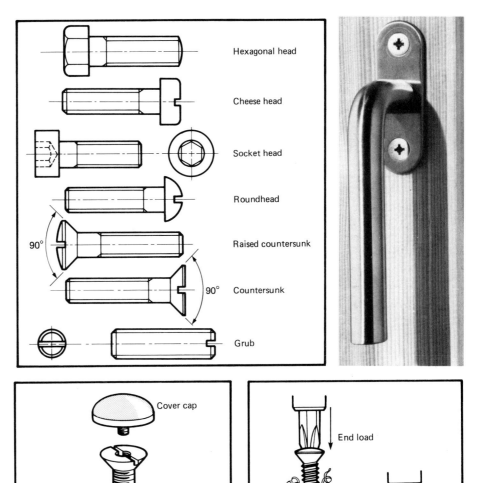

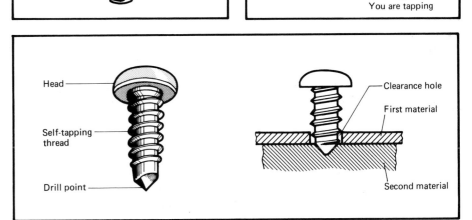

Manufacturers of these screws supply detailed charts about the capacity of screws — the simple chart here relates to three common sizes from the 'King Klik' range.

Screw number	Minimum thickness for thread cutting	Maximum penetration in metals	Minimum clearance holes in first materials
6	0.9	2.3	3.7
8	1.0	2.5	4.4
10	1.2	2.8	5.1

Hardware

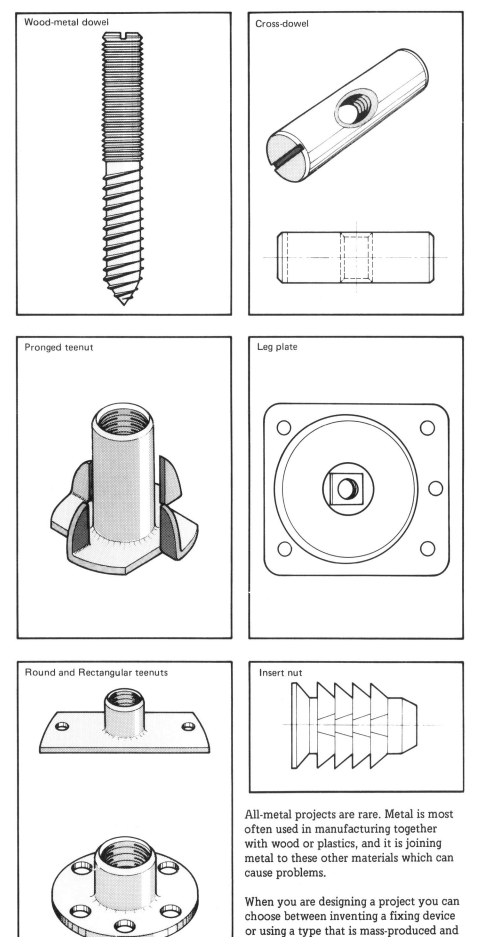

Wood-metal dowel

Cross-dowel

Pronged teenut

Leg plate

Round and Rectangular teenuts

Insert nut

The hardware shown here is suitable for joining metal to wood components – the plates are pre-drilled for screws. However, these plates can also be fixed to metal using metal thread screws or rivets. Fix them permanently to metal by brazing (see page 61).

Each of these fittings is threaded to allow components to be detached from each other. The systems are often used in knock-down (KD) or quick-assembly (QA) items such as furniture or toys. Used correctly, they make constructions simple and enable them to be dismantled for easier storage, transport and delivery. Another advantage is that damaged parts can be removed and replaced, or separated for a fresh finish to be applied.

Wood-metal dowel

Screw the wood thread into the wood component so that the metal thread projects to accommodate nuts. These dowels are usually 38–75 mm long.

Cross-dowel

An aluminium barrel nut is used as a cross-dowel in the rails of a leg-and-rail construction. Bore the rail to fit the barrel nut. Pass a screw through the leg and into the nut to pull the components together.

Leg plate

This is a steel plate fitted with a nut into which a screw is fixed. It can be straight, or offset to give sloping legs.

Pronged teenut

Hammer the nut into a pre-drilled hole in the wood and insert a metal screw from the other side. These nuts are usually 13–25 mm wide with M3 to M10 threads.

Round and Rectangular teenuts

These work in the same way but are pre-drilled for screw fixing – use on wood, metal or plastics.

Insert nuts

These are made in steel, brass or nylon and are designed to resist withdrawal from soft materials such as wood and chipboard.
Carefully bore holes of the recommended size, and consider using appropriate adhesive to strengthen the joint.
Use when Teenuts cannot be inserted from the opposite side.

All-metal projects are rare. Metal is most often used in manufacturing together with wood or plastics, and it is joining metal to these other materials which can cause problems.

When you are designing a project you can choose between inventing a fixing device or using a type that is mass-produced and cheaper. These fittings are called 'hardware'.

Hardware (continued)

Because metal can be made to precise sizes and does not shrink and warp like wood, it is ideal for making into a 'system'. The parts of a system can be put together in different ways depending on the needs of the user. The designer quickly learns how the system works and rarely meets design problems that cannot be solved. Systems are often simple enough for the user to construct using basic tools and limited skills.

A lot of wood furniture is built with quick-assembly (QA) joints, needing only a screwdriver to make them. 'Speedframe' is a metal framing system using standardized units which are joined by plastics fittings. A hacksaw is used to cut the tube to length. Burrs are removed with a fine file and a soft hammer drives the joints together. You will see 'Speedframe' used in shop displays because it is strong and can be taken apart and reconstructed.
'Speedframe' can be used for partitioning and furniture making.

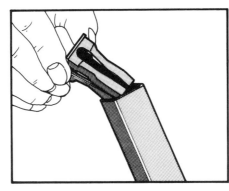

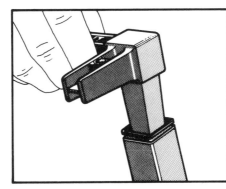

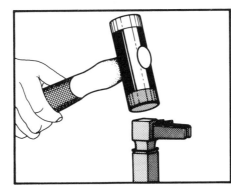

Use the principle of the 'Speedframe' system to make up your own designs. Use the tube in the following way:

1. Select the tube. Choose from steel or aluminium 19 or 25 mm square.
2. Select the finish. Choose from black, grey or satin chrome.
3. Cut the tube using a hacksaw, preferably in a saw guide.
4. Remove any rough edges with a fine file.
5. Check for squareness. Then insert a soft plastics insert.
6. Select the joint. Choose from seven aluminium alloy joints.
7. Push the joint into the insert and drive it in with a soft-faced hammer. (PVC plastic extrusions can be fitted to the tubing so that frames can be fitted with 19 mm chipboard or 4–6 mm glass.)
8. Give the ends of tubes a neat finish using a polyethylene plastics cap.
9. Fit a steel cap into the framework so that an adjustable foot can be used.
10. When the frame is used as a trolley or portable unit, fit a polyethylene cap. A tapered socket fits into this into which a castor can be inserted.

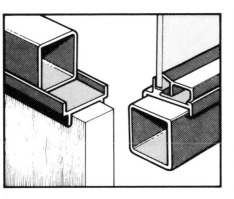

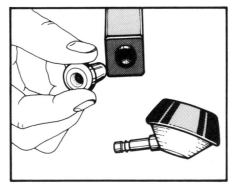

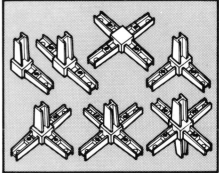

Hardware (continued)

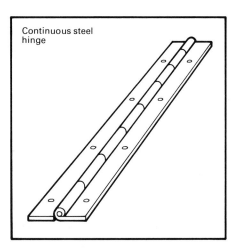

Continuous steel hinge

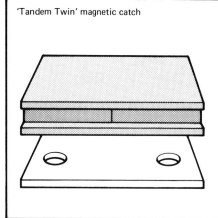

'Tandem Twin' magnetic catch

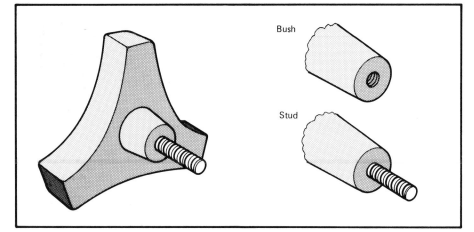

Bush

Stud

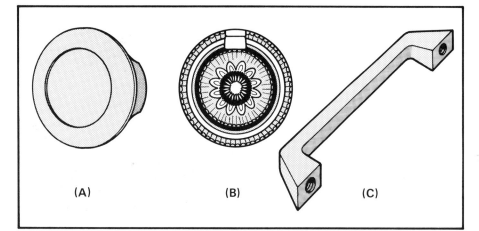

(A)   (B)   (C)

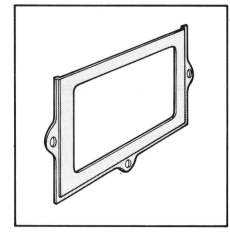

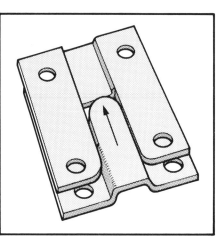

Metal objects are often used as extras on furniture. For example, my desk is made from hardwood and plywood. The top is held on by simple metal plates. The top drawer is fitted with a brass lock and opened with a metal handle. The lock and the handle are made by craftsmen using special metals and specialist techniques. The metal plates could easily be made at the work bench, but even that might not be worth while as mass-production methods make them cheap to buy. It may be best to spend more time on the *design* of objects and *learn how standard hardware fittings can best be used.*

Continuous steel hinge can be purchased in 1800 mm lengths. Cut it to length and either screw, rivet, braze or spot-weld it on to metal constructions.

Magnetic catches are the neatest way of temporarily closing surfaces together.

Handwheels are often fitted on machines — a triangular type is shown. It is made in black plastic and can be covered in an alternative metallized chrome finish. The bush fitting has an internal thread cut directly into the plastic to receive a bolt.
The stud fitting has a projecting metal thread to receive a nut.

Handles

I have a hardware catalogue with sixty-two different styles of handle in it. The choice is enormous. The filing cabinets, cupboard doors and drawers in my study are fitted with seven styles. Three contrasting styles are illustrated:
(A) is a cabinet knob, cast in aluminium and given a brushed finish. This contrasts well with a dark painted door.
(B) is a drop-ring pull, cast in brass and given an antique finish to harmonize with dark wood drawer fronts.
(C) is a cabinet handle, cast in aluminium and given a bush fitting to be screwed to a metal filing cabinet from inside the drawer.

Choose handles, knobs and pulls with care. There is a style and size to fit most design needs.

A **card frame** is riveted to each of my filing drawers — a neat labelling device.

The **Flushmount** is a two-part fixing device useful for locating wood or metal units together. The bright zinc-plated interlocking pieces can be fixed with countersunk screws or riveted.

Soft Soldering

Soldering is the process of melting solder into the gap between metal parts to form a joint. The solder must adhere to both parts and fill the gap. It is a suitable method of joining most metals (but not chrome–steel or aluminium) provided that the joint does not need to be strong. Solder is a mixture of tin and lead and is a relatively weak alloy. Use this alloy for soft soldering.

The **straight bit** or **hatchet bit** are traditional soldering tools. A solid piece of copper is fitted because it is big enough to conserve the heat and keep the joint hot whilst the solder melts.

Use a small **soldering iron** for electrical work – this small copper bit has a heating element of 40 watts.

The **soldering gun** shown has a 250 watt element which is instantly heated or cooled by the trigger. Additional tips enable it to be used on thermoplastic and polystyrene materials – damaged plastics can be repaired.

The **soldering torch** shown has a gas cylinder as the heat source. Use it with a flame on large joints to be soldered, or with the copper bit attachment in the traditional way.

A **gas burner** is traditionally used to heat a bit quickly and economically. *A gas soldering iron stove is safer.*

Solder types

The melting point of solder changes with the change in its tin content:

1. The softest solder has about 60 per cent tin. It runs easily, sets quickly and is ideal for electrical work.
2. Solder with about 50 per cent tin content is for general use on copper, brass and tin-plate.
3. The hardest solder has about 40 per cent tin. It takes longest to melt and is usually used when the heat source is a soldering torch or blowpipe.

Flux

Flux is a material which prevents oxidization around the joint and helps the solder to flow. A zinc-chloride liquid flux (active flux) is used for most metal work – the residue is rinsed off to prevent corrosion.
Resin flux (passive flux) is used on electrical work.

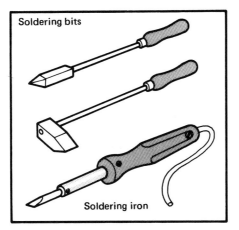

Soldering bits

Soldering iron

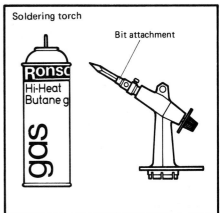

Soldering torch

Bit attachment

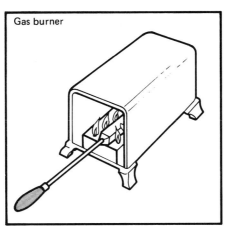

Gas burner

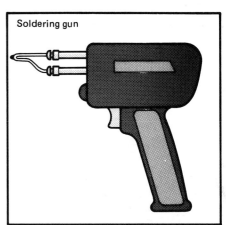

Soldering gun

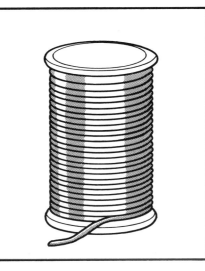

One of the difficulties in soldering is to ensure that the correct amount of flux is used in the right place. This problem is solved by a 'Multicore' solder. The coil of solder has fine flux cores along its length. The flux cores melt before the solder, ensuring that the joint is wet and that the solder makes reliable joints.

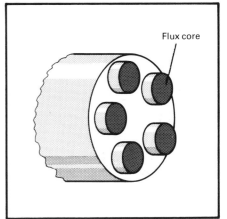

Flux core

Soft Soldering (continued)

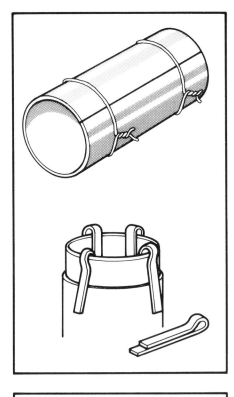

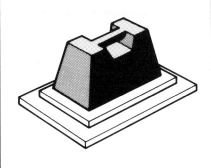

A **sweated joint** can be used for temporary fixing such as when two sheets of metal need to be cut out together and then separated. Clean, flux and tin both surfaces. Put the surfaces together and reheat with a blowpipe or gas torch. When the solder runs apply weights to ensure good contact between the surfaces.

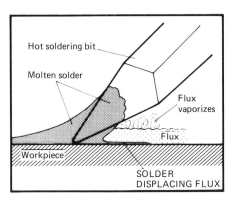

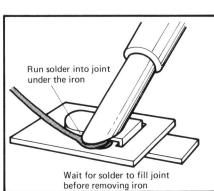

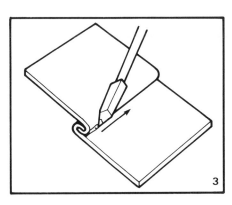

Use emery cloth to clean the surfaces to be soldered. Choose a method to hold the work whilst the joint is made. Binding wire will secure a cylinder and prevent the joint from opening when heat is applied. Clips are used when the pieces cannot be wired, as when soldering one cylinder inside another. Use weights when large surfaces have been 'sweated' together.

This soldering method describes the traditional way of making a double lap or lockseam joint — one of the strongest ways of making a side seam on tin-plate:

1. Prepare the joint, allowing only a fine gap between the metal. The correct gap is one which will just accept a thin sheet of paper. Heat the bit electrically or in a stove. Then dip it into the flux and 'tin' it — this means coating the bit with a thin layer of solder.
2. Use an old brush to apply the flux to the joint.
3. Reheat the bit and lay it on the joint. As the joint reaches the heat at which the solder will flow, run it slowly along the joint in the direction of the arrow. There should be sufficient solder on the bit to complete the joint, but add more solder if required. Large joints and thick metal can be pre-heated by a torch before the flux is applied.
4. Rinse the joint to wash away surplus corrosive flux.

The enlarged section shows the soldering process. The hot bit vaporizes the flux, which allows the molten solder to adhere to the materials.

An electrically heated bit maintains its heat throughout the operation and makes soldering easier.

The drawing shows the way in which Multicore solder is applied to a small area. The soldering iron bit must be cleaned and tinned as described.
Place the end of the multicore solder on the joint with the bit firmly on it. As the solder melts it carries the heat from the iron to the joint surfaces — the heat precedes the melted flux and the solder follows. If the joint is a good fit capillary action will ensure that the solder reaches all parts of the joint.

Hard Soldering

Hard soldering is the process of joining metals using a copper, zinc and silver alloy.
Solders with high amounts of silver in the alloy melt at lower temperatures. This is extremely useful if more than one soldering process is needed when making something — the solder with the least silver content is used first, and solder with more silver and a lower melting point is used last.

Hard solders can be used on most metals. The joint is strong, ductile and resists corrosion.

Brazing is a similar process for making a very strong joint in steel using a copper and zinc alloy called 'spelter'.
Spelter with high amounts of zinc in the alloy melts at lower temperatures, so that using different spelters allows more than one brazing process to be carried out on the materials. Appropriate fluxes, usually mixed into a paste, are available for each type of solder or spelter.

Work to be joined is heated to red heat by a gas torch on a brazing hearth. There are two types of torch used to supply gas and blown air to produce the high temperatures necessary.

A section through a traditional torch shows separate controls for gas and air and an air nozzle which can be changed. The modern torch has a separate pilot light burner and is operated in the following way:

1. Ensure that all the torch valves are closed and that the gas valves on the hearth are horizontal.
2. Turn on the isolating switch. This allows sufficient gas to flow for the pilot light to be lit.
3. Turn on the gas valve and light pilot.
4. Press the *green* start button to operate the combustion fan.
5. Hold the torch and turn the valve wheel clockwise to obtain a flame. Turn it further to increase the flame.

To shut down the apparatus, reverse the procedure. First turn the torch valve wheel anticlockwise, press the *red* stop button, then turn off the isolating switch.

The shape of a flame is important in brazing and hard soldering. Start with the largest flame, with the valve wheel turned fully clockwise. Then reduce it to a smaller pointed flame as the required temperature is reached.

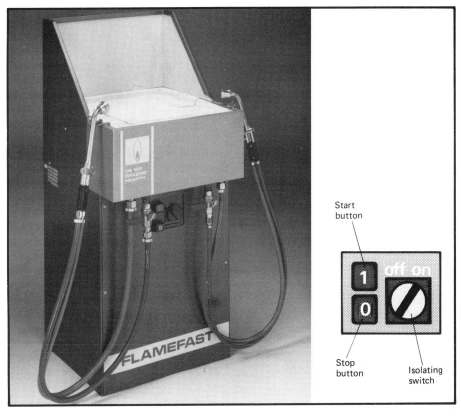

Start button

Stop button

Isolating switch

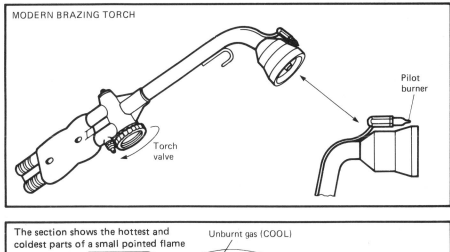

TRADITIONAL BRAZING TORCH

Section through head

Air

Air

Gas

Gas

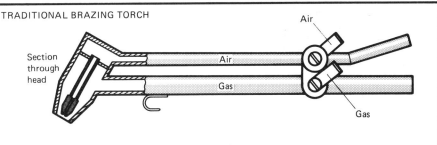

MODERN BRAZING TORCH

Pilot burner

Torch valve

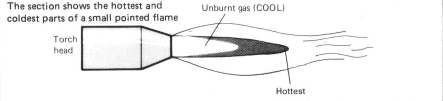

The section shows the hottest and coldest parts of a small pointed flame

Torch head

Unburnt gas (COOL)

Hottest

Hard Soldering (continued)

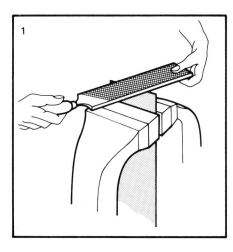

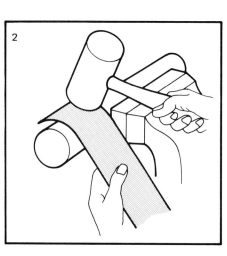

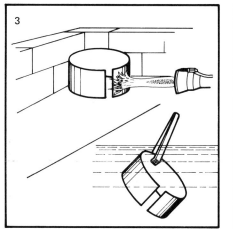

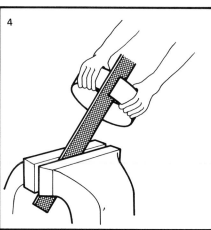

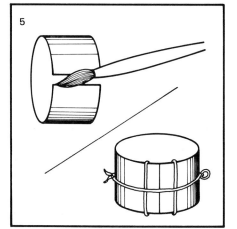

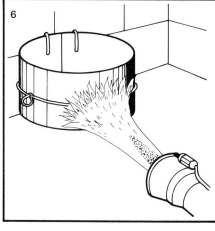

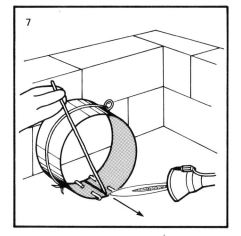

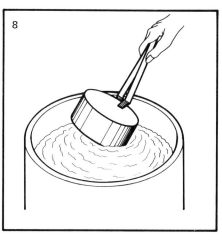

Copper is a metal commonly used in jewellery and box making. A cylindrical shape can be made as follows:

1. Cut some sheet copper approximately to size and hold it in a soft-faced vice to prepare the edges with a file. Check for squareness.
2. Use a soft mallet to work the copper strip from each end around a suitable stake.
3. Beating the copper makes it 'work-harden' so that the metal becomes more difficult to bend. Soften the metal by annealing it. Heat the copper to a dull red, using a soft flame from the torch. Then quench it in water.
4. Fix a second-cut file in a vice, open the joint and place it around the blade. Obtain perfect joint alignment by rubbing carefully up and down the file.
5. Mix the appropriate flux and apply it to the joint with a brush.
   Use binding wire to wire up the joint. Two vertical wires prevent the main wire from touching the joint. Arrange the tightening loops opposite each other, the same distance from the joint, so that pressure is even.
6. Fix a soft flame on the torch and heat the material on the *opposite side* from the joint. The metal will then expand towards the joint.
7. When the cylinder is evenly hot, turn it over in the hearth and adjust the torch to produce a smaller, harder flame. Concentrate the flame on the joint area. Then, at the right temperature, put a little solder to the inside of the joint. Draw the flame slowly along the joint in the direction of the arrow. Allow the solder to flow along, following the heat.
8. Allow the cylinder to cool. Remove the binding wires and place the cylinder in a pickle bath (dilute sulphuric acid) to remove surface oxides which discolour the copper. After a few minutes remove it and rinse thoroughly in running water.

Clean up the hearth, removing any solder which remains. This would spoil later work.

Brazing

Brazing can be used on copper but is most often used when joining steel parts together.

Tubes and rods used in constructing table, stool and chair frames will usually be brazed. The copper and zinc alloy spelter gives a strong joint.

1. Clean the surfaces with emery cloth and degrease with acetone or methylated spirit.
2. Paint the borax flux on the joint. Wire up or cramp the pieces together leaving a very small gap (0.1 mm). Place the work on the brazing hearth surrounded by insulating bricks which will reflect the heat back on to the material.
   The cylinder shown would be brazed with grade A spelter (melting point 885°C) and the cylinder fixed to the base using grade B spelter (melting point 880°C). This would ensure that the first joint did not melt when the second joint was made.
3. Use a gas torch to heat the work to an even 'cherry red' colour.
   As both pieces of metal must be at the same temperature the thickest piece must be heated first. Dip the end of the spelter rod in the borax flux and apply it to the joint. When the rod reaches the correct temperature a small amount will run off around and into the joint. Remove the spelter and flame immediately so that too much spelter is not used.
4. Quench the object in water whilst it is still hot so that the flux will flake off.

A problem with larger work is holding joints together whilst a thin layer of spelter binds the material together. Use cramps and wire where possible.

The occasional table shown is made from tubes, bars and rods. The detailed drawings show how three brazed joints may be made.
In joint A a slot is cut in the tube to locate the bar.
In joint B a spigot is turned on the rod to locate it in the bar.
In joint C a disc foot is screwed into the bar.

When working with such hot materials you **must** wear protective clothing:

1. Wear a face shield to protect your eyes and face.
2. Wear leather gloves to protect your hands.
3. Wear a leather apron to protect your body.

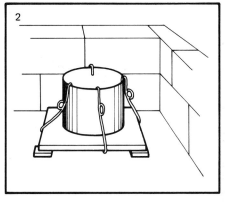

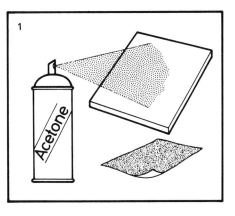

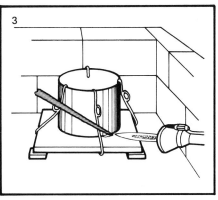

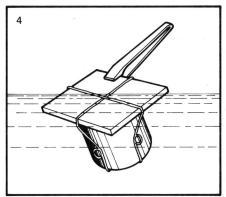

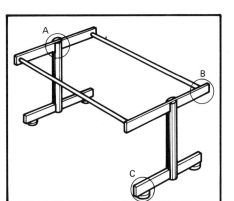

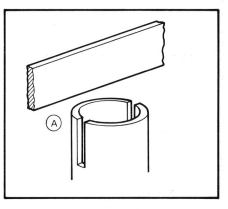

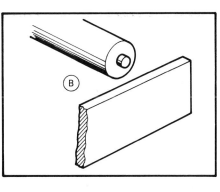

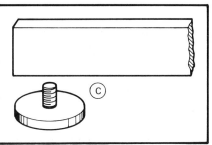

Welding

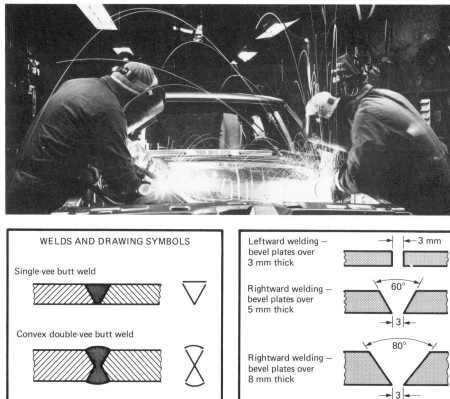

Fusion welding is a process where the edges of two pieces of metal to be joined together are melted. The filler rod is similar to the base or parent metal.

The high temperatures needed for welding steel are produced by either:

1. the oxygen/fuel-gas (acetylene) process, known as *gas welding,* or
2. the manual metal arc (MMA) process, known as *arc welding.*

Gas welding

This is commonly used to join mild steel plate. The diagrams show how plate edges can be left square or bevelled according to thickness and direction of welding. The heat to melt the metal is provided by the burning of the oxygen/acetylene mixture.

The strength of mild steel welds can be improved by *normalizing* the weld.

Use the same equipment for welding cast iron and aluminium.

Cast iron must be pre-heated to a dull red and the joint fluxed.

Aluminium edges may have oxide deposits which must be removed with a wire brush. Apply an appropriate flux to the edges and tack at frequent intervals to prevent distortion. (A tack weld is a small temporary weld between the edges — the equivalent of a stitch or pin.)

Arc welding (MMA)

This is a cheaper modern method of welding. It uses light, mobile equipment which runs from mains electricity. The transformer requires little maintenance and only uses up the electrode. The *electrode* provides the filler and carries the electric current to make the welding arc.

The power needed to 'strike' the arc and to melt and deposit the filler varies in direct proportion to the diameter of the electrode. The Murex DC130, for example, uses electrodes up to 3.25 mm diameter.

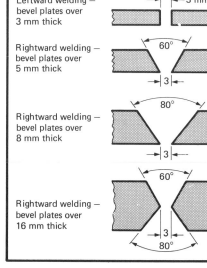

WELDS AND DRAWING SYMBOLS

Single-vee butt weld

Convex double-vee butt weld

Concave fillet weld

Leftward welding — bevel plates over 3 mm thick

Rightward welding — bevel plates over 5 mm thick

Rightward welding — bevel plates over 8 mm thick

Rightward welding — bevel plates over 16 mm thick

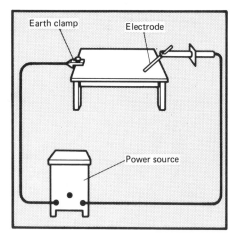

Earth clamp   Electrode

Power source

The diagram shows the welding lead and electrode holder and the return lead clamped firmly to the work.

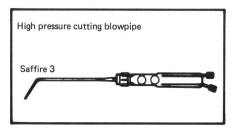

High pressure cutting blowpipe

Saffire 3

Cutting mild steel plate

The 'Gate' by Alan Evans is an example of the use of the oxygen/fuel-gas equipment to cut mild steel plate using an *oxygen lance attachment.*

1. Pre-heat the metal using the blowpipe.
2. Press the handle to release a fine jet of oxygen from a central nozzle. This oxidizes the metal.
3. The fierce pressure of the oxygen jet blows the oxidized metal away to make a slot (kerf).

Hold the torch at right angles to the metal and cut towards the user.
The method is especially useful for large diameter circles and irregular shapes.

Welding (continued)

The diagram shows a typical set of high-pressure gas welding equipment. The supply cylinders of oxygen (black) and acetylene (maroon) are held upright in a stand or trolley and secured by chains. Each bottle is fitted with a pressure-regulating screw. This helps to regulate a changing *inlet* pressure to provide a constant *outlet* pressure. The screw is a precision instrument to be treated with care.

The drawing shows Murex 3 equipment. The oxygen has a 3.5 bar maximum outlet pressure, and the acetylene a 1.5 bar maximum outlet pressure.
There are two dials on each cylinder. The right-hand dial shows the contents of the cylinder. The left-hand dial shows the outlet pressure setting.
On each dial 'USE NO OIL' reminds the user not to use oil or grease to lubricate screw threads — *this could lead to an explosion.*

Flashback describes the return of the flame through the blowpipe. This mixes the gases in one of the rubber hoses and creates danger.
A flashback arrester is a second safeguard. It protects the pressure-regulating screw and automatically cuts off the gas supply from the cylinders.
Hose check valves fitted between the blowpipe and hoses are designed to prevent gases mixing in the hoses.

Do not expose the hoses to heat, oil or grease. Do not wrap the hoses around the cylinders.
All threads on the oxygen side are normal right hand. All threads on the acetylene side are left hand.

The blowpipe shown is able to weld mild steel plate up to a thickness of 8 mm. Its hole must be clean, sharp and square with the nozzle end to maintain a good flame.

Safety

In addition to the care of equipment already mentioned, operators should wear protective clothing, including substantial footwear and a leather apron.
Wear double-lensed goggles to protect your eyes from glare and sparks.
Check for gas leaks using a detergent solution only.
Weld in a well-ventilated area, especially when galvanized metal is being worked.
When flashback occurs, first TURN OFF THE OXYGEN. Second TURN OFF THE ACETYLENE.

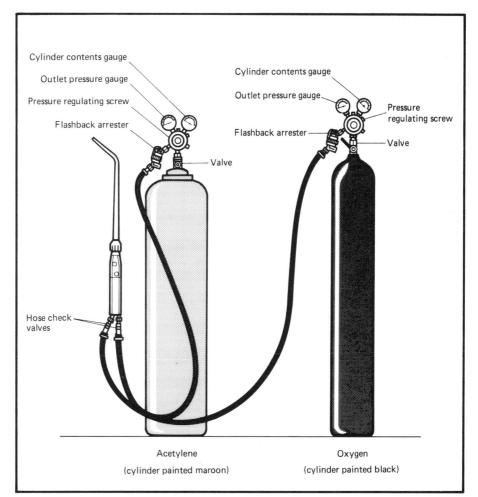

Cylinder contents gauge
Outlet pressure gauge
Pressure regulating screw
Flashback arrester
Valve
Cylinder contents gauge
Outlet pressure gauge
Pressure regulating screw
Flashback arrester
Valve
Hose check valves

Acetylene
(cylinder painted maroon)

Oxygen
(cylinder painted black)

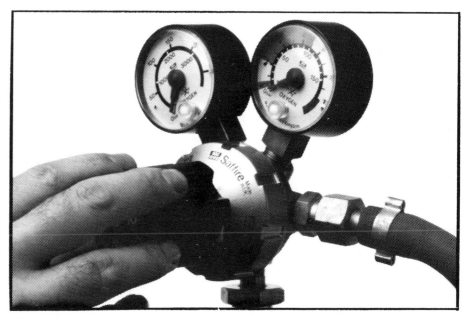

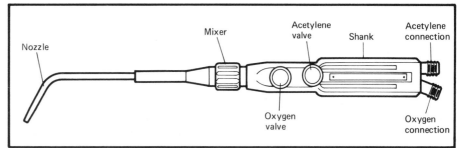

Nozzle
Mixer
Acetylene valve
Shank
Acetylene connection
Oxygen valve
Oxygen connection

The Gas Welding Process

Saffire high-pressure blowpipes							
Saffire A-NM acetylene nozzles							
		Operating pressures				Approx. cutting speeds	
Plate thickness (mm) (in)		Nozzle size	Oxygen (lbf/ (bar) in²)		Acetylene (lbf/ (bar) in²)		(mm/ (in/ min) min)
6	1/4	1/32	1.8	25	0.14	2	430 17
13	1/2	3/64	2.1	30	0.21	3	360 14
25	1	1/16	2.8	40	0.14	2	280 11
50	2	1/16	3.2	45	0.14	2	200 8
75	3	1/16	3.5	50	0.14	2	200 8
100	4	5/64	3.2	45	0.14	2	150 6

OXIDIZING FLAME (excess oxygen)

An oxidizing flame is necessary for welding brass

NEUTRAL FLAME (equal quantities oxygen and acetylene)
For steel, stainless steel, cast iron, copper, aluminium, etc.

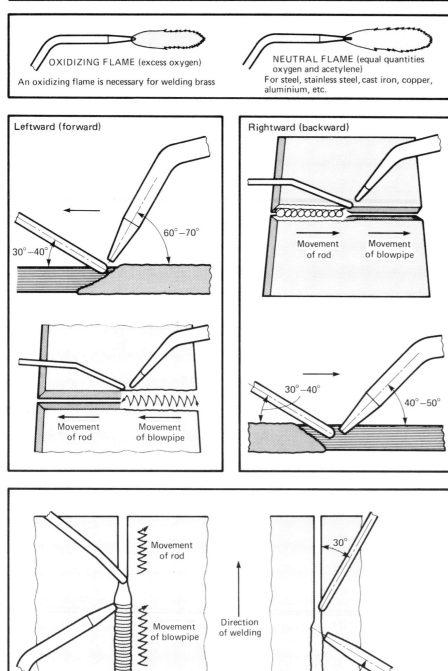

Leftward (forward)

30°–40°   60°–70°

Movement of rod   Movement of blowpipe

Rightward (backward)

Movement of rod   Movement of blowpipe

30°–40°   40°–50°

Movement of rod   Movement of blowpipe   Direction of welding

30°

1.6 mm (1/16in) 30°
3.2 mm (1/8in) 60°
4.8 mm (3/16in) 80°

No movement of blowpipe on plate up to 3.2 mm (1/8in) thickness
Slight movement of blowpipe as above on plate thicker than 3.2 mm (1/8in)

Select a nozzle size suitable for thickness of mild steel to be welded.

Lighting-up procedure

1. Use a spindle key to open the valve on the acetylene cylinder.
2. Open the acetylene valve on the blowpipe.
3. Adjust the regulator to give the correct working pressure.
4. Close the acetylene valve on the blowpipe.

Repeat on the oxygen side

To ignite

1. Open the acetylene valve on the pipe.
2. Light with a spark-lighter.
3. Adjust the valve until the flame stops smoking.
4. Slowly turn on the oxygen valve on the blowpipe to make a *neutral flame* suitable for most welding on mild steel, cast iron and aluminium.

To shut down

1. Close the acetylene valve on the blowpipe.
2. Close the oxygen valve on the blowpipe.
3. Close the valves on both cylinders.
4. Open, then close the oxygen valve on the blowpipe to reduce pressure to zero.

Repeat on the acetylene side

Setting up work

Make sure that work is fixed securely, with the correct gap and with a fireproof backing strip to support the weld.

Leftward (forward) welding is used for thinner material and bevelled plates up to 5 mm thick, cast iron and non-ferrous metals.
The slight sideways movement of the blowpipe in leftward welding pre-heats the material.

Rightward (backward) welding is used on material over 5 mm thick.
Note the small circular movement of the filler rod.

Welding positions

1. Flat on a horizontal plate — weld on the upper side of the joint (leftward or rightward)
2. Horizontally on a vertical plate — horizontal joint (rightward travel)
3. Vertically on a vertical plate — vertical joint (upward travel)

Arc Welding (Manual Metal Arc)

The photograph shows the Murex DC130. This is a light-duty transformer ideal for relatively light welding work such as car body repairs. It is powered from the mains supply and is transportable.

The **electrode** is made up of a rod (core wire) and an outer coating (flux). This coating is mixed with silicate into a paste and extruded on to the rod. Both ends are kept clean, one to be gripped in the holder and the other to strike an arc.

The **flux coating** protects the weld deposit from the oxygen and nitrogen in the air. It can also contain alloying elements for the weld.
One electrode coating is *rutile*, producing a stiff slag which is easy to remove when solid. This is best used in the flat position. Another coating is *basic*, providing a carbon dioxide shield to ensure a clean weld. This can be used in all weld positions.

The **rod** (core wire) carries the current to make the welding arc and provides the filling metal.

The process

A high amperage (current) is needed to deposit the weld metal. The model shown has a current output from 10 to 130 amperes. This is enough to use mild steel electrodes up to 3.25 mm diameter.
On vertical welds use a smaller electrode for control and reduce the amperage to the minimum recommendation.

Open-circuit voltage (OCV)

This describes the *potential voltage* which exists between the electrode and the workpiece when the transformer is switched on but *before* an arc is struck. The OCV must be high enough to strike an arc. Set too low the electrode will tend to stick to the work.
The OCV of the model shown is 42 volts.

Safety

Wear full safety clothing and ensure adequate ventilation.
Have the position of the return lead checked before switching on.
Flash blindness is a real danger. Where possible arc weld between metal screens.

Weld spatter release

This is an aerosol fluid which is sprayed on work and working surfaces to prevent spatter from the welding process sticking to the surface.

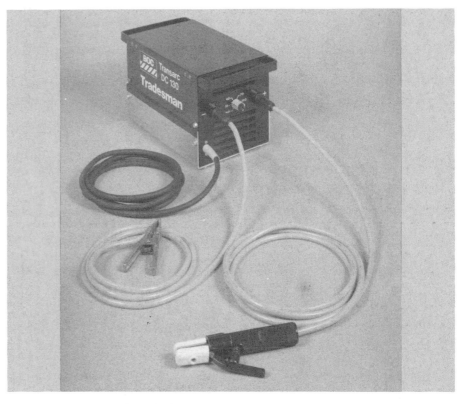

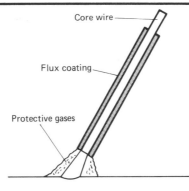

Core wire

Flux coating

Protective gases

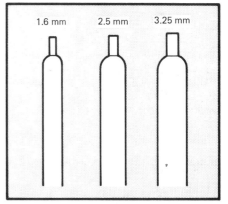

1.6 mm   2.5 mm   3.25 mm

spectra

weld spatter release

Protects welding equipment and work pieces from spatter adhesion.

Adhesives

Adhesives for joining metals are a comparatively modern alternative to traditional methods of joining such as riveting, soldering and welding. Adhesives are now so reliable that they *could* be used for almost any joints. They *should* be used where:

1. rivets would look unsightly
2. rivet holes would weaken the structure
3. access to a joint with soldering or welding gear is difficult
4. heat would distort or seriously mark the surface of the material
5. materials with different rates of expansion are joined, such as aluminium and glass
6. Bimetalic corrosion may be a problem with mechanical fixing devices.

This list of uses for adhesives does *not* mean that adhesives should replace riveting, soldering or welding, because they do have disadvantages. While the bond takes time to strengthen, the components must be held together, whereas a weld is immediately strong. Successful joining of the surfaces with adhesive may be difficult and a faulty joint is difficult to correct.

The photograph shows a perfect use of adhesive, a stiffening panel being bonded to the underside of the bonnet of an Aston Martin sports car.

Of all the modern adhesives available to the metalworker, epoxy resins are probably the easiest to use and the most versatile. Most epoxy adhesives consist of a resin and a separate hardener. 'Araldite' is generally available with a choice of two hardeners — one which allows joints to be adjusted and takes a day to set (cure), and another which sets in a few minutes. The photograph shows a joint between an aluminium casting and extrusion secured with Araldite. (The Race chairs are used on the QE2.)

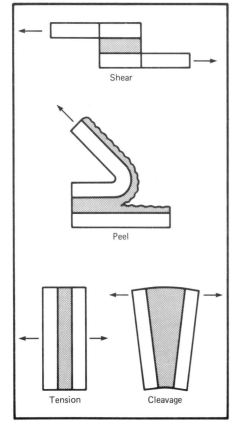

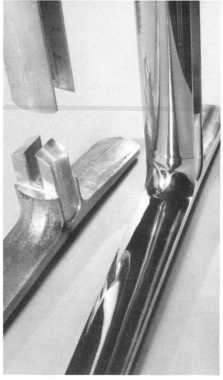

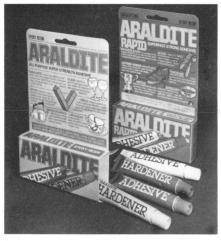

When designing joints to be stuck together with epoxy resin, consider the loads which may have to be supported. The adhesive is particularly strong where the load exerts *shear* or *tension* forces to the joint. It may not be strong enough if *peel* stress (where one of the components is flexible) or *cleavage* stress (where stress is concentrated on one end of a joint) is likely.

Always design joints so that stresses will be directed along the lines of the adhesive's greatest strength.

Correct **surface preparation** is vital. Remove dirt or corrosion and lightly 'key' the surface with a file or abrasive. Degrease with a brush or cloth pad soaked in trichloroethane or trichlorotrifluoroethane.

Mix quantities of resin and hardener according to the manufacturer's instructions. Apply the mix to both components and exert pressure until the adhesive sets. Heat speeds up setting.

Adhesives (continued)

Epoxy resin need not only be used in the technology workshop as an adhesive. Two other uses for it are shown.

Small patterns which need to be tough for frequent use can be cast from plaster. The surface of the plaster must be treated with a mould release, and the pattern itself made with a special Araldite resin and hardener.
Use yet another type of Araldite to make stakes or moulds using chalk, sand or chopped glass fibre to increase its bulk and reduce costs.

Protect small electronic assemblies, which may be liable to damage from excessive vibration or impact, by encapsulating them in epoxy resin adhesive. Ensure that the circuit is working, then enclose it with thin card walls and pour in sufficient epoxy resin to cover it.

In each instance, the manufacturer supplies full details of suitable uses, preparation of surfaces, mixing the adhesive and curing times. Follow the directions carefully.

Make a sheet of epoxy resin by casting it between two sheets of glass coated with Araldite mould release. Use these sheets with a polarized light source to show how stress occurs when a material is loaded. The illustration here shows the stress pattern of a bonded lap joint.

Synthetic resin glue (e.g. Aerolite 306) is a two-part adhesive you may need to use when constructing wood components. The powdered resin is mixed with water and the acid hardener is supplied separately.
Apply the resin to one side of the joint with a spatula and the hardener to the other with a felt pad. Setting begins when the surfaces are brought together and takes about three hours.
The adhesive is resistant to water and is stronger than the wood itself.
This glue is ideal for laminating veneers and thin plywood, as shown in the stacking chair.

Contact or impact adhesive is a neoprene/rubber compound in an inflammable solvent. You may need to use it to apply a sheet or non-structural plastics laminate to a base e.g. 'Formica' to chipboard.

The glue is ready for use and is spread on both surfaces with a plastic 'comb'. When the adhesive has become 'touch dry', position the laminate and press it firmly into place. Adjustments cannot be made.

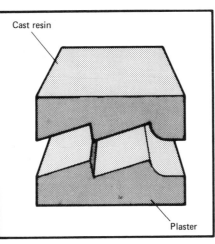

Cast resin
Plaster

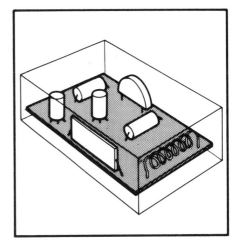

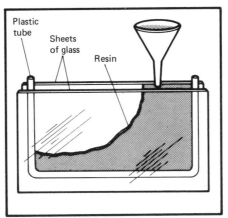

Plastic tube
Sheets of glass
Resin

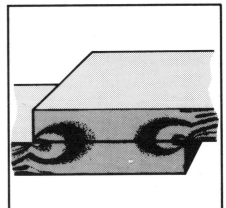

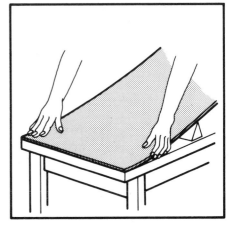

Adhesives (continued)

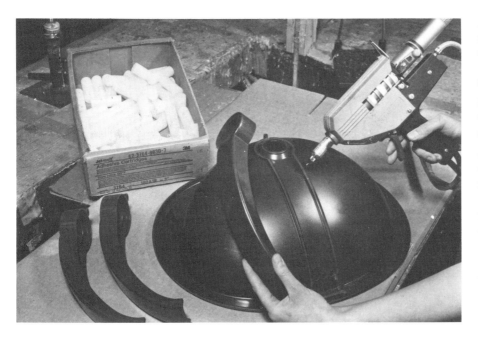

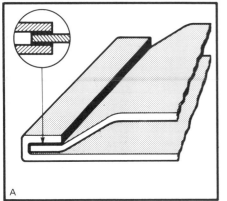

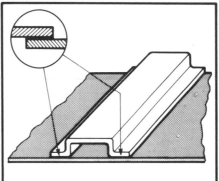

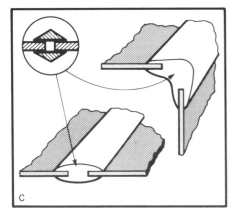

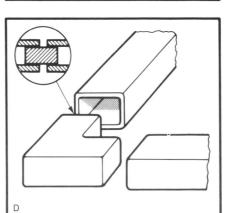

A group of synthetic resins known as **acrylics** form the basis of many modern adhesives. The **anaerobic** type is used as a 'locking compound' or 'sealant' to secure, seal and retain a screw in a thread.

Polyurethane adhesives are usually two-part adhesives which cure rapidly and are most useful when bonding GRP.

Modified phenolics have been used since the Second World War in aircraft manufacture. They give a high-strength bond for wood-to-metal and metal-to-metal joints. Heat and pressure are required for successful curing.

Hot melts are based on modern **polymers**. They are applied from the nozzle of a heat gun which melts the stick of adhesive. Use these where fast assembly of parts is more important than strength.

Some of the adhesives are sold in DIY shops in small quantities suitable for domestic use. A chart may be provided to help the layman to select the correct adhesive.

For example, Bostik products may be used as follows:

Metal-to-metal	*Hyperbond* or *Quick set* epoxy
Metal-to-wood	*Hyperbond*
Metal-to-rigid PVC	*Hyperbond* or *Clear Mending* adhesive
Metal-to-glass	*Hyperbond* or *Quick Set* epoxy
Metal-to-laminate	contact

Joint types

The breaking load of a simple lap joint is directly proportional to its width. This means that the widest joint is the strongest.

The principle of producing the widest possible gluing area is applied to all joint designs. Four are illustrated:

1. sheet material joined using a toggled joint (A)
2. sheet material of a thin-gauge stiffened by using a top-hat section (B)
3. sheet material which cannot be bent or folded can be successfully joined using purpose-made profiles (C)
4. frame constructions may use plugs to secure tubing (D).

Safety

Wear PVC gloves and eye protection.
Do not use cleaners close to open frames.
Ensure adequate ventilation of the fumes.

Shaping – Shaping Sheet Metal

Tinplate is low-carbon steel sheet which is thinly coated with a protective layer of tin to stop it from rusting. Store tinplate with care to prevent it from being scratched, because scratches rust.

Sheet iron is of similar quality and is finished 'black' when used for shovels. It is galvanized by being dipped in molten zinc after it has been made up into an object. Dustbins are a common example.

Shears and snips for cutting sheet metal are described on page 33. The extra tools needed to work sheet metal are simple enough.

Steel **folding bars** are held in a vice and grip the sheet along an edge which is to be bent over at right-angles — the first stage in producing a safe edge or seam joint.
Use two lengths of hardwood bolted together at each end to bend sheet over a curve — the first stage in producing a wired edge.
A pencil line shows the line of fold. Put this line level with the edge of the folding bar and tap over the upstanding metal using a rawhide **mallet** or a hammer with rawhide faces. Traditional mallets have water-buffalo hides tightly coiled and fixed to a cane shaft.

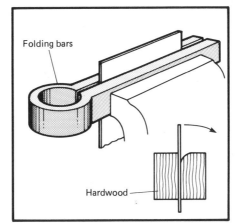

Folding bars

Hardwood

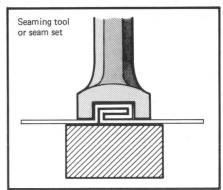

Rawhide mallets

Use a **seaming tool** or **seam set** to close down a seam joint so that the underside surface is flat. It is important that the set is the correct size for the seam or the joint will be damaged.
Seam joints are sometimes soft-soldered to make them watertight.

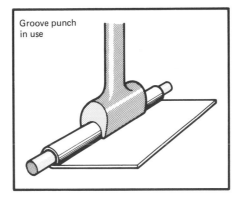

Groove punch in use

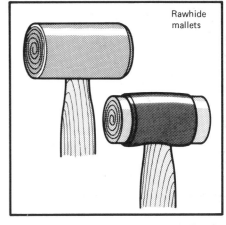

Seaming tool or seam set

Use a **creasing hammer** with a **creasing iron** to prepare edges for wiring or for forming semicircular grooves.
Use a **paning** or **tucking hammer**, which has acute corners, for tucking-in the plate over the wire.
Finish off the wire edge with a **groove punch** or **grooving tool**. It is important that the tool is the correct size to match the wired edge.

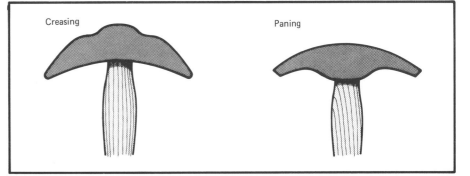

Creasing

Paning

Sheet Metal (continued)

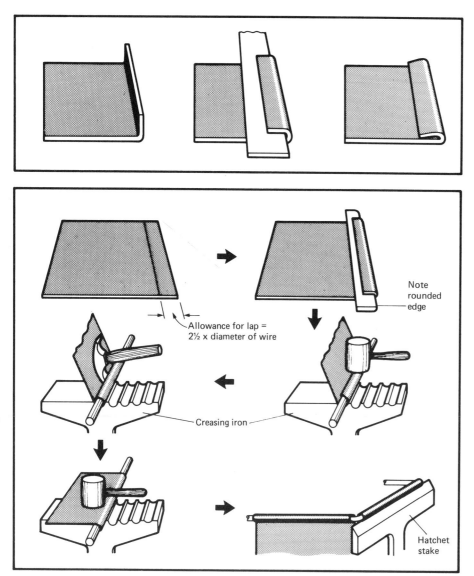

Tinplate edges are sharp and weak. A **safe edge** stiffens the material and improves its appearance.

1. Mark out the lap width from the edge and hold the metal in folding bars to bend it at right-angles.
2. Close-down with a mallet over a steel rule or strip of waste metal.
3. Remove the metal strip and gently mallet down. Do not flatten the edge.

Use a safe and strong **wired edge** on boxes and trays. You will see them used on baking equipment.

1. Mark out the lap width from the edge allowing 2½ times the diameter of the wire. Hold the metal in folding bars to bend it at right-angles.
2. Close-down with a mallet over a metal former the same thickness as the wire.
3. Support the work on a creasing iron. Insert the wire and turn the edge over.
4. Use a tucking hammer to tuck in the edge.
5. Reverse the material and set down with a mallet.
6. Finish the tuck using a mallet and hatchet stake.

Allowance for lap = 2½ x diameter of wire

Note rounded edge

Creasing iron

Hatchet stake

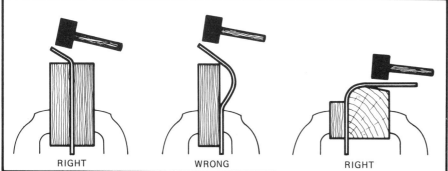

RIGHT   WRONG   RIGHT

Sheet metal being bent must be supported on both sides. Do not try to bend over a single former — if you do the sheet will bow away and distort. Make hardwood formers to the appropriate section when making curved surfaces.

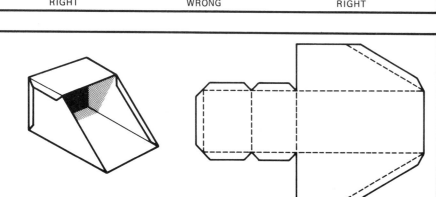

Most objects made from sheet metal are constructed from a single sheet. It is helpful to make full-size accurate drawings of the **development** of the object. This will ensure that allowances are made for jointing flaps and safe edges. Mark folding lines with a fine felt-tip marker and cutting lines with a scriber.

Sheet Metal (continued)

A box seam is used to produce a strong box corner which is flush on both outside surfaces.

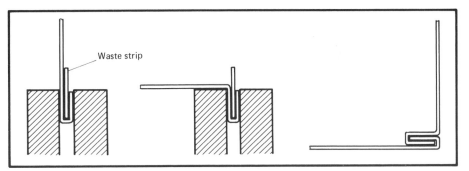

First make a folded seam in opposite directions on each end of the sheet. Insert a waste strip of metal into one fold and secure between folding bars. Bend over the box side to produce a folded seam at right-angles to the box side and into which the other folded seam will lock.
Make sure that marking-out allowances are made for each of these seams.

A folded seam used to make a sheet into a cylinder must have the folds in opposite directions.
The seam is set in the same way as a flat seam, to give a flush surface on the inside of the cylinder. Support the cylinder on a side stake when using the seam set.

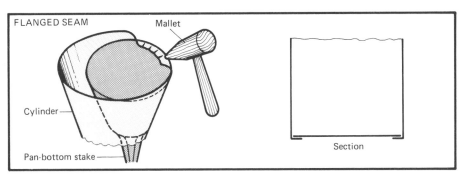

Cylinders with wired edges will normally be wired whilst flat. The sheet is then curved on a mandrel, starting with a hide mallet, then continuing using hand pressure only. Use a set of rolls if these are available.

Two ways of fixing a base to a cylinder are shown:

Flanged method

Support the cylinder on a pan-bottom stake and use a boxwood mallet to gradually knock over the edge to form a flange. The base is a disc which is dropped into place and soldered.

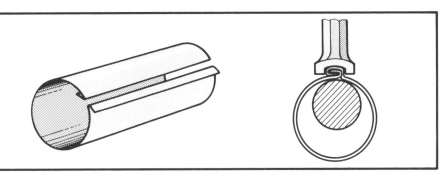

Circular lap method

Cut a disc to size with an allowance for a lap. Mark on it the external diameter of the cylinder and knock over the flange with a boxwood mallet. Do this on a half-moon stake as shown. Alternatively, hold the disc between two hardwood or mild-steel discs, which have been turned to the cylinder size, cramped in a vice. Knock over the flange with a boxwood mallet.

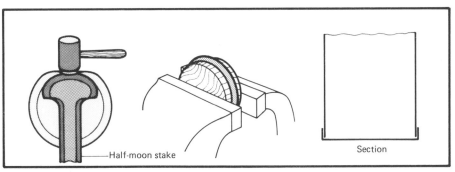

Large folds and folds in thick sheet are best done in a folding machine. The one shown will fold sheet up to 600 mm long in 18-gauge mild steel or 16-gauge aluminium. Narrow brackets can be bent up in mild steel 6 mm thick.
There are limits to box depths according to size, but a radiused clamp bar with one edge reduced to 3.2 mm can be used to prepare wired edges and hinges. These have to be closed by the hand method.

Beaten Metalwork

The making of sheet metal into what is called **holloware** is now mainly an industrial process.

The aluminium baking trays have been stamped into shape with a powerful press before being given a non-stick finish.

Both **stamping** and **spinning** are used on a small scale by craftsmen who work on industrial pieces, but they also use the traditional methods of making holloware — shaping the metal by striking it. Two processes are common:

Raising can be done from a flat disc. Elizabeth Clay made the silver decanter by raising the shape from a cylinder which was open at both ends. The silver beaker was spun before being decorated.

Hollowing is a simpler method used for making shallower shapes — because the metal stretches and can become thin. These are the processes used in the silver-plated bronze vegetable serving dish. The dish is raised and the shallower lid with a rim is hollowed.

The materials already mentioned — aluminium, silver and bronze — can be hammered (malleable) and can be stretched (ductile) whilst cold without fracturing. Copper is commonly used because it is easily brazed or soldered, annealing is simple, and it can be given a plated finish. Gilding metal and brass are two copper/zinc alloys with rich colouring.

Vegetable Serving Dish

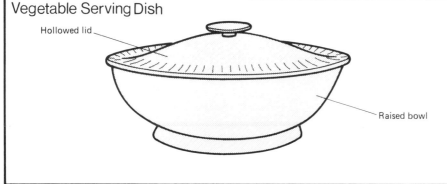

Hollowed lid

Raised bowl

Tools

Hammers and mallets come in all shapes and sizes. The **blocking hammer** has two domed faces with different diameters. The **Bossing mallet** consists of a cone-shaped boxwood head fixed to a flexible cane handle. Both these tools are used for hollowing or sinking metal.

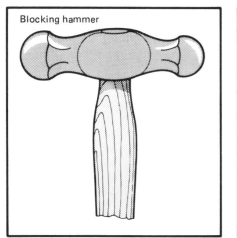

Blocking hammer

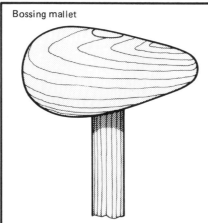

Bossing mallet

The sheet is supported in one of two ways. Larger, freer forms are usually beaten over a leather-covered **sandbag**. Smaller, exact forms are beaten over a former specially cut into hardwood. A hollow in the end grain is ideal, though in practice most hollows can be cut into the side grain.

Choose the hammer or mallet according to size and need.

Sandbag

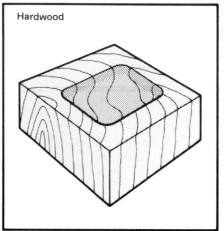

Hardwood

Beaten Metalwork (continued)

The differences between some hammers and stakes for metal working are subtle. They will only become obvious when doing practical work. This page illustrates some of the most common tools and indicates their uses.

The **collet** hammer has curved faces and rounded corners. Use it with a bick iron or funnel stake to flare a cylinder.

The **bick iron** is conical in shape. Use it to support work being expanded, such as flaring. It can be used as a former for cones — a flat development being formed around the bick before it is soldered together.

The **raising mallet** is made of boxwood fitted with a cane handle. It has a flat end, used for truing-up dish rims that have been hollowed, and a wedge-shaped end. Use this for raising a large-diameter shape with a raising stake to support the work.

The **raising stake** can have two cones of contrasting diameters. Sometimes it is also a side stake, with the cylindrical bar used to support straight-sided work.

The **raising hammer** looks similar to a collet hammer but it has oblong flat faces and rounded edges. Use it in the same way as the wedge-shaped raising mallet. It is often used on smaller work which may be raised on a **round-headed** stake.

Planishing heads fit into a vice horse held in the vice. As well as the shapes shown, some planishing heads are oval or horn-shaped with varying radii. Use a box head with square edges for working into the corners of containers.

Planishing hammers have flat faces for working curved surfaces, and slightly convex faces for working flat surfaces. The faces are highly polished. Use them with work supported on highly polished heads suited to the work.

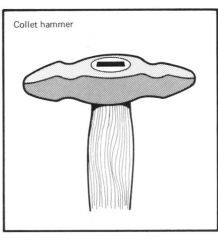

Collet hammer

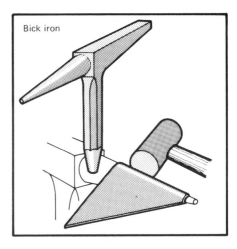

Bick iron

Raising mallet

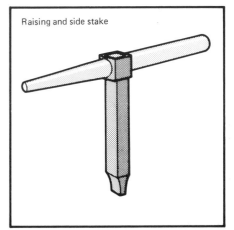

Raising and side stake

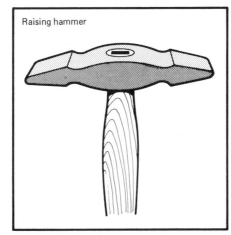

Raising hammer

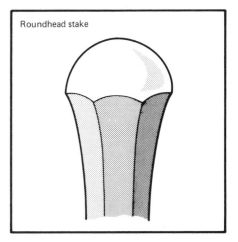

Roundhead stake

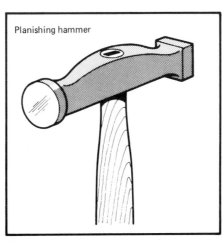

Planishing hammer

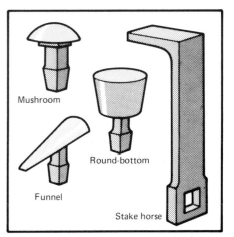

Mushroom

Round-bottom

Funnel

Stake horse

Beaten Metalwork (continued)

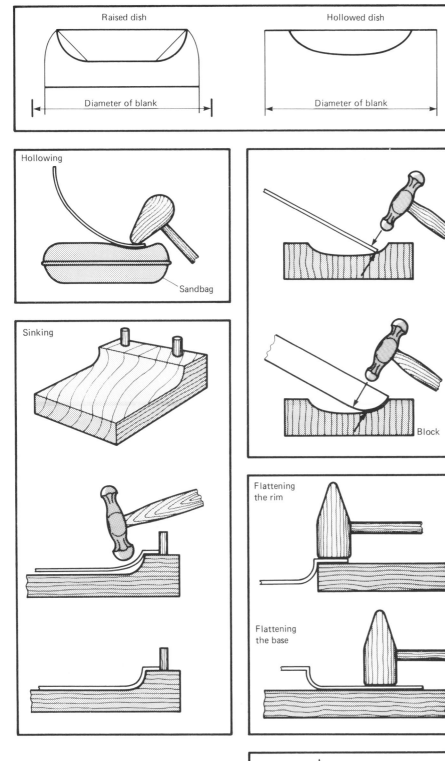

Raised dish — Diameter of blank

Hollowed dish — Diameter of blank

Hollowing — Sandbag

Sinking

Block

Flattening the rim

Flattening the base

Doming block

Use the brass or steel **doming block** to make very small hollows. Metal can often be hollowed with one blow of a wood punch of the correct size. A doming block has a variety of diameters machined on its six surfaces.

Metals suitable for hollowing, sinking and raising are worked cold. Beating the metal hardens it (work-hardening). It frequently has to be softened (annealed) so that the shaping can continue.
Heat copper to a dull red heat and quench it in clean, cold water.
Heat brass to a dull red heat and allow it to cool in the air. Cover the surface of aluminium with soft soap — when the soap darkens quench in clean, cold water.

Pickle copper and brass in dilute sulphuric acid (one part acid added to seven parts water) using non-ferrous (brass) tongs. Rinse in water and remove remaining oxide with a brass wire brush.

In estimating the sizes of sheet metal for fabricating, it is necessary to draw developments of shapes.
Work which has a rim and is to be hollowed is stretched, so cut the disc to the finished size needed.
Work to be raised is contracted, so that surplus material is needed. This has to be estimated and will depend on the size of the job and complexity of its shape.

Hollowing

Prepare the disc by marking on it with a pencil concentric circles about a centimetre apart. These will act as guidelines when striking the metal with a mallet.
Rest the disc on the sandbag and begin hammering at the edge. Rotate the disc anticlockwise until one circumference is completed. Repeat this procedure for each marked line.
Anneal the work and repeat as necessary.

Hollowing with a blocking hammer and block is done in the same way. The metal is stretched because the point of contact with mallet or hammer should be just beyond the point of contact with the sandbag or block.

Sinking

Use this method to make a shallow hollow for a small dish or plate with a rim. Prepare a hardwood former with two dowel stops which will locate the disc and keep it in place during forming.
Mark out the disc with concentric circles and progressively stretch the metal into shape with a blocking hammer.
The rim tends to distort easily and may need flattening after each turn. Use the flat end of a raising mallet with the work supported on the edge of a hardwood block. Use the surface of the hardwood block at a later stage to flatten the base.

Beaten Metalwork (continued)

Raising

Relatively *shallow* dishes are raised on a roundhead stake using the wedge-shaped end of a raising mallet.

Prepare the disc by marking out the base in pencil and drawing a series of concentric circles to act as guidelines for beating the metal evenly.

At this stage the base may be hollowed slightly on a sandbag and flattened later on a round-bottom stake.

Hold the disc at an angle of about 30° to the stake. Strike it at a point slightly beyond the point of contact. This has the effect of *contracting* the metal. Turn the disc anticlockwise until one circumference is completed. Repeat this procedure for each marked line, to produce a shallow form.

Anneal the work and repeat this process. Tilt the work at a progressively steeper angle to produce steeper sides.

Raise a *steep-sided* container on a raising stake using a raising hammer. Prepare the disc in the way described above and work in the same way. Make sure that the base circle is in contact with the corner of the raising stake when the first round of hammering is done.

Expanding a steep-sided container (opening out) is possible using a collet hammer. Support the container on a **funnel stake.**

Contracting the shallow dish (closing in) is possible using a flat-faced hammer on a roundhead stake.

For expanding and contracting, the profile of the chosen stake should be as near to the finished shape as possible.

Planishing takes place after the work has been shaped, annealed, pickled and washed thoroughly. Planishing with polished hammers on polished stakes hardens the metal ready for polishing.

Ensure even working by marking concentric lines with a pencil. Start at the centre and work outwards. Overlap the small facets as the work is slowly rotated. Hammer gently and evenly, trapping the metal between the stake and hammer head. This slightly expands the metal. If the blow is uneven or inaccurate, distortion will occur.

True the rim of the raised object using a scribing block and surface plate.

Remove waste with curved snips. File the irregularities. Finish by inverting on a sheet of abrasive on the surface plate.

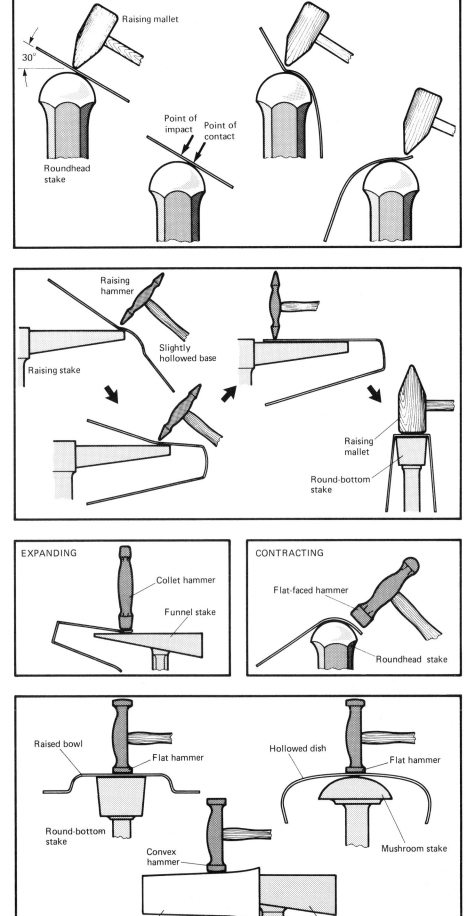

Repoussé

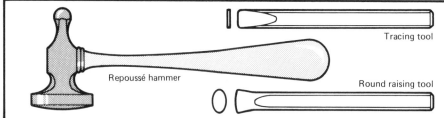

Repoussé hammer

Tracing tool

Round raising tool

Repoussé is a French word we use to describe the decorating of beaten metalwork by embossing or stretching it from the reverse side with shaped punches and a lightweight hammer. The metal starts by being annealed, but eventually the surfaces work-harden.

The photograph shows Elizabeth Clay working on a shallow silver dish shape using a punch and repoussé hammer.

The metal is supported on a bed of 'pitch' to which it sticks. The bed is hard enough to support the metal but soft enough to accept the impression made by the punch. The 'pitch' is a mixture of pitch, plaster of Paris, resin and tallow which is melted and poured into a hemispherical bowl. The bowl is supported on a leather ring (or grommet) so that it is easily rotated and tilted to make working easier.

Coat the surface of the work with wax, and press it firmly into the warm pitch. Release the work by warming the pitch with the soft flame from a torch.

A wide range of punches are available, but any shape can be made using 6 mm-square high-carbon steel, hardened and tempered. The corners are removed to prevent the thin metal sheet from being pierced. Two common shapes are shown.
The tracing tool is sometimes used to outline a pattern. This process is known as **chasing**.

Source material

Elizabeth Clay uses the surroundings in which she lives in Cumbria as one kind of inspiration for her work. She photographs and draws waterfalls, animals and flowers which then appear on some of her designs.

The waterfall is clearly the source material for a bowl. The repoussé work is on a hollowed piece of metal set into a raised bowl.

The hexagonal boxes are fitted with lids. Chasing of stems and leaves from bushes appears on both the box and the lid. The berries and plant leaves are punched into the lids from the reverse side.

The sheep's head is punched deepest and the body and legs less so. Chased marks made on the top give it a woolly appearance.

Introduction to Forgework

There used to be a blacksmith in every village, now they are few and far between. The things blacksmiths used to make and mend belong to a way of living before mass industrial production and the motor car.

Alan Evans calls himself an Artist Metalsmith. Like many of the new generation of metalworkers, his work is individual in style and usually made to commission. He has had the support of the Crafts Council and was chosen to make gates to the Treasury of St Paul's Cathedral.

Alan Evans says: *'I like the plastic quality of hot steel — its ability to change section and flow to different forms under the hammer, and as it cools, to 'freeze' that flow. The power hammer enables me to work at the same magical speed as the potter at his wheel or the wood turner at his lathe.'*
Forging steel by hand methods is slower but still gives great satisfaction.

This page illustrates some of his domestic work in steel, and a processional candlestick using forged brass on an ash stave.

A

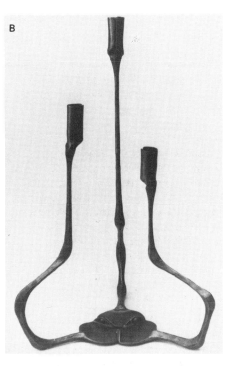

B

C

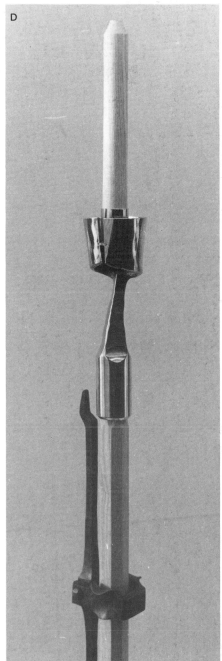

D

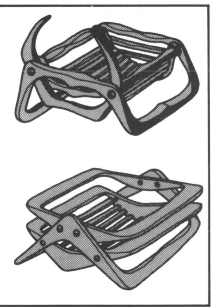

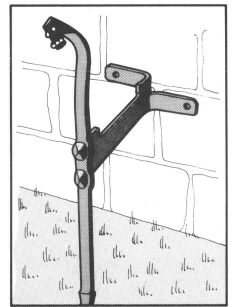

Introduction to Forgework (continued)

The 'plastic' quality of hot steel was appreciated by a famous Scottish architect and designer, Charles Rennie Mackintosh. He made use of it on a small scale in his designs for houses and cafes — but in his design for the Glasgow School of Art it became a main feature.

The photograph shows an iron finial on the roof of the School. The wrought iron strip looks like a birdcage. The other picture shows an iron support for a beam where the girder has been cut and scrolled — it is both functional and decorative. On the North face of the building, long stalk-like iron rails decorate the windows but also act as ladder-rests for the window cleaners!

A century ago the designs of Mackintosh were made from wrought iron. This is 'pasty' when very hot. It develops an iron-oxide surface which is a self-protection against rust. The modern blacksmith is more likely to work with mild steel which has a uniform texture, bends easily and works well when hammered.

Otherwise the forging process is little changed. The metal is heated in a hearth, held with tongs and hammered on an anvil. The craftsman must work quickly, especially when the metal is thin, because it loses its heat quickly.
He re-heats the metal as few times as possible because metal loses its best qualities when kept at high forging temperatures for a long time.

Safety

Working with hot metal can be very dangerous.
The hearth and the anvil must be close to each other and the floor clear of obstructions.
The craftsman must wear a leather apron with a bib and leather gloves which extend beyond the elbow.
Protect the eyes with glasses or with a shield which protects the whole face.

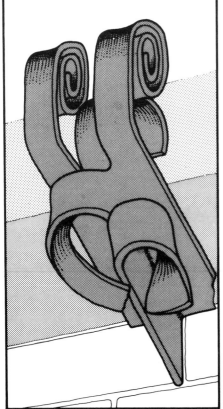

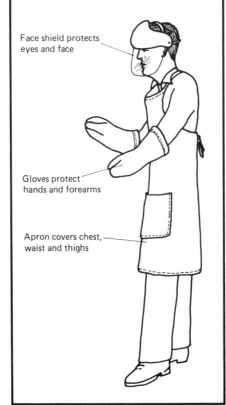

Face shield protects eyes and face

Gloves protect hands and forearms

Apron covers chest, waist and thighs

Forgework Tools

One photograph shows a traditional blacksmith's hearth. The section drawing helps to explain its construction and the way it works.

Coke breeze is placed on top of a bed of fire bricks and sand and can conveniently be lit with a gas poker or kindling. The air supply to increase the temperature of the fire is provided through a water-cooled tuyère.
The hearth is fitted with an extractor hood.
A water tank in which hot metal can be quenched may be hung from the edge of the hearth.

There is a tendency for clinker to form near the air supply, and this should be removed before lighting up the hearth. If the clinker reforms during working, shut down the air supply. The clinker will solidify as it cools and can be lifted away in one piece.

The Flamefast ceramic chip-forge is a modern hearth. Supplied with both gas and air the ceramic chips can quickly be heated to a high temperature and cooled quickly by running air through the chips. The chips burn without the dirt, smoke and fumes associated with coke, and there is no fuel to store.
Remove slag and clinker from around the ceramic base fire before lighting with a torch.

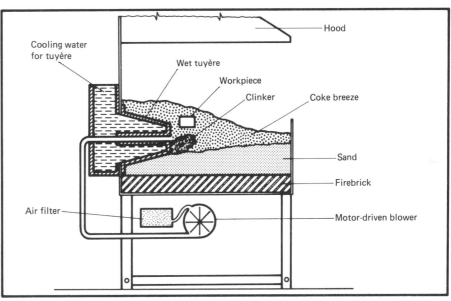

Mild-steel anvil

This is given a hardened face which must never be directly struck with a hammer. The table is left soft and work to be cut with a chisel should be rested on that part. The tapered bick is soft and is used for bending, drawing-down and flattening. A round punch hole allows holes to be punched through hot metal. A square hardie hole is for holding bottom tools such as swages and sets.

The anvil rests on wood boards set into a cast iron stand. This brings the anvil up to a comfortable and safe working height.

Leg vice

This holds metal to be bent. It also holds a scrolling iron when scrolling.
Its rugged wrought iron construction fixed to both bench and floor makes it ideal for withstanding hammer blows and extreme leverage.

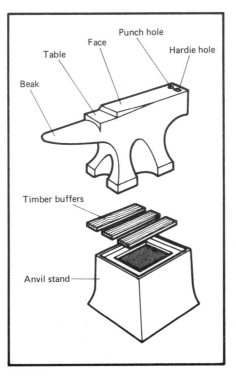

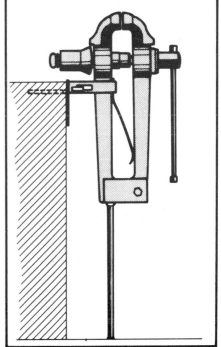

Forgework Tools (continued)

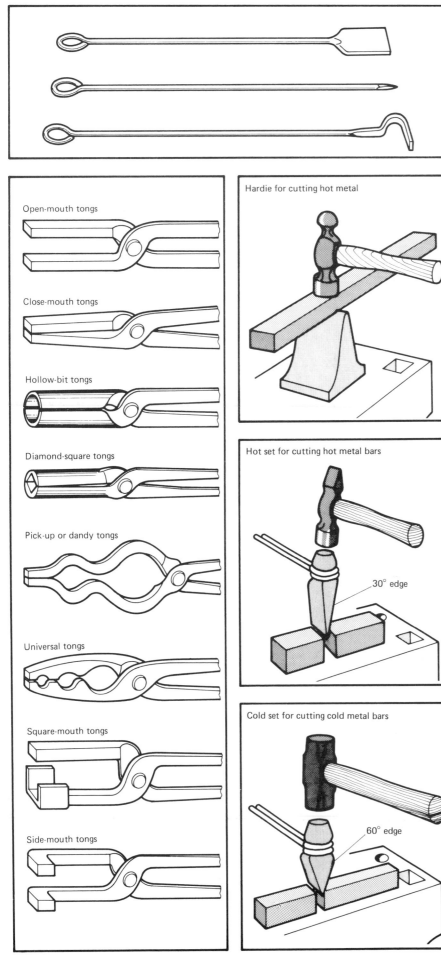

Open-mouth tongs

Close-mouth tongs

Hollow-bit tongs

Diamond-square tongs

Pick-up or dandy tongs

Universal tongs

Square-mouth tongs

Side-mouth tongs

Hardie for cutting hot metal

Hot set for cutting hot metal bars

30° edge

Cold set for cutting cold metal bars

60° edge

Hearth tools are used to control the amount of coke and its arrangement around the tuyère. Use the poker for breaking up clumps of fuel. Use the slice (spade) for tamping fuel down to avoid having a hollow fire.
Use a rake to feed in fresh fuel and to remove clinker.

Tongs

There may be as many as twenty-four tongs in a full set. A basic set of eight tongs is shown. Lengths vary from 460 to 560 mm.
Use **open-mouth tongs** to hold flat material which is fairly thick. Mouth openings are from 6 to 25 mm.
Use **close-mouth tongs** to hold flat material which is thinner than 6 mm.
Use **hollow-bit tongs** to hold round rod from 6 to 19 diameter.
Use **diamond-square (vee) tongs** to prevent square rod from twisting when being worked. The closed shape is 10 mm wide.
Use **pick-up tongs** for picking up hot material and awkwardly shaped metal.
Use **universal tongs** to side-hold rod of varying diameters.
Use **square-mouth tongs** to hold square bar and flats up to 16 mm wide.
Use **side-mouthed tongs** to hold flat material.

Quench tongs in water to keep them cool. Slip a ring over tong handles to hold work firmly and relieve the strain of gripping the tongs tightly.

Hammers

Several types of hammer are in common use.

The **ball pein** hammer is shown in use with a hardie to cut hot metal.
The **straight pein** hammer is shown in use on a hot set for cutting a hot bar. It can also be used for fullering.
The **sledge** hammer is shown in use on a cold set for cutting cold bars when more weight is needed. Heavier sledges may need two hands to be used properly.

Ball and straight pein hammers for forging usually weigh about 900 to 1800 grams. Sledge hammers are from 1800 grams upwards.
A short-handled sledge hammer called a clump or mason's hammer weighs 1000 grams and can be used one-handed.

Forgework Tools (continued)

A **swage block** is a heavy cast iron block which will stand on any face on an anvil stand.
All four sides have grooves cut into them to support materials of different sections. The flat faces are pierced with square, round and rectangular holes into which work is fitted for bending or through which holes can be punched.

Swages are forming tools made in matching pairs. Each swage has a female half-round section cut across the face with diameters from 6 mm upwards. The **bottom swage** has a square shank which fits in the hardie hole in the anvil. The top swage is fitted with a wood or wire handle.

Use the swaging process to reduce the diameter of a round bar or to change a square of hexagonal bar to round. Position the hot metal in the grooves between the swages and strike the top swage with a heavy hammer.

Fullers are forming tools made in matching pairs. Each fuller has a male half-round section at one end. The **bottom fuller** has a square shank which fits in the hardie hole in the anvil. The top fuller is fitted with a wood or wire handle.

Use the fullering process to draw-down large sections of material. Strike the top fuller with a heavy hammer.

Flatters and smaller **sets** are used for finishing a surface. The striking face must be smooth and the edges rounded to prevent marking the surface.
A face of 50 mm square is useful for most work. Use the flattering process to remove the irregular marks left by fullering. The hot metal is trapped between the hard, smooth surface of the anvil and the flatter. Strike the flatter with a heavy hammer.

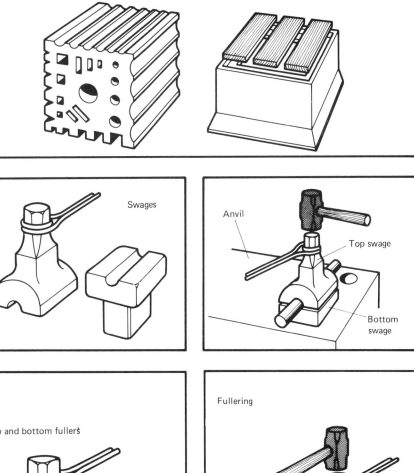

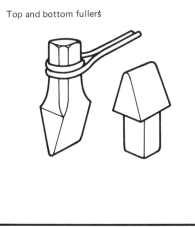

Top and bottom fullers

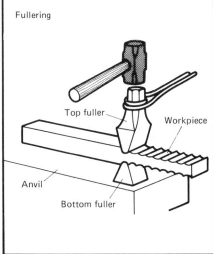

Fullering

Top fuller

Workpiece

Anvil

Bottom fuller

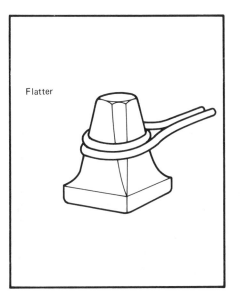

Flatter

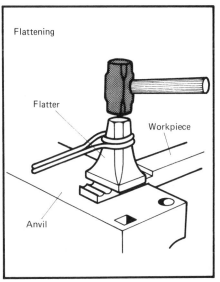

Flattening

Flatter

Workpiece

Anvil

Forgework Techniques

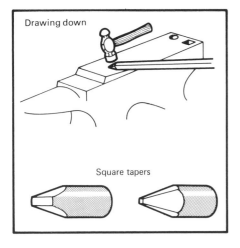

Drawing down

Square tapers

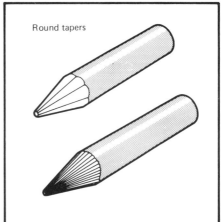

Round tapers

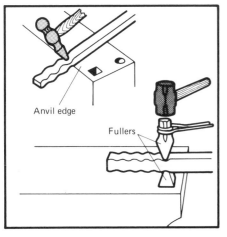

Anvil edge

Fullers

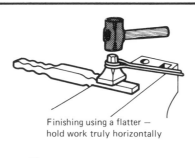
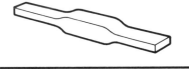

Finishing using a flatter —
hold work truly horizontally

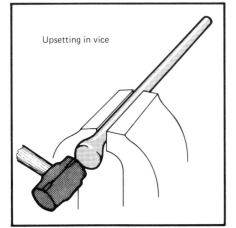

Upsetting in vice

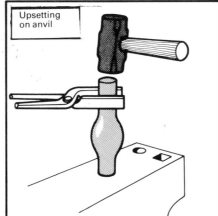

Upsetting
on anvil

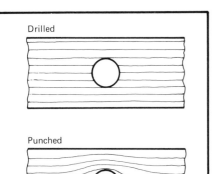

Drilled

Punched

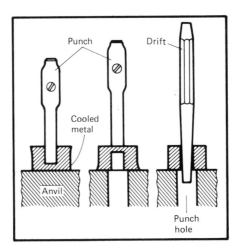

Punch

Drift

Cooled
metal

Anvil

Punch
hole

Drawing-down

Drawing-down is the most common forging process. The process not only reduces the thickness of the metal but also increases its length.

To make a short **square taper** on a bar, heat the metal and hammer it on the anvil face at the angle required. This will produce a small flat surface. Turn the bar through 90° and repeat the hammering to form a square taper. At this stage, a square taper can be finished using a flatter.

To make a short **round taper,** re-heat the bar and forge each corner in the same way to form an octagonal taper. Repeat the process until the bar is reduced to a round, even taper.

To reduce the thickness of a bar, heat the metal and fuller it. On small-sectioned material, fuller with a cross-pein hammer on the anvil edge. On thicker material, use a set of fullers and have a helper to strike the blows. Finish the reduction with a flatter on the face of the anvil.

Upsetting (jumping-up)

Upsetting is the process used to *increase* the thickness of the material. The process reduces the length of the metal.
To upset the end of a bar heat it to yellow heat. Hold a short piece in tongs and drive it on to the anvil face, striking it with a hammer if necessary. Hold a longer piece in a vice and hammer it to shape.
To upset the bar part-way along its length — where extra thickness may be needed to allow a sharp bend to be made, heat only that part of the bar to yellow heat. Pour on water to cool each side of the area to be upset. Drive the bar on to the anvil face.

Punching

Use hardened punches to make round, square or rectangular holes in hot metal. The grain structure is not destroyed by forging — the metal is stronger than if it is drilled.

Heat to almost white heat. Rest the metal on the anvil face and quickly punch a hole through most of the thickness. Reverse the material. Punch the hole through over the anvil, and use a drift to open up the hole.
The punch may need cooling during the punching process.

Forgework Techniques (continued)

Twists

The twist is a decorative feature of much ironwork such as railings and gates. A simple, even twist actually adds strength to the rod or strip.

To make a simple twist hold one end of the bar in a vice and fit a twisting bar over the other end. Use both hands to make the twist in one even movement between 90° and 360°. Work quickly before the heat is lost.
The drawing shows a twist being made in a mild steel strip. When several identical pieces are needed a loose-fitting steel tube ensures that the twists are exactly the same length.
Heat the metal to an even dull red over an area slightly longer than the twist. An even heat will produce an even twist.

Bends

Heat the area to be bent to a bright cherry red.

Make a curved bend in steel strip by bending it over a former held in a leg vice. Forging over the edge of an anvil produces a sharper bend but the material is distorted.
To make a sharp-cornered bend, first upset the area to be bent and work the metal to the outside. Knock-over the rod on the sharp corner of an anvil and work the corner square.

Making an eye

Calculate the length of metal needed to make the eye and mark it with a punch. Heat the area around the mark to yellow heat and bend it at right angles in a vice jaw.

Re-heat the metal which will become the eye and quench the right-angled bend with water. Begin to turn-over the end on the bick of the anvil. Begin at the end of the rod and work back towards the right-angled bend to make a half-round loop. Re-heat the metal and quench the corner. Reverse the metal on the bick and begin to close up the eye.
Check that the eye is flat and, if necessary, flatter on the anvil face. The eye can be trued on a mandrel.

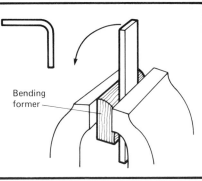

TWISTING

Heat this portion to a dull red

Strip

Tube

Apply even turning pressure

Bending former

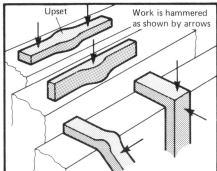

Bulge forms on edge

Slight hollowing across width

Upset

Work is hammered as shown by arrows

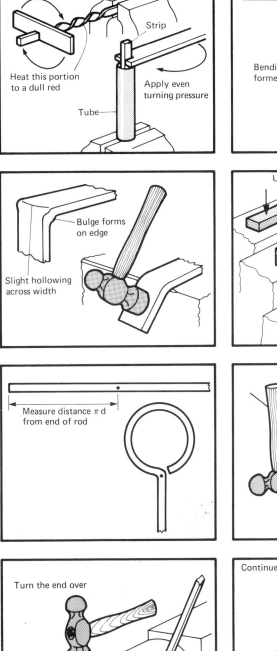

Measure distance π d from end of rod

Bend to right-angle

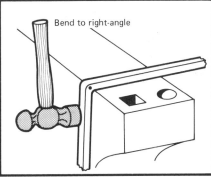

Turn the end over

Cooling point

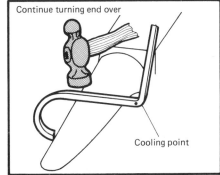

Continue turning end over

Cooling point

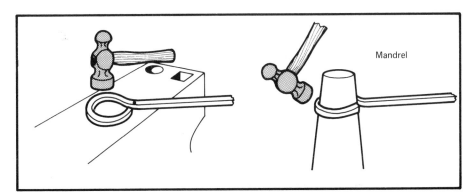

Mandrel

Scrolling

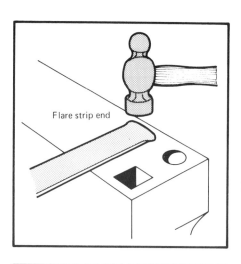

Flare strip end

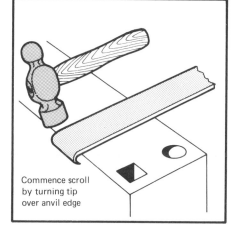

Commence scroll
by turning tip
over anvil edge

Modern design in metal had followed the trend in design in most other materials. There has been a demand in the home for objects that are easier to clean. This has been convenient for the manufacturer who can mass-produce objects which are plain and simple without the need for old-fashioned craftsmanship.

But there has been a reaction to this modern simplicity, which soon begins to look barren and uninteresting. People begin to want 'natural' shapes — the kinds of curves and patterns visible in the structure of plants and animals. Good design has been referred to as 'getting the best out of the material'.

Forging is a traditional craft in which the process of scrolling extends the material and lightens it, bends it and strengthens it, and produces a finished design which is always interesting. Some traditional forgework seen on garden gates is amongst the best and most satisfying craftsmanship in the world.

The photograph shows details of scrollwork on a garden gate designed and made by Alan Dawson in Maryport.

Use the scrolling technique to strengthen and decorate mild-steel frames used as railings, screens or gates.

The process

Spread the end of the strip using a process known as **flaring.** It is similar to drawing-down except that only two opposite sides are worked on the face of the anvil.
Bend over the tip on the anvil corners.

A **scrolling iron** is a perfect scroll former of heavy iron which is held in a vice. Heat the strip to yellow heat and fix it to the scrolling iron with scroll tongs. Pull it firmly round the former.
If you need to re-heat the metal quench that part of the scroll which is already curved. Re-heat as few times as possible.

When it leaves the scrolling iron former, the newly made scroll rises in the middle. Flatten this on the face of the anvil.

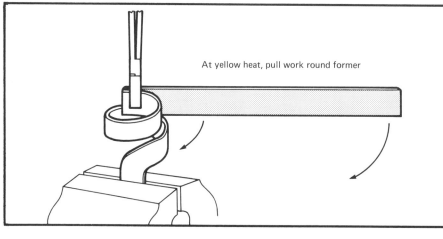

At yellow heat, pull work round former

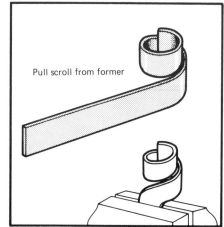

Pull scroll from former

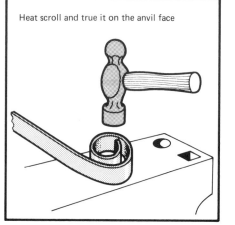

Heat scroll and true it on the anvil face

Foundry Work – Introduction to Casting

In foundry work, molten metal is poured into a mould made from a pattern. The solidified metal is referred to as a **casting**. In the workshop, patterns are often made from wood and the mould from sand. Aluminium is a relatively cheap and reliable metal to melt and pour.

For the Great Exhibition of 1851 the Crystal Palace was constructed from beams and arches made from grey iron.

Taps are complicated shapes made from brass, which resists corrosion and is easy to machine.

The Jonathan Clarke sculpture No.8112 is a unique aluminium casting from a polystyrene pattern, and the Paul Bridge brooch pattern was made from wax and cast in expensive silver. These are excellent examples of casting as an art process on a small scale.

The Glynwed Foundries 'Action Man' demonstrates the variety of industrially produced castings for drainage.

The Victor nutcracker shows a domestic product which is mass-produced in a metal mould.

The John Taylor Foundry is famous for its bells. This mould is for a 7-ton bell cast in **bell metal** – an alloy of copper and tin which resounds when struck.

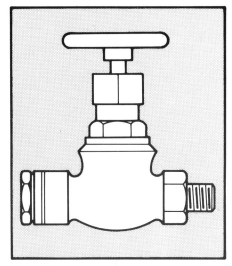

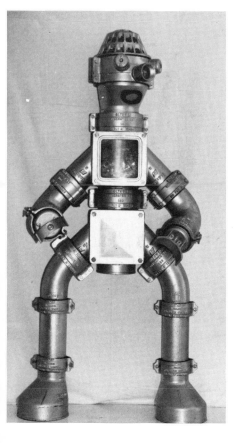

Safety

You know how hot metal becomes when it is heated so that it glows. Imagine the kind of temperatures needed to actually melt metal so that it can be poured, and the great care needed to make a casting safely.

The photograph shows the casting of a bell in the John Taylor Bell Foundry. All the men are wearing protective clothing consisting of helmet, eye shield, gloves, apron, leggings (gaiters) and heavy shoes or boots, all made from leather.
Of course, the amount of metal you will melt and pour in the workshop is small in comparison. But it is just as hot and dangerous!

YOU MUST WEAR PROTECTIVE CLOTHING

Increase your safety by preparing the foundry area properly:

1. Clear the floor of any obstructions.
2. Make sure that the floor is dry.
3. Ventilate the area.
4. Clean and dry all equipment and pre-heat lifting, degassing and skimming tools.
5. Set the moulding boxes on a bed of dry sand.

Work in pairs — one operator and one helper only.
Work methodically. DO NOT RUSH.

Leather **leggings** and **gloves** are made to a British Standard and are marked either 'All Metals' or 'To 780°C'.
Those marked 'To 780°C' should only be used when casting aluminium or lead. Both metals melt below this temperature. Other metals are hotter when molten.

Polystyrene patterns are left in the mould and the material evaporates when the metal is poured. The styrene fumes are unpleasant and can be very dangerous. When using a polystyrene pattern, have maximum ventilation and wear a **face mask** or **respirator.**

Legging

Glove

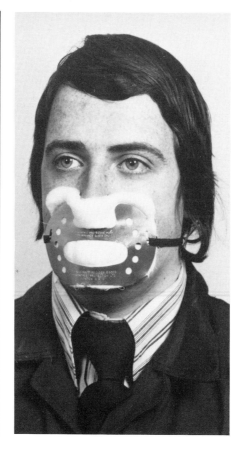

Casting

Basic equipment

A moulding bench has a metal-lined working surface. The moulding flasks are supported on it whilst sand ramming takes place. Moulding sand is stored in a recessed area and is riddled into the flasks through one of two sieves — coarse or fine.

A **ceramic crucible** is heated in a furnace. The Flamefast furnace shown has insulating and refractory materials which help to rapidly heat the full range of metals beyond their melting points. The furnace is heated with a mixture of air and gas. It shuts off safely if either the mains electricity or gas supplies fail.

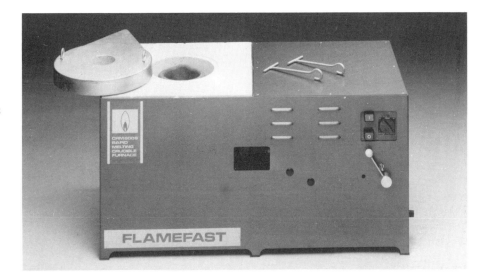

Use **lifting tongs** to transfer the crucible and molten metal from the furnace to the **pouring ring shank**. The tongs must grip evenly to avoid uneven pressure on the fragile container.

The pouring ring shank is used by two people. The helper holds the single handle, acting as a pivot. The operator holds the double handle which controls the pour from the crucible.

The **degassing plunger** is inverted to hold down a tablet in the melt until unwanted gases are released.

Use the **ladle** to remove slag (impurities) from the surface of the melt before it is poured.

Use hardwood **peg rammers** to pack moulding sand firmly around the pattern and sprue pins.

Use a **drawer spike** to remove a wood pattern and sprue pins from the mould.

Use a **spoon** to shape the pouring basin and a **gate cutter** to cut a channel from the cavity to the sprue.

Taper, flat and heart-shaped **trowels** are useful for repairing any damage caused to the mould by the removal of the pattern.
Any sand which falls into the mould can be removed by gentle use of a pair of **bellows**.

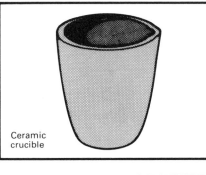

Ceramic crucible

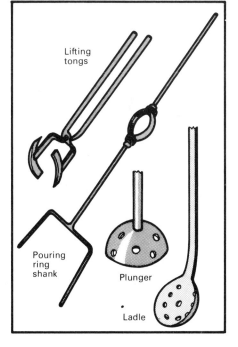

Lifting tongs

Pouring ring shank

Plunger

Ladle

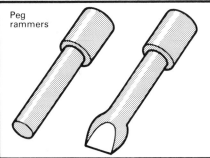

Peg rammers

Drawer spike

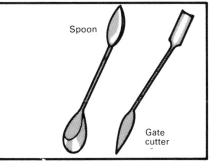

Spoon

Gate cutter

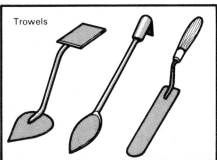

Trowels

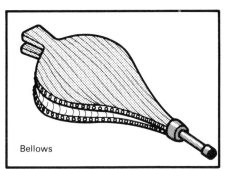

Bellows

Moulding

The quality of the mould affects the finished casting more than anything else. To achieve a good mould you must have a well-made pattern. The casting will come out of a well-made mould an exact copy of the pattern around which the mould was formed – in the same way that a fancy jelly for a childrens' party is produced from a mould!

Industrial castings are often much larger than workshop work, but the principle is the same. The photograph shows a mould maker from Holcroft Castings taking great care to give a perfect finish to the moulding sand with a trowel.

The moulding flask or box is in two parts. The bottom half is called the **drag** and the top half is called the **cope**. Each half of the flask has lugs on it through which a peg locates it accurately in place.
The drawing also shows a hardwood snap flask which is useful in a busy foundry. After the mould has been carried to the casting area the fastening clips are released and the flask can be used immediately to make up another mould. Use this method to make up a number of identical moulds which can then be cast at the same time.

Preparing sand for moulding

Moulding sand is usually supplied ready for use and should be stored in lidded bins. Cover the sand with a damp sack to keep it moist.

1. Re-use sand by breaking down lumps and mixing in some fresh sand.
2. Use a coarse sieve to riddle out solid lumps and metal slag.
3. Check the moisture content by squeezing the sand into a ball.
4. Break the sand ball. If the break is clean, and does not crumble, the sand is ready for use.
5. If the sand crumbles, spray on water. Dry sand will produce a weak mould.
6. If the sand sticks to your fingers, it is too wet. Add dry sand.

Wet sand is *dangerous*. Gases may be trapped, causing 'blowholes' in the casting.
Worse still, molten metal may generate steam which could *explode* the molten metal.

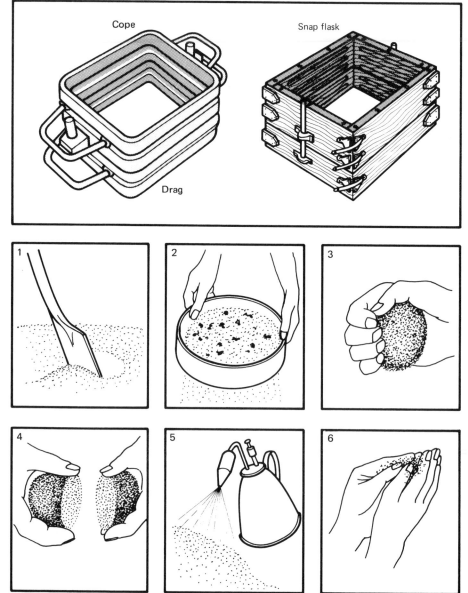

Cope   Snap flask

Drag

Patterns

The pattern must be carefully and accurately made. The casting is almost an exact copy of it, the only difference being that, as metal shrinks as it cools, the casting will be slightly smaller than the pattern. Where surfaces will have to be machined, the pattern should be enlarged.

Patterns are usually made from wood, but metal patterns can be made if a large number of castings are to be produced.

The polystyrene pattern is for a piece of sculpture, 'Helmet' by Jonathan Clarke. Polystyrene is an ideal material for casting 'free' shapes which are complicated and which do not have to be an exact size.

A well-made wood pattern will:

1. have a small draft or taper (1:100) to allow the pattern to be easily taken out of the moulding sand
2. have no sharp corners — fit internal corners with fillets and slightly round the outside corners
3. be designed to give a fairly even thickness of metal
4. be well-finished — seal and fill the grain.

If patterns are painted, use the following British Standard colours:

Non-ferrous metals
Cast finish — red
Machined surface — yellow
Core print — black

Ferrous metals
Cast finish — black
Machined surface — yellow
Core print — red

Cores

Use cores to make holes and internal shapes in a casting. They are made in a core box traditionally from a mixture of moulding sand and linseed oil, hardened in an oven. Ready-made cylindrical cores can be bought.

The core print is a projection on a pattern which will make a recess in the mould. Fit the core into this.

The section shows a core held in place by only one core print. It is supported at the other end by a pipe chaplet. A chaplet is a distance piece positioned to support a core (the simplest is like a square-headed nail) and is made from a similar metal to the melt.

Wood

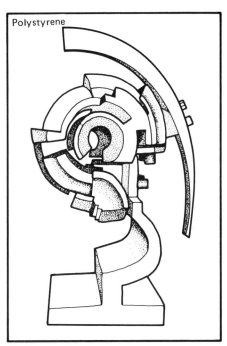

Polystyrene

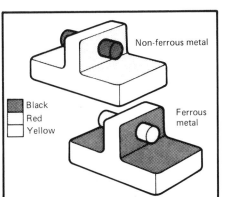

Non-ferrous metal

Black
Red
Yellow

Ferrous metal

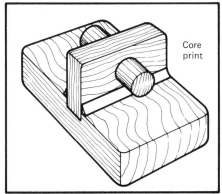

Core print

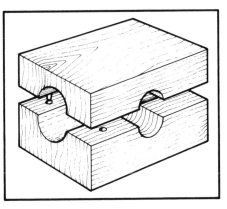

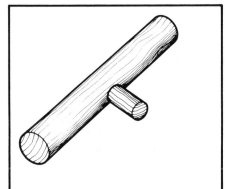

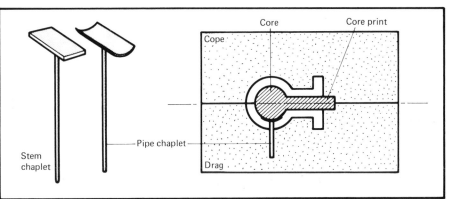

Stem chaplet

Pipe chaplet

Cope

Core   Core print

Drag

Patterns (continued)

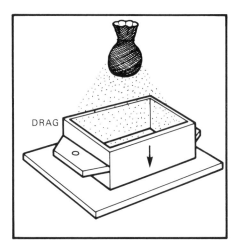

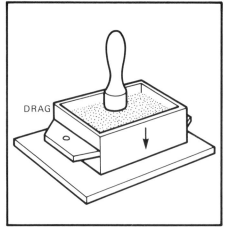

Moulding a one-piece pattern

Sprinkle parting dust on to the moulding board and place the drag on it, upside down. Place the pattern in position making sure that there is a space of at least 50 mm around it. Sprinkle the pattern with parting dust.

Riddle sand through a fine sieve to cover the pattern by 20 mm and ram this with care. Do not over-ram.

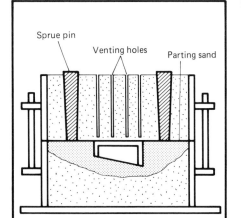

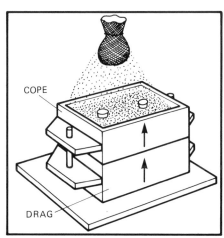

Fill the drag with coarse sand and ram. Remove the surplus sand with a strickling rod.

Invert the drag on to a moulding board sprinkled with parting dust and fix the cope in position. Position the sprue pins and sprinkle with parting dust.

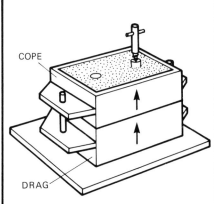

Gradually fill the cope with coarse sand and ram it down at each stage. Remove the surplus sand with a strickling rod. Vent holes are put into the cope either with a fine rod or by laying in waxed string which will burn out as the melt is poured.

Tap the sprue pins to loosen them, then take them out with a draw pin. Use a spoon to cut a pouring basin and round the edges with your fingers.

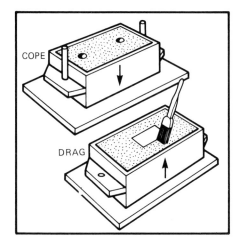

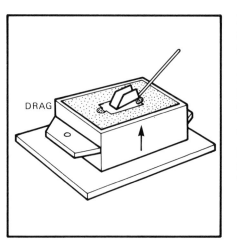

Remove the cope and invert it on to a moulding board. Dampen the sand around the pattern.

Insert draw pins into the pattern. Tap them to loosen the pattern then lift the pattern out of the drag.

Use a square or spoon to cut channels (gates) from the sprue holes to the mould. Use bellows to clean out any sand which has fallen into the mould.

Patterns (continued)

Preparing for casting

To obtain an extra-fine finish, spray a **mould coating** on to the mould.

Skin-dry the mould using a **soft** flame from a blow torch.

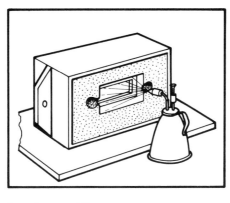 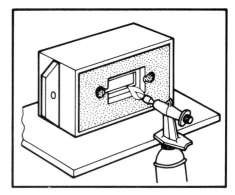

Close the flask by replacing the cope on top of the drag.

The drawing has half of the cope cut away to show the moulding flask fully prepared ready for the cast to be made. The labelled section shows the sprue hole into which the melt is poured. This is referred to as the **runner**. The other sprue hole is called the **riser**. At the base of the runner a basin has been cut to collect any loose sand which may come down when the melt is poured.

Metal melting

Check that tools are free from rust and dirt. Place ingots or scrap metal on top of the furnace to pre-warm them before putting them in the crucible. Do not overfill the crucible.

When the metal begins to melt cover it with a suitable melting flux.
Use a pryometer regularly to check the temperature.
The *pouring temperature* of the melt is higher than the temperature at which the metal melts. For example, aluminium melts at around 600°C, but needs to be at about 750°C for pouring.

If you are melting aluminium, at this stage de-gas the melt with a de-gaser. Use a perforated plunger to hold the degassing tablet at the bottom of the melt until the reaction stops.

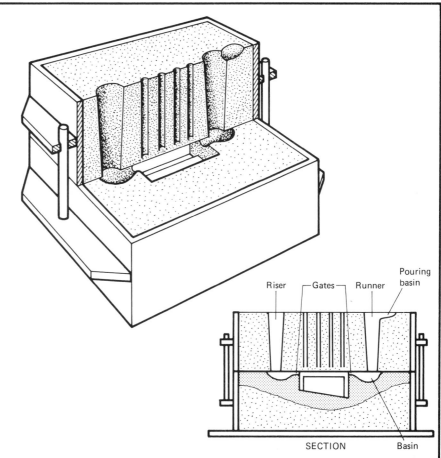

Riser — Gates — Runner — Pouring basin

SECTION   Basin

Lift the crucible from the furnace and place it in the pouring ring shank. Then use a ladle to remove the slag from the top of the melt.
Add in and stir a suitable flux.
The melt is then ready to pour.

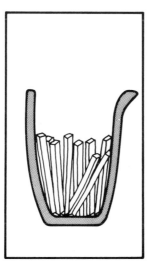 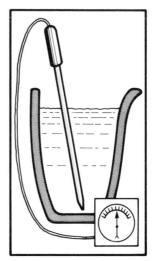 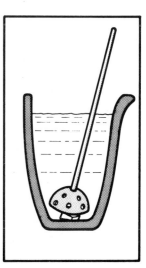

Patterns (continued)

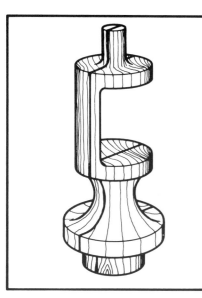

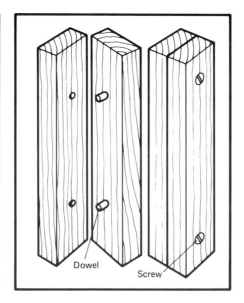

Dowel

Screw

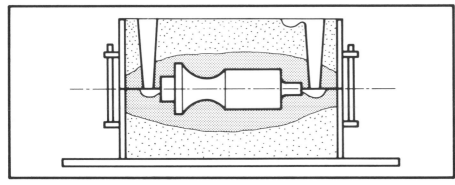

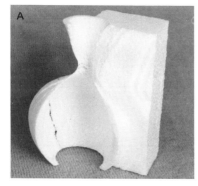

A

B

C

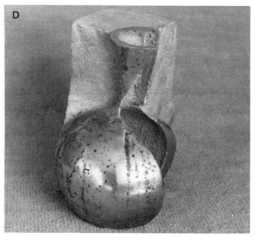

D

Two-piece patterns

A two-piece pattern is referred to as a **split pattern.** A split pattern is used in a design where it would be impossible to draw out a one-piece pattern from a mould without damaging it.

A split pattern is often used when the pattern has been turned on a lathe. The pattern for a nutcracker is an example.

1. Make the pattern from two pieces of wood which locate each other with dowel rod. Hold them together with screws for turning.
2. Prepare the drag, as for a one-piece pattern, using one half of the split pattern.
3. Turn the drag over and fix the cope.
4. Locate the second half of the split pattern and the sprue pins and cover with fine sand. Ram and fill the cope, as for a one-piece pattern.
5. Separate the cope from the drag. Tap and remove both halves of the split pattern.
6. Complete the preparation of each half of the mould and close up the flask ready for casting.

Polystyrene patterns

Polystyrene is an excellent pattern material for free shapes such as sculpture. Cut and shape it using a hot-wire cutter (ensure good ventilation), a hacksaw blade, Surform tools and abrasives.

Glue a fairly large polystyrene runner to the back or base of the pattern and position it in the closed moulding flask. Fill with sand and use a sprue pin to provide a riser.
DO NOT ram the sand as this may damage the fragile pattern.

The photographs on this page show various stages in the production of a metal sculpture by Jonathan Clarke.

The polystyrene pattern for the piece of tabletop sculpture (A).

The casting removed from the moulding. The thick runner and the thin riser have to be sawn off and the surfaces finished. This process is known as fettling (B).

The sculpture after it has been fettled and some parts of it highlighted by grinding and buffing (C).

Jonathan Clarke finished this piece using a black wax polish to exaggerate the difference between the smooth and rough (machined and cast) surface (D).

Power Tools – Safety

A workshop can be a very dangerous place in which to work. There are the dangers of burns and fire when metal is heated for forging or melted for casting. Far less obvious are the dangers of acids and fumes created when etching metal or working with plastics. The most basic source of danger is the power of electricity which is invisible, and the most obvious is the rapid and powerful movement of cutting machinery.

The dangers of working in a place surrounded by heat and movement can be reduced by simply learning to work safely. *Workshop safety is a skill to be learned.*

The way in which your workshop is designed, constructed and managed is controlled by Government regulations introduced in the last century, and since changed to improve the safety of workshop users.
The drawing shows Victorian machinists working a planer with open pulleys and drive wheels and without cutter guards. The men are wearing neckties, loose jackets and are without eye protection. One is so small that he has to stand on a box to operate a wheel!

It is your teacher's responsibility to provide such things as guards and protective clothing.
Remember: It is *your* responsibility to *use* guards and wear protective clothing. *Obey rules and follow recommendations.*

General safety

There is less danger if everybody works in a quiet and sensible way, walking with care along clearly marked gangways. Keep benches and machines clean and tidy. Store away tools and brush-up swarf.

Machine safety

The Royal Society for the Prevention of Accidents (ROSPA) says that, when an accident happens, the person responsible will probably say one of the following:

'I didn't think'
'I didn't look'
'I didn't ask'

THESE ARE *NOT* EXCUSES.

Do not use a machine unless you have been shown how to use it and understand how it works. If in doubt *ask*.

Electrical faults are the cause of many burns and deaths where machines are used. There is greater danger if an area is damp, so work only in dry conditions.

Do not use machines which you *think* are faulty or which *look* faulty. Tell-tale signs include a supply of power which is intermittent and a pilot light which isn't lit.
Report these symptoms to your teacher.

Portable electric tools are most likely to be dangerous. Before using them look to see that wiring is not loose or frayed and that the plug is in good condition.
Look to see if goggles are provided. If they are you must wear them.
Ask if hand protection is needed to move heavy workpieces or tools.
In some conditions you may need to protect your mouth and ears.

REMEMBER

Fix guards over cutting areas.
Stop machines to adjust or clean them.
One operator for each machine.

DO NOT distract or be distracted by other people.
DO NOT leave a machine which is working.

Pillar Drills

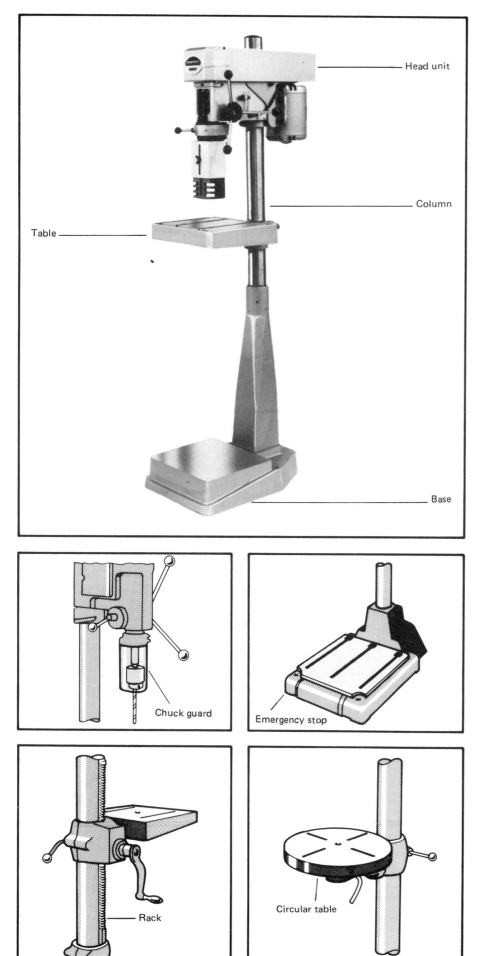

Head unit

Column

Table

Base

Chuck guard

Emergency stop

Rack

Circular table

Pillar drills are usually floor-mounted but bench models are available. They have the same specification but have a different length of steel column.

The pillar drill shown consists of a **base** and **column** which supports a **head unit**, and a **table** which has been machined flat and slotted. Both are held at right-angles to the column.
The head unit contains the **motor** and **drill spindle**.
The spindle holds the drill or a chuck which is operated on a rack and pinion by a **feed handle**. It is fitted with a simple depth stop — knurled nuts on a screw thread.
A vee-belt pulley transfers the motor drive to the spindle. It can produce a range of drilling speeds. These vary according to the model. A typical 5-speed drill will range from about 350 to 2500 rpm (revolutions per minute) and an 8-speed drill from 80 to 3000 rpm. The model shown has 10 speeds from 65 to 3830 rpm.

A **chuck guard** is essential for safe use. A clear plastic guard may hinge upwards for easy access to the chuck. Slide down the telescopic guard to cover the drill in use.

A floor-mounted pillar drill may be fitted with a foot-operated **emergency stop**.

Work tables may be **rack operated** for easy and safe height adjustment. When adjusting tables on a plain circular column use a table support for safety — a length of thick softwood is ideal.

A circular table is an alternative to a standard square table. It has four radial slots and a central hole. It can be rotated about its centre and can be tilted.

Twist Drills

Most holes in metal are cut with twist drills. A twist drill with a parallel shank is called a **jobber** and is usually used in a hand drill. A twist drill with a tapered shank will fit directly into the appropriate spindle on a pillar drill or the tailstock of a lathe.

There are three types of spiral. The **normal** spiral is used on most steels. Choose a drill with a **slow** spiral when drilling brass, bronze or plastics. Choose a drill with a **quick** spiral when drilling copper or aluminium.

The **chisel edge** of a drill penetrates the material.
The **lip** is the cutting edge. If the lips are ground unequal the hole being cut may become irregular or oversized.
The **land** is a cutting edge raised above the body of the drill so that it runs clear of the side of the hole. This reduces friction.
The **flutes** form the spiral. They allow cutting fluid on to the cutting edges and allow waste swarf to work itself out of the hole.
See diagram p. 40

A taper-shank drill is automatically aligned in the spindle. The small flat at the end of the tapered shank engages with a slot in the spindle to ensure a direct drive without slipping. Most spindles are fitted with a no. 2 morse taper. Use a twist drill with a no. 1 morse taper by fitting it into a no. 2 **sleeve**, tapping it 'home' with a soft-faced hammer.

Use a **drift** to eject a twist drill from the spindle.

Fit a morse tapered chuck to hold parallel-shanked twist drills up to about 12 mm diameter.
The twist drill is held by three jaws which slide up and down in a conical body when the chuck key is turned.
If the twist drill does not run true, check that the jaws are clean.
Safety note: Remove the chuck key before starting to drill.

Countersinking and **counterboring** are done at a slow speed using special drill bits.

Countersink to accommodate conical screw heads with an angle of 60° or 90°.
Counterbore to accommodate cheesehead screws or bolt heads. The bit has a pilot to fit a pre-drilled hole made for the bolt shank.

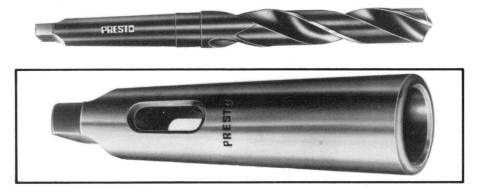

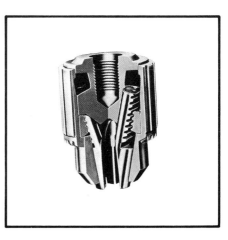

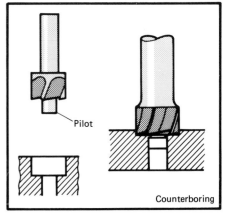

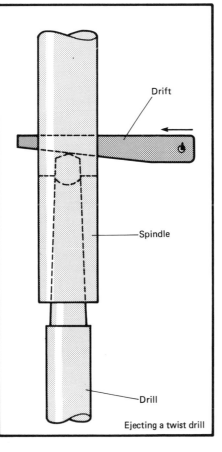

Drift

Spindle

Drill

Ejecting a twist drill

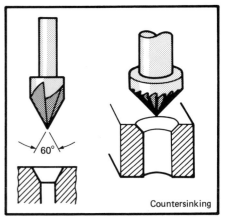

Pilot

Counterboring

60°

Countersinking

Drilling

If metal is hand-held it can be dangerous. When the drill breaks through the material it may jam and drive the work round. A workpiece which is not firmly held may fly off the drill. Both could cause serious injury and damage the drill. Use a hand vice (see page 29) to hand-hold small, light or thin material.

Clamping plates are held parallel to the table by bolts fixed into the table T-slots. They are supported by packing pieces the same thickness as the workpiece. The drawing shows a clamping plate and supporting bar supporting work over the edge of the machine table.

Angle plates are especially useful to hold awkward shapes such as castings which have to be drilled.

Sheet metal

When drilling sheet metal these faults may occur:

1. The hole may not be round. Make the chisel edge smaller and reduce the feed pressure.
2. The drill may jam in the metal. Change the point angle so that it cuts the full diameter before breaking through.
3. The underside of the hole may be burred. When accurate location is not vital, clamp the workpiece between two pieces of thicker scrap metal.

Drilling for screws

Clamp the two workpieces together. Drill a clearance hole through the top piece and into the bottom piece to leave a shallow counterbore. This will give a lead for the tapping drill.

Large holes

Use a **hole saw** when extreme accuracy is not important. The saw was designed for pipe fitting in sizes from 14 to 152 mm diameter. Arbors have an hexagonal shank to fit a three-jaw chuck. When using a pillar drill support the sheet material on a wood block.

Use a **tank cutter** in a Carpenter's brace to cut by hand (25 – 125 mm diameter). Cut washers in the same way.

Drilling for bolts

Clamp the two workpieces together, drill clearance holes and ream if necessary.

Drilling blind holes

Use the depth stop.

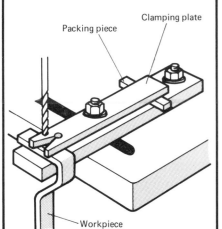

Packing piece — Clamping plate
Workpiece

Angle plate
Casting

Modified drill for aluminium — Standard drill

140° 118°

The standard point angle is 118°. Use 125° for copper, 130° for brass and 140° for aluminium.

Drilling for screws

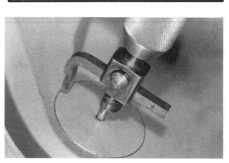

Drilling (continued)

Drilling a bar

First mark a centre-line and locate the position of the hole using a centre punch. A pilot hole may help when drilling into a curved surface.

The Eclipse **magnetic machine vice** will hold a variety of sections in its case-hardened jaws. It is accurately ground to be usable on its base, sides or end. Holes can therefore be bored at right-angles to each other without the workpiece being removed.

Magnetic Vee blocks are often used in line as matched pairs for holding lengths of bar. They are accurately ground to stand on end. The small vee holds bars up to 20 mm diameter — the large vee holds bars up to 65 mm diameter.

Vee blocks are also used as matched pairs. Each can be fitted with a clamp to secure the material. Both the blocks and the material are securely held with clamping plates. These plates are positioned as near as possible to the hole to be drilled. A **vee clamp** follows this principle — holding material at both sides of the hole.

Reaming

A hole drilled with a twist drill is not always accurate enough. Use a reamer to ensure a perfect hole.
A reamer will not drill a hole. It will enlarge an existing hole, but it will not alter the direction of the hole.
Use the reamer to make a fine cut of about 0.1 mm. Use plenty of cutting fluid.

Reamers

Both hand and machine reamers are available. Machine reamers have *either* a morse tapered shank to fit the drill spindle or lathe tailstock — or a parallel shank to fit a three-jaw chuck.

The reamer shown has a parallel shank and is made in ten diameters from 2.5 to 12 mm.
Note that the flutes of the reamer have a left-hand spiral — opposite to those of a drill.

Reamers are *precision* tools. Store them separately in boxes or suitable racks.

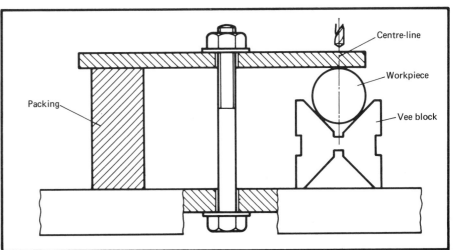

Centre-line

Workpiece

Vee block

Packing

The Power Hacksaw and Bandsaw

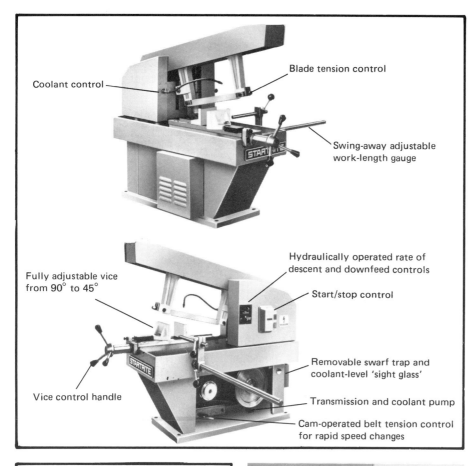

Coolant control

Blade tension control

Swing-away adjustable work-length gauge

Fully adjustable vice from 90° to 45°

Hydraulically operated rate of descent and downfeed controls

Start/stop control

Removable swarf trap and coolant-level 'sight glass'

Vice control handle

Transmission and coolant pump

Cam-operated belt tension control for rapid speed changes

BANDSAW

Mitre cutting

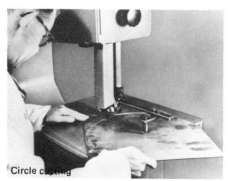

Circle cutting

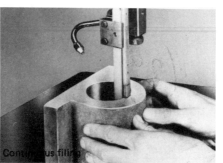

Continuous filing

The power hacksaw shown will cut solid bars up to 150 mm diameter. It has two cutting speeds of either 100 or 150 strokes per minute. The blade is 350 mm long and 32 mm wide. It may have 6 or 10 teeth per 25 mm.
The rate of feed (the speed at which the material is cut) is adjusted to provide the best cutting conditions.

On the return stroke the blade is raised to clear the work to avoid unnecessary wear. Coolant is circulated by a pump and the swarf is filtered by a removable swarf trap.

On the completion of each cut the bow automatically raises clear of the material and the machine stops.

The vice jaws are adjustable from 90° to 45° when the cutting capacity is reduced to 90 mm diameter.

The bandsaw

The continuous running blade of a bandsaw reduces cutting time. The narrow blade allows curved cuts to be made. The narrower blade will cut the smallest diameters.

The bandsaw shown has a throat size of 335 mm. The blades are made in continuous lengths up to 45 m, then cut and welded to the correct length. Blade speeds are measured in units of 300 mm per minute and can be varied from 50 to 3000.

Three different tooth profiles are available, and the teeth are either set wavy or with a rake to give even wear. Blade qualities are similar to those for hand hacksaws — carbon steel for general work, HSS for heavy duty, and one with a hardened cutting edge and a softer flexible back.
The maximum blade width is 16 mm with 3 – 18 teeth per 25 mm.

Functions include:

1. mitre cutting of tube using the universal holder
2. circle cutting using a disc cutting attachment
3. continuous filing using a file guide and support assembly. Files have a snap joint to make internal filing possible.

Safety

Ensure that blades are properly guided and that the cutting speed suits the material. Clamp the material to be cut.

The Shaping Machine

The shaping machine is used to produce flat surfaces, square-bottomed slots and vee-grooves by moving a cutting tool across the surface of the material. The work remains stationary as the tool cuts on its forward or power stroke, then it moves across during the return stroke.

The size of a shaping machine is measured by the length of its **ram stroke**. The shaper shown has a ram stroke of 200 mm. The ram can be adjusted to cut at 35, 60, 100 or 160 strokes per minute with a maximum cutting speed of 33 m per minute. The tool slide has a vertical adjustment of up to 90 mm and will swivel through 360°.

The **base** is either an iron casting or is fabricated in sheet steel. Doors give access to tools and to the driving mechanism. The **saddle** fits across the vertical slides and carries the table and the machine vice. It is raised and lowered by hand. The **table** is a hollow casting machined with vee-slots on the top and sides. Work can be fixed either directly to the table or be held in a machine vice with a swivel adjustment. The table can be moved by hand or fed automatically.
The **ram** is a heavy iron casting which moves horizontally, in slides on top of the pedestal, at right-angles to the table.

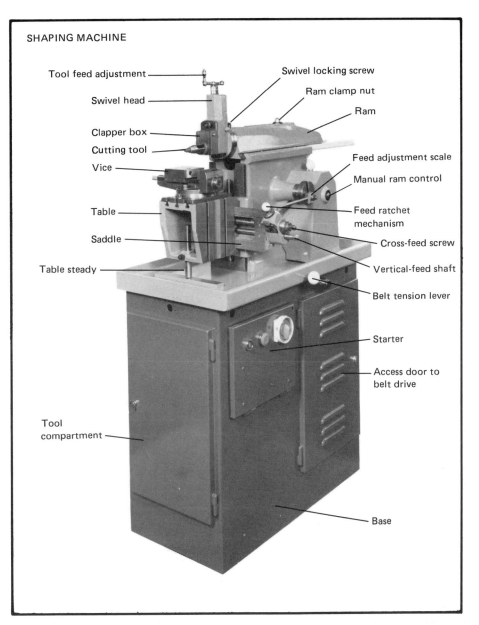

SHAPING MACHINE

- Tool feed adjustment
- Swivel locking screw
- Swivel head
- Ram clamp nut
- Ram
- Clapper box
- Cutting tool
- Feed adjustment scale
- Vice
- Manual ram control
- Table
- Feed ratchet mechanism
- Saddle
- Cross-feed screw
- Table steady
- Vertical-feed shaft
- Belt tension lever
- Starter
- Access door to belt drive
- Tool compartment
- Base

The shaper in use

The photograph shows a heavy industrial shaper at work. The material is being held on a magnetic vice with an end stop. The quality of the finish produced depends on:

1. the shape of the cutting tool
2. the cutting speed
3. the feed speed (a slow feed produces the best surface)
4. the use of a cutting solution to suit the material being cut.

The Shaping Machine (continued)

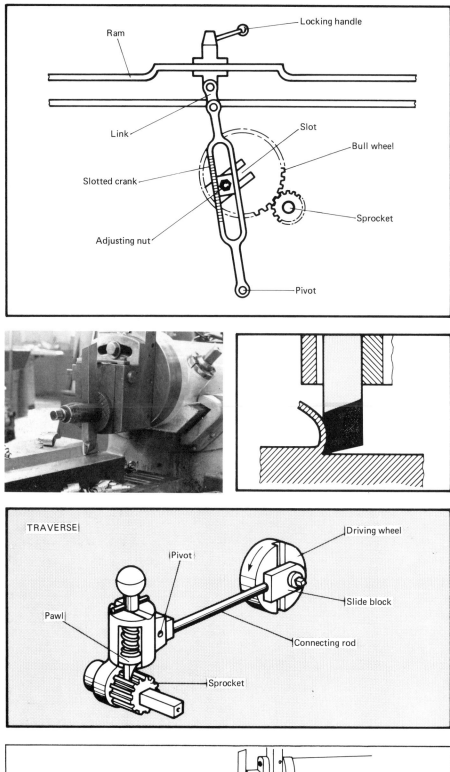

How it works

The **ram** is driven by a slotted crank attached to a large driving wheel called the **bull wheel.**

A link connects the ram to the slotted crank and compensates for the variation in distance as the crank swings through an arc.

The **pivot** provides the point about which the complete arrangement rotates.

Adjustment to the length of the cutting or power stroke is made by the adjusting nut on the bull wheel; the nearer it is to the centre of the wheel the shorter the stroke.

The driving mechanism gives a long, slow cutting stroke at *maximum* power and a quick return stroke at *minimum* power.

Cutting tools are held in the **tool post.** The tool post is held on the **clapper box** and is hinged so that it is free to pivot upwards on the return stroke. This helps to preserve the cutting edge of the tool.

Cutting tools have basically the same shapes as lathe tools, but they are usually larger and deeper in section to give added strength.

The table traverse operates automatically with the **pawl** engaged in the **sprocket.** The amount of movement depends on the position of the **connecting rod** on the **driving wheel.**

Do *not* move the table during a cutting stroke — the nearer it is to the centre of the wheel the finer the feed.

As the driving wheel rotates it causes the rocker to move backwards and forwards. The position of the pawl governs the direction of the table. Turn the pawl through 180° to change the direction of feed.

Disengage the pawl to traverse the table by hand.

Swivel and tilting tables allow angled surfaces to be machined. A 'Universal' table combines both a swivel and tilting mechanism.

The table is supported on an adjustable leg or table-steady. Slacken this off, set the table height, then adjust the support with the table at the mid-position on the cross-slide. Lock the leg in position.

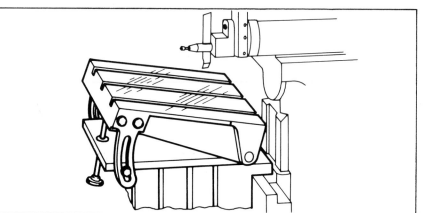

The Shaping Machine (continued)

Holding material

In the **machine vice**, use parallel packing strips to support work which would otherwise be too low in the vice.

Work is thrown out of true if the movable jaw of the vice lifts. Prevent this by inserting a length of rod as shown.

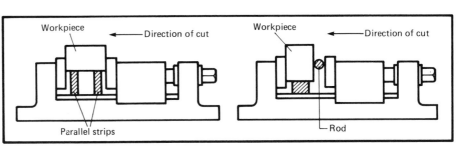

Ensure that the work is properly bedded on its packings and that the cutting stroke is *across* the vice jaws.

An **angle plate** can be used to hold small castings and awkwardly shaped material. Larger work can be clamped directly to the table using tee-bolts and packing pieces, which are slightly thicker than the work to give leverage. Where possible, fix an end stop to resist the thrust of the cutting stroke.

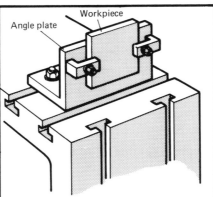

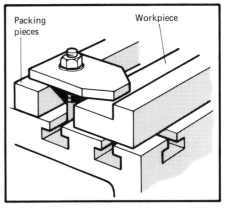

Work may also be clamped directly to the side of the table.

Magnetic parallels are precision ground blocks supplied in matching pairs, but they can be used singly or in multiples. They are used to support previously machined surfaces.

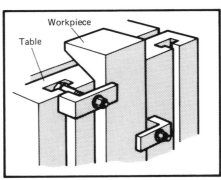

Testing tools and methods

Test the table for parallelism using a feeler gauge.
Test the slide for squareness in the same way.

Check that work is set parallel to the table traverse in the same way, or more accurately using a dial-gauge set in the tool post.

Check that previously machined surfaces are at right-angles to the table by using a surface gauge.

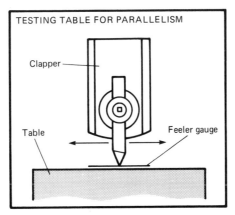

TESTING TABLE FOR PARALLELISM

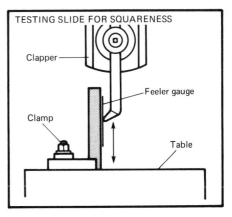

TESTING SLIDE FOR SQUARENESS

Setting up tools

The smallest possible overhang of the tool reduces the strain on the tool post and makes the tool more rigid.

Tool bits are cheap and easily ground to shape. Use them in a tool holder clamped in the tool post.

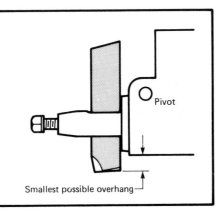

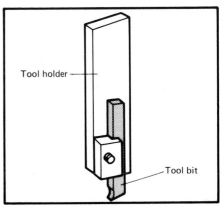

The Shaping Machine (continued)

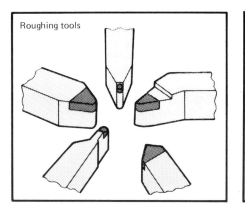

Roughing tools

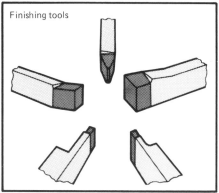

Finishing tools

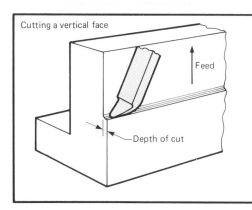

Cutting a vertical face

Feed

Depth of cut

Toolbox set well over

Allow small clearance here

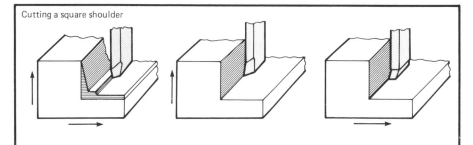

Cutting a square shoulder

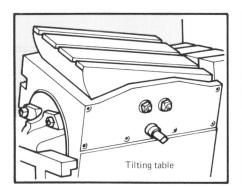

Tilting table

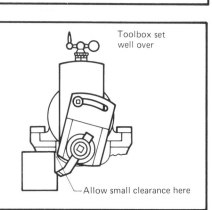

Roughing

Feed per stroke

Depth of cut

Feed

Finishing

Feed per stroke

Depth of cut

Feed

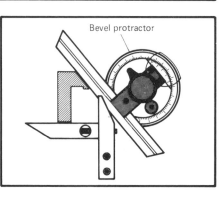

Bevel protractor

Roughing a flat surface

A roughing tool is round-nosed and is most suitable for the fast removal of metal.

Set up the workpiece in a machine vice or clamp it directly to the table.
Fix the round-nose tool in the tool post with the smallest possible overhang.
Set the stroke length.
Check the clearance of the clapper box at the beginning and end of each stroke.
Check also that it will run clear of any fixing clamps.
Adjust the feed to the capacity of the machine.
Raise the table height to give the correct depth of cut.
Use a cutting fluid.

Finishing a flat surface

A finishing tool is flat-nosed and is most suitable for removing ridges left by the roughing tool.

Leave the work set up as for roughing, and replace the roughing tool by a finishing tool.
Adjust the machine to the lowest feed rate.
Set for a shallow depth of cut, and use plenty of cutting fluid.

To cut a *vertical face* the workpiece would normally be hand-fed.
Set the toolbox over so that the clapper clears the surface of the work on both the cutting and the return strokes.
Check that it will not hit the main casting on the return stroke.

To cut a *square shoulder* set up as for shaping a vertical face, and rough cut most of the waste.
Replace the roughing tool with a knife tool, first to finish the vertical surface, and then to finish the horizontal surface.

To make an *angled cut*, secure the work on a tilting table set to the appropriate angle. The toolbox may need setting over to achieve the necessary clearance between the work and the clapper box.

Testing work for accuracy is essential. The **bevel protractor** is ideal for testing angled surfaces.

The Milling Machine

The milling machine is fitted with rotating HSS cutters and the workpiece is secured to a movable table. The table is adjusted so that the work passes the cutters and the waste metal is removed.

There are two main types of milling machine.
In the **horizontal** type the cutter is held on a horizontal arbor.
In the **vertical** type the cutter is fixed to the end of a vertical spindle.

Horizontal milling machines

The **spindle** is fitted into a heavy cast column and is driven by the motor fitted below. The БEC machine shown has eight speeds from 100 to 1700 rpm.
The spindle has a steep taper (no. 3 morse taper) at one end to fit an **arbor**. The arbor is pulled into the spindle by a **drawbolt**. The overarm has a bracket which supports the arbor and stops it from bending.

The **knee** casting slides on the front of the column and is adjusted for height by a handwheel. (On larger machines it is supported by an adjustable leg.)
The **saddle** fits on to the knee and is moved in line with the spindle using the cross traverse handwheel.
The **table** fits on to the saddle and is moved at right-angles to the spindle either by hand, using the long traverse handwheel, or by a power unit in the saddle.
The model shown has eight rates of feed, ranging from 25 to 230 mm per minute.
The table is fitted with a series of T-slots into which clamps and other holding devices can be fitted.
Trip dogs automatically restrict the long traverse movement.

Milling cutters are positioned on the arbor using a series of spacing collars.

Milling machines in use

Up-milling describes the process where the work is fed in the opposite direction to that of the revolving cutter. The cutter begins at the bottom of the cut.

Down-milling describes the process where the work is fed in the same direction as the revolving cutter. Heavier cuts can be made on robust machines.

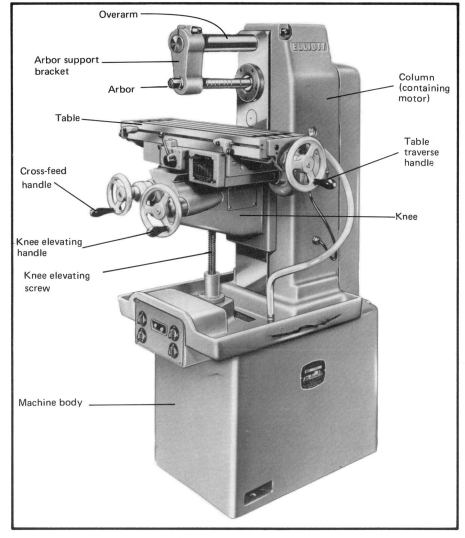

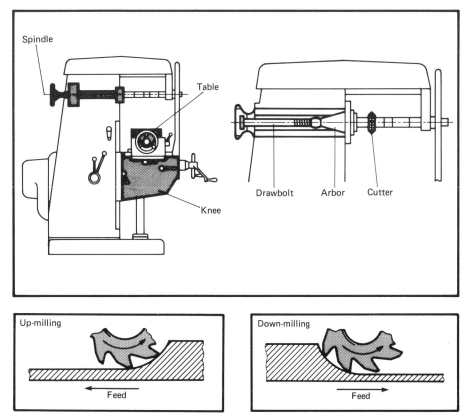

The Milling Machine (continued)

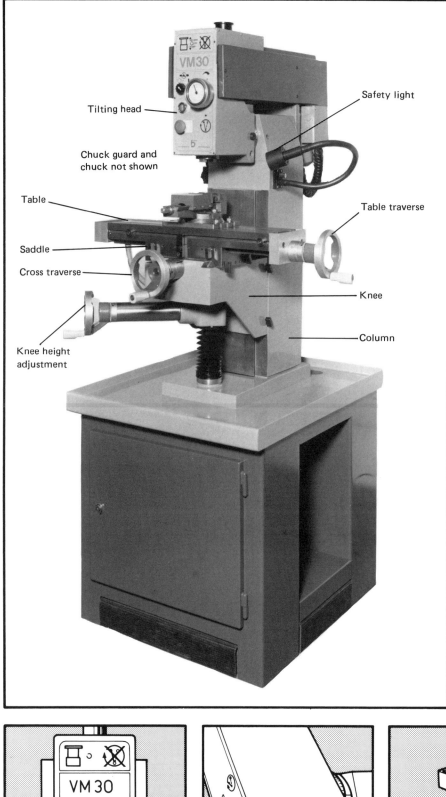

Tilting head

Safety light

Chuck guard and chuck not shown

Table

Table traverse

Saddle

Cross traverse

Knee

Column

Knee height adjustment

Vertical milling machines

The machine has an upright spindle which fits into the **machine head**. The machine head can be swivelled up to an angle of 45° on either side of the vertical.

Apart from the machine head, the vertical milling machine is constructed in the same way as the horizontal milling machine. The knee, saddle and table may be identical in the ways in which they are made and controlled.

The photograph shows a Boxford VM30 milling machine. It incorporates three necessary safety features :

1. a clear, adjustable cutter guard
2. a spotlight to brighten the work area
3. an emergency foot switch in the base.

The machine head contains the controls. This model has an infinitely variable spindle speed from 55 to 3000 rpm. (In the range 55–500 rpm, the gear at the top of the head is engaged.) This fine control over cutting speed allows better finishes to be produced and makes milling cutters last longer.
There is a coolant switch and the usual stop/start buttons.

The head may be tilted. It is here shown swivelled at 45°. A slitting cutter is protected by a clear adjustable guard.

Note the adjustable stops which can be set to limit the long traverse of the table.

In both horizontal and vertical milling, the quality of the milled surface depends on selecting :

1. a sharp cutter
2. the correct cutting speed
3. the correct feed speed
4. a cutting solution to suit the material being cut.

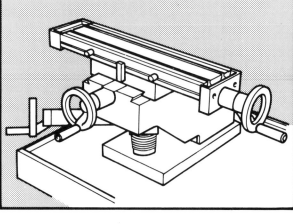

The Milling Machine (continued)

Holding tools

The machine vice will hold work with parallel sides. The direction of feed must be across the jaws and towards the fixed back jaw. Fix to the table with nuts and bolts fitted into the T-slots.

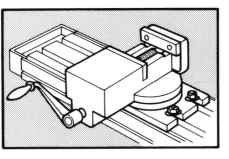

The traditional method of holding work uses T-bolts, clamping pieces and packing strips. The diagram on page 30 shows how such an arrangement may only be more or less 50 per cent efficient.
In comparison a Carver clamp pivots so that all the energy is transferred to the workpiece. This allows fewer fixings to be used, it adjusts easily and can be used with columns to hold down tall workpieces.

The Eclipse magnetic vice holds work without the danger of clamps interfering with milling. It is available in sizes from 255 × 125 mm upwards.
A recent development is the Eclipse electronically controlled electromagnetic chuck. This is linked to the machine head, so the miller will only work when the electromagnetic chuck is switched on.

Most milling cutters have skew teeth. The angle ensures that each cut is progressive, so that there is less **chatter**.
The detailed drawing shows the small primary clearance behind each cutting edge to give the edge maximum support.

Setting-up on the horizontal milling machine

1. Select the type and size of cutter.
2. Select an arbor or adaptor to hold the cutter.
3. Clean the arbor taper and spindle.
4. Screw a drawbolt into the taper and tighten the locking nut.
5. Decide on the best method of holding the workpiece.
6. Mount the work in position on the table.
7. Mount the cutter in position.
8. Clean some spacing collars and fit them.
9. Fit the cutter as near to the spindle as possible.
10. Check the cutting direction.
11. Fit an arbor support bracket as near to the cutter as possible.
12. Tighten all locking nuts.
13. Select the correct speed and feed.

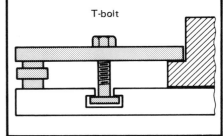

T-bolt

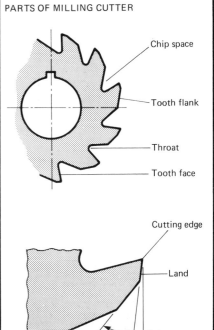

PARTS OF MILLING CUTTER

Chip space

Tooth flank

Throat

Tooth face

Cutting edge

Land

Secondary clearance

Primary clearance

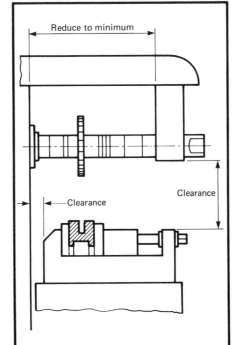

Reduce to minimum

Clearance

Clearance

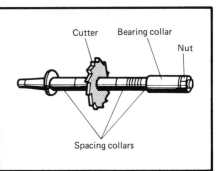

Cutter   Bearing collar

Nut

Spacing collars

To cut a *central slot:*

1. Adjust the table to the correct position.
2. Put the side of the cutter to the edge of the workpiece and note the reading on the cross-slide dial.
3. Lower the table until the cutter is clear of the workpiece.
4. Move the cross-slide by a distance 'd' (centre-line of slot from edge).
5. Move the cross-slide by half the thickness of the cutter.
6. Adjust the depth of cut.

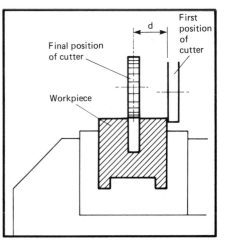

First position of cutter

Final position of cutter

d

Workpiece

The Milling Machine (continued)

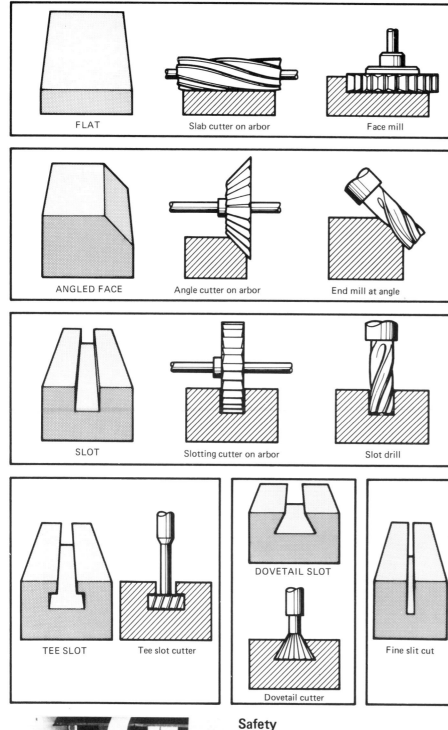

FLAT   Slab cutter on arbor   Face mill

ANGLED FACE   Angle cutter on arbor   End mill at angle

SLOT   Slotting cutter on arbor   Slot drill

TEE SLOT   Tee slot cutter   DOVETAIL SLOT   Dovetail cutter   Fine slit cut

Milling cutters

Side and **face** mills are designed to cut surfaces at right-angles to each other at the same time.

Flat faces
Horizontal: The cylindrical cutter is often called a slab cutter.
Vertical: Mills more than 100 mm diameter are large enough to have cutting teeth inserted.

Angled faces
Horizontal: A variety of angled cutters are available. The simplest is the single angle cutter with angles from 60° to 85° (in steps of 5°).
Vertical: It is possible to use the side-cutting facility of an end mill with the machine head tilted to the appropriate angle.

Straight slots
Horizontal: The slotting cutter has teeth on the edge only and is hollow-ground for clearance. The narrower cutters may have straight teeth. Wider cutters have angled teeth.
Vertical: The slot drill can be fed straight into the work to make closed ends.

Tee slots
Tee slots are cut on the vertical milling machine using two processes. First cut a slot to accommodate the shank of the tee-slot cutter. Then make the second cut.

Dovetail slots
Dovetail slots are made in the same way as tee slots. First cut a slot to remove most of the waste. Then run through with a dovetail cutter. Choose from three angles – 45°, 60°, 90°. Feed slowly to avoid damaging the fragile teeth.

Slitting
Slitting is done on the horizontal milling machine with a hollow groundcutter from 0.25 to 6 mm thick. Use for deep and narrow slits and parting off.

Safety

The photograph shows a clear guard on a horizontal machine.
In addition to normal workshop safety precautions:
Before milling –

1. Check the workpiece is secure.
2. Clean working surfaces.
3. Isolate the machine when fitting cutters.
4. Handle cutters with a cloth.
5. Check the direction of cutters.
6. Ensure a soluble oil supply faces the cutter.

During milling –

7. Ensure the guard is in position.
8. Stop the machine to brush away swarf.
9. Disengage the table traverse handle before engaging the autofeed mechanism.

The Lathe

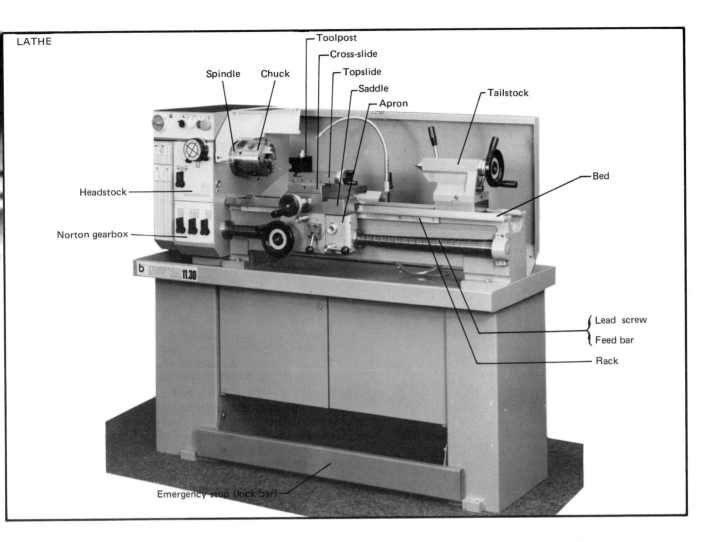

LATHE

Toolpost
Cross-slide
Topslide
Saddle
Apron
Spindle
Chuck
Tailstock
Headstock
Norton gearbox
Bed
Lead screw
Feed bar
Rack
Emergency stop (kick bar)

The lathe is used to turn materials into cylindrical shapes by traversing the tool parallel to the lathe bed.

Traverse the tool across the lathe bed to produce a flat surface.

You can also use the lathe to produce tapers, bore holes and cut threads.

The size of a lathe is described by the swing — twice the height of centres above the lathe bed — and the distance between centres.

The **lathe bed** is made of cast iron and carries the other components.

The **headstock** has a hollow spindle which will take a morse taper. Chucks and faceplates are attached to the headstock nose by a screw thread.

The **tailstock** is fully adjustable. The spindle is bored to receive a morse-tapered centre or a drill chuck.

The **saddle** fits across the lathe bed and consists of the carriage and the apron.

The **carriage** carries both the cross-slide and the compound slide. It is moved along the lathe bed by a rack fitted to the front.

The **apron** is fitted with a handle to engage the lead screw and a wheel for hand-traversing.

The **cross-slide** is moved at right-angles to the bed by rotating the cross-feed handle.

The **compound slide** swivels around a heavy pin mounted on the cross-slide. It can be locked at any angle so that short tapers can be turned. Its position is calibrated in degrees.

On many lathes the motor is mounted in the base. Then it is connected to the headstock spindle by a belt and drives via a clutch and gearbox.

Screw-cutting lathes have a lead screw and feed bar. This is driven by a separate gearbox or, on a simpler lathe, by direct gearing from the spindle.

The carriage can be moved automatically by the lead screw or feed bar.

The cross-slide can be moved at right-angles across the lathe bed either automatically or manually.

The 11.30 lathe shown has a swing of 11 inches (280 mm) and a distance between centres of 30 inches (750 mm).

Speeds range from 40 — 2240 rpm and both the spindle and lathe's lock have No. 3 morse tapers.

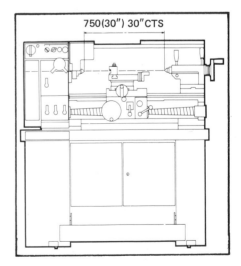

750(30") 30"CTS

The Lathe (continued)

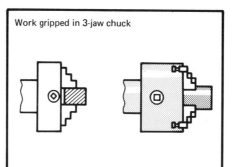

Work gripped in 3-jaw chuck

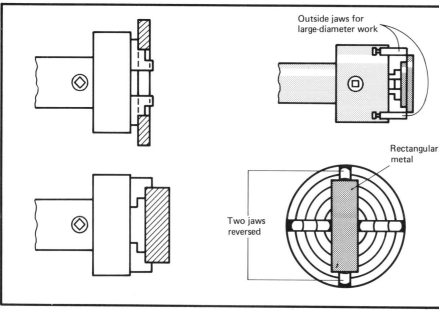

Outside jaws for large-diameter work

Rectangular metal

Two jaws reversed

Chucks

The **three-jaw self-centring** or **concentric** chuck is used to hold round or hexagonal bars.

The three jaws open or close together as the scroll is turned by the chuck key. Each jaw is matched to the scroll and must be fitted into the correct numbered slot. They cannot be interchanged.

To fit the chuck, use a wood block to support its weight. Clean the threads on both the chuck and spindle nose. Then screw the chuck on tight.

To remove the chuck, first set the gearbox to the lowest speed and put the wood block in position. Place a strong metal bar through the open jaws and push downwards. Unscrew the chuck carefully by hand.

Large-diameter work is held in a spare set of jaws with reversed steps, which must also be fitted into the correct numbered slots.

A **draw-in collet chuck** is a quick and accurate means of holding small-sectioned square, round or hexagonal bars. Use when making small items for models and instruments.

The **four-jaw independent chuck** is used to hold square-sectioned bar or irregular shapes.

The work can be set up centrally or off-centre (when balancing weights may be used.) Each jaw is adjusted separately and can be reversed when necessary. It holds work more firmly than the three-jaw chuck, but it takes longer to set up.

Magnetic chucks use permanent magnets to establish the magnetic lines of force which pass through the ferrous workpiece and hold it in place.

To release the workpiece, turn a lever to break the circuit.

Face plates are screwed into the spindle nose.

Use them for mounting irregular shaped workpieces and work which is too large for a four-jaw chuck.

Use balance weights when necessary.

The Lathe (continued)

Holding work between centres

Centres are made from high-speed steel and are ground to fit the morse taper of either the headstock spindle or the tailstock.

Centres designed to fit the tailstock have hardened centre points to resist the rubbing of the material which tends to wear the 'dead' centre.

A **full centre point** is ground at an angle of 60°.

When end-facing material, use a **half-centre** which is shaped to allow the tool to be fed further in.

Revolving centres rotate on bearings. These reduce the friction caused by both the radial and the thrust loads.

Remove a 'live' centre from the spindle by pushing a mild steel rod through the spindle bore.

Remove a 'dead' centre from the tailstock by screwing the barrel back — the centre is self-extracting.

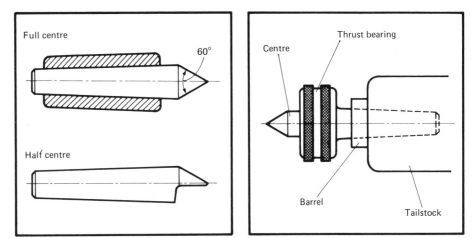

Full centre

60°

Half centre

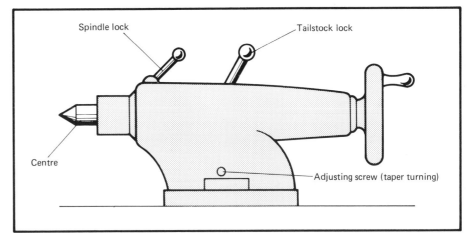

Centre

Thrust bearing

Barrel

Tailstock

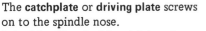

The **catchplate** or **driving plate** screws on to the spindle nose.

It is either fitted with a driving pin or slotted to receive a cranked carrier or dog.

Carriers or **dogs** are fastened to the end of the workpiece.

A straight carrier engages the catchplate driving pin.

A cranked carrier engages a slotted catchplate.

Spindle lock

Tailstock lock

Centre

Adjusting screw (taper turning)

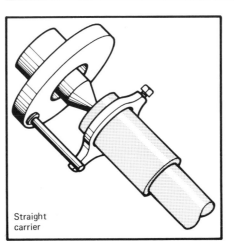

Straight carrier

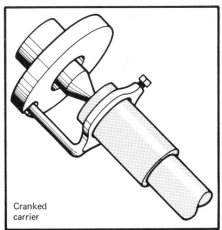

Cranked carrier

A **fixed steady** has three jaws which can be adjusted to the workpiece and locked in position on to the lathe bed.

Use it to support work which projects a long way out from the chuck.

A **travelling steady** has two jaws which contact the workpiece just behind the tool.

It bolts to the cross-slide or carriage and travels along with the tool.

Use it to support long, small-diameter work which would otherwise bend under the pressure of the cutting tool.

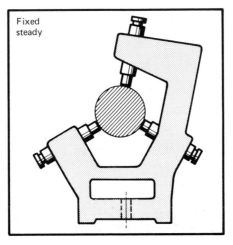

Fixed steady

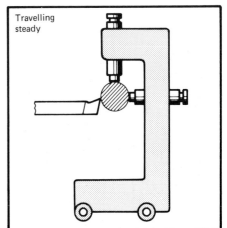

Travelling steady

Lathe Tools

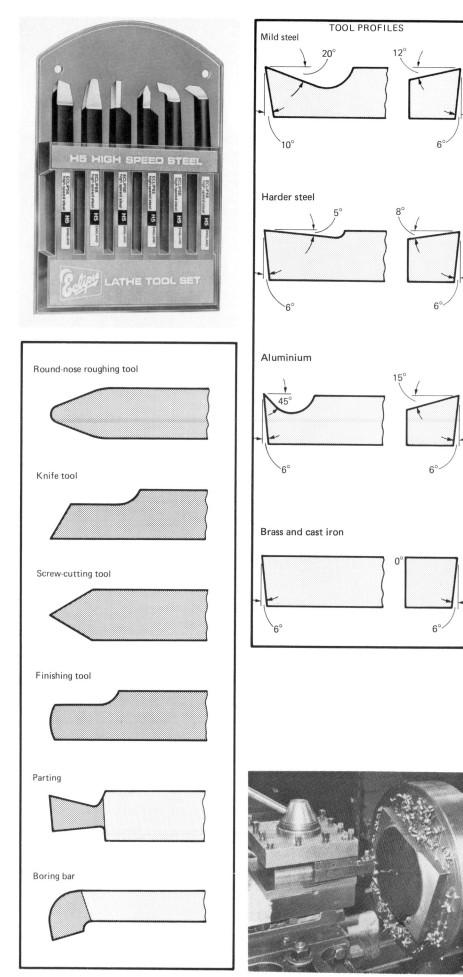

Round-nose roughing tool

Knife tool

Screw-cutting tool

Finishing tool

Parting

Boring bar

TOOL PROFILES

Mild steel
20°   12°
10°   6°

Harder steel
5°   8°
6°   6°

Aluminium
45°   15°
6°   6°

Brass and cast iron
0°
6°   6°

Lathe tools must be hard and tough. They are usually made from high-speed steel or other alloys which will hold the cutting edge even when heavy cuts raise the working temperature at the tip. Solid one-piece tool bits are held in a tool bit holder at an angle of 15°.

Use the round-nose **roughing tool** for making heavy waste cuts and general shaping.

Use the **knife tool** to face-off work and turn square shoulders. Make a light, fine cut to produce a good finish.

The **screw-cutting tool** has a profile ground to the angle of the thread required. Use it to cut an external thread.

The **finishing tool** has a curved tip to make light finishing cuts to the workpiece

Use a **parting-off tool** to separate the completed workpiece from the stock.

Use a **boring bar** to cut internal diameters.

Holding lathe tools

A **four-way tool post** enables four different tools to be placed in position ready for subsequent cutting operations. Rotate the tool post into each position.

The **tool post** (ring and rocker) allows the tool to be tilted until the tip is at the correct centre height.

Shims are thin pieces of steel which may be needed to pack the tool to the correct centre height.

Tool angles

Clearance angles allow all the tool, except the cutting edge, to clear the workpiece.

Rake gives the tool a wedge-like form, and is varied according to the metal being cut.
Use a **high top rake** on ductile metals, and a **low top rake** on hard and brittle ones. (If a tool nose is sloped sideways as well, this is called side rake.)
To produce a good surface finish consider the tool angle in relation to the cutting speed.

Lathe Tool Setting

Set the cutting tool to the centre height by:

1. swivelling the rocker on post-type holders
2. using packing pieces (shims) on fixed-tool holders

A tool which is set *too high* reduces the clearance angle. The workpiece then rubs on the tool front.
A tool set *too low* effectively reduces the top rake angle. This gives a poor cutting action. Workpieces, especially of small diameter, will tend to ride over the top of the tool.

To check the tool height use one of these methods:

1. Close the jaws of the three-jaw chuck and set the tool to the jaws' centre.
2. Set the tool to the head or tail centre.
3. Protect the tool tip with a thin piece of card. Position a steel rule between the tip and the workpiece. When the rule is vertical the setting is correct.

Facing-off

To set the cutting tool:

1. Allow minimum overhang to reduce possible vibration.
2. Adjust the tool to give the correct top rake angle.
3. Set to the correct centre height.
4. Give the tool 6° side clearance.
5. Lock the saddle to the lathe bed.

Face-off by feeding the cross-slide forward to the work centre. Withdraw the tool.
Traverse the compound slide approximately 1 mm and repeat the process.
Apply cutting fluid on each cut.

Centre-drilling

To drill holes to accommodate a centre, use the combination or slocombe drill. The hole at the bottom of the countersink leaves clearance for the centre point and provides a reservoir for the lubricant.

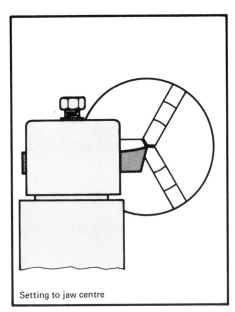

Setting to jaw centre

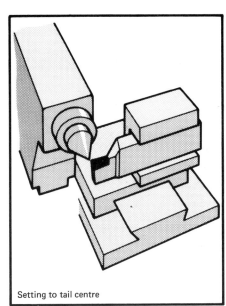

Setting to tail centre

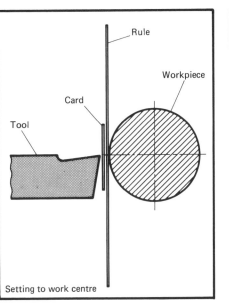

Rule

Workpiece

Card

Tool

Setting to work centre

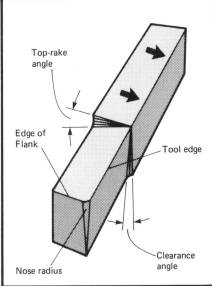

Top-rake angle

Edge of Flank

Tool edge

Nose radius

Clearance angle

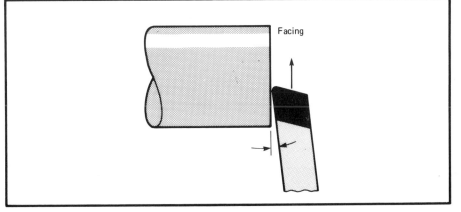

Facing

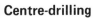

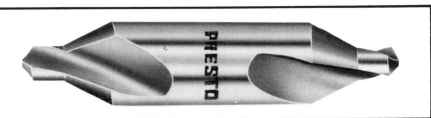

Using a Lathe

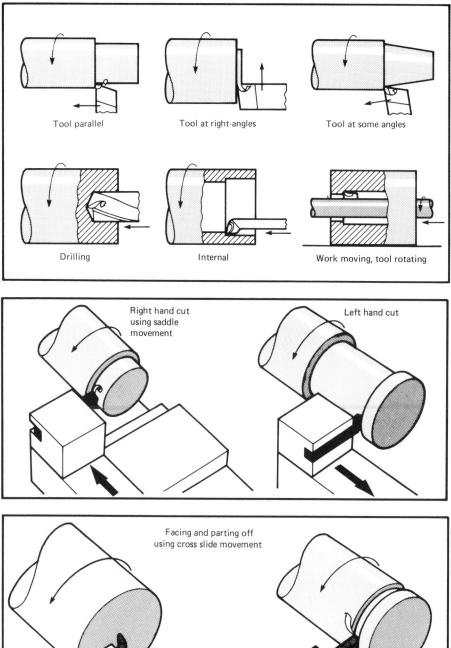

Tool parallel

Tool at right-angles

Tool at some angles

Drilling

Internal

Work moving, tool rotating

There are six basic principles in metal turning:

1. The tool may move parallel to the lathe bed.
2. The tool may move at right-angles to the lathe bed.
3. The tool may move at another angle to lathe bed.
4. The work may rotate while being drilled.
5. The tool may move internally and parallel to the lathe bed.
6. The tool may rotate, with the workpiece moving along the lathe bed.

Right hand cut using saddle movement

Left hand cut

Parallel turning

It is best to hold short workpieces in a chuck.
Set the cutting tool for facing.
Long work must be supported by the tail stock centre.

1. Face the workpiece and centre drill it at one end.
2. Support this end with the tailstock centre.
3. Lubricate the tailstock centre with a suitable high-melting-point grease.
4. Prevent the work vibrating by mounting a two-point travelling steady to take the thrust of the cutting tool.
5. Use a cutting fluid to help provide a clean cut.

Facing and parting off using cross slide movement

Checking the cut

After the first roughing cut has been taken, check the diameter at each end of the workpiece. Use either calipers or a micrometer. If the measurements are equal the lathe is turning parallel.

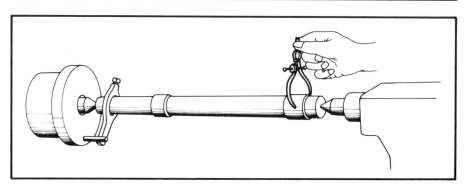

Using a Lathe (continued)

Turning a short taper

Set up the workpiece in a chuck.
Loosen the locking screws of the compound slide, so that it can be swivelled to the angle needed for the taper.
Set the tool to the centre height. Then tighten the screws to lock the compound slide in position.
Lock the saddle to the lathe bed.

To achieve feed, rotate the handle on the compound slide. This can be in either direction and will depend on the cutting angle of the tool.
The length of the taper is restricted to the length of travel of the compound slide.

You can work out the setting angle using the equation

$$\frac{D-d}{2} \div \text{length} = \text{tangent of setting angle}$$

Subtract the small diameter (d) from the large diameter (D) and halve it. Divide this figure by the length of the taper. This figure represents the tangent of the base angle. Find the angle from tangent tables.

Turning a long taper

Offset the tailstock by an amount calculated as follows:

$$\text{Amount of offset} = \frac{\text{length of work in mm}}{1000}$$

$$\times \frac{\text{taper per metre}}{2}$$

The tailstock can only be adjusted a small amount before the centre binds in the pre-drilled hole.

Use a special taper-turning attachment for tapers of more than $2°-3°$.

Parting-off

Do this while the workpiece is still in the lathe.
Set the tool to the correct centre height.
Reduce the overhang to a minimum.
Set the rake to less than that of a shaping tool for the same material.
Lock the carriage against movement along the lathe bed.
To part off a washer:

A. Set tool to face, note top slide reading and wind back on cross slide.
B. Traverse top slide to distance required.

Reduce the speed to half that for shaping. Feed in the parting-off tool by hand, using the appropriate cutting fluid.

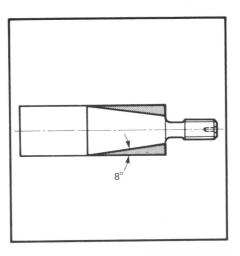

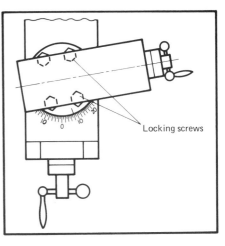

Locking screws

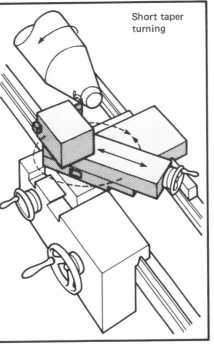

Short taper turning

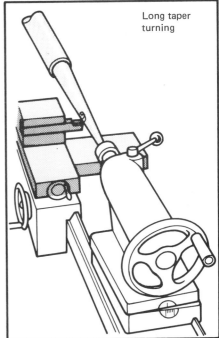

Long taper turning

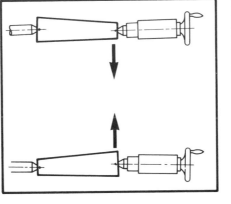

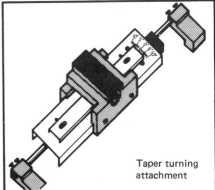

Taper turning attachment

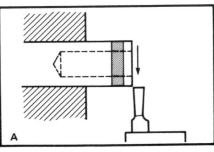

A

B

Using a Lathe (continued)

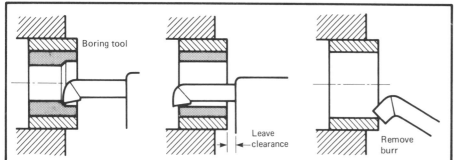

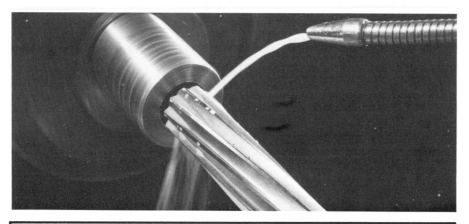

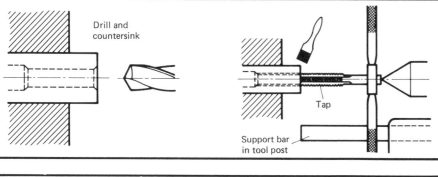

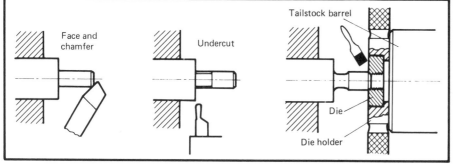

Drilling

Face-off the workpiece.
Set the lathe to a high speed and centre drill. Use cutting fluid.
Replace the centre drill with a twist drill. Use the tailstock handwheel to feed in the twist drill. Use cutting fluid.
Calculate the depth of hole using the graduations on the tailstock barrel.

Boring

Holes which are too large to be drilled should be bored.

Set up for drilling and drill a hole.
Set the boring tool at the centre height and use the tailstock handwheel to feed in. Use cutting fluid.
Make final light cuts. They must be light to reduce the tendency for the tool to spring.
Do not measure the diameter while the workpiece is rotating.
Remove burrs as shown in the diagram.

Reaming

A drilled or bored hole may be reamed to ensure an accurate finished diameter.

Drill or bore a hole 2 mm less than the required finished diameter.
Fit the reamer into the headstock.
Set the lathe to a slow speed and use the tailstock handwheel to feed in. Use cutting fluid.

Tapping

This is cutting an internal screw thread.

Set up the work and drill a tapping size hole.
Countersink the lip of the hole.
Set up a taper tap as shown and apply cutting fluid.
To make the cut use the tailstock handwheel to apply light pressure and turn the chuck by hand towards yourself. Repeat the process using a second tap and then a plug tap.

Threading

Turn the workpiece to the full diameter.
Face and chamfer the end. Undercut.
Open the die to its full extent and set it into the stock.
Support the stock and die on the face of the tailstock barrel and move the tailstock up against the workpiece.
To make the cut, use the tailstock handwheel to apply light pressure and turn the chuck by hand towards yourself.
Repeat the process with the die closed to form the thread fully.

Using a Lathe (continued)

Chamfering

A chamfer is a bevel cut on the edge of the work.

Face and turn the workpiece to the diameter required.
Set the tool to the angle of the chamfer required – usually 45°.
Feed in the tool from the cross-slide until the chamfer is the required width.

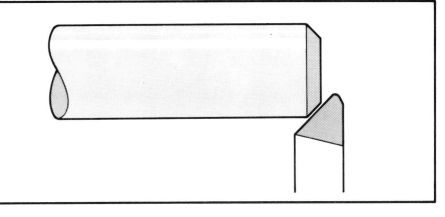

Doming

Doming is forming a rounded end to the workpiece.

Grind the shaping tool to the radius required.
Set up the tool to approach the work to give the correct shape.
Feed in slowly. Use a cutting fluid.

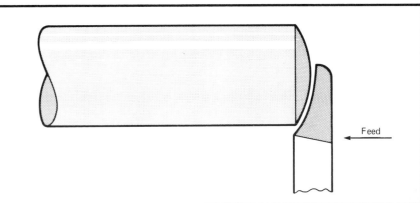

Undercutting

Undercutting allows an external thread to be cut right up to a shoulder.
It removes any radius which stops the spigot entering a hole right up to the shoulder.

Use a cutting fluid.

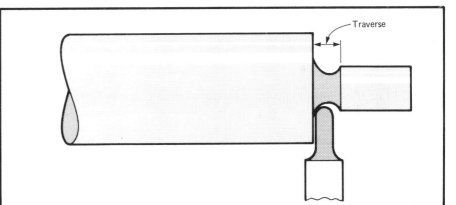

Knurling

Knurling is the method of embossing a pattern on the surface of the workpiece to form a surface that can be gripped.

Set the knurling tool at the centre height.
Feed the tool on to the workpiece furthest away from the chuck.
Run the lathe slowly, and apply cutting fluid.
Apply enough pressure to make the knurl completely in one traverse, feeding slowly and evenly towards the chuck.
Finish by lightly chamfering the ends of the knurl.

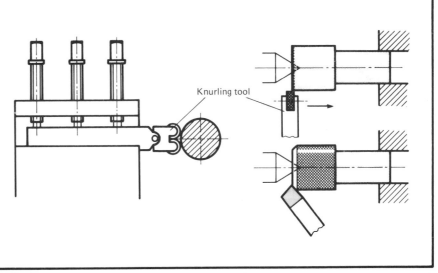

The Electric Drill

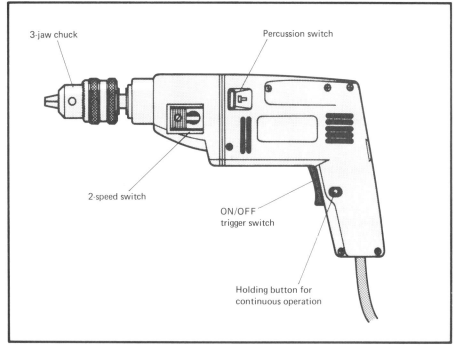

3-jaw chuck

Percussion switch

2-speed switch

ON/OFF trigger switch

Holding button for continuous operation

An electric drill is also known as a **power unit.**

Its main use is to drill holes in a whole range of materials, including wood, metal and masonry.

To do these jobs safely both indoors and outside, the most suitable electric drill would have:

1. a double-insulated case identified by this symbol $\boxed{\square}$
2. a three-jaw chuck to hold drill shanks up to 13 mm diameter
3. two or more speeds
4. a percussion facility
5. a holding button for continuous operation
6. an automatic cutout to prevent overloading
7. a palm-grip handle to ensure that pressure is exerted directly in line with the drill bit

Approximate drilling capacities (diameter)

Steel	13 mm	Hardwood	50 mm
Masonry	16 mm	Softwood	50 mm

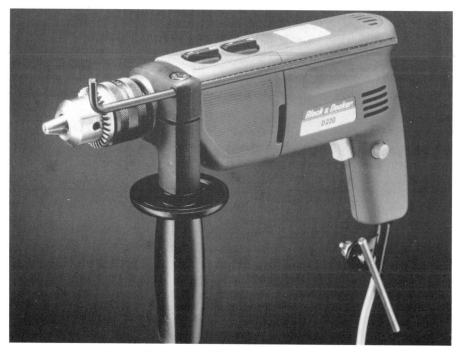

The power unit shown has two speeds:

2500 rpm	(1500 rpm on full load)
1250 rpm	(750 rpm on full load)

The faster speed is used for drilling softwoods, plywood and polishing. The slower speed is used with dense hardwoods, metal and masonry.

Some drills can be adjusted to run at speeds which allow a choice of optimum speed for each job. This is usually between 200 and 3000 rpm. The photograph shows a drill fitted with a handle which will swivel through 360° and a nose-mounted stop.
Note that the chuck key is safely stored in the cord grip secured in the handle.

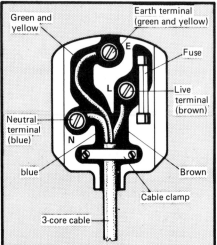

Green and yellow

Earth terminal (green and yellow)

Fuse

Live terminal (brown)

Neutral terminal (blue)

blue

Brown

Cable clamp

3-core cable

Wiring a plug safely

Connect the wires to the correct terminals. A mistake in the wiring would be dangerous.

1. Connect the earth wire (green and yellow) to terminal E.
2. Connect the live wire (brown) to terminal L.
3. Connect the neutral wire (blue) to terminal N.
4. Secure the power cable with the clamp.
5. Insert a fuse of the correct size and capacity.
6. Replace the top of the plug.

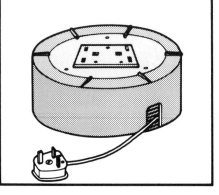

When using an extension lead avoid excess wire. If possible use a reel which has additional safety features — both a thermal and current overload cutout.

Power Unit Accessories

The electric drill can be used as a portable power unit to drive a range of accessories. This is particularly useful in the home workshop.

Use a variable-speed unit fixed to the bench to power a belt-driven **abrasive sheet.** At a slow speed this will remove metal.

Use a unit to power a 100 mm **dry grindstone.**
The grinder is fitted with a protective eyeshield.

Another photograph shows a 180 mm portable **grinding machine** being used to dress steel welds at a speed of 6000 rpm. The grinder is fitted with an adjustable **spark guard.**

Use the smaller **angle-grinder** to cut and grind all types of metal, and different forms such as pipe, rod, sheet and angle iron.

Fit a **rubber backing pad** and abrasive disc for rough sanding of wood and plastics.

Fit a **wire cup brush** to de-rust material at high speed.

Notes
Abrasive discs for metal grinding, metal cutting and stone cutting are similar in appearance. Check the information given before using the disc.
Wear appropriate protective clothing.

Power Unit Accessories (continued)

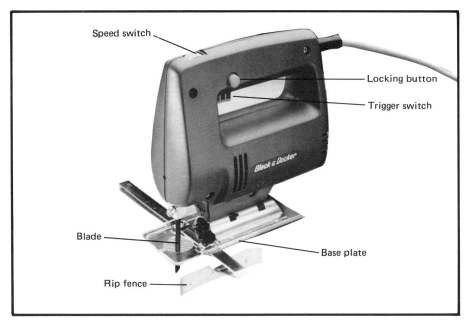

Speed switch

Locking button

Trigger switch

Blade

Base plate

Rip fence

The **jigsaw** is a versatile saw which can cut through steel, soft metals, plastics and wood.
It is usually used to cut curves, but a rip fence is fitted to cut parallel to an edge. The base plate can be tilted to 45° on both sides.

The unit shown:

1. has a double-insulated case
2. has a two-speed switch (2400 and 3000 rpm)
3. will cut mild steel up to 3 mm thick.

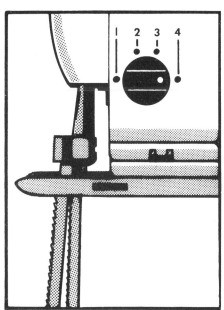

A heavy-duty jigsaw unit may have a pendulum action which can be set at four different angles.
The angled blade on the upward-cutting action increases the cutting speed and the capacity of the saw.
The unit shown will cut steel up to 10 mm thick, aluminium up to 20 mm thick and 70 mm softwood.

Use different blades for cutting wood, metal and plywood/plastics.

Engraving

An engraving tool is shown in use with a plastics stencil.
A bicycle frame is being engraved for security.
The carbine-tipped tool cuts at 6000 strokes per minute.
An abrasive tip is used for textured decoration on metal.
A diamond tip is used for work on glass.

Finishes – An Introduction

Metal surfaces are given a **finish** which will improve their appearance. Surface coatings are applied which will prevent the metal from **corrosion**.

Corrosion is a chemical reaction between oxygen and the metal. On steel this oxidization appears blue/black when joints are welded. On copper which is heated, a surface scale forms.
Corrosion is increased by the presence of moisture — steel rusts and copper becomes green.

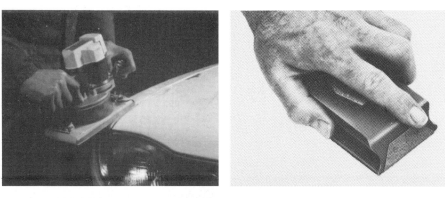

Metals are finished or prepared to be given a surface coating using abrasives and/or degreasing fluids.

Abrasives

Emery abrasive is bonded to a cloth backing and is commonly available in eight grades from 3 to 00 (grits 40 to 280) in sheet and roll form. On a mild steel surface which has been properly draw-filed, grade 1 would be the coarsest needed, followed by the finer abrasives. Grade FF emery cloth and a light oil lubricant gives a fine finish.

Silicon carbide abrasive bonded to a waterproof paper backing is called 'wet and dry' paper.
Use the coarsest grit (60–120) to etch the surface. Use finer grits up to 600 to produce a perfect finish on paint.

Tungsten carbide abrasive bonded to a thin metal sheet is ideal for rapid removal of wood and GRP.

On non-ferrous metals remove deeper surface marks with a scraper and then work over with a **Water of Ayr stone**.

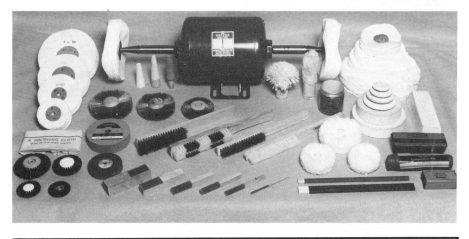

Power-driven abrasives remove material quickly and can give a very fine finish.

Use **aluminium oxide** grits on disc sanders supported by a rubber backing pad to descale welds etc. Use **silicon carbide** for non-ferrous work including plastics.

Use a **buffing machine** to power a **polishing mop** to attain a high polish. The calico mops are fitted to tapered screws and are charged from a bar of lubricant and abrasive. Finish with a soft clean cloth.

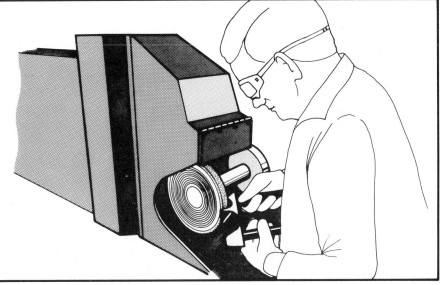

Work safely. Wear eye protection. Work below the centre of the wheel, and avoid edges which may 'snatch'. If the metal becomes hot from friction, allow it to cool. Do not hold it with a piece of cloth.

Metal Surface Finishes

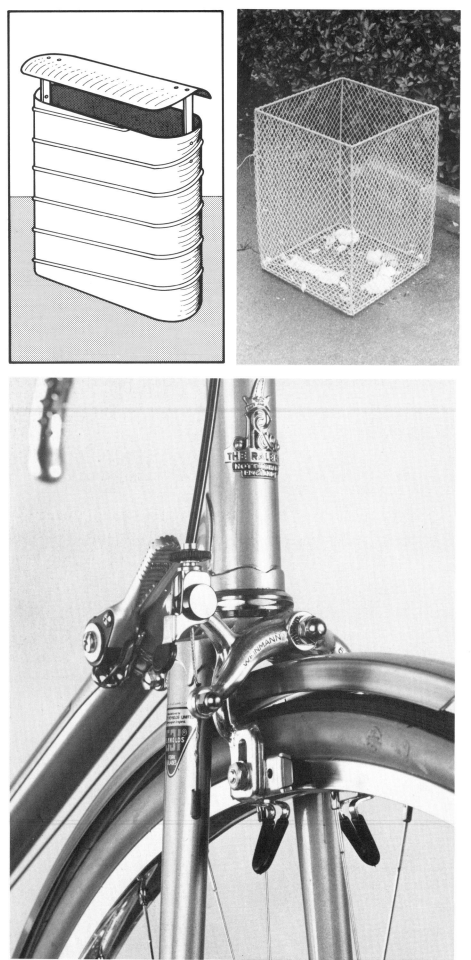

The drawings show two litter bins seen at the seaside. One was made from coiled mild steel plate and coated in a bright-yellow plastics material to prevent corrosion threatened by damp, salty seaside weather. But the coating has been scratched and rust is rapidly spreading underneath the layer of plastics.
The other bin was made from wire heavily galvanized with zinc to prevent corrosion. It looks less attractive but is ideally finished for the job it has to do. Choose *your* finish with care.

Engine turning

This produces an attractive patterned finish on steel. Use a dowel rod in a pillar drill to rotate a carborundum paste abrasive, and work an even pattern.
DO NOT use engine turning in an attempt to cover-up a poor finish.

Hot dipping

This is a common method of coating metals in industry. A good example is tinplate. Thin mild steel plate is cleaned in acid and dipped into molten tin. Surplus coating is removed as it passes through rollers.

Galvanizing is the process of coating ferrous metal with molten zinc. It is recognizable by its bright spangled appearance on items such as metal dustbins.

Electroplating

This is a method of coating metals with another metal using an electrolytic action. It is used to apply chrome-plating on brass taps and steel bicycle components.
An electric current is passed through a solution of metallic salts. The solution is decomposed and deposits pure metal on the object suspended in it.
Obtain a satin chrome finish by careful, even brushing with fine brass wire brushes.

De-greasing

Surfaces to be coated with another metal must be thoroughly de-greased.
Large workpieces are usually washed down with a hot sodium salt solution. Smaller work may be cleaned using a solvent such as carbon tetrachloride. Take special care to provide adequate ventilation of the toxic fumes.

Coatings

Ferrous metal kept in store is likely to rust, simply because it is damp after being handled. Prevent this by lightly spraying surfaces with a rust-prevention fluid. More permanent surface rust can be neutralized chemically:

1. First use a wire brush to remove loose rust.
2. Protect your hands with suitable plastic gloves.
3. Apply white 'Neutra-Rust' with a brush. Stop brushing when it turns purple.
4. The liquid dries black and provides a primed surface on which to apply paint.

Metal primer

Primer with a zinc chromate base is best used before finishing with an oil-based paint.
Apply it by brush to steel which has been de-greased and rinsed.
Aluminium and zinc-coated steel, such as that used for seaside railings, must first be coated with an etching primer.

Etching primer

This is a two-pack water-sensitive paint. It must be applied in dry conditions and primed at a critical stage — between 12 and 14 hours.

Quick-dry enamel

This is the most popular metal finish on machinery, equipment and fittings which are to be used indoors. It is not affected by machine oils, battery acid and cutting fluids.
Apply it with a brush over a light-grey primer—surfacer. Apply a second coat either in less than an hour, or after 24 hours. Between these times a second coat will 'lift' the first coat.

Aluminium paint

This gives a lustrous finish which will resist high humidity and condensation. Pure aluminium is contained in 'Hammerite' paint — one-coat finish which can be brushed on to rusted surfaces. Galvanized surfaces must be etch-primed.
The paint dries in 15 minutes.

Plastics coatings

These coatings are a good finish for metal which must be kept hygienic or handled, but which will not suffer from direct heat or abrasion.

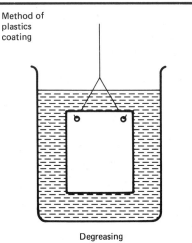

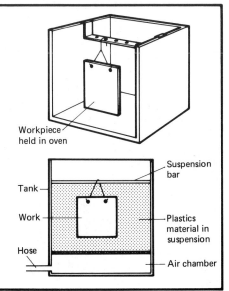

Method of plastics coating

Degreasing

Workpiece held in oven

Suspension bar

Tank

Work

Plastics material in suspension

Hose

Air chamber

Coatings (continued)

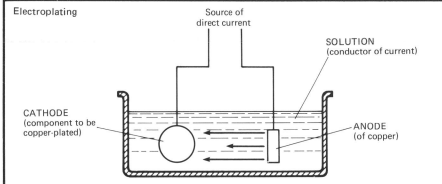

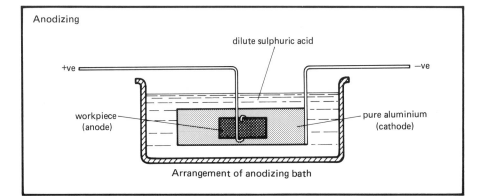

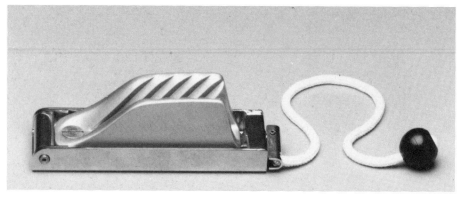

Lacquering

Lacquer will preserve the surface finish of any metal, but it is most effective in preventing *non-ferrous metals* from tarnishing.

A colourless lacquer may be used on trophies and jewellery which is made of silver or which is silver-plated.

With hot lacquers the work must be heated. Synthetic lacquers may need stoving.

A cold cellulose-based lacquer is applied with a soft brush in a dust-free atmosphere. It dries in air very quickly.

Remember that for all coating methods the metal must be clean and de-greased, and good ventilation is essential.

Electroplating

This process is the electro-depositing of more expensive or attractive metal on to a cheap or less attractive one.

Chrome is used to plate brass bathroom fittings and steel kitchenware.

Industry uses cadmium to electroplate nuts and bolts.

Sculptors use the process so that their work will reflect the surroundings.

A plate of the metal to be deposited (the *anode*) and the object to be plated (the *cathode*) are hung in a tank of electrolyte. An electric current is passed through the electrolyte from the anode to the cathode. The anode dissolves, and is deposited on to the cathode (the object).

Anodizing

This is a process used on aluminium and aluminium alloys. The process thickens the natural oxides which form on the surface.

It is an ideal finish for architectural fittings such as window frames, and for the rope cleats used on sailing boats.

The process is the *reverse* of electroplating. Now the aluminium article is the anode. It is hung in a bath of dilute sulphuric acid, which is the electrolyte. The oxygen bubbles set free on the surface of the anode produce the protective oxide film.

The highest current gives the thickest film — although this might only be 25 microns (0.001 in) thick.

The process can be used to give a wide range of colours from pale yellow to black. Old-gold, bronze and pewter are commonly used on aluminium extrusions used for picture frames.

Coatings (continued)

Colouring is applied to ferrous metals using paints and enamels. Aluminium may also be dyed.

The Italian floodlamp has an anodised aluminium reflector and a black stove-enamelled support.

Non-ferrous metals such as copper have attractive natural colours and are often simply coated with transparent lacquer. However, copper and its alloys of brass and bronze can also be coloured, using a variety of chemicals in different combinations.

Paul Bridge finished 'Two Birds' with a green patina using a copper nitrate solution.

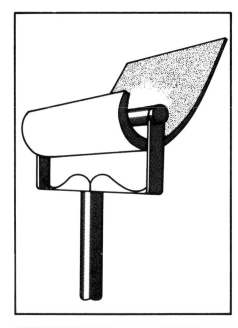
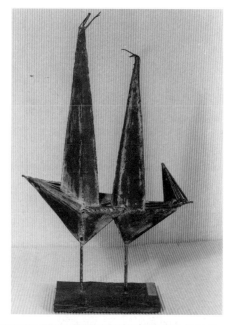

Paint spraying

Paint sprays work by using the energy supplied by compressed air or electrically operated pistons.
The method is superior to brushing when used on flat surfaces such as car panels or the intricate castings of garden furniture. The unit must always be held vertically. Clean the unit by spraying the appropriate solvent through it.
Aerosol spray paints are expensive, but are easy to use and readily available in a wide range of colours.
Spray only in a well-ventilated area.

Brushes

The quality of a finish depends on the care taken in applying it and on the equipment being used.
Best-quality brushes give the best results. They are expensive but, if cared for properly, they last a long time.
Clean brushes thoroughly *immediately* after use. Wash them in detergent, rinse them in clean water, and hang them up to dry.
The list opposite indicates the brush cleaner which is appropriate to the type of finish used.

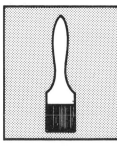

Oil paint	White spirit
Polyurethane paint	White spirit
Cellulose paint	Cellulose thinners
Acrylic paint	Water
Preservatives	White spirit
Creosote	Paraffin
Brush/French polish	Methylated spirit
Polyurethane varnish	White spirit
Acid-catalyzed lacquer	Special thinners

Removing finishes

Unwanted paint, varnish, shellac, cellulose, enamel and epoxy finishes can be removed using either a liquid or a paste solvent.
Apply the paint stripper in a well-ventilated area.

Wood – Hardwoods

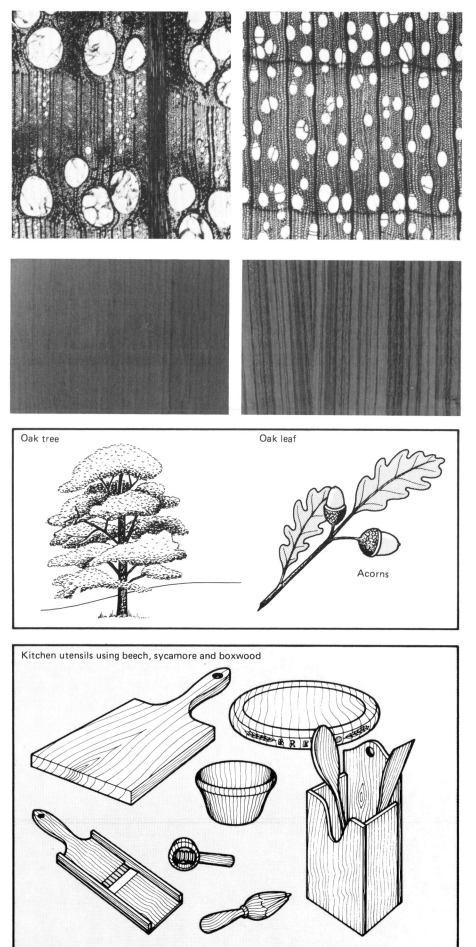

Oak tree

Oak leaf

Acorns

Kitchen utensils using beech, sycamore and boxwood

Most hardwoods are harder, heavier, darker and more varied in appearance than softwoods. Magnified views of the end grain show clearly the small holes (pores), which transport the sap from the roots to the leaves. Hardwoods are either ring-porous e.g., Oak, or diffuse-porous, e.g. Beech, depending on the formation of these pores.

An example is English Oak which takes over a 100 years to mature. It is an expensive, hard, tough and durable wood which can be cut in such a way as to produce a silver figuring which many people find attractive. Its leaves and acorn fruits are easily recognised.

Major uses of european hardwoods

Beech veneers are used for the laminates of chairs and in solid form for childrens' toys. Tool handles, ladders and sports equipment are best made of springy Ash. Elm is a heavy, durable wood traditionally used for coffins and Oak is ideal for fencing posts and so on. Musical instruments utilize many fruit woods including Lime, and Sycamore kitchen tools are common.

Major uses of tropical hardwoods

West African trees grow large and relatively free from knots. Sapele is one wood which, because its stripey grain is difficult to plane, is cut into facing veneer to decorate our plywood furniture. Cheaper tropical woods like Gaboon provide the core material.

Large sections of durable wood, such as Opepe, which will withstand constant exposure to water, wind and salt are excellent for marine work.

Teak comes from the Far East and before becoming popular for household furniture, it was used for bench seating, ships' decking and, because of its natural resistance to acids, laboratory bench tops.

Note: Do not use steel screws in oak, chestnut or mahogany as the acids in the wood will corrode the screw and cause staining. Steel fittings must be galvanised or plated.

Softwoods

Softwood is the name given to timber which comes from coniferous trees. Coniferous trees grow mainly in the cooler regions of the world (temperate climates).

Magnified views of the end grain show clearly the distinctive alternate dark and light growth rings and the presence of resin ducts.

Softwood forests grow quickly. Young trees are planted near to each other and are 'thinned out' after 25 years, to give each of them space to grow. Softwoods are less than a 100 years old when they are felled, by which time some are enormous.

An example is Douglas Fir (Columbian Pine) which grows mainly in British Columbia and western USA. It is reddish-brown in colour with distinctive spring and summer growth. This is used as a feature by interior designers and architects.
Very sharp chisels are needed to cut *across* the grain. It glues and screws well, but take care when nailing to avoid splitting. It is used mainly for making plywood, paper pulp, vats and tanks (as it resists acids).
Large sizes make it ideal for heavy construction work — roofing and laminated arches.

Other uses of softwoods

Some softwoods (Western Red Cedar is a good example) have a high resistance to rot when exposed to the weather. It looks attractive, is an excellent insulating material and so has become popular in Britain for cladding parts of houses.

Softwoods do not split easily when nails and staples are driven in. Joiners use them for roofing timbers, fencing and packing cases.

One of the harder softwoods, Parana Pine, is not suitable for outdoors. It is commonly used for interior joinery such as window sills, stair treads and door frames.

Standard sizes

Standard sizes are available from any local timber merchant. It makes sense if your design preparation and planning takes into account the standard sizes available.

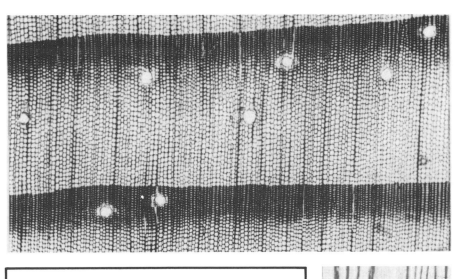

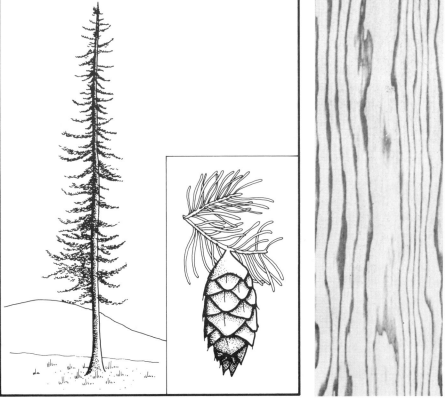

	Standard sizes for softwoods														
	Nominal widths (mm)														
Nominal thickness (mm)	12	19	25	32	38	50	75	100	125	150	175	200	225	250	275
12	•	•	•	•	•	•	•	•	•	•					
19		•	•	•	•	•	•	•	•	•	•				
22					•			•	•	•	•				
25			•		•	•	•	•	•	•		•	•		
32				•	•	•	•	•	•	•	•		•		•
38				•	•	•	•	•	•	•	•	•	•		•
50						•	•	•	•	•	•	•	•		

The sizes given are for softwood PAR (Planed All Round) standard lengths from 1.8 m × 0.3 to 6.3 m

Manufactured Boards

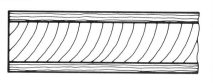

Stoutheart

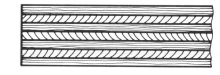

Multiply

Sheathing. Thin sheets can form the basis of exciting architectural features of houses such as roofing.

Flooring. Large, flat stable surfaces for specialized flooring — indoor running tracks.

Plywood

The photographs show plywood being manufactured. A steamed log is rotated on a lathe. A knife cuts a continuous length of veneer which is rolled up on a cylinder to dry out.
The process is continuous, there is little waste and the veneer is relatively cheap t produce.

These rotary-cut veneers are cut to size, and glued by rollers. Several layers (with the grain of alternate pieces at right-angles to the next) are put in a hot press for the glue to set. Plywood has an odd number of veneers in each sheet.

Properties

Plywood is made in large sizes with perfect surfaces. It does not shrink or twist much and is exceptionally strong. Thin sheets are flexible and can be 'formed'. Plywood furniture is made using simple constructions.

Materials

Rotary-cut plywood veneers are made from Birch, Beech, Gaboon or Douglas Fir. Knife-cut facing veneers are used on the best boards.

Grades

Cheaper plywood is graded according to the quality of its external veneers.
This depends on surface blemishes and or the number of knots which have been removed and patched. Grades are A, B and BB.

Adhesives

The large gluing surface of all plywood veneers gives all the boards exceptional strength. The type of glue used determines in what conditions the plywood should be used:

WBP Weather and boil-proof
MR Moisture resistant
INT Interior use only

Blockboard and laminboard

The boards are made by edge-jointing narrow strips of softwood and sandwiching them between sheets of veneer.
This construction gives the boards great strength. The thicker sizes are cheaper than plywood. Laminboard is the best quality.

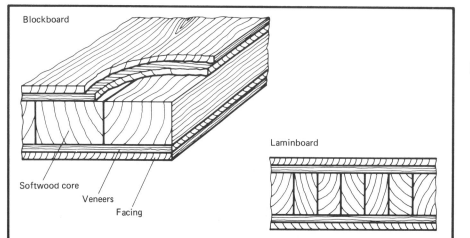

Blockboard

Softwood core

Veneers

Facing

Laminboard

Manufactured Boards (continued)

Particle boards

Manufacture

Particle board is made from wood thinnings and trimmings which are shredded and mixed with a synthetic glue. This mixture is squeezed between rollers and then pressed between heated plates to the required thickness.

Properties

This continuous mechanized process produces a finished board which is of guaranteed quality and is comparatively inexpensive. In the manufacturing process additives in the glue—wood mixture can give the finished board resistance to water and fire.
The particle board is itself quite weak. It gains considerably in strength if its surfaces are covered with a veneer.

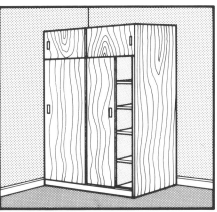

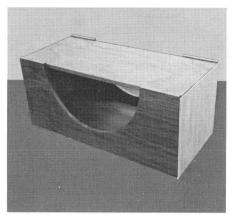

Uses

Veneered particle board is in world-wide use as the basic material for most forms of cabinet making, like sideboards and wardrobes.
The unit on castors is used as an occasional table. This simple design is quickly made up from standard sized edged boards.

Fibreboards

Fibreboard is made from a timber and fibre mix which is refined and formed into homogenous sheets of material.

Softboard is made from sheets of dried fibres which are not compressed. It is lightweight. Use it for insulation or sandwiching between metal sheets.

Medium-density fibreboard (MDF) includes a synthetic resin binder. The sheets are compressed to thicknesses between 4 and 35 mm and are as dense as most hardwoods. They have no grain and can be machined to a high finish. Use for panels which need good edges — usually painted.

Standard hardboard is the most common board. It has one smooth face. It is cheap, will not split when nailed or riveted and can be bent.

Perforated hardboard is pierced with holes or slots.

Tempered hardboard is treated with oils to resist damp.

The white table is machined from 10 mm **duo-faced hardboard**. Both sides have a smooth surface which finishes well.

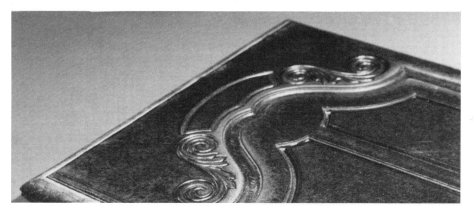

Veneers and Edge Treatments

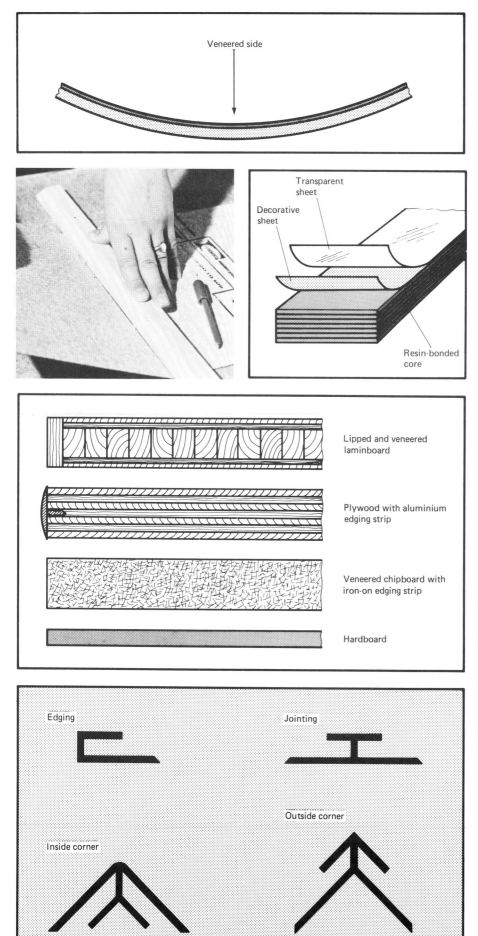

Veneered side

Transparent sheet

Decorative sheet

Resin-bonded core

Lipped and veneered laminboard

Plywood with aluminium edging strip

Veneered chipboard with iron-on edging strip

Hardboard

Edging

Jointing

Outside corner

Inside corner

Decorative veneers are thin sheets of material bonded to a thicker piece called the 'ground'. Traditionally, veneers were slices of expensive wood chosen because of their attractive grain or colour. Much modern furniture and fittings are covered with plastics veneers.

Plastics surfaces can be laminated on to most types of manufactured board. A protective veneer glued on to a surface will tend to bow the board. This is avoided by backing the board with a similar but usually cheaper material called a **balancer**, so that it remains flat.

Melamine veneer is often referred to by a trade name such as 'Formica'. It produces a hard synthetic finish which is resistant to most household chemicals and normal abrasive wear. Adhered to blockboard or laminboard, chipboard or plywood it is ideal for horizontal working surfaces. However, the pressure and heat used in manufacture make the material brittle. To obtain a neat cut, score the surface heavily and lift one piece upwards to obtain a clean break.
The normal thickness is 2 mm but thinner material for forming is available.

PVC veneer is a softer plastics coating which can be laminated to a fibreboard (e.g. hardboard) without the need for a balancer. Use it for vertical surfaces such as panels where its light weight is an advantage.

Edge treatments

Most manufactured boards need edge treatment. Where edges may be liable to damage, cover them with a hardwood lipping before veneering, or insert an aluminium cover-strip. Edge pre-veneered chipboard with a matching iron-on strip of veneer.

The sections also show aluminium extrusions which are used to protect the edges and to join hardboard.

Frames and Box Constructions

Frame constructions are common in the home.

Interior house doors are often light constructions consisting of a softwood frame sandwiched between sheets of hardboard or plywood. Exterior house door frames are usually constructed with traditional mortise and tenon joints. The illustrations show three types of frame joint which can be used in furniture making — the cross, tee and corner.

In a halving joint, half the thickness of each piece of wood is removed to fit the other.

The round table shows a use of the joint cut on the edges, but the joint can just as well be cut on the faces to produce a flat frame.

Here one half of the joint has been cut in the shape of a dovetail. The joint is called a dovetail halving and is a typical tee-joint.

Bridles are simple framing joints with large gluing surfaces. The centre third of one piece and the outside thirds of the other piece are removed — a kind of 'open' mortise and tenon.

The *corner* bridle is used on flat frames and is shown pegged with a dowel to give extra strength.

The tee bridle is a popular method of joining legs to rails of occasional tables.

Box constructions vary from the crudely made packing crate to the most exquisitely jointed jewellery box. They require different jointing techniques to be effective.

The nailed butt joint is one of the simplest constructions but is crude.

The lapped joint reduces the amount of end grain showing. Also, because of the shoulder and increased gluing surface, it is stronger.

Both these are examples of corner joints.

Tee-joints in box constructions usually take the form of shelves or partitions. When these are fixed they give rigidity to the construction. The through-housing shown, cut to one third the thickness of the wood, is a common method for fixed bookshelves.

Modern dowelling jigs which guarantee true alignment of holes have made the use of corner dowel joints popular.

Use them mainly for frame corners in solid wood and box corners in manufacturer's board (e.g. veneered chipboard).

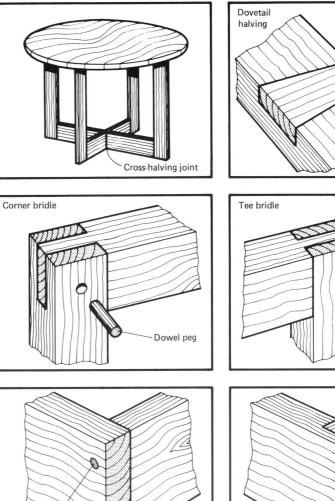

Cross-halving joint

Dovetail halving

Corner bridle

Dowel peg

Tee bridle

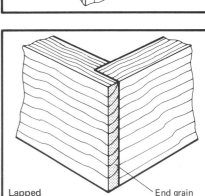

Nails

Nailed butt

Lapped

End grain

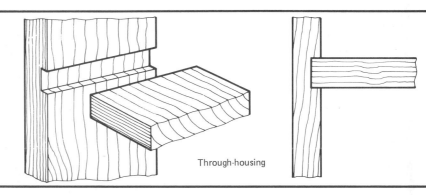

Through-housing

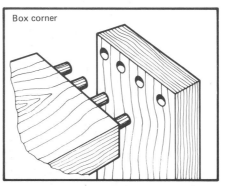

Box corner

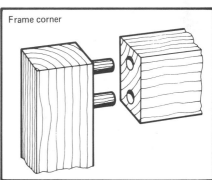

Frame corner

Permanent Jointing

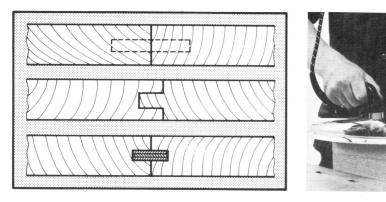

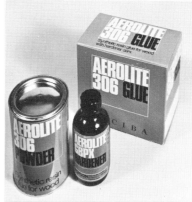

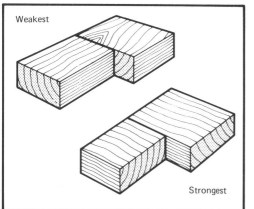

Weakest

Strongest

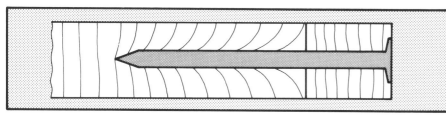

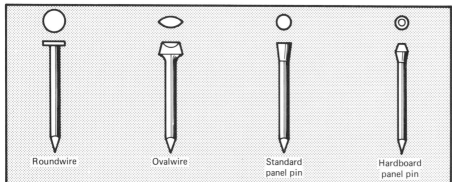

Roundwire   Ovalwire   Standard panel pin   Hardboard panel pin

Solid timber is often too narrow for box constructions or for table tops and must be joined at the edges. Both edges have to be carefully trued with a large metal try plane.

The butt joint is simplest, but it is weak and is usually strengthened by the use of dowels.
A traditional method is the tongue and groove joint which is prepared with a set of matching cutters.
A modern method is to cut a groove in each edge and insert a loose tongue made from plywood.

Permanent Fixings

Adhesives

Joints are strongest when adhesive can be used on the side grain of each piece of wood. Do not try to glue end grain to end grain.
There are two kinds of cold adhesive:

1. *one-pot type:* a milky PVA liquid suitable for almost all indoor work.
2. *two-pot type:* such as Aerolite 306 which consists of a powder resin to be mixed with water and a chemical hardener. Each is applied to opposite sides of a joint. It is waterproof when set.

Nails

Nails work by pushing the wood fibres away from the nail head. These fibres grip the side of the nail to resist attempts to withdraw it.
The nail length should be equal to three times the thickness of the wood being fixed.

Four common nails are illustrated:

Roundwire	Round shank, flat head
Ovalwire	Oval shank, narrow head, easily punched in – joinery
Panel pin	Thin round shank for strengthening joints
Hardboard pin	Made from non-rusting copper, self-sinking

Dowels

Dowels are often called 'wooden nails'. Use them where holes can be jigged. Plain dowel (A) should be grooved with a saw cut (B) before it is glued into a joint. Multigrooved dowel (C) is ready prepared – made slightly oversize it makes a tight fit and allows excess glue to escape.

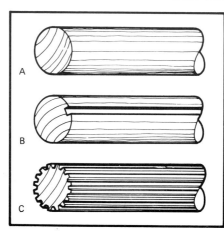

A

B

C

Temporary Jointing

'Temporary' fixings

Factory-made furniture is now available in 'flat packs' ready for DIY quick assembly in the home. Most of these designs rely on modern screw technology and the use of KD (knock-down) or QA (quick-assembly) fittings.

Some designers are really inventive. The photograph shows a plywood chest of drawers slotted together without the help of KD or QA joints!

Fittings

Surface fittings used to join two pieces of manufactured board are often plastics mouldings attached with 'Twinfast' screws. These screws have two threads instead of one and have greater holding power in man-made materials.

Wood screws

Wood screws are the most common 'temporary' fixing of wood to metal and for fixing hardware fittings.
The drawing shows the three main head shapes:

Lengths are measured from the tip to the surface of the material.

The **GKN chipboard screw** is designed as a one-piece fastener for joining chipboard at right angles. Sockets are not required. Accurate pilot holes are critical to ensure maximum strength.

A **chipboard fastener** is a three-part fitting. Glue the nylon socket into the chipboard. Insert the machine screw through the other material. Hide the head with the brass or chrome-plated cover cap.

Table tops may be made from manufactured board and can be fitted to a wood top rail in one of the three following ways:

Metal plates: Make these from 3 mm thick steel or brass. Fix to the rail with a countersunk screw and to the top with a roundhead screw through the slot.
Plastic KD fittings: These are two-part surface fittings, one screwed to the top and the other to the rail. They are located by projecting dowels and secured with a roundhead machine screw.
Counterboring: Bore a hole equal in diameter to the screw head in the edge of the top rail. Drill a smaller pilot hole to accommodate the shank of the screw thread.

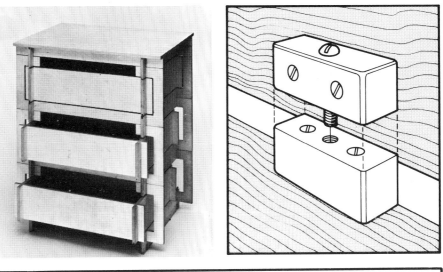

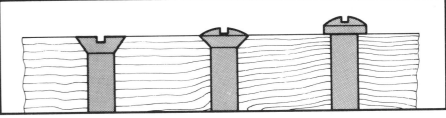

A. *Countersunk* — the material is prepared so that the head can be driven below the surface.
B. *Raised countersunk* — often finished in chromium-plated brass and used on high-quality metal fittings.
C. *Roundhead* — a steel screw used for securing metal fittings. Often coated in black paint (japanned) to prevent rust.

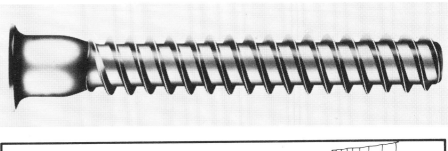

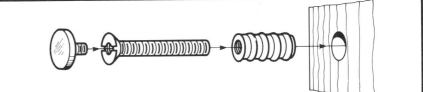

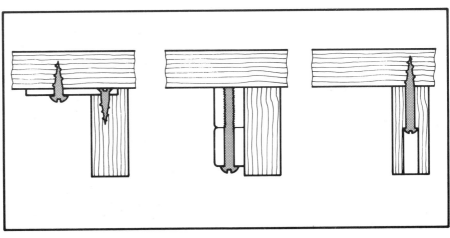

Wood Finishes

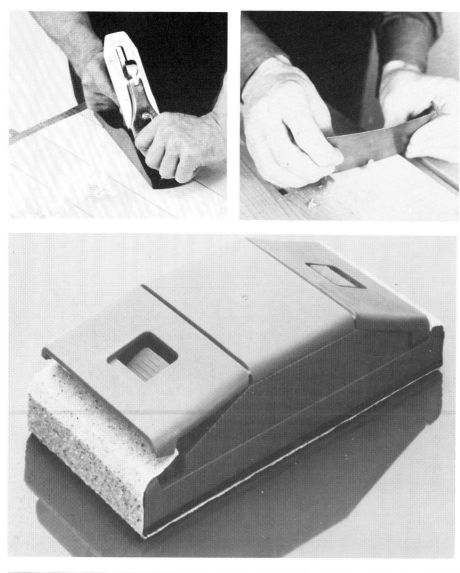

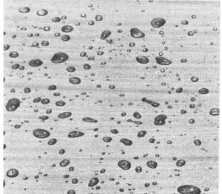

Surface preparation

Solid wood has usually been machine planed, but for high-quality work such as furniture making it must be smoothed further before a finish is applied.
A finely set metal smoothing plane is usually used.
Rough patches of grain — where the fibres lie in different directions — may need scraping. A metal scraper is sharpened with a burr on its edge — it is slightly bent to remove a fine shaving. Finish the surface with a fine abrasive. Veneered chipboard and surfaces of other manufactured board do *not* need planing.

Hand sanding

'Sanding' is the name given to the use of abrasive grits on timber — so called because glasspaper looks like a coating of sand. Glasspaper is relatively soft and does not last as long as the red-coloured garnet paper.
Small sheets of abrasive paper may be wrapped around a cork block or fixed into a holder. Use the abrasive only along the direction of the grain.

Finishing the surface

Some woods have properties which prevent rot without a surface finish being applied (e.g. Teak and Western Red Cedar). All woods discolour or mark easily if they are not protected, so finishes are nearly always applied either for protection or decoration.
Untreated wood will absorb liquids quickly and stain — a finish seals the wood fibres so that liquids stay on the surface.

Power sanding

The Orbital sanding machine makes a small rotation of about 2 mm × 4000 rpm and is most useful on large, flat surfaces such as doors and table tops.
It is important to use the correct type of abrasive — nothing softer than aluminium oxide. Use tungsten-carbide abrasive bonded to a flexible aluminium sheet to finish plastics laminate and GRP work.

Grades of abrasive

Abrasives for machines are usually open coat (OC) or closed coat (CC). Follow the manufacturer's instructions.
Coarseness is measured by a number, very coarse being about 20 and very fine about 200. Choose the coarseness according to your needs.

Surface Treatments

Softwoods are commonly protected by paint. It is a tough finish available in unlimited colours and is easy to apply. Knots in softwood contain resin which can damage the finished surface. First seal them with a 'knotting'.

After priming the wood, 'make good' cracks or surface blemishes with a suitable filler.

Then apply undercoat and finishing coats according to the manufacturer's instructions.

Allow all fillers and each layer of finish to harden.

Hardwood or softwood surfaces which do not have to be heat- or water-resistant can be given an attractive satin finish. First seal the grain with two thin coats of brush or white polish. Then apply wax with a pad of steel wool. Polish lightly with a soft cloth.

Two types of oil are used to protect hardwoods.

Teak oil dries quickly and can resist heat. Vegetable or olive oil is used on woodware which comes into contact with food.

Both types need to be applied regularly to maintain an attractive surface.

Outdoor preservatives vary from being a clear liquid to a variety of staining colours.

The brush-on or spray-on liquids are designed to give full protection to sheds and weather-boarding by repelling rainwater. Apply extra maintenance coats according to the manufacturer's instructions.

Wood dyes give permanent colour to the fibres, do not fade when exposed to the sun and can be covered with all types of wood finish.

They are available in various wood shades. Use brightly coloured dyes on light timbers — for example, the birch plywood of a child's playroom furniture. The surface must be very well prepared before the dye is applied — in cream or liquid form.

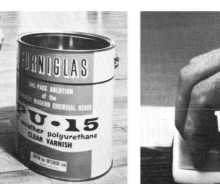

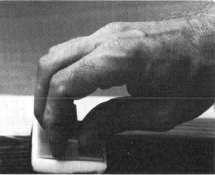

Polyurethane

One-pack polyurethane varnish dries on exposure to air to give a hard, durable finish.

Coloured polyurethanes do not stain the wood fibres as effectively as dyes. They are available in high gloss, satin (eggshell) and matt finishes.

Do not use on thermoplastic, PVC or rubber surfaces.

Care of brushes

Best-quality brushes give the best results but are expensive.

Take care of brushes by washing them thoroughly immediately after use. Wash them in liquid soap, rinse them in clean water and hang them up to dry. Use the cleaner indicated.

Brushes in regular use may be temporarily suspended in water as shown.

Oil paint	White spirit
Polyurethane paint	White spirit
Cellulose paint	Cellulose thinners
Acrylic paint	Water
Preservatives	White spirit
Creosote	Paraffin
Brush/French polish	Methylated spirit
Polyurethane varnish	White spirit
Acid-catalysed lacquer	Special thinners

Plastics – Workshop Safety

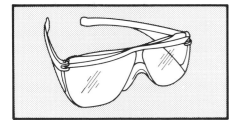

Workshop safety is a mixture of common sense and knowing the properties of the materials with which you are working. Plastics are *different* from other materials because they are based on chemicals. It is important to read the manufacturers' instructions for storage and handling and to follow them.

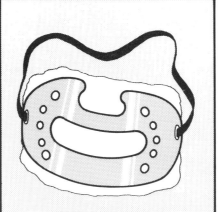

Storage

Most plastics are best stored in cool and dry conditions away from attack by frost. Sheet materials should be stacked on edge. Rolls of film or glass-fibre should be fixed on and dispensed from a stand. Resins and other inflammable liquids must be stored in fire-safe metal cupboards.

Skin

Prevent soreness of skin by using a barrier cream and/or disposable polyethylene gloves.
Use thick leather gloves to handle hot plastic or it may stick to your skin and burn.
Wash your hands frequently.

Eyes

Use goggles or spectacles to protect your eyes from plastics dust and flying particles.
Avoid splashes from liquids, especially catalysts, by using them from a dispenser.

Breathing

The solvents used in forming plastics produce vapours which can damage your lungs. The effect is not always immediately obvious. Make sure that rooms are properly ventilated.

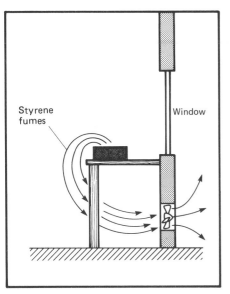

Styrene fumes

Window

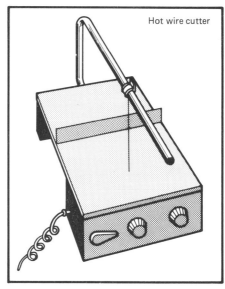

Hot wire cutter

Styrene fumes are common when working with glass reinforced plastics (GRPs) or when cutting expanded polystyrene. The fumes are heavy and should be ventilated from below bench height.

Cut GRP at the 'green' stage before it becomes brittle. When cutting and finishing edges which have hardened, reduce the effects of dust by using water as a lubricant.

Wear a mask to avoid inhaling fine dust.

Fire

Most plastics catch fire easily. The effects can be disastrous – deadly fumes are given off.

Avoid the risk of fire, especially when handling catalysts, resins and cleaning fluids:

1. Allow liquid waste to evaporate.
2. Allow catalysed resin to harden.
3. Dispose of waste cured resin in plastics sacks.
4. Put cleaning rags in a metal bin.
5. Rags soaked in catalyst *must* go in a separate bin.
6. DO NOT pour liquids into a sink.
7. DO NOT expose any materials to a naked flame.

Uses of Plastics

Many objects traditionally made from metal are now made from one of the large selection of modern plastics. Large metal objects such as buckets were heavy. Lightweight, cheap and hygienic plastics is an obvious replacement.

Small metal objects such as cameras were expensive to fabricate from bent sheet metal. They needed careful finishing. A plastics materials which could be moulded to fine tolerances, with a ready finish, was an obvious replacement. Non-conductive plastics were a safer alternative to the metal casings of electric drills and hairdryers. Childrens' plastics toys became almost entirely safe.

Modern plastics each have specific qualities which can be used by the designer, but they have two things in common. Because they are not natural materials, plastics are reliable and have uniform quality.
Early plastics were used to replace wood and metal in the wrong way. They were coloured or plated to imitate wood and metal and often were too brittle or too soft for the job they had to do. Modern plastics have stopped pretending to be something else, and we have benefited enormously.

The IMI Opella tap and fittings is made completely from plastics. It resists extremes of heat, abrasives and extreme hard wear. It requires no maintenance. The plastics 'Kematol' will not discolour, is completely hygienic and remains cool even when running near boiling water.

The woman in the ICI cartoon has discovered that everything made of plastics in her new kitchen has disappeared! Floor tiles and work surfaces, all the plumbing, buckets and basin; handles and hinges from cupboards, wiring insulation, plugs and sockets; the curtain rail, curtains and fridge fittings; the coatings from the non-stick pans, handles from the cutlery and even the paint from the walls!

The latest fuel-efficient vehicles use the strength–weight advantage of plastics over metal.
A major feature of the Fiat 'Panda' is the deep protective bumpers and side panels made from corrosion- and impact-resistant resin. Inside the car, softer plastics for the instrument panel, handles and steering assembly make it safer for the occupants in the event of a crash.

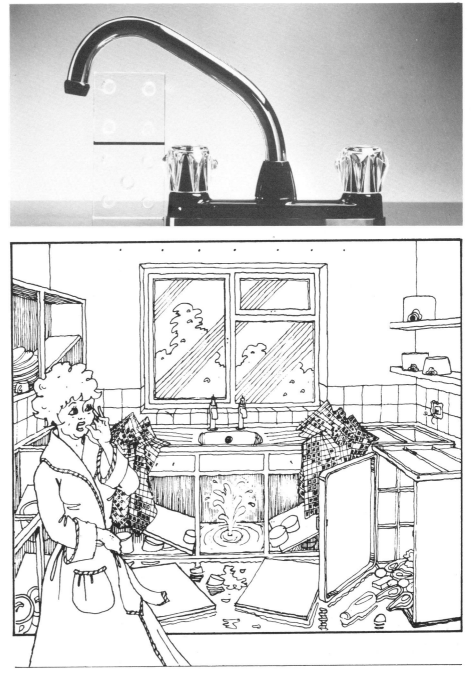

Types of Plastics

Plastics have replaced many natural materials. A generation ago a running shoe was made from leather, possibly with a cotton lining and some rubber padding. The 'Nike' running shoe is a complex lightweight plastics construction with some rubber in the sole.

The heel counter is of stable *polyvinyl chloride* (PVC) to give support. This is held in place by a moulded *polyurethane* (PU) collar. The mid-sole of *ethylene vinyl acetate* (EVA) is light and shock-absorbent. The heel impact is reduced using a 'Sorbothane' heel pad of *visco-elastic polymer*. The upper consists of a non-stretch woven nylon which is flexible and porous.

Plastics have transformed shoe design and encouraged better running performances.

The shoe contains examples of the two main types of plastics:

1. *thermoplastics*, which can be re-softened
2. *thermosetting*, which cannot be re-softened

You can use a simple re-heating test on a sample to discover which type it is.

Thermoplastics

Most plastics products in every-day use are made from thermoplastics. These are formed or moulded into complex shapes ready for use.

The 'Prestige' carpet sweeper is made from a hard, opaque plastic *acrylonitrile butadiene styrene* (ABS) which will take knocks and has a smooth finish.

The 'Proform' stadium seats have a high resistance to impact and common solvents. They can be any colour and are moulded from *polypropylene* (PP).

The 'Ambig' bird feeder is a combination of transparent *polystyrene* (PS) for the tube, with the coloured ends and perches moulded from a high-density *polyethylene* (HDPE).

The IMI Opella tap top is cast in crystal-clear *poly-methyl-methacrylate* (PMMA), generally referred to as *acrylic*. It is brittle but can be given a high surface polish.

The 'Clamcleats', used to hold ropes on sailing yachts, are of *nylon*. High-impact strength and flexibility make them reliable and long-lasting.

The characteristics of thermoplastics in common use

	Colour		Feel					Cutting		Burning		Floating	
	Clear	Opaque	Rigid or semi-rigid	Soft	Hard or medium-hard	Waxy	Dry	Smooth	Jagged or chipped	Easy	Difficult	Sinks	Floats
Acrylic	X	X	X		X		X		X	X		X	
ABS		X	X		X		X	X		X		X	
Polystyrene	X	X	X		X		X		X	X		X	
Expanded polystyrene		X	X	X			X	X	X	X			X
HD polyethylene	X	X	X		X		X			X			X
Polypropylene		X	X		X		X	X		X			X
PVC	X	X	X		X		X	X			X	X	
Nylon		X	X		X	X	X	X			X	X	

Types of Plastics (continued)

Expanded polystyrene

Apart from acrylic sheet, the two main thermoplastic materials used in the workshop are **expanded polystyrene** and **PVC**.

Expanded polystyrene can be cut smoothly using a hot-wire cutter. Use it for making complex patterns for casting. The pattern can be any shape and does not need a two-piece moulding box. It can, of course, only be used once. The surface finish is not smooth but it is ideal for sculptural shapes, such as the presentation boot.

PVC

Use PVC in paste form to coat metal which needs to be protected from rust. Cold-dipping in a fluidizer is suitable for thin coats, but heavier protection must be applied when the metal is hot. PVC is an attractive finish applied to wire baskets and for handles etc., but it only covers the metal. If the metal is first coated with an epoxy resin, the coating will bond to it.

Thermosetting plastics

Polyester resin

This is available in a casting quality from which solid blocks can be made. These blocks can be worked on in a similar way to aluminium before they become really hard (in about four weeks).

Polyurethane foam

This inflexible foam is available in different densities and has the advantage over expanded polystyrene in that it is not affected by the application of resins. It is used as a **mould** for sculptural forms and the forming of thermoplastic sheets. Use it as a **core** when making resin-coated seats for steels and chairs as it is easy to shape with Surform tools, and as a *structural* material such as buoyancy compartments in a boat.

Melamine formaldelyde (MF)

This is a resin used in the manufacture of 'Formica' and similar sheet materials.

Epoxy resin

This is familiar as an adhesive (e.g. Araldite), but it can be used for casting and as a surface coating. Use polyester resins to give a hard, decorative finish to metal surfaces such as boxes or small trays. Lip the edge of a flat surface with masking tape. Pour on a layer of undercoat resin, allow to gel then pour on the decorative resin. Allow this to cure, then finish with wet-and-dry abrasive and polishing compounds.

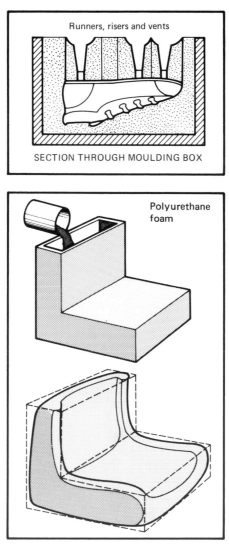

SECTION THROUGH MOULDING BOX

Runners, risers and vents

Polyurethane foam

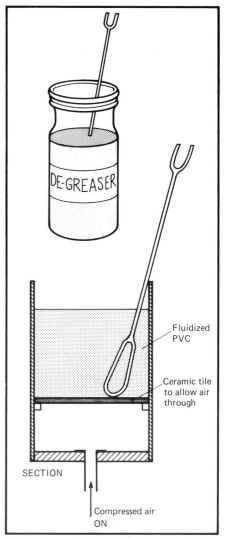

DE-GREASER

Fluidized PVC

Ceramic tile to allow air through

SECTION

Compressed air ON

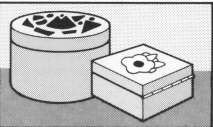

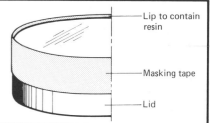

Lip to contain resin

Masking tape

Lid

	Colour		Feel					Cutting		Burning		Floating	
	Clear	Opaque	Rigid or semi-rigid	Soft	Hard or medium-hard	Waxy	Dry	Smooth	Jagged or chipped	Easy	Difficult	Sinks	Floats
Polyester resin	X	X	X		X		X		X	X		X	
Polyurethane foam		X	X	X	X		X	X	X	X			X
Melamine	X	X	X		X		X		X		X	X	
Epoxy resin		X	X		X		X		'X	X		X	

Glass-reinforced Polyester

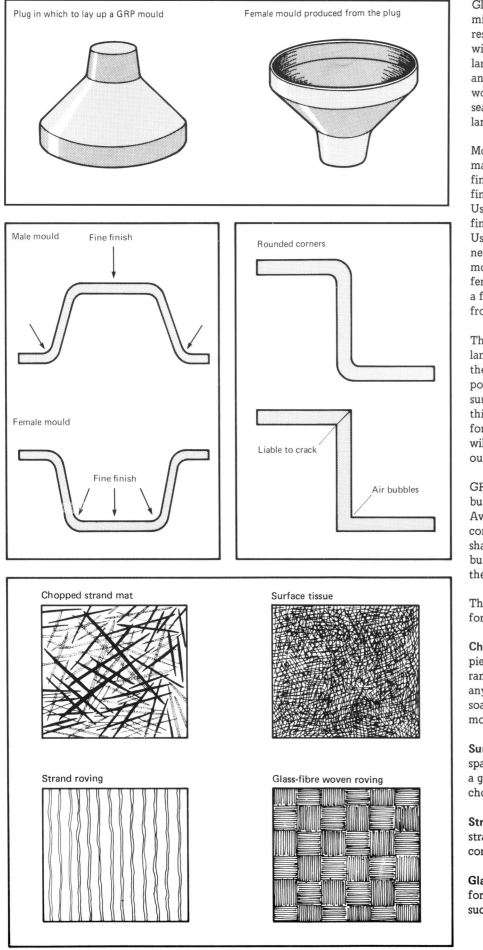

Plug in which to lay up a GRP mould

Female mould produced from the plug

Male mould   Fine finish

Female mould

Fine finish

Rounded corners

Liable to crack

Air bubbles

Chopped strand mat

Surface tissue

Strand roving

Glass-fibre woven roving

Glass-reinforced polyester (GRP) is a mixture of stranded glass and polyester resin, in the form of non-corrosive sheet with high tensile strength. It is used on a large scale to construct swimming pools and car bodies, and in the school workshop to construct canoes, stool seats, and small complex shapes, such as lampshades.

Moulds can be made of almost any material, but the quality of the surface finish depends entirely on the surface finish of the mould.
Use a male mould if the inside needs a fine finish.
Use a female mould if the fine finish needs to be on the outside. Where male moulds are often easier to make than female moulds, a male 'plug' is made and a female mould (often in GRP) taken from it.

The mould shown is for an adjustable lampshade. It is turned on a wood lathe, the grain filled and sealed with polyurethane paint to give a smooth surface. A GRP lamination is made from this which, in turn, acts as a female former. The lampshade layed-up on this will have the finished surface on the outside.

GRP can be made into complex shapes but it must not have a reverse slope. Avoid sharp external corners which concentrate the strains on setting. Avoid sharp internal corners into which air bubbles will gather when laying-up. Both these faults will weaken the structure.

The glass reinforcing is available in several forms:

Chopped strand mat consists of short pieces of stranded glass glued together at random so that it has equal strength in any direction. It becomes pliable when soaked in resin and forms the bulk of most laminations.

Surface tissue is made up from closely spaced fine strands. Use it to strengthen a gel-coat and to give a smooth finish to chopped strand mat on the lay-up side.

Strand roving: continuous lengths of strand glass are used to strengthen corners. Tape is an alternative.

Glass-fibre woven roving is interwoven for extra strength where impact is likely, such as on boat hulls.

GRP Moulds

Mould-making and the laying-up of GRP can be complex. The major suppliers of materials always give valuable advice.

Some simple moulds with perfect surfaces can be bought. So can complex flexible moulds for the casting of jewellery and chess sets.

You can best practise using the materials by laying-up a flat mat of GRP. This could then be cut up for drinks mats or for making fashion jewellery. You can make up your own design on paper or use patterned cloth as a ready-made design. Lay-up the mat on a flat sheet of plate glass.

1. Make sure that the glass is perfectly clean. Then apply three coats of mould release wax, polished to a clear hard finish. Mark the unwaxed side.
2. Prepare the gel resin using the amounts recommended by the manufacturer. Add 2 per cent of catalyst from the safety bottle.
   If colour is to be used it should be added to all resin mixes.
3. Apply a generous but even coat of gel resin to the surface and allow it to cure. Prepare the lay-up resin using the amounts recommended by the manufacturer for two layers of chopped strand mat.
4. Apply a coat of lay-up resin. Place the design face down on to the wet resin, taking care to avoid trapping air. Stipple evenly all over this with a brush until the resin comes through.
5. Apply another coat of lay-up resin. Place a layer of chopped strand mat on to the wet resin and stipple through in the same way. The mat softens as the resin dissolves the binder which holds the strands together.
6. Repeat the procedure with a second layer of chopped strand mat. Finish with a layer of tissue to give a finer surface.
   At this stage use a ribbed roller to remove surplus resin and air, making the lamination of even thickness. Clean brushes and rollers in cleaning fluid and soap and water.
7. Release the mat from the plate glass first by lifting one corner then prising it away gradually. Do not use a sharp tool or it may damage the surface — a wood wedge is ideal.
8. Whilst the mat is 'green', that is not fully cured, mark out the final shape and cut with snips or a guillotine. Protect work in a vice to file the edge.

AT ALL TIMES OBSERVE SAFETY PRECAUTIONS.

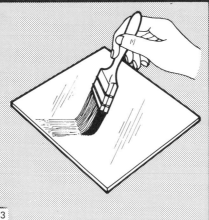

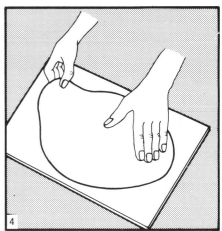

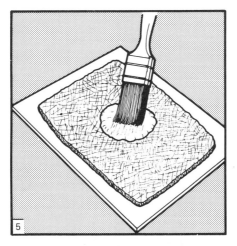

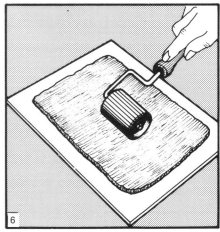

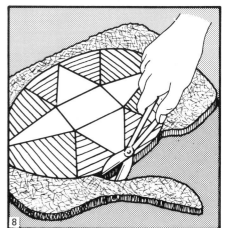

Forming Sheets

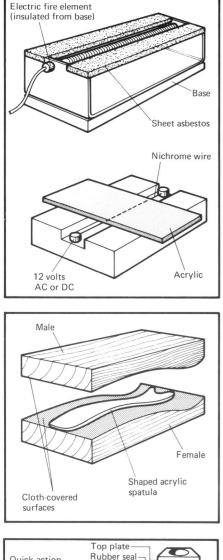

Electric fire element (insulated from base)

Base

Sheet asbestos

Nichrome wire

12 volts AC or DC

Acrylic

Male

Female

Shaped acrylic spatula

Cloth-covered surfaces

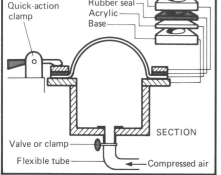

Quick-action clamp

Top plate
Rubber seal
Acrylic
Base

SECTION

Valve or clamp

Flexible tube

Compressed air

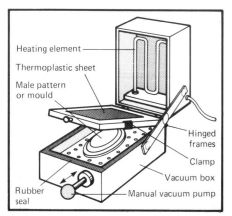

Heating element

Thermoplastic sheet

Male pattern or mould

Hinged frames

Clamp

Vacuum box

Rubber seal

Manual vacuum pump

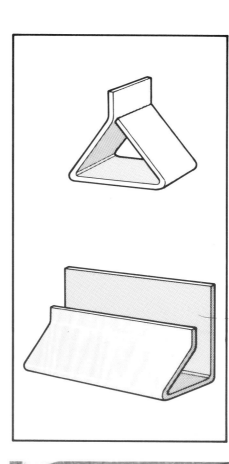

Thermoplastic material in sheet form varies from the thin and flexible to the thick and rigid — from 'plastic bags' to aircraft windscreens.
Between these extremes are sheets of acrylic, PVC and polypropylene which are used for protecting paintings and as a lightweight roofing material.

The surfaces of sheet material are covered by a protective sheet. This must be retained until the edges are cut and shaped. Remove the protective sheet before applying heat to material.

Make straight cuts in material up to 1.5 mm thick with a craft knife. Make cuts in thicker sheet with fine-toothed saws. Use files or coarse abrasive discs to shape material. Polish with abrasive compounds.

Heat rigid acrylic sheet (3 mm thick) above a hot-wire strip or domestic fire element when the material is to be bent straight with a small radius.
Use this method for small jobs such as napkin rings and letter racks.

Heat rigid acrylic sheet in a heat transfer press or a domestic oven until it is uniformly soft. In this state it can be cramped between matching male/female formers until it cools.
This method is best for gentle bends and shallow forms, such as spatulas and dishes.

Blow-moulding

To produce a deep hollow, acrylic sheet is blow-moulded. This process is used on a large scale to make a bubble cockpit. The apparatus is simply constructed from 19 mm blockboard and a rubber mat forms a seal. Sufficient air pressure can be exerted with a foot pump. A valve or clamp is used to maintain the pressure until the material sets.

Vacuum-forming

Vacuum-forming of thick acrylic to make a bath requires expensive equipment, but the process is the same for smaller objects. Use thin material (up to 1.5 mm) to make complex shapes such as model car bodies.

The thermoplastic sheet is clamped in a frame and held against a heater until it is soft and flexible. The frame is lowered on to the vacuum box. A vacuum pump withdraws the air through holes in and around the former so that the soft sheet is pulled on to it. The vacuum is maintained until the sheet cools and is set.

Joining Plastics

A thermoplastic material can be welded to an identical material. This produces a joint that is stronger than cementing. The joint is suitable for blocks and rods where enough heat is produced by friction to melt the materials. A pillar drill or lathe is used, one piece to turn and the second to be held stationary until the weld takes place, when it must then rotate with the first piece.

Solvent and cementing are used to join rigid thermoplastic sheet material. One-part and two-part cements vary in their gap-filling qualities. Consult the manufacturer's guide for the most suitable cement.

The 'Tensol' cements are commonly used on acrylic. Surfaces must be clean, dry and free from grease. Butt joints should be taped with masking tape to allow slight overfilling. Corner joints should be tapered to allow the cement to penetrate, then rubbed to make a neat corner fillet.

Unlike PVC, some thermoplastics bond to metal. the 'Prestige' kitchen knives have matt-black polyurethane handles moulded permanently on to the stainless-steel blades. (Wood handles used previously had to be riveted in place.)

The 'Tefal' bun tray is spray coated with non-stick PTFE (*polytetraflouroethylene*) on to an etched aluminium surface. It will never blister or peel in normal use.

Cements

PVC cement A solvent applied to both surfaces. Use light pressure. Good ventilation necessary.

Polystyrene cement Highly toxic — good ventilation. Use on hard polystyrene only.

Expanded-polystyrene adhesive A heavy wallpaper paste applied to both surfaces.

On thermosetting plastics use contact or epoxy resin adhesives. *ALWAYS* follow the manufacturer's instructions.

Injection and extrusion moulding

Injection moulding is a technique used for large-scale production — from bowls, buckets and milk-bottle crates to toy soldiers and chess pieces. The simple diagram shows the principle of manufacture. Granules of a thermoplastic are fed into a cylinder. Heat elements plasticize the material, which is rammed by a spreader into the metal mould.

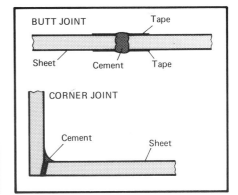

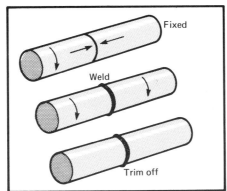

BUTT JOINT — Tape — Sheet — Cement — Tape

CORNER JOINT — Cement — Sheet

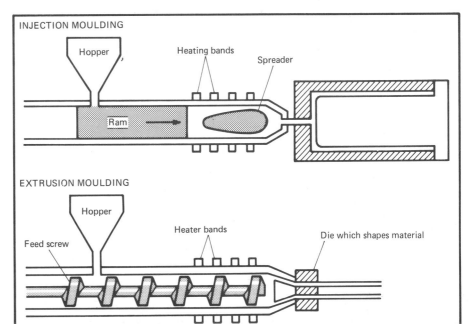

INJECTION MOULDING — Hopper — Heating bands — Spreader — Ram

EXTRUSION MOULDING — Hopper — Feed screw — Heater bands — Die which shapes material

Extrusion moulding works in a similar way. A screw feeds the plasticized material through a die to produce pipes, rod or tubing.

The body of the 'Screwball' drinking glass is injection moulded and the straw formed from extruded tubing.

Sculpture – An Introduction

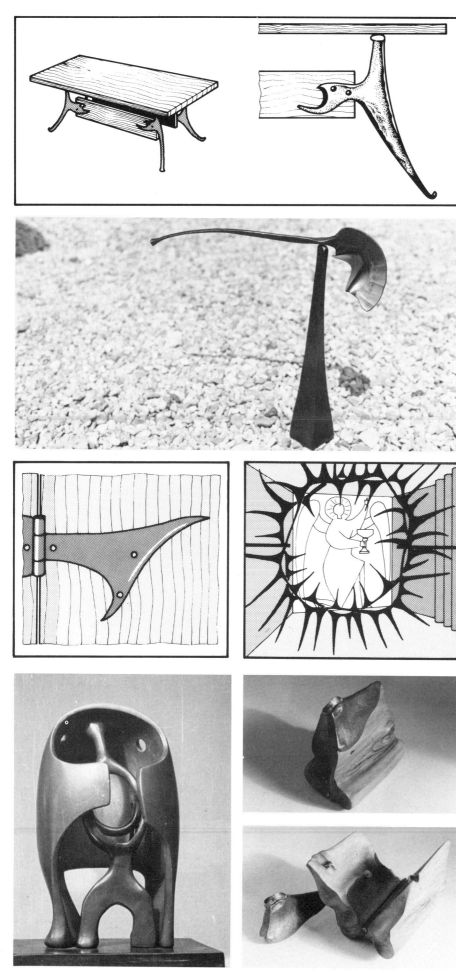

Sculpture can be made in any metal but is traditionally cast in a bronze alloy. Much modern sculpture is comparatively large and is constructed from much cheaper steel. The newest techniques involve the use of polyester resin containing a metal filler. This is either poured into a mould or on to a former.

Sculpture is a creative form which does not necessarily have a function. Some forms made of metal do have a job to do but have a sculptural shape.

Clay is the traditional material in which sculptors have worked, and forgework is the nearest the metalworker gets to such modelling. The artist working directly with the material can use heat to soften it, then stretch and contract it into almost any shape.

Paul Bridge has successfully used a forged sculptural form as a functional leg of a low table.
Alan Evans has forged steel into a balanced sculptural form which rotates and rocks. It is intended to be a toy. Although this sculptural toy and the forged hinge shown use the same skills and are similar in appearance, one *has* to be functional – its appearance is not so important.

Some sculpture has to be made to a specific size. The Royal Engineers made the 'Crown of Thorns' – a screen to fit the opening in a Coventry Cathedral Chapel.

The famous British sculptor Henry Moore now has large work cast in bronze. As a student he cast small pieces in cheaper lead melted on a kitchen stove. The 'Helmet' is such a sculpture in two pieces. It is one protective form surrounding another – perhaps an abstract 'Mother and Child'.

Diana Hobson has made a small box which does not hold very much, but is a most interesting sculptural shape.
It makes use of an offcut of juniper wood. The hinge is a brass ballpoint cartridge and the rod is copper wire. The beaten copper catch is an important part of the whole form as it fits the 'natural' flow of the wood grain.
It combines a useful and decorative object with a sculptural shape – or is it a useful piece of sculpture?

Free Forms

Traditional bronze casting is a complicated process which is expensive, but many of the techniques used by modern sculptors are simple and cheap. Sculpture can be formed or constructed in the workshop using readily available materials and tools. The photographs show some ways in which modern British sculptors have made sculpture.

Kenneth Martin made the 'Screw Mobile' from thin rods. The mobile is constructed with regular spaces and regular angles based on the development of the drawing of an eclipse. The idea is mathematical but fascinating. Visual forms are created as the suspended mobile turns and casts shadows on nearby flat surfaces.

Henry Moore made a series of small castings based on the human figure. This one is the abstract head and shoulders of a reclining figure only 220 mm in length. Strings or wires are used as straight lines as a contrast to the solid rounded metal. The lines seem to cross at different angles as you move around the sculpture, creating their own changing patterns — an idea taken from mathematical models Moore had seen at the British Science Museum.

David Annesley made 'Orinoco' by shaping the mild steel with a rolling machine and welding the parts together. The painted finish protects the surface, makes the sculpture seem lighter and hides the character of the material from which it is made.
This sculptor's work is abstract and has precise shapes and lines, in complete contrast to the unprecise shapes and textures of traditional sculpture. He works out his ideas directly in metal, but the final piece is constructed from a full-size drawing.

Robert Adams made 'Large Screen Form' from steel plate and rod and gave it a bronzed finish. Rods of varying diameters are fixed into some of the holes bored through the plates. The welds joining the four plates are not ground down, so that they appear as lines on the surface.

Anthea Alley made 'Spatial Form' by coiling and joining strips of sheet metal from which circles had been stamped in an industrial process. She has made use of *found* materials.

The common tin can is an easily found source of material that is easily cut and rejoined.

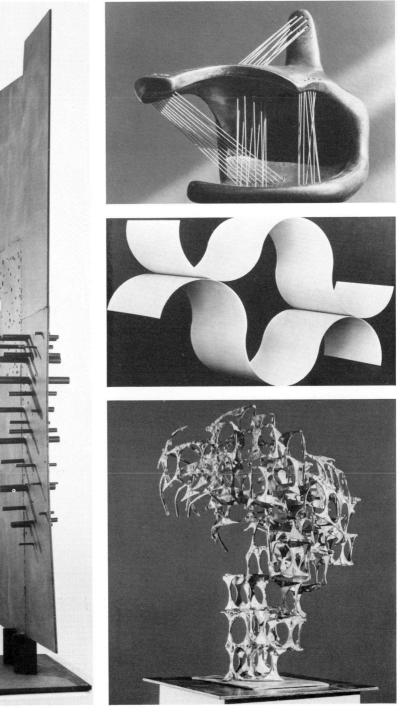

Machined Forms

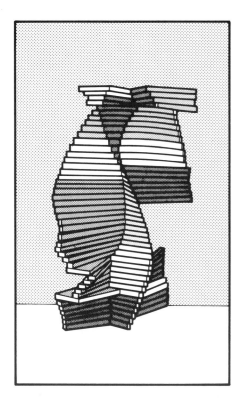

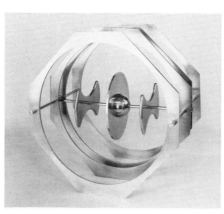

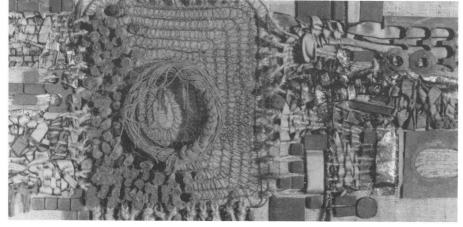

Some of the 'found' objects used in sculpture have already been machined as part of an earlier manufacturing process, but some sculptors do use machines to shape materials to fine tolerances. Kenneth Martin made 'Oscillation' from carefully machined lengths of phosphor bronze. It is part of a series which, unlike his 'Screw Mobile', is static but gives a feeling of movement. Although it seems large it is only 220 mm high.

Bryan Kneale made 'Marina' from precisely machined and constructed brass parts. He works directly in metal because he says: 'From a purely practical point of view, the use of metal is an extremely direct way of making sculpture. I can become involved in the actual making of a piece almost instantly, in the same second as I have the idea.'

Anthony Hill made his 'Relief Construction' from extruded aluminium with a coloured edge. Lengths vary according to mathematical proportions, explained in his book about the relationship between non-figurative art and mathematics.

Drawing is traditionally used as a means of generating ideas for sculpture or, as Henry Moore puts it, 'thinking on paper'. He made the pen, ink and chalk exploratory drawing shown before making 'The Helmet'. (See page 142.)

André Wallace is an artist who uses drawings as a shorthand for exploring problems related to scale and form for a new piece of sculpture and works out the possible variations until enough information has been discovered to begin making it.

But drawings are not essential. Some sculptors let an idea become 'drawn in the mind' — then when all the problems are solved, get on with making it. Now that computer graphics are available, other artists fix points in space, use a program to make them three-dimensional and then have them printed out.

Sculptors traditionally use people and places as inspiration, and modern artists have made industrial waste, mathematical data and computer-aided drawings as starting points.

In 'Heptonstall', a collage of woven fabrics and industrial waste (springs, stampings and heavy swarf), Brenda Shepherd used a map of the Yorkshire town of Heptonstall as inspiration.

Finishes and Presentation

The non-ferrous materials used in sculpture — such as bronze — have not needed protection from weathering and handling. Over the years such materials have developed a patina — a covering of an oxide film which appears green where copper has reacted to weathering.

Paul Bridge gave 'Two Birds' this appearance of age by coating it with a copper nitrate solution and allowing it to stand outside to 'weather'. Ferrous metals will rust if not protected. Paul Bridge made 'Two Birds II' in mild steel and kept the steely appearance by covering it with a transparent lacquer.

Eduardo Paolozzi made his two-metre tall sculpture 'Amir Amor' in steel and gave it a chromium finish to reflect its immediate environment in a distorted way. The form is purer because it no longer seems to be made from a material as common as steel.

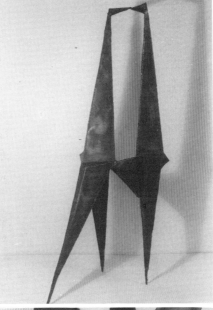

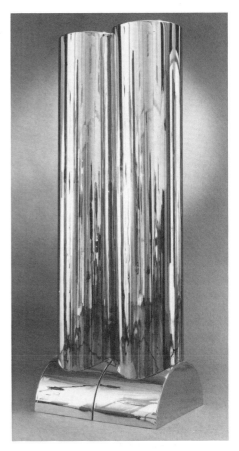

The way in which a piece of sculpture is displayed or presented is important. 'Amir Amor' is large enough to simply stand on the floor. 'Two Birds' is made from copper rod which Paul Bridge has inserted into a slate base for stability. The base has a covering of felt to protect table surfaces on which it is put.

Alexander Calder invented the *mobile*. His 'Antennae with Red and Blue Dots' is suspended from a ceiling and is carefully balanced so that it moves in very many ways whilst the onlooker stands still.

Anthony Caro is a British sculptor who was responsible for some of the very largest pieces of modern sculpture. As these were far too big for most people to buy he then made a series of table-top works which would fit in houses.
In the piece shown, the thick steel has been cut and shaped to fit on to and over a table — the table being part of the sculpture. He called it 'Piece LXXXII', which makes a change from some of the odd titles that sculptors have given to their abstract work!

Jewellery – Enamelling

Enamelling is a process in which powdered glass is fused to a metal ground by intense heat.

Before the introduction of cheap plastic buckets, some steel buckets were white enamelled, and enamelled coffee pots can still be bought.

Cast iron is not suitable for enamelling in the workshop but it is a common industrial process used to give a fine finish to high-quality casserole dishes. The ones shown are white on the inside and flame red on the outside.

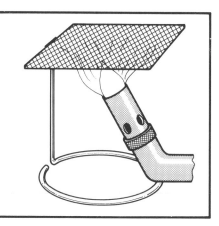

The gas-fired enamelling oven has simple controls which quickly bring the temperature up to a little over the 800°C at which glass melts. A glazed slot in the sliding door allows the craftsman to observe the process safely.

It is possible to raise the same temperature on a small area such as a pendant using a brazing torch. The work rests on a metal mesh and the heat is applied from below.

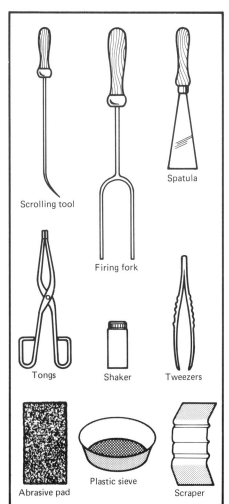

Scrolling tool

Spatula

Firing fork

Tongs

Shaker

Tweezers

Abrasive pad

Plastic sieve

Scraper

Enamelling is a decorative workshop process which requires very few tools and materials.

A century ago a textbook read: 'I would venture to call the attention of ladies to the pretty things they can make out of gold and enamel with no other tools than scissors, pliers, a few jeweller's files and a spirit lamp and blowpipe.'

The writer referred to some of the best sixteenth-century work which was made by the 'whitest of fingers in the most tidy of drawing rooms'. A modern beginner's kit contains similar tools.

Copper blanks can be cut and shaped in any way and enamelling is a creative way to use up some of the waste from 20 gauge sheet after larger shapes have been cut from it. Repeated shapes of an individual design can be cut on a press. One manufacturer supplies as many as forty different ones.

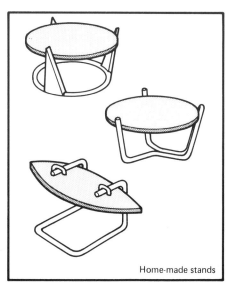

Home-made stands

Some metalworking skills will be needed to make stands and supports – hard stainless steel sheet or wire is best. These are used when the metal is counter-enamelled. Flat or thin metal should be enamelled on the reverse side to prevent warping of the blank and cracking of the enamel.

Enamelling (continued)

Traditional enamelling methods

The process of enamelling has been known for at least two thousand years, but the traditional techniques are known by the French names given to them. Two of these methods can be used in the workshop.

Champlevé

This is the oldest technique of them all. Hollows are beaten, carved or etched into the surface, then filled with wet opaque enamels and fired. The process is repeated until there is surplus enamel. The surface is ground flat and refired to finish.

Cloisonné

This is the technique of using wire to contain small reservoirs of wet enamel. In high-class work silver or gold wire is hard-soldered to the blank.
A simpler method is to fire a base enamel on to the blank. Cut and shape the copper wire to the required pattern and set this into the molten base enamel.

The drawing shows part of a necklace in an Egyptian style which combines the two processes. The circular surround is hard-soldered and the hieroglyph is formed using the base enamel method.

Modern Enamelling Methods

Sgraffito is drawing with a pointed tool such as the scroller. A base enamel is fired. Then an opaque second coat is applied on gum. When dry, the pattern is drawn and fired a second time.

A **stencil** is usually a paper cut. A base enamel is fired. The stencil is wetted and laid on the surface and a second colour is shaken on. The paper is removed. Subsequent coats are applied in the same way.
The flower design from a William Morris fabric needs four separate stencils.

Scrolling is done when the enamel is molten. A second colour is dragged through the base enamel with a scrolling tool — just like working wet slip in the pottery.

Texture is obtained in two simple ways:

1. Create an overall rough texture by deliberately under-firing the work — perhaps for only about 60 seconds.
2. Create high points within a pattern by setting lumps of enamel into a base colour — withdrawing the work before they melt completely.

Champlevé

Punch   graver

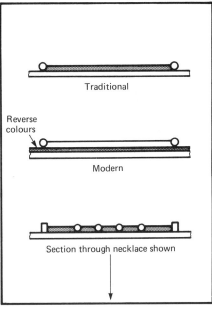

Traditional

Reverse colours

Modern

Section through necklace shown

William Morris Medway

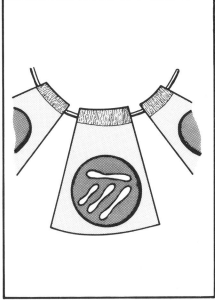

Scrolling

Texture

An Example of Enamelling

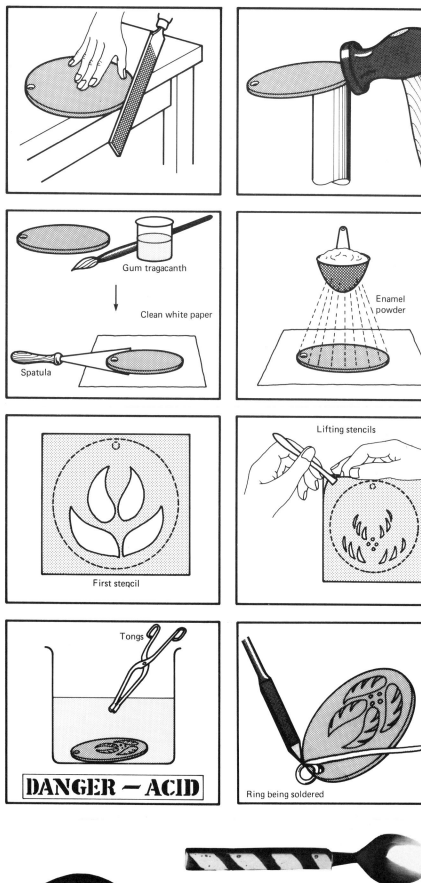

Ideas for designs can either be original or taken from existing work. Whatever the source of the idea you must draw out a full-size colour design. Remember that enamels do not always turn out the colour you expect, so a series of test firings is a good idea.

This is a description of one method of making a pendant, using the flower design from 'Medway', a Victorian curtain fabric.

1. Cut the blank disc from 20 gauge copper. Drill the hole for a jump ring. Finish the edges with a file and abrasive.
   At this stage the disc should be slightly domed using a mallet and sandbag, and the edges turned down or counter-enamelled to prevent distortion.
2. Clean both surfaces with abrasive cloth. Heat in the kiln to a dull red (about 700°C). Quench in cold water.
3. Dry the disc carefully without touching it — your fingers are greasy. Place it on a sheet of clean paper and paint the top surface with gum or cellulose adhesive.
4. Shake base enamel over the surface, taking care to cover the edges. When this is dry, fire for not more than about 60 seconds. Then allow the disc to cool on a safe mat.
5. Wet the surface and apply the first stencil. Shake on the colour and allow it to dry. Dust off excess enamel and fire for about 60 seconds.
6. Repeat this procedure for each colour. When the last colour is applied the firing should be long enough to let the enamels form a flat surface. Keep a constant visual check to avoid over-firing.
7. Clean fine scale from the back either with abrasive or by immersing in dilute sulphuric acid. Rinse, dry and apply a lacquer to prevent discolouring.
8. Fix a jump ring or loop, which can be soldered for security. Hang the pendant from a chain or leather thong.

Metal and Ceramics

David Hilton designed the ceramic handled cutlery called 'Spiral'. The metal is pressed nickel steel which is held in the stoneware handle by means of a special cutler's cement. This is not an adhesive. It expands in the curing process to create a watertight bond.

Etching

The drawing shows a small box made from gilding metal (an alloy of copper and zinc). It is gold in colour. The domed top has a beaten plaque set in enamel, and both the lid and base are etched.

Etching is the method by which metal is dissolved away in dilute nitric acid. The amount of metal that is 'eaten away' depends on the strength of the acid solution and the length of time the metal is immersed.
The equipment needed to make a pendant is simple. In addition to normal shaping tools all that you need are detergent, a paint brush, cellulose paint or lacquer and brush cleaner, and a bath of acid.

1. Cut a blank disc from 20 gauge sheet. Drill a hole for a jump ring. Finish the edges with a file and abrasive.
2. Use detergent to thoroughly clean the surfaces and take care to avoid touching them — your fingers are greasy.
3. Use cellulose varnish or lacquer to cover the areas of the metal which do *not* need etching. Make sure that the back and edges are thoroughly covered. A coloured cellulose paint is recommended so that the design can easily be seen.
4. Immerse the disc in the acid bath and leave it for several hours. Do not try to etch it too quickly. Check the depth of the etch. When it is deep enough, remove the disc from the acid.
5. Thoroughly rinse the disc and remove the cellulose with cellulose thinners on a rag.
6. The flower design shown is taken from the William Morris design 'Medway'. Some of the richness of the design could be achieved by making the etching on several levels. To do this, paint out new areas of the pattern again, leaving exposed only those areas to be etched to a deeper level. Repeat this process as often as necessary.
7. Finally clean off all the cellulose and use an abrasive polish to give a finishing shine to the surfaces.
8. Apply a clear lacquer to prevent discolouring.

Safety

ACID is dangerous — TAKE CARE.
Follow ALL safety precautions.

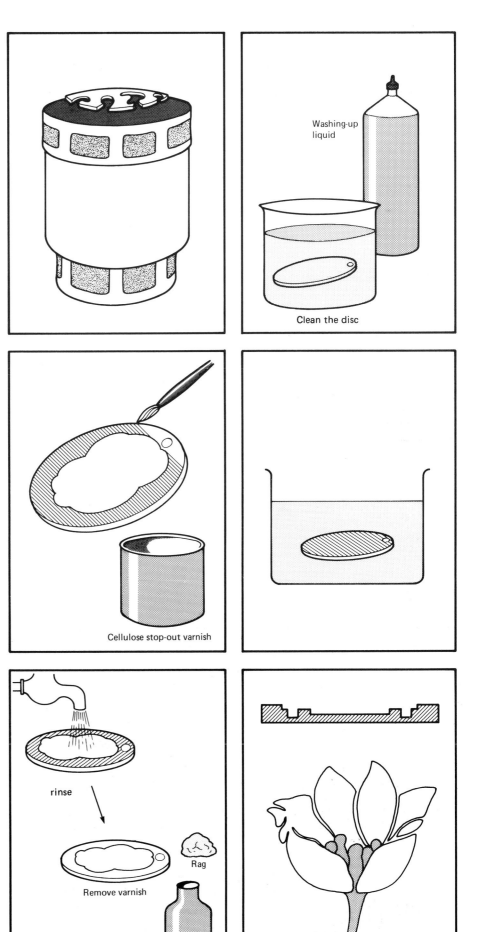

Washing-up liquid

Clean the disc

Cellulose stop-out varnish

rinse

Remove varnish

Rag

Cellulose thinner

Settings

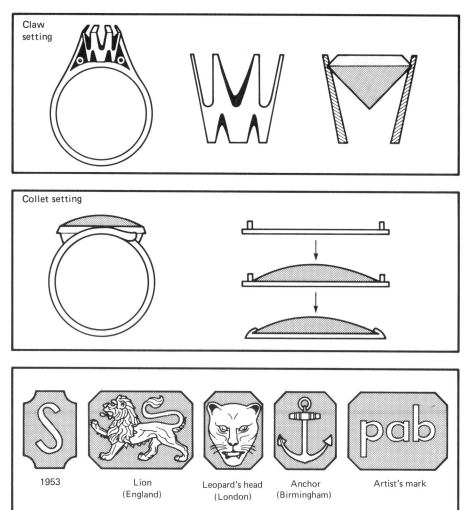

Claw setting

Collet setting

1953   Lion (England)   Leopard's head (London)   Anchor (Birmingham)   Artist's mark

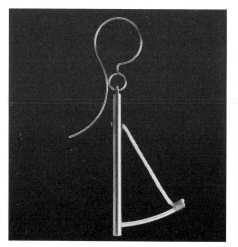

Jewellery is often thought of as an expensive luxury. For many people the first visit to a jeweller's shop is for an engagement ring — often a precious stone, such as a diamond, set in gold. Diamonds are transparent stones held in a **claw-setting** which allows the light to pass through and show their brilliant cut. The setting can be made from a cone which is tapered on a mandrel. The claws are formed by cutting material away with needle files. The stone clicks into a vee-notch engraved on the inside (as shown on the section). The claws are turned over with a burnisher.

A **collet setting** is used to mount opaque stones which are usually polished to a cabachon section. The collet is made to fit the stone exactly. It is soldered to a base and reduced to the height required. The processes of pickling, cleaning and polishing are carried out before the stone is put in place.
The collet is gradually turned over on to the stone with a burnisher to avoid creasing the thin material.

Jewellery materials

Silver is cheaper than gold. The purity of silver is guaranteed by the system of hall-marking by an Assay Office which will test and stamp authentic work with four marks.
The lion *passant* denotes English Sterling silver. The leopard's head is the symbol for London (the anchor found on much mass-produced work is for Birmingham). A letter in a shield represents the date. for example, the S is for 1953.
The fourth mark is that of the craftsman, e.g. Paul Anthony Bridge.

Kenneth Hartwell cast the silver chrysanthemum brooch as part of a set based on a theme of Autumn.

Joël Degan used four different materials — each a different colour — for his ear-ring. Stainless steel rod or wire, titanium rod (pale blue), terylene string (yellow) and polyester thread (red). For the bangle he used anodized titanium sheet, corrugated in a bench vice and secured with pop rivets.

Today, jewellery has become fun and need not be expensive. For beginners malleable copper is ideal. Gilding metal works like silver but looks like gold! Jewellery uses small quantities of material — and allows the designer plenty of freedom.

Jewellery Tools

The basic jewellery tool kit for beginners shown here was provided by Charles Cooper Ltd. You will see that many of the tools are part of basic workshop equipment. These will include some of the marking-out tools, shears, pliers and files.

Cutting tools include a fine hacksaw for straight cutting and an adjustable piercing saw for cutting curves. Needle files are used for intricate shaping and finishing. The making of rings is made easier by using the tapering triblet and soft-jawed ring clamp. Soldering techniques demand borax, binding wire, a charcoal block and tweezers. Soft mops and abrasive rouge are used for polishing.

The safe pad is made from a ceramic fibre mix designed to replace asbestos sheet. It will withstand very high temperatures without burning.

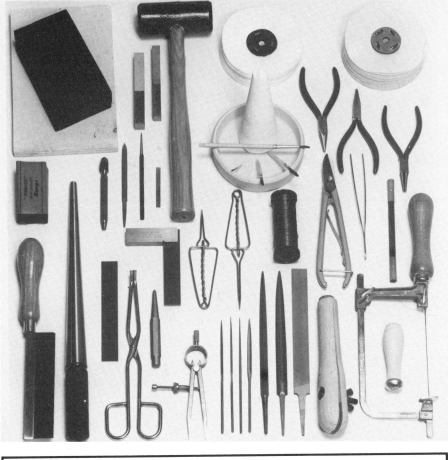

A pin vice is used to hold round or square wire.
A hand vice is used to hold small pieces of flat work.

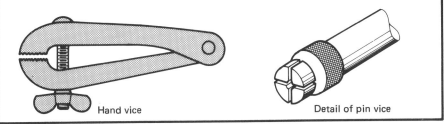

Hand vice   Detail of pin vice

Pickling

Pickling is the process by which oxides and other impurities are removed from the surface of the metal. The dilute sulphuric acid solution or safety pickle can be heated before use to reduce the risk of splashing – hot pickle is also more effective in removing borax flux after soldering.
Use only non-ferrous tongs.

The photograph shows copper tongs, brass tweezers, brass wire-brushes and mop, and a copper pan.

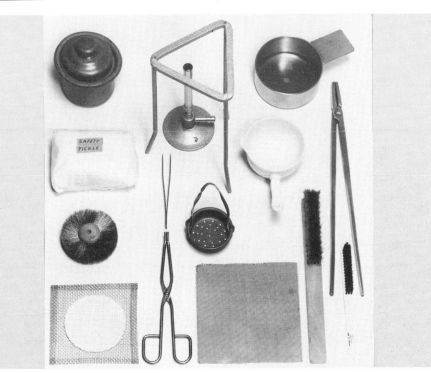

Using Wires

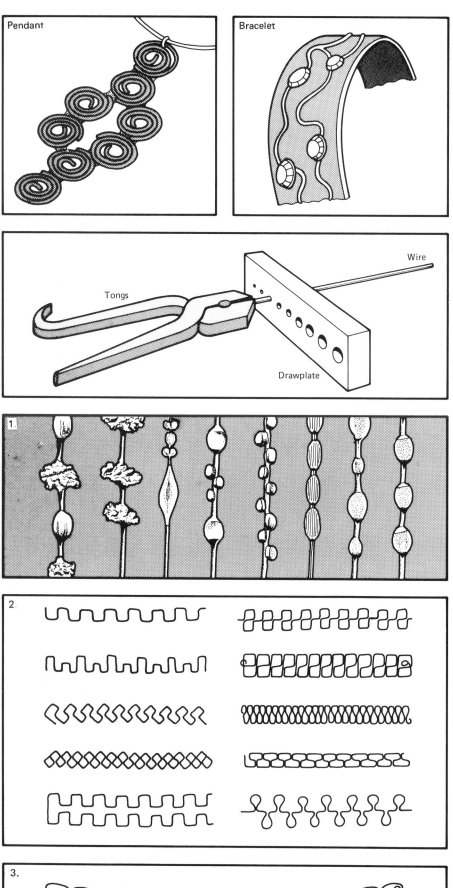

Pendant

Bracelet

Tongs

Wire

Drawplate

1.

2.

3.

Wire is a ready-made material which can be used to create all types of jewellery — from the simplest to the most complicated, from the cheapest to the most expensive.

It can be used to construct chain, make fastenings (such as brooch-pins), or simply applied to surfaces as a form of decoration.

A schoolgirl used simply-coiled copper wire soldered together to make a large pendant.

Stuart Wharton designed the gold bracelet using gold wire to link together his settings of precious stones.

A **drawplate** is made from hardened steel and contains a series of tapered holes through which wire is drawn or pulled. Use the holes either to reduce the diameter of wire or change its section. Holes can be round, half-round or oval; square, triangular or star-shaped. It is possible to pull two wires at the same time — two square wires pulled through a round hole will produce two half-round wires.

To use the drawplate, first estimate the length of wire required. Allow for stretching.

Prepare the wire by annealing and repeat this as necessary. Coil and tie the wire during the annealing process.

Taper one end of the wire with a hammer. Insert it into the smallest lightly oiled hole which will accept it.

Grip with the draw tongs and if possible make *one* steady pull.

Repeat in progressively smaller holes to achieve the finished size.

The drawings show:

1. Heavy-gauge wire annealed and beaten with a variety of home-made steel punches to produce decorative effects.

2. Thin wire given added strength by being worked into a rich variety of shapes around different shapes of former.
   Work out your own designs on squared paper.

3. A bracelet made up from a series of identical wire shapes linked together by small jump rings.

Using Chains

Small chain is made by machine, but you can use wire to make individual chains which form part of the design of the jewellery.

To make links, wrap annealed wire around a suitable **former**. Formers for oval, rectangular and round links are shown.
Coils must be removed from metal formers and carefully held in a vice for cutting with a piercing saw. Coils around wood formers can be cut in place (e.g. jump rings on wood dowel rod).

To make a secure chain all the links must be **soldered**. Do this by first soldering half the number of links needed. Then join these together with alternate open rings. Peg out the chain on a charcoal block to separate the links and complete the soldering with great care.
There is a correct way to open and close a link which will not distort the shape. Open and close the link **sideways.**

The pendants show two contrasting uses of wire. In one the chain links and jump ring are made around formers and the pendant is made from a series of concentric wire circles. In the other the chain loops are linked by jump rings and wired to an enamelled plate from which bound wires dangle.

Bold and simple jewellery can be made with horseshoe nails. The brooch here is made from nine nails soldered together. The pendant is made from eleven small nails, five large nails, fourteen jump rings, binding wire and a ready-made chain with a clasp.
Bend the nails around a suitable former such as a length of tube. Grip a nail on to the former with slip-joint pliers and bend it through 90°. Turn the nail head to the original position and repeat to close-up the end.
The techniques for making nail jewellery are simple, and pieces can be quickly made up. Design pieces carefully to avoid making them too heavy!

The nails and wire may *rust*. Avoid this by protecting the surfaces with a cellulose lacquer (e.g. hairspray). Spray this on taking the usual safety precautions — ventilate the area, and do not use lacquer near a naked flame.

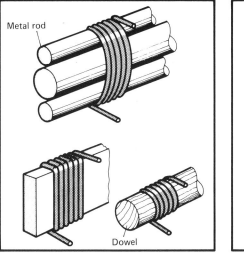

Metal rod

Dowel

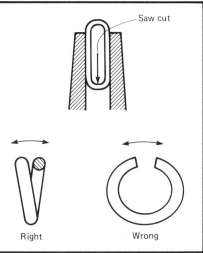

Saw cut

Right   Wrong

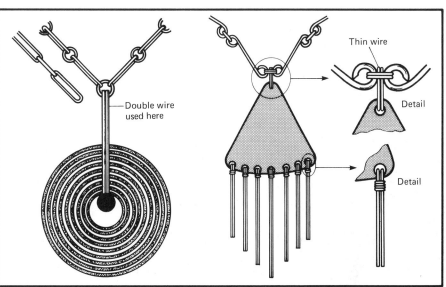

Double wire used here

Thin wire

Detail

Detail

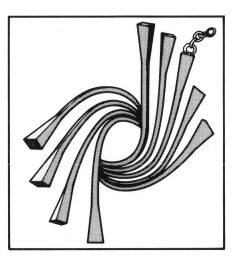

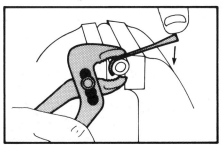

Sawing

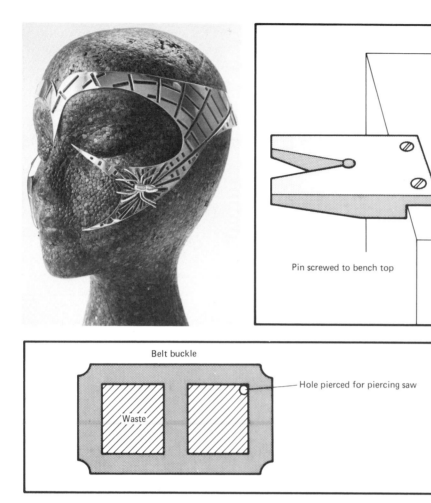

Pin screwed to bench top

Belt buckle

Hole pierced for piercing saw

Waste

A century ago the piercing saw was used to cut the most elaborate patterns in silver, but modern designs are much simpler. The silver headband, designed and made by Kenneth Hartwell, is pierced with rectangular slots and further decorated with a lost-wax cast of a spider in gold.

The piercing saw illustrated on page 144 has an adjustable frame which allows broken saw blades to be re-used. The maximum depth of cut (70 mm) is 15 mm less than that of a fixed-frame saw. The 125 mm long standard blade is available in five teeth sizes: 80, 60, 52, 44 and 32 teeth per 25 mm. The choice of blade depends on the thickness of the material — as with a hacksaw, at least three teeth should be in contact with the material. Choose a high number of teeth for thin material.

The jeweller's pin can be used as shown or with the sloping surface on top. A bored hole at the base of the slot helps with sawing. Jewellers will make different slopes on the pin to help them cut and file particular shapes and angles.
Fix the blade with teeth facing the handle, and cut metal on the downward stroke.
Do not force the saw — if you do the blade will break. Keep the blade straight. At corners, keep the blade moving and gradually turn the metal. Finish square with a file.

To pierce metal — that is to cut out an inside shape — centre-punch and drill a small hole in the waste metal. Insert the saw blade and re-tension it in the frame. Then cut in the usual way using long, even strokes. Beeswax can be used as a lubricant.

Findings

Findings can be bought from the jewellery trade. It is usual for a jeweller to buy items such as coin mounts, padlocks, bolt rings in diameters from 5 to 12 mm and ready-made jump rings in bulk.
Earclips and ear wires are available in silver and rolled gold, and cufflink mechanisms (silver or gilt plated) are available which can be soldered to the back of your design.

Fine chain is mass-produced in a variety of weights and in the four main designs shown. Consider the chain designs available when designing a pendant.

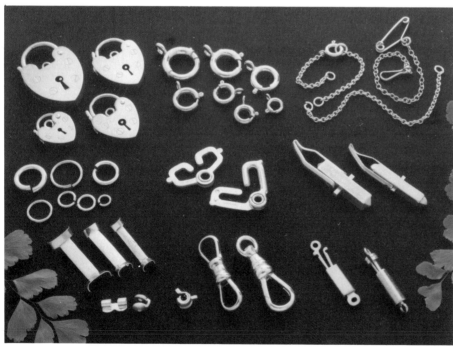

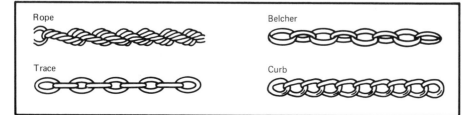

Rope

Belcher

Trace

Curb

Casting

Nigel Edmundson designed and made the two-part necklace. It is cast in pewter and attached by jump rings to a length of curb chain.

Casting is the process of forming molten metal into the shape of a prepared mould. There are four main methods of producing small cast items.

1. The **lost-wax** method uses a **wax** pattern which is destroyed by the casting process.
2. The **centrifugal** method spins the mould to force the metal into it. It is best for detail, such as toy soldiers.
3. The **investment** method uses a master pattern from which a silicon rubber mould is prepared. The mould is re-usable.
4. The **direct-casting** method is one of the easiest and most effective methods. Cuttlefish casting is an example.

To make a cuttlefish casting:

A. Obtain a piece of cuttlefish bone from a pet shop. Trim it and grind it flat on abrasive paper. Then 'face' it by rubbing it against the charcoal block which will become the second half of the mould.
B. Strips of pewter are readily bent to shapes which can be impressed into the cuttlefish bone to form the design. Small ready-made objects such as tube, 'Lego' and 'Scrabble' pieces can be used in the same way.
The mould can also be formed by cutting with sharp tools such as lino cutters. An inlet is cut.
C. The prepared bone is firmly wired to its charcoal block ready for casting.
D. The metal — in this case pewter — is put into a ladle and melted by the heat from a butane gas torch.
When the low melting point is reached, remove any oxide dross which may have formed and pour it quickly into the mould. Fumes are not given off.

Pewter is an ideal metal with which to cast. It is relatively inexpensive, works easily and can be given a rich satisfying sheen. There is no waste as excess metal or faulty castings may be re-used.

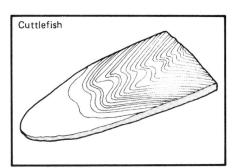

Cuttlefish

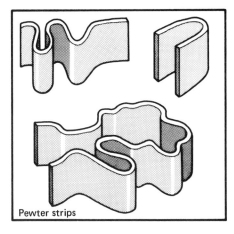

Pewter strips

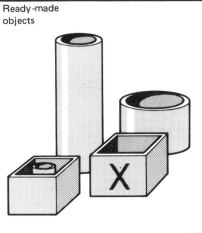

Ready-made objects

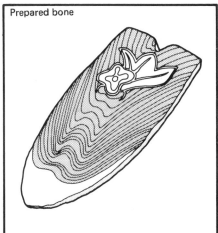

Prepared bone

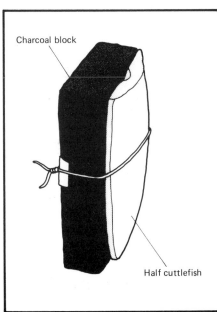

Charcoal block

Half cuttlefish

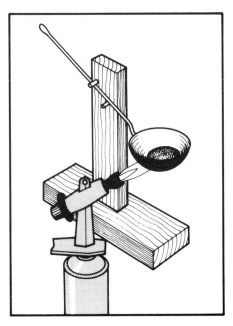

Use of Resins

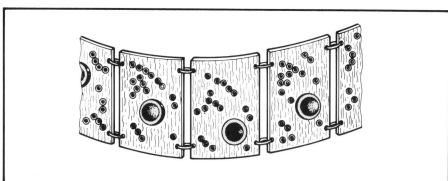

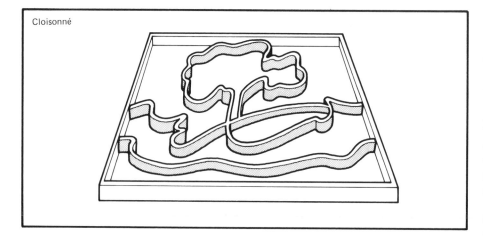

Cloisonné

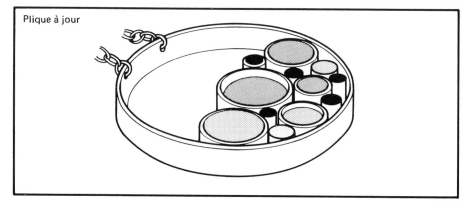

Plique à jour

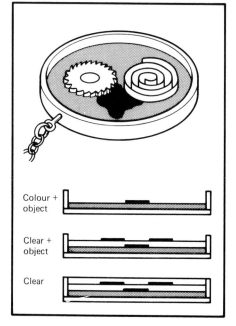

Colour + object

Clear + object

Clear

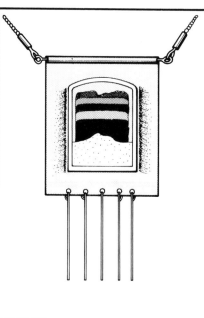

Paul Bridge designed and made a silver bracelet from six convex shields of equal size, linked by jump rings and fastened with bolt rings. The hollow plaster mould was carved to give the surfaces a rippled texture. Pieces of tube of varying diameters were soldered into place. Each tube was filled with a transparent resin in a range of colours from yellow to deep red.

Use the type of resin designed for encapsulating objects. This is transparent but can be coloured with a translucent coloured paste.
Although the liquid resins set by a chemical reaction, heat is not applied. They can be used in a way similar to enamel.

Areas of different coloured enamels can be separated by low walls of metal – the cloisonné method of enamelling. The walls can either be soldered in place or embedded in a layer of clear coat resin (the base enamel method).

Obtain a stained glass effect – the plique-à-jour method of enamelling – by filling the tubes with transparent resins. The metal piece rests on plate glass polished with a release agent.
Brooches and pendants can be made from embedding interesting objects – such as the parts from an obsolete watch – into resin. The sections show:

1. the metal base and retaining wall on to which a coloured resin is poured over an object
2. a layer of clear embedding resin into which further objects are set
3. a second and final layer of clear embedding resin which is given a highly polished surface.

Since this method uses only a small quantity of material, avoid wasting surplus resin by embedding several pieces at the same time.

Opaque resin is used in the copper pendant shown. Copper wires are suspended from the base plate.
The layers of different coloured resins are made in the form of a small 'loaf' which is sliced to make similar slices – a mass-production method. The slice of resin is embedded into the copper retaining wall, ground flat on a belt sander, smoothed with fine wet-and-dry abrasive, and finished with a polishing compound.

Upholstery – An Introduction

For twenty centuries only the very rich had padded seats. The seats were padded with horsehair, and cushions were filled with feathers.

The craft of upholstery has changed dramatically in the last thirty years with the introduction of foam fillers, Pirelli webbing and covers made from synthetic material. The most adventurous furniture designers have made full use of the new materials, and padding traditional furniture is now more simple and fairly cheap.

Upholstery was originally used to soften hard surfaces and then to give support to various parts of the body — head, arm and foot rests.

The covering material was nearly always decorated by woven cloth or tooled leather. Times change!

Laurent Dioptaz designed the Isotope chair in 1969, making full use of the different qualities of foamed polyurethane. The combined back and arm rests and the firm base are of high-density chipfoam. The sitting area is of the softest foam which will mould to the shape of the sitter.

The cube-like finished foam is covered in a knitted nylon fabric.

Kenneth Grange designed the net seat used on the prototype British Rail Advanced Passenger Train. The net seat was developed for Apollo II and is stretched on an aluminium frame so that the passenger does not feel carriage vibrations. Springs, rubber suspension and padding have been rejected and the seat weighs less than half that of the normal train seat. There is a traditional padded arm and headrest but the overall effect is strikingly modern.

Alan Tilbury designed the 'ilia 2' chair in chrome-plated steel tube. The seat platform is designed to link two identical side frames and is roundly upholstered in foam with a stitched leather cover. The arms are wrapped in plastics cord to give warmth and to add a distinctive pattern to the design. Black is the chosen colour. The 'ilea 2' chair is typical of most metal-framed designs — the upholstery is applied to a separate wood platform or frame.

Tools used

Modern materials are used, but traditional tools are still useful. A spring-loaded **staple gun** has often replaced the upholsterer's **tacking hammer,** but the

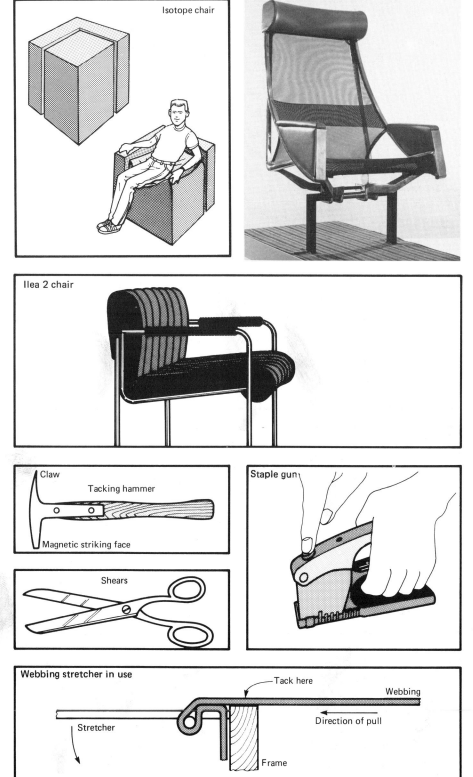

Isotope chair

Ilea 2 chair

Claw — Tacking hammer
Magnetic striking face

Shears

Staple gun

Webbing stretcher in use — Tack here — Webbing — Direction of pull
Stretcher — Frame
SECTION

claw end of the hammer is useful for removing unwanted tacks.

A large pair of **shears** (heavy scissors) will cut foam filler and all types of covering material.

Use a carving knife to slice latex foam. Trim excess covering materials with a **trimming knife.**

Sundry tools include adhesive tape, a ball-point pen, flexible adhesives and talcum powder.

A **webbing stretcher** is an invaluable appliance.

Webbing and Platforms

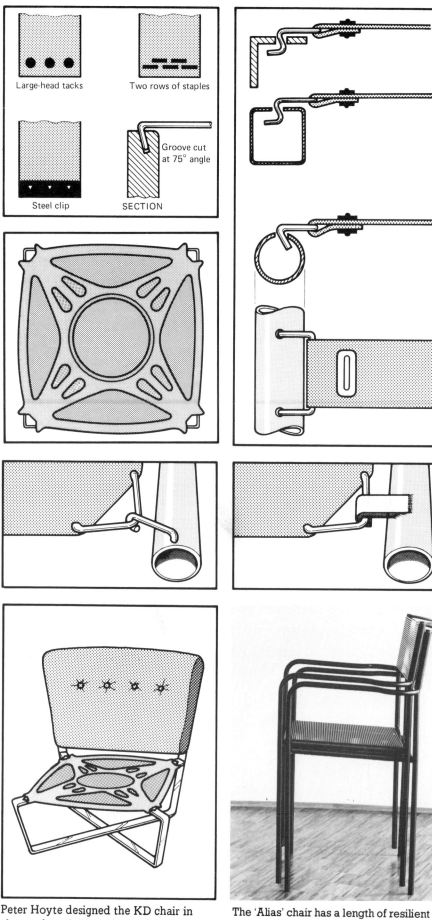

Construct a solid base (platform) from a manufactured board that has holes drilled through it. These holes allow the filling material (filler) to 'breathe'.
Use perforated hardboard, with additional supports for large areas such as beds, divans and settees.
Use plywood or blockboard on chairs and stools. It is self-supporting but must have 15 mm diameter ventilation holes bored at 100 mm intervals.

Pirelli resilient webbing is a lamination of bias-cut rayon and rubber which forms a flat 'spring'. Use the widest and thickest webbing for seats (which support 80 per cent of bodyweight) and narrower and thinner webbing for backs.
To fix Pirelli webbing to *wood* either:

1. insert large-head tacks
2. insert two rows of staples
3. groove rails to hold the metal clips.

Radius the inside edges of supporting rails to prevent damage to the webbing.

To fix Pirelli webbing to *metal*, use either:

1. a hook into angle iron or square tube
2. a hook into tube of not less than 20 mm diameter.

Place the appropriate hook into the webbing and secure with a Pirelli staple.
In tube, drill 3 mm holes top-dead-centre (67 mm apart for 51 mm webbing).
In angle iron or square tube, drill 3 mm holes 13 mm from the inside edge of the frame (54 mm apart for 51 mm webbing). Ensure free movement of the hooks.

Estimate webbing lengths in the following way:

1. Measure the span (the distance between holes) — for example, 560 mm.
2. The resilient length would be 500 mm (less for harder seating).
3. Deduct 10 per cent for tension (leaving 450 mm).
4. Add 70 mm for staple assembly (cut a 520 mm length).

The Pirelli four-point platform is a resilient plastics diaphragm which is suspended from four points to support a loose cushion. The size of the supporting frame is critical and tensioning must be considered at the design stage.
Hooks can be inserted into or welded on to the metal frame.

Large-head tacks

Two rows of staples

Steel clip

Groove cut at 75° angle

SECTION

Peter Hoyte designed the KD chair in chromed steel. It is shown with the back and Pirelli platform in place.

The 'Alias' chair has a length of resilient plastic wrapped around the metal frame, for both support and decoration.

Fillers

Foamed rubber has been in use for half a century, but foamed synthetic materials are a more recent development. This new generation of foams can be carefully controlled and are very reliable.

Plain sheet

This is smooth on both sides. Use it for walling, seats and chair backs.

Cavity sheet

This is smooth on one side only. Use it for seating, with walling round the edge.

Pin-core sheet

This is perforated on both sides. It is a reversible, heavy-duty material which does not need walling.

Polyether (plastic) foam is cheaper than **Latex** foam but softens more easily in use. It is available in a wide variety of density and hardness values and may be cut to any shape or size.
The two main types are *slabstock foam* and *bonded (reconstituted) foam*.

Selecting foam

Whether a hard or soft seat or bed is preferred will depend on personal taste. Allow for loss of hardness with time. Seats must not 'bottom' on a solid platform.

The high-density foams give the best performance but are expensive. Use bonded foam where a very high density is needed. Allow 10 per cent extra thickness in flat cushions to allow for thickness loss.

Latex and polyether foams both deteriorate in bright sunlight. Use calico undercovers under open-weave cover fabrics.

Adhesives for foams

Select with care adhesives for bonding upholstery materials. The photograph shows some of the adhesives listed below in the various sizes and packs in which they can be purchased.

Recommended adhesives

Evostik Impact (528) is a general-purpose adhesive that can be used to join all the materials listed. Adhesives made especially to join these materials are shown opposite.
In addition Dunlop adhesive S758 will stick leather, PVC-coated fabrics, polyether foam and latex to most metals.

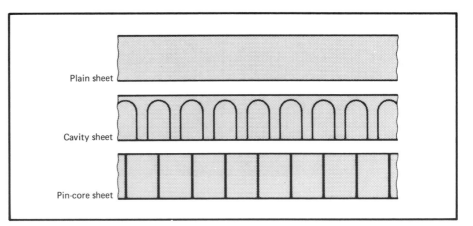

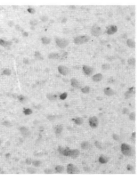

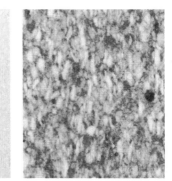

slabstock foam – examples of low-sponge and high-upholstery density types (A and B)

bonded (re-constituted) foam – offcuts of slabstock foam are shredded and bonded with a liquid polyether foam to produce a high-density slab (C)

	PVC to Wood	Fabric to Latex	Fabric to Foam	Fabric to Wood	Foam to Wood	Latex to Wood	Foam to Foam	Latex to Latex	PVC to PVC
Evostik clear (5183)	X			X	X				X
Dunlop upholstery (L107)	X	X		X				X	
Dunlop foam building (S834)					X	X	X		
Copydex			X	X	X	X	X	X	
PAC (Copydex)		X				X		X	X
Unistik	X		X				X		X

Covers

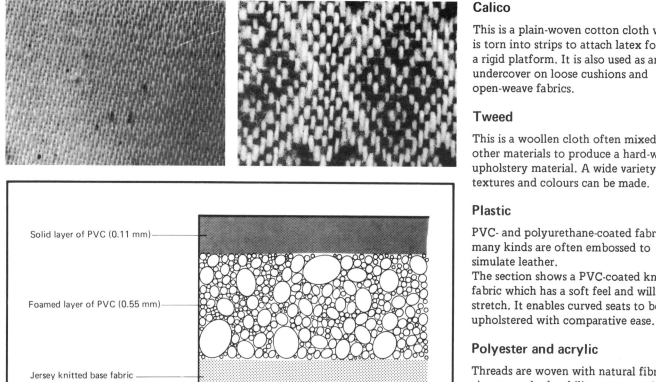

Solid layer of PVC (0.11 mm)

Foamed layer of PVC (0.55 mm)

Jersey knitted base fabric

Calico

This is a plain-woven cotton cloth which is torn into strips to attach latex foam to a rigid platform. It is also used as an undercover on loose cushions and open-weave fabrics.

Tweed

This is a woollen cloth often mixed with other materials to produce a hard-wearing upholstery material. A wide variety of textures and colours can be made.

Plastic

PVC- and polyurethane-coated fabrics of many kinds are often embossed to simulate leather.
The section shows a PVC-coated knitted fabric which has a soft feel and will stretch. It enables curved seats to be upholstered with comparative ease.

Polyester and acrylic

Threads are woven with natural fibres to give strength, durability, crease-resistance and easy care.

Cover care

Each fabric must be cleaned with care, following the manufacturer's cleaning instructions.
DO NOT use solvent-based cleaners as these will damage the foam filler.
Clean plastics-coated covers with mild soap and a damp cloth. Avoid using excessive amounts of water.

'Cassis' seating by OMK is an example of modern upholstery techniques incorporated into a metal seat frame. The seat has a tubular framework supporting a perforated steel plate – all epoxy coated. The removable upholstery covers are printed in a washable cotton and linen fabric, fastened by zips. The filler is a medium-density polyether foam sandwiched between layers of 'Dacron' to give a feeling of luxury. Matching cushions give added support.

Adhesives for covers

To stick fabrics direct to metal, hot-melt adhesives (e.g. 3M 3764 and 3783) can be used. Alternatively, use double-coated 3M Scotch tape which will adhere to metal, polystyrene, ABS and acrylics.

Brand names of some man-made fibres			
Acrylic	Acrilan	**Nylon**	Bri-nylon
	Courtelle		Celon
	Orlon		Enkalon
	Dralon		
		Polypoplyne	Courlene
Polyester	Dacron		Cournova
	Terylene		
	Trevira		

Fastenings

Velcro

Velcro is a touch-and-close fastener made of Bri-nylon. One strip has hooks and the other has loops which hold when pressed together, yet can be peeled apart.

Use this fastener on loose cushions, and to secure detachable covers to chair frames.

Stitch it or glue it on to fabric. Glue it to foam or metal. Staple or glue it to wood. The chart suggests suitable adhesives from major manufacturers.

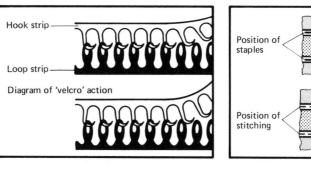

Hook strip
Loop strip

Diagram of 'velcro' action

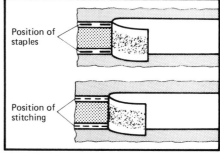

Position of staples

Position of stitching

	Adhesives to stick Velcro to:						
	Wood	Steel	Aluminium	Hardboard	Leather	Polystyrene	PVC
Bardens Polytak 240						Polytak 860	
Dunlop 708				Dunlop S1115			
Tretabond 200 + C31							
Bostik Boscoprene 2762							Bostik 1

Fitting a zip

Zips are mostly used on woven seat covers which need to be removed for cleaning.
The instructions and diagrams here refer to fitting a zip into the seat cushion cover of the chair shown in the photograph.

1. Cut two pieces of cushion fabric (A and B) according to the pattern. Turn under the amount allowed for the seam and press with an iron.
2. Select a zip and sewing thread to colour-match the cover fabric.
   Place piece A over the zip fastener so that the folded edge rests on the centre of the fastener and tack in position.
   Stitch on a sewing machine. A zipper foot attachment may be helpful but it is not essential.
3. Place piece B over the zip fastener to meet the edge of piece A. Tack B in position, and machine stitch in the opposite direction (as shown).
4. Make sure that the zip fastener is closed, joining pieces A and B together. Then stitch this combined piece to the other sides of the cushion cover (C).
   Complete the cover by machine stitching the remaining seams.

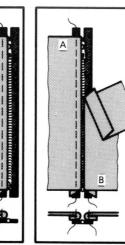

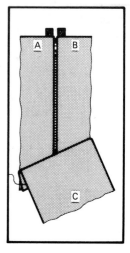

Covering A Stool Seat

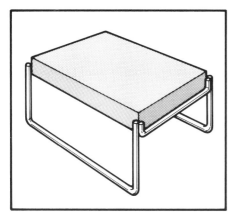

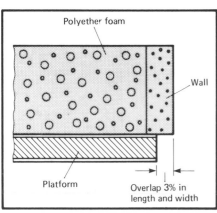

Polyether foam

Wall

Platform

Overlap 3% in length and width

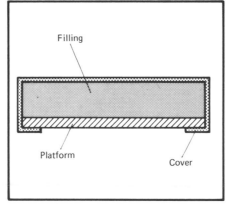

Filling

Platform

Cover

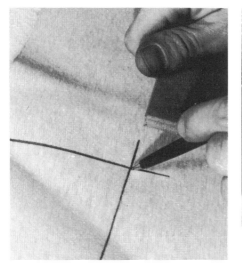

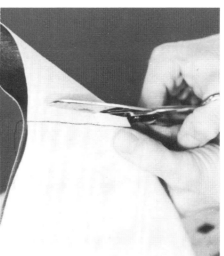

The tubular-steel stool frame shown is fitted with a square-edge drop-in seat made from materials already described. The seat is supported on metal lugs which are brazed to the frame. Two alternative methods are shown.

The platform

Cut the blockboard or plywood to size. Round the sharp corners and bore sufficient ventilation holes.

The filler

Select a medium-hard density polyether foam.
Cut this oversize (to allow for thickness loss) with a bandsaw or sharp knife. If necessary, allow for the addition of dense walling.

The cover

Calculate the size to allow for twice the thickness of filler, platform and underlap. An undercover is not necessary as a PVC-coated knitted cover is used.

Marking out

Lay the platform on the reverse side of the cover and mark the position of the corners.

Sewing

Machine- or hand-stitch the corners. Cut off excessive waste material.

Fitting

Use adhesive, calico strips or 3M double-coated foam tape to position the filler on the platform.
Fix centre staples to position the cover. Ensure an even tension.
Staple the sides, leaving the corners free.

Corners

The material is easily cut and will stretch. Remove some surplus material to prevent a bulk of cover at the corner. Fold the remainder over and neatly staple it. Trim all round.

Other Furniture

A cavity foam seat

To produce a rounded-edge seat in cavity foam, cut away the bottom edge of the filler at an angle of 45°. (A polyether foam filler can be shaped on the top edge using an abrasive disc in a power unit.) Glue a calico strip to the top surface. Staple this to the underside of the platform and powder the joint. Fix a calico undercover, achieving an even curved edge with careful tensioning. Finally fit a woven cover material.

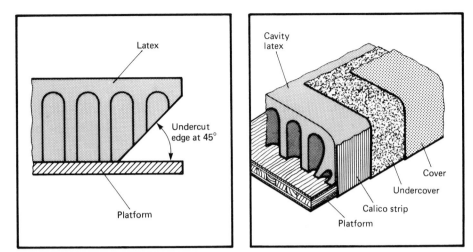

A Single Bed

Brightly painted steel tube is a popular material for bed-ends. They are usually attached to a framework made from angle-iron.
The frame can be used (angle downwards) to support a Pirelli webbing platform — five long and nine short lengths are recommended. The frame is strengthened by two cross-braces 150 mm deep, brazed to the framework.
The frame can be used (angle upwards) to support a perforated hardboard platform.

Glue a layer of hard-density polyether foam (up to 25 mm thick) to the hardboard.
Choose a mattress with a degree of hardness which suits you from the range of polyester foams, or use walled-cavity Latex foam.
Cover both the platform polyether foam and the mattress with a woven material which will allow the filler to 'breathe'.

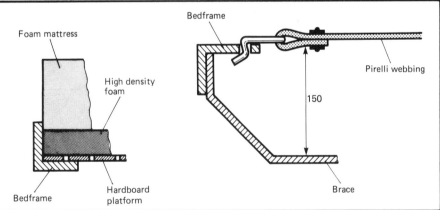

Chairs without frames

The first illustration in this section showed a French chair in the shape of a cube — it looked rather uncomfortable! The last illustration shows quite a different chair from the same year. In 1969 a team of Italian designers invented 'The Sacco' — a leather 'sack' containing more than ten million expanded-polystyrene granules, which adapt instantly to the shape of whoever sits in it. The manufacturer described it as having 'one thousand positions by day and one position by night — marvellously comfortable!' The photograph shows the cotton-canvas Habitat version — the 'Sagbag'.

Upholstery patterns

When covering new furniture make accurate paper patterns from which to cut the material.
When re-upholstering use the old cover material as a pattern.

Design – An Introduction

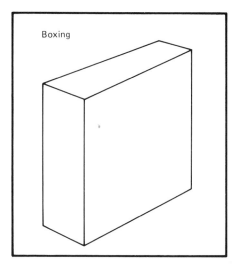

Boxing

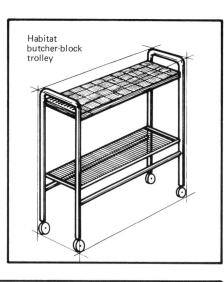

Habitat
butcher-block
trolley

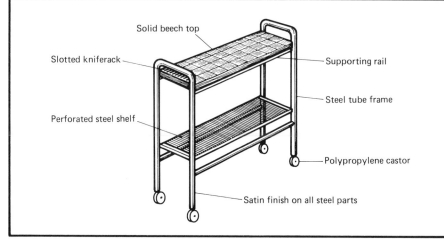

Solid beech top

Slotted kniferack

Supporting rail

Steel tube frame

Perforated steel shelf

Polypropylene castor

Satin finish on all steel parts

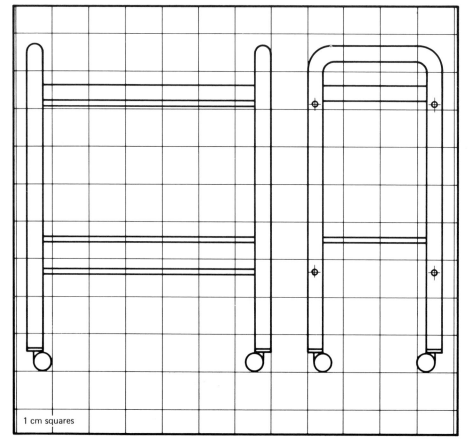

1 cm squares

Designing is a creative process. It is the visual and technical solution to a problem.

Solutions to design problems are only useful if other people can understand them. You must be able to communicate your ideas to someone else — using written notes, making drawings or constructing models. The emphasis in this section is on communicating by drawing.

Sketching

Freehand sketching is the quickest and most convenient method of drawing. To be effective the proportions of an object need to be reasonably accurate. The sketch need only be large enough to show essential detail.

The technique of **boxing** is useful. Imagine a cardboard box into which the object would be an exact fit. Draw the box outlines. Make any alterations necessary to make it look 'right'.

An example is shown for the Habitat butcher-block trolley.
Draw the box outline to indicate the proportions of length, height and width. Use the box outline as a guide to put in the main shape of the trolley.

The **labelled sketch** is a boxed drawing which gives a good impression of the finished design. The parts, materials and finishes are carefully labelled. It is *not* a working drawing but forms a good basis for discussion. Make a labelled sketch when your ideas for a solution to a design problem have been fully worked out.

A **scale drawing** is made to show the exact proportions. It could be a labelled sketch to a given scale — perhaps one-fifth (1:5) or one-tenth (1:10) of the full size.

Either make the drawing on *plain paper* and insert overall dimensions, or make the drawing on *squared paper*.

Scale drawings allow direct comparisons to be made visually between the proposed new design and any existing items — for example, between a new chair design and an existing table.

Projections

There are three main methods of making a formal drawing from which an object can be made. They consist of **orthographic, isometric** and **oblique projections**.

Orthographic

An orthographic drawing or projection describes the bookend using a number of views — elevations — of different faces. Not all the views are necessary.

The drawing can be made without the use of formal drawing instruments. You can use a ruler and pencil and draw on squared paper.

First angle projection is traditionally used in the UK and Europe. It is indicated by the symbol shown in the bottom right-hand corner.
The side view, in the direction of arrow A, is drawn on the *opposite* side of the front view. The plan view, in the direction of arrow B, is drawn *below* it.

Third angle projection would be indicated by the other symbol shown. The side view is then drawn on the *same* side of the front view. The plan view is drawn *above* it.

Isometric

This is a method of drawing an object in three dimensions. The front, end and top are shown in one drawing. This isometric drawing shows a Habitat single bed made from metal tube.
The isometric drawing is *not* a sketch and it does *not* use perspective. It is accurately dimensioned. Parallel edges of the bed ends and mattress are represented by parallel lines drawn along one of the 30° axes. Vertical edges are represented by vertical lines.
Use a ruler and pencil and draw on isometric grid paper if possible.

Oblique

This is an alternative method of drawing an object in three dimensions and is developed from orthographic drawing. One face has a true shape and size. The other faces are projected back at an angle of 45°.
When these faces are drawn to their full length it exaggerates the depth of the object (see bed A). Halve these measurements to produce a more realistic appearance (see bed B).
Use a ruler and pencil and draw on oblique grid paper if possible.

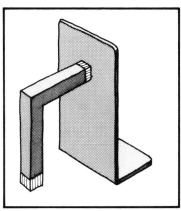

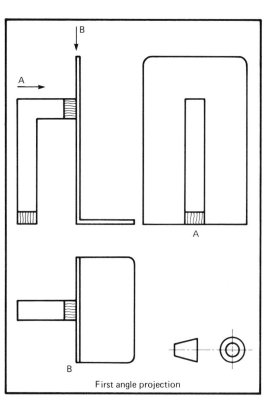

The structure and appearance of a bookend made from sheet steel and square tube with hardwood inserts

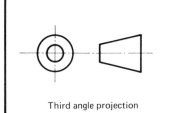

Third angle projection

First angle projection

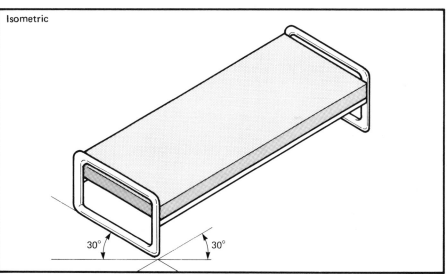

Isometric

30°   30°

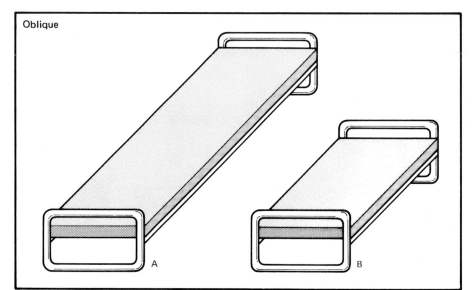

Oblique

A   B

Standard Practices

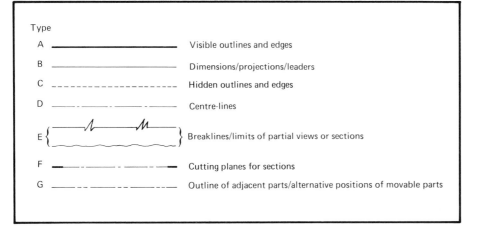

Type		
A	──────────	Visible outlines and edges
B	──────────	Dimensions/projections/leaders
C	----------	Hidden outlines and edges
D	─·─·─·─·─	Centre-lines
E	{ ⌐ ⌐ }	Breaklines/limits of partial views or sections
F	▬─·─·─▬	Cutting planes for sections
G	── ── ──	Outline of adjacent parts/alternative positions of movable parts

British standard 308

Standard practices for working drawings are set out in British Standard 308: *Engineering Drawing Practice*.
This Standard recommends that all drawings are made in a similar way. Then anyone who knows the 'language of drawing' can understand them. The Standard makes sure that a drawing can be 'read'.

All types of line should be sharp and dense so that they can be reproduced by machine. When drawing pens are used the 'thick' lines should be two or three times the thickness of the lines specified as 'thin'.
The third-angle orthographic projection of the bookend shows how some of these different types of line can be used.

Sections

A sectional view is normally used when the object contains hidden details which are difficult to show using broken lines. It represents the remainder of the object after part of it has been cut away.
Cut surfaces are shown by section lining (cross-hatching), which are thin parallel lines drawn at an angle of 45°. Adjacent parts are lined in opposite directions.

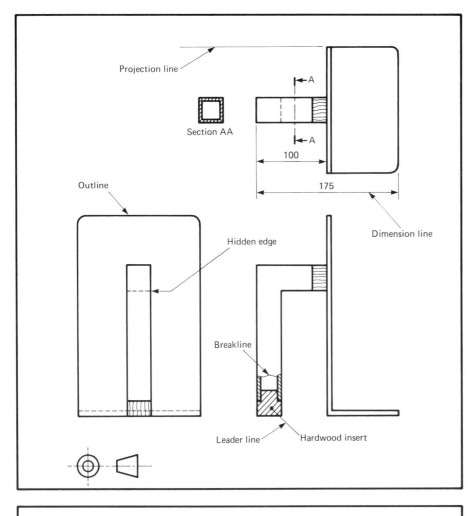

Projection line

Section AA

100

175

Dimension line

Outline

Hidden edge

Breakline

Leader line

Hardwood insert

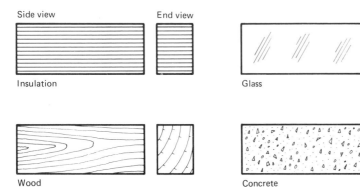

Side view · End view

Insulation

Glass

Wood

Concrete

Methods of representing four common materials are shown. They are not always used – for example, side grain is often omitted from wood components. End grain should indicate the preferred grain direction, if any.

All types of section lining can be omitted if this makes the drawing clearer and easier to 'read'.

Standard Practices (continued)

Screw threads

For **visible screw threads** the crests are shown by a continuous thick line (type A) and the roots by a continuous thin line (type B). On an end view the root is represented by a continuous thin line forming more than three-quarters of a circle.

For **hidden screw threads** the crests and roots are drawn as dashed lines (type C). The end view is represented in the same way.

For **threaded parts shown in section**, hatching extends to the line defining the crests. Where tapping-drill holes are shown a continuous thick line is used. The **limit of useful length** of a screw length is shown by a line at right angles to the length.

Other features

The drawing shows a side view of the bookend. The parts are drawn full-size but it fits into the small space by using irregular breaklines (type E). It is called an **interrupted** view.

The tube cross-section AA is drawn full-size. The line which shows the cutting plane for the section AA is a long chain, thickened at each end (type F) and labelled with capital letters.

The limit of the partial section is shown by an irregular **breakline.**

The section shows hatching spaced differently — larger parts have wider spacing — and a countersunk-head woodscrew.

Thick parallel lines show the shank diameter. A thin centre-line indicates its length.

A **welding symbol** indicates the type of weld used to join the square steel tube.

A **machining symbol** indicates the type of finish applied to a particular surface.

Interrupted views are commonly used for long objects. Tube is interrupted to show that it is hollow. For solid rod use conventional methods (type E).

Enlarged features are used when a drawing is so small that details of a particulars feature either cannot be shown or cannot be dimensioned clearly. The feature is framed or encircled and identified with a capital letter. The feature is redrawn to a stated scale and identified by the letter.

When **repeated features** such as holes, bolts, and rivets are needed in a regular pattern, the number and position may be shown by their centre-lines only (type D).

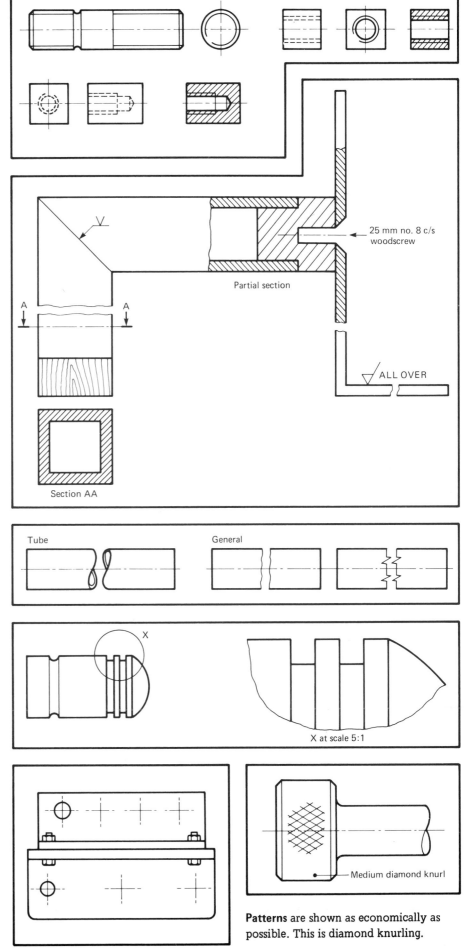

25 mm no. 8 c/s woodscrew

Partial section

ALL OVER

Section AA

Tube   General

X at scale 5:1

Medium diamond knurl

Patterns are shown as economically as possible. This is diamond knurling.

Standard Practices (continued)

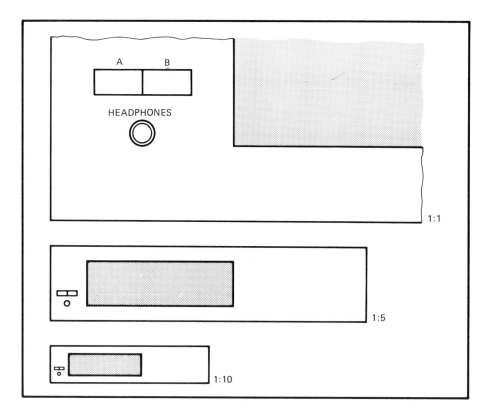

1:1

1:5

1:10

The scale is the length of part of an object as represented on a drawing, divided by the real length on the object itself. Scale is therefore a *ratio*.

All formal drawings — those to be used as working drawings — should be drawn to a definite scale. The chosen scale is stated in the drawing title block where it can easily be 'read'. Scale drawings can be accurately reduced or enlarged by reprographic processes.
When convenient a drawing should be made full-size (scale 1:1). Some reduction scales are half full-size (1:2), one-fifth full-size (1:5) and one-tenth full-size (1:10). Some enlargement scales are 2:1, 5:1 and 10:1.

The effect of scale is shown on the drawings of the Sony stereo receiver.

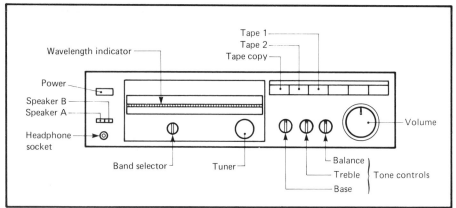

Labels and Leaders

Labelling is a useful addition to a small drawing. Use it to indicate parts and functions of an object.

Leaders are the thin lines used for labelling.
Leaders ending on a line must be arrowed. Those ending on the surface of the part end in a dot.
Leader lines should not cross each other.

Drawing layout

The scale drawing of the bookend uses many of the standard practices described in the previous pages.
Note the information contained within the **title block**.
Notice also the positions of dimensions and alternative methods of dimensioning.

Dimensioning

The main purpose of dimensioning is to make the manufacture of an object possible.
All the necessary measurements must be included and clearly numbered.
Overall dimensions must be stated and measurements can be 'taken off' full-size working drawings.
Dimension and limit lines are thin lines.
Arrow heads must be neat and sharp.
There must be ample space between the object outline and the dimension line for the number to be inserted.

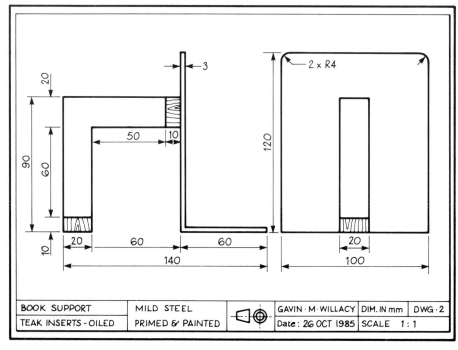

| BOOK SUPPORT | MILD STEEL | | GAVIN · M · WILLACY | DIM. IN mm | DWG · 2 |
| TEAK INSERTS - OILED | PRIMED & PAINTED | | Date: 26 OCT 1985 | SCALE 1 : 1 | |

Standard Practices (continued)

Lettering

The efficiency and appearance of a formal drawing will be spoiled if written dimensions, title blocks and notes are badly done.
Freehand lettering can be drawn clearly and can be easy to read. But if you have a really shaky hand, use a stencil!

For titles on paper sizes A1, A2 and A3 letters should be not less than 7 mm. On paper size A4 it is 5 mm.
Dimensions and notes — on all paper sizes — should not be less than 2.5 mm high. The spacing between lines of lettering should not be less than half the height of the letters themselves.
Underlining is not recommended. To emphasize a note, make it bigger.

'Letraset' is one make of instant lettering which is rubbed down on to the drawing surface. There are more than five hundred different styles available, one of which **Isonorm 3098** is the standard for drawings.
Use it for presentation drawings, especially in the larger sizes which are difficult to letter freehand.
Sizes available: 2.5, 3.5, 5, 7, 10, 14 mm.

Tone

Letratone and **Instantex** are patterned, self-adhesive film. They were used to make the line drawing of a speedway rider more interesting.

Templates

My catalogue contains details of more than one hundred plastic templates which help draughtsmen to produce precise drawings. Many of them have specialist uses — they include symbols for electronic data-processing, plumbing fixtures and standardized welding symbols.
The simplest templates have circles, squares and triangles. Each contains 34 shapes from 2 to 35 mm in 1 mm increments.
Two sets of templates are of special value:

1. a set of three or four French curves containing most curves needed
2. a set of ten ellipse templates with angles from 15° to 60°.

Each ellipse template contains: sizes 2 mm to 15 mm in 1 mm increments, 16, 18, 20, 22, 24, 25 and 28 mm, as well as 30 mm to 50 mm in 5 mm increments — a choice of 260 ellipses!

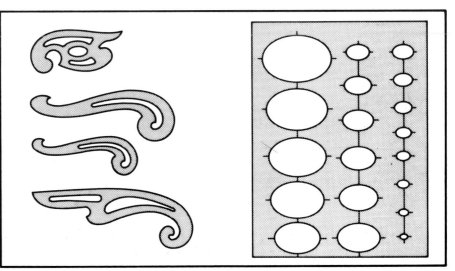

Sketching

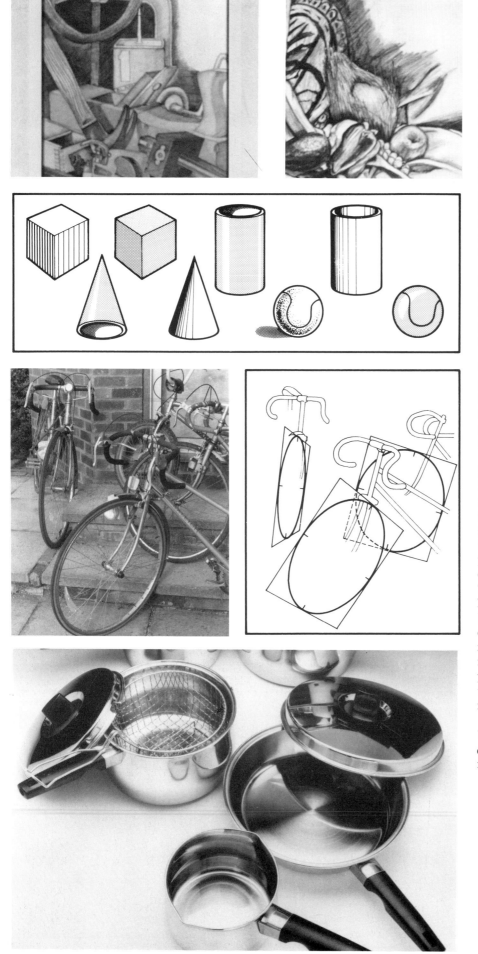

A sketch is an informal drawing which can be done quickly either to explain an idea to someone else or to record information for your own use. If you find sketching difficult, practice will help you to improve. The only equipment needed is a soft pencil (2B or 3B). This will enable you to produce lines which vary in thickness and blackness.

Your art teacher will often have a still-life group set up which will help you to observe the differences in size and shape between objects.
Note the differences between hard and soft materials, and between rough and smooth surfaces. Notice also the ways in which some materials reflect light.

Many still-life objects are based on three-dimensional geometric shapes — cubes, cylinders, cones and spheres. For example, balls and fruit are based on the sphere.

Try to show the differences without using colour. Outlines will indicate the solidity, but **tone** is used for emphasis. Use a torch light to show how the nearest surface reflects most light — then exaggerate the darkest parts in your sketch.

Ellipses are circles seen in perspective. They are not easy to draw freehand.
A circle fits inside a square and touches the centre-points of all four sides. If the square is first drawn in perspective, *then* the shape of the ellipse can be more easily plotted. The ellipse also touches the centre-points of all four sides.
The photograph shows bicycles which have identical wheels. They look different because different amounts of each wheel can be seen — each ellipse has a different minor axis. (An ellipse has two axes. The major axis is a line through the longest part, and the minor axis is a line through the narrowest part. Axes are at right-angles to each other.)

Use a group of circular or cylindrical objects, such as pans and lids to practise freehand drawing of ellipses.

Sketching (continued)

The bookend is shown in use by making a freehand line drawing. It is a formal sketch.

A line drawing such as this could be made more realistic by the addition of **texture** and **pattern**.

Presentation drawings of a final design can be finished in 'Letratone'. The transparent sheets are laid over the line drawing and cut with a sharp stencil knife. The bits required are then rubbed down.

Use lines and dots to give the effect of reflective metal.

The samples below show just a few of the plain, graduated and variable sheets available.

Sheets of perspective lines and concentric circles can be used to indicate both shape and surface finish.

The eight patterns and textures show bricks, concrete, softwood, hessian, tile, sand, basketweave and striations. These have been selected from a range of more than five hundred different designs.

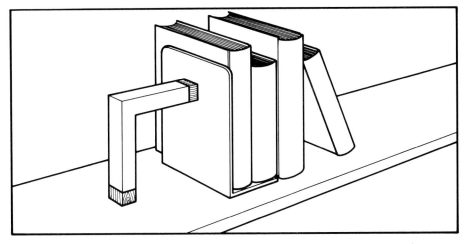

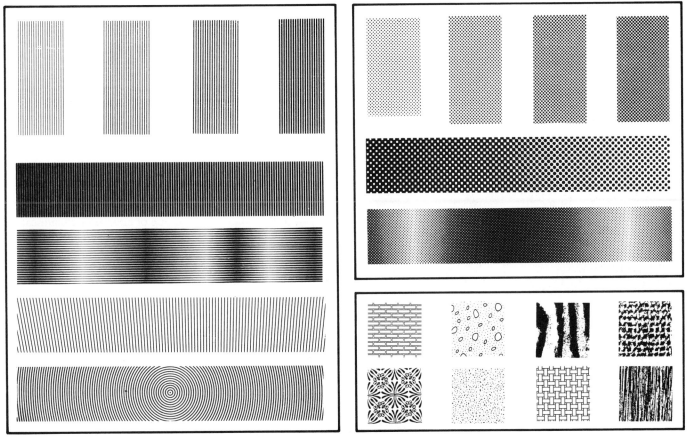

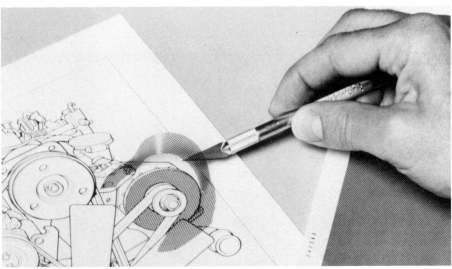

Perspective Views

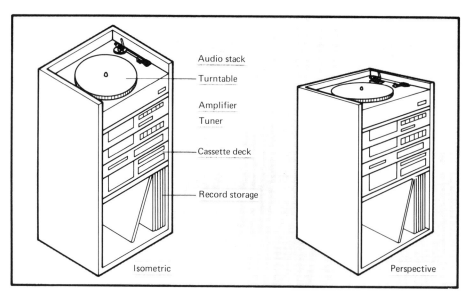

Audio stack
— Turntable

Amplifier
Tuner

— Cassette deck

— Record storage

Isometric   Perspective

The Sony audio stack consists of a turntable, amplifier, tuner, cassette deck and record storage.
The turntable on the isometric sketch seems to stick up in the air. This is because the lines are drawn parallel to each other.
The **perspective** sketch of the same audio stack looks more natural because the lines are made to converge at **vanishing points**, fixed on a line representing **eye level**.

The nearest corner of the object coincides with a vertical line called the **centre of vision**. The vanishing points need not be the same distance from the centre of vision.

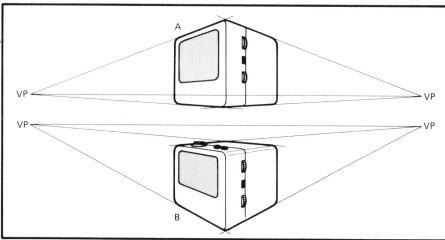

A

VP   VP

VP   VP

B

The Sony cube radio is drawn with *two* vanishing points at equal distances from the centre of vision. This method is called two-point perspective.
Drawing A shows most of the cube radio *above* eye level, so the top cannot be seen. This makes the radio look larger and more important than it really is, and only two sides are visible. Use this method to draw objects which are normally taller than yourself, such as buildings.
Drawing B shows all the cube radio *below* eye level. Now the top can be seen. This gives a more normal view, as it would usually be seen on a bedside table. Three sides are visible.

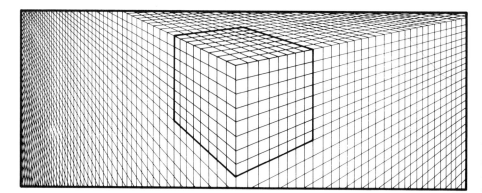

The cube radio can be drawn using one vanishing point. This method is called **one-point perspective**. One face is shown accurately, as in oblique projection, and receding lines converge on one vanishing point. Only two sides are visible.

The drawing shows a cube drawn in two-point perspective with unequal vanishing points. Each surface is divided into perspective squares to form a grid. Make a grid like this — but larger — to use as an underlay to guide you when making drawings in two-point perspective.

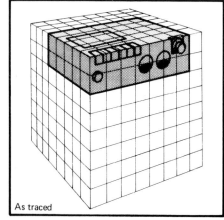

As traced

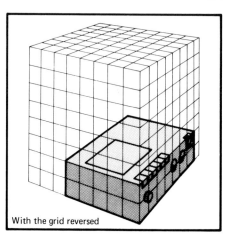

With the grid reversed

The grid is shown in use when making a perspective sketch of a cassette-recorder. One drawing emphasizes the front. The same object drawn on the reversed grid gives a different emphasis. It picks out different features.

Choose the perspective view with care.

Room Setting

The way in which people live is reflected in their home furnishings and how these are arranged.

It is not necessary to be wealthy to achieve and maintain living conditions whick work well and look good. Secondhand furniture can be reconditioned — stripped pine shows attractive natural grain, and uninteresting wood can be painted to fit into a scheme of decoration.

Wood furniture is particularly simple to make.

For example, fifty years ago Gerrit Rietveld designed some crate furniture — elegant and efficient chairs, tables and storage units, simply nailed together from re-used wood and painted. Today, cheap units can be purchased for quick home assembly.

Attractive fabric offcuts can be used for scatter cushions and walls emulsioned with subtle colours.

If the basics are carefully chosen, money may be available to spend on one or two well-designed and distinguished pieces of furniture and equipment. In a room which is simply furnished and decorated, 'high-tech' products — such as the OMK tractor stool or the OMK black-framed plate-glass table and black-metal table lamp — may look quite stunning.

Designing a Study Bedroom

If you are able to design or re-design your own room, begin with an outline plan, drawn to scale. Draw a plan view of each item of furniture to the same scale, placed anywhere in the room.

The drawings show plans of a study bedroom. A close look at plan A shows that the units are badly arranged. For example, the bookcase and writing desk are too far apart, and there is wasted space.

Plan B shows the same study with the same furniture arranged or 'zoned' according to its function. There is no wasted space and the unused central floor area makes the room seem larger.

The items illustrated — except the television — are based on the minimum recommendations for a study bedroom contained in the booklet *Space in the Home* (HMSO).

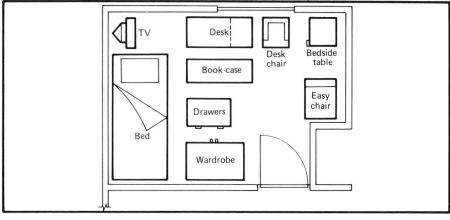

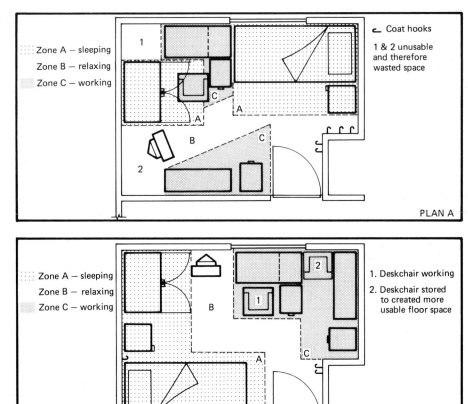

Room Setting (continued)

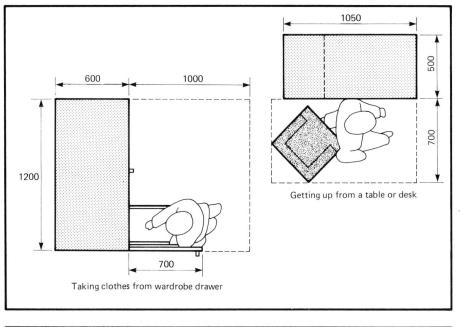

600   1000

1200

700

Taking clothes from wardrobe drawer

1050

500

700

Getting up from a table or desk

The use of space in modern houses and flats must be carefully planned to avoid clutter and congestion. The sizes and positions of items of furniture are equally important.

Space in the home shows clearly the spaces needed to do jobs like preparing food and disposing of refuse. These will help you to plan your own rooms.

To summarize:

1. Consider the function(s) of a room.
2. When possible, create 'zones of activity'.
3. Position the furniture using a scale plan.

It can be useful to make drawings of your rooms in *one-point perspective*. Draw a rectangle, in the correct proportions, to represent one wall of the room. Next draw on it an eye-level horizontal line and a vertical centre-of-vision line.
The point at which these lines cross is called the vanishing point. All the lines at right-angles to the wall will go to the vanishing point.

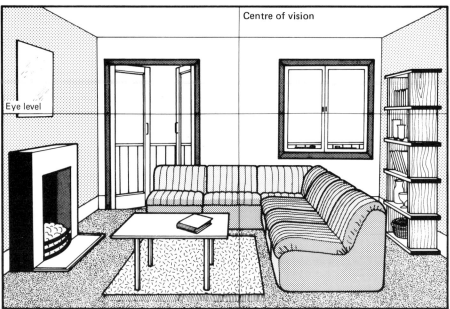

Centre of vision

Eye level

The example shows a sitting room of a flat. There is a fireplace and framed print on one wall and a bookcase on the opposite wall. The window in the end wall is partly covered by a blind, and the French window opens up to a balcony. A coffee table rests on a fringed rug which fits between comfortable modular seating. All lines at right-angles to the end wall converge on the vanishing point.

Another drawing shows the study bedroom plan using one-point perspective. The drawing is made looking from the entrance of the room, so that the centre-of-vision is not central to the room.

Suggested design method

1. Draw your own empty room in one-point perspective.
2. Use overlay sheets of tracing paper to work out the positions and shapes of furniture.
3. Produce a final black line drawing.
4. Print this on a sheet of OHP transparent film.
5. Use LetraVision self-adhesive film, coloured markers, PVA or acrylic paints to add suggested colour schemes.

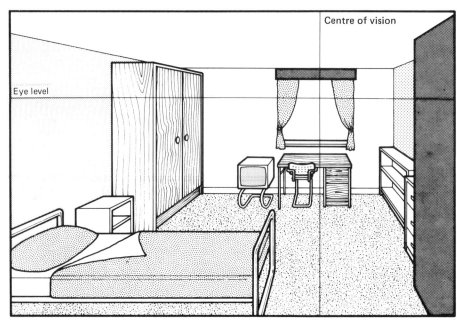

Centre of vision

Eye level

Time taken to do this will help you to avoid making expensive mistakes.

Working Surfaces and Walls

Horizontal surfaces such as floors, table tops, seats and shelves are **working surfaces.** Choose with care the materials for working surfaces to ensure that they do their jobs well.

Each of the materials illustrated is available in a wide range of colours with patterns and textures to satisfy individual needs.

Carpet

This is the most expensive item in most rooms. It is available in grades to suit all needs. A wool and nylon mix is recommended.

Cork

This is a warm, quiet floor covering used in bathrooms. It can also be used as a vertical pinboard.

Wood

It is basically reddish-brown or cream in colour, with various grain markings. Used for furniture and shelving.

Vinyl

This is a hard-wearing seating material which may look like leather. It is easily cleaned.

Plastics laminate

This is a heat- and scratch-resistant surface for table tops. It is available with multi-coloured patterns.

The strips of 'cane' shown comes from 'The Natural Collection', and the beaten copper from 'The Metallic Range'. Both are made by Formica.

Vertical surfaces are used both to insulate and to decorate. They can be made up into screens which divide room spaces.

Hessian

This has a rough, textured surface which will help to hide irregular plasterwork. It is made in many colours.

Wallpaper

Vinyl papers are washable and suited to the damp conditions of bathrooms and kitchens.

Glass

Glass is available in many textures and patterns for use in doors, windows and screens. There is a limited colour range.

Ceramic tiles

Tiles are used in kitchens for hygienic reasons and in bathrooms because they protect walls from condensation.

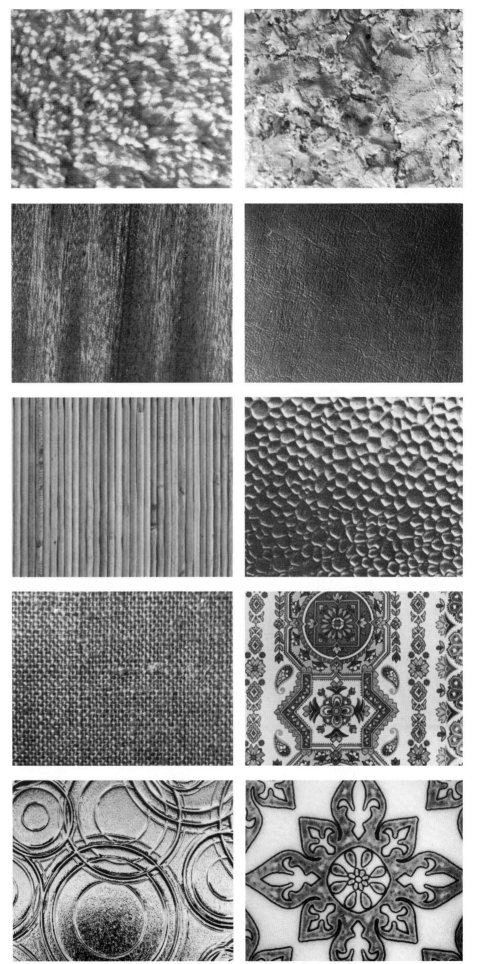

Furniture to Fit People

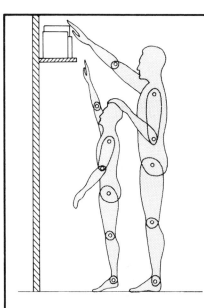

You should consider smaller people, so use the fifth-percentile figure. Ninety-five per cent of the population can then reach it.

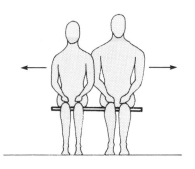

You should consider larger people, so use the ninety-fifth percentile figure. Then there is room on it for two people from 95 per cent of the population.

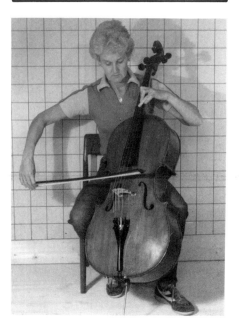

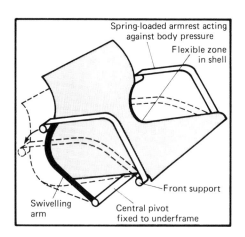

Spring-loaded armrest acting against body pressure
Flexible zone in shell
Swivelling arm
Central pivot fixed to underframe
Front support

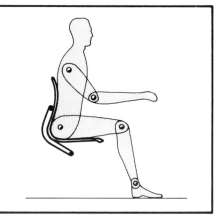

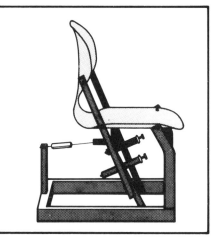

Most people buy furniture ready-made in the same way that a dress or jacket is bought — 'off the peg'. To have a suit 'made to measure' is expensive as it requires individual measurements to be made and a unique pattern to be cut. To have furniture 'made to measure' could also be expensive.

But furniture is *not* made to fit the 'average man' — measurements that relate to the *fiftieth percentile* of the population. If it was a chair it would either be too high or too low for a large number of the population. Instead designers try to make furniture to fit people between the *fifth and ninety-fifth percentiles*. In this way only 10 per cent of the population is inconvenienced!

Two examples are shown, fixing the height of a shelf and fixing the width of a double seat.

These measurements of the body are used to make up 'anthropometric data'. Such data have been collected ever since a nineteenth-century Englishman called Edward Muybridge made photographic sequences of men and women in action. The study of spaces needed for food preparation, sleeping, getting dressed, etc., has been useful in setting minimum needs for *Space in the Home*.
To collect your own data, take photographs against a 100 mm square grid.

The measurements of body movement are used to make up **ergonomic data**. The designer can then make use of such data to make up models, prototypes and testing jigs.
The illustrations show some of the stages in designing the Ergonom 'FS-Line' chair.
The annotated sketch shows the features which the designer wishes to use.
A hinged figure (one of a series) is used to assess the effects of body position on the seat.
A testing jig is fitted with a prototype seat shell to measure the actual effects of body position. These include inclination of seat and back rest, the amount of flexibility in the seat, and the strength of the spring-loaded armrest.
Using the test information, the designer modifies the design so that the finished chair can go into mass production.

Design Processes

All items of furniture must be functional and should be carefully positioned in a room. New furniture should be considered in relation to the style of decoration and the existing furniture. It must do its job and look 'right'.

The 'Spaghetti' armchair is an Italian design by Belotti. It is likely that the chair would be out of place in the Georgian room-setting shown. Would the chair have to be a copy of a chair of that period for it to harmonize?

The list below suggests a number of design processes. Not all of them are used when preparing a design. The design outlines on pages 179–183 show how and when some of these processes are used.

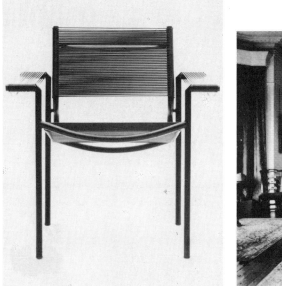 

Written notes stating the function(s) of the end product	Specification
Data collected by measuring existing items of a similar kind and consulting manufacturer's catalogues	Research
Sketch notes which are worked into a labelled drawing indicating the materials and finishes to be used	Ideas
Use a suitable scale and choose the necessary number of views. Check proportions and make changes quickly on a tracing paper overlay	Scale Drawings
Select easily worked materials such as Balsa, card, paper, etc., joined by pins, glue and tape. Take measurements from the scale drawing	Models
A full-size drawing on hardboard is a check on proportions before constructing a mock-up in cheap or waste materials for testing. This technique is often used in chair making	Mock-up
Study tests on mock-up and make necessary adjustments. Survey materials available — make a choice, and 'cost' the product	Analysis
Prepare a full-size (scale 1:1) drawing where convenient. Make out a cutting list of material required	Working Drawing
Make up sample joints to check strength and appearance. Make necessary alterations on an overlay. For group work design a flow chart	Construction
Construct and finish the product. Note that a machine-made product prototype may be constructed by hand methods	Prototype
Do this under test or normal working conditions. Report on relative success of construction, appearance and finish in relation to the original specification	Testing-report

Design Processes (continued)

Scale models

Prepare scale drawings and use them as working drawings in the manufacture of scale models. Make models from wire (to represent tubing), balsa wood (to represent wood) and cardboard (to represent sheet metal).
Common scales for models are one-fifth full-size (scale 1:5) and one-tenth full-size (scale 1:10).

Working drawings

The scale drawings of a large item of furniture will include important overall dimensions. Full-size details of joints and fittings should be added to this to produce a drawing from which the table can be made.

Fittings

Large items of furniture are often designed so that they pack flat for easy carriage and are then assembled using KD (knock-down) or QA (quick-assembly) fittings. These include wood to metal dowels, frame connectors and tee nuts as shown on page 54.
These fittings are usually concealed or designed so that they are unobtrusive. 'Kee Klamps' are designed to join tube with an outside diameter from 13.5 to 60.3 mm. Cast in either malleable iron or aluminium and fixed by a socket set screw, they give great strength to constructions. They are practical, economic, simple and reliable, but *not* unobtrusive. However, they can be painted to match the framework, or be ready-finished with an epoxy coating or chrome-plated.

Cutting list

A cutting list is an important checklist of all the materials and fittings to be used. Attach it to the working drawing.
The cutting list shown is for the table shown in the flowchart (left).

Construction

A large item of furniture such as a table may be made by a group of people working as a team. A flowchart indicates the work to be done on each component. This helps the practical work to be understood and coordinated.
The system works best where a series of identical items has to be made.

Part or item	Number off	Length	Width	Thickness	Material
Top	1	1800	1000	25	Chipboard
Edging strip	2	1850	30	19	White deal
	2	1050	30	19	White deal
Long rail	1				
Short rails	2	800	100	37	White deal
Legs	4	900	25	25	Mild steel tube
Stoppers	4				Black polypropylene to fit tube
Fittings	4	100	09		Coach bolts
	4	45	32	14G	Shrinkage plates

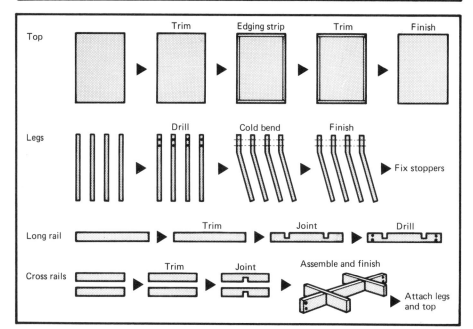

Design Study 1

'Bob' is a Habitat folding chair made in epoxy-coated metal. It is designed to be sat on for a short length of time and will fold up into a small space. It is ideal as a kitchen chair.

The 'GS 40/4' is a Seid International stacking chair made in chromed steel with seat and back panels of either steel or plywood. It is designed for use in halls. These are just two examples of the hundreds of different designs available in the form of an upright or activity chair. Apart from differences in style and materials, the needs of the sitters are different. It is possible to use the same chair for dining or for working at a sewing machine — but analysis of the sitting movements would produce different data and should produce different designs.

Make use of known anthropometric data. Pressure on the skin between the buttocks and a hard platform may be 40 pounds per square inch (psi), inches away it may only be 4 psi. Sitting in one position for a long time interferes with blood circulation, is painful and may cause numbness. First spread the body weight more evenly using proper padding.

Make use of known ergonomic data. Ensure that the space on and around the seat is large enough for the sitter to frequently change the sitting position. The sitter is always active, adjusting to achieve a compromise between two needs — stability and variety.

The 'Vertebra' chair by Ambasz and Piretti makes the fullest use of ergonomic and anthropometric data. Designed especially for use at a keyboard, it fully supports the operator but the seat and back move independently of each other so that comfortable positions can always be achieved.

Steel tube is ideal for upright seating. The 'OMSTAK' chair on the left in the group photograph has a perforated steel platform and backrest. Both are curved to give correct support to the sitter and strength to the construction. The back is at the recommended rake of about 105°.

The 'OMK T8 tractor stool' in the centre is a high seat with rubbered footrests at the recommended distance from the seat. It is designed for short-stay sitters.

The 'OMK dining chair' on the right is firmly padded. The curved front edge and space at the back allow the sitter to lean forward in comfort, but there is little back support.

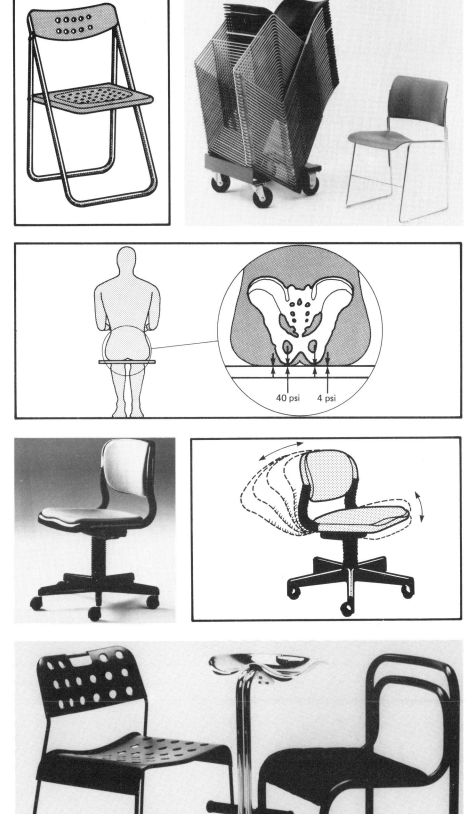

40 psi   4 psi

Design Study 1 (continued)

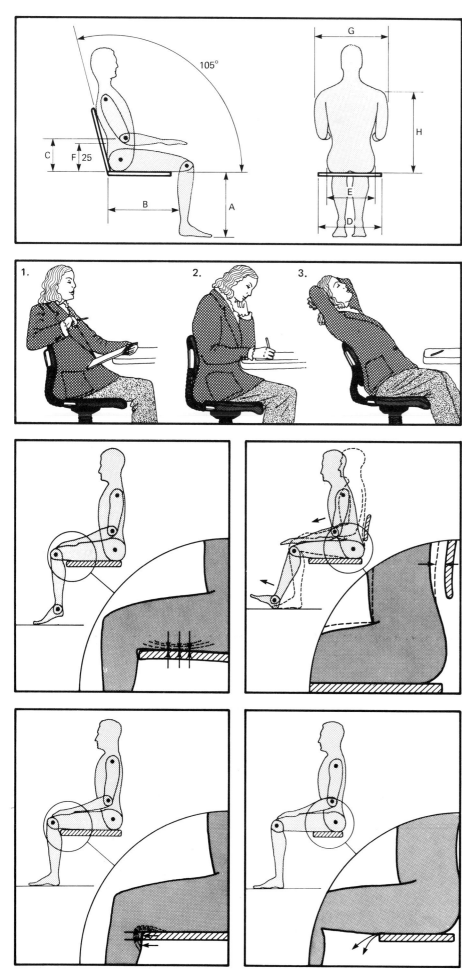

The full-size drawing

Full-size drawings are not only used for
final working drawings. Make full-size
drawings, based on known data, as soon
as your sketch ideas have been developed.
These drawings will help you to make
revisions to the appearance of the chair
and to show details of the construction.
Constructional detail is particularly
important if the chair is to have a
mechanical system. The 'vertebra' chair
is shown when the sitter is:

1. in the normal upright position
2. in a writing position – the seat and
   back tilt forward 6°
3. stretching to relax muscular tension.

A **mock-up** or **prototype** of the design
should be made at this stage so that
estimated sizes can be properly tested.
For example, you may have to make
extra allowances for clothes and shoes
which are not in the data.

Determine the following

If the seat platform is too high the thighs
will be compressed and blood circulation
will be restricted. If soles do not rest on
the floor then the person loses stability.

If the seat is too low the legs are
extended, the feet cannot provide
stability and the back moves away from
the backrest. This is uncomfortable.
A tall person is better on a low seat than
a small person on a high seat.

If the seat is too deep the front edge
presses behind the knees. This causes
discomfort because blood circulation is
restricted. The sitter eases this by moving
forward but then loses back support.
Other muscles make up for this but
eventually they become tired and back
pain occurs.

If the seat is too shallow there is no
support for the lower thighs and the
sitter has the sensation of sliding off the
front of the chair.

The **backrest** is the most difficult to
assess – experts cannot agree. It should
be curved to fit the curvature of the spine
and should have a space below it to
accommodate the buttocks.
The **armrest** should be between 180 and
250 mm above the seat platform.
Cushioning will distribute the pressure
felt by the sitter. A 15 mm layer of dense
foam and a 35 mm covering of
medium-density filler is a successful
combination.

Design Study 2

Design a dining table to accommodate four adults

There doesn't seem to be much of a problem to solve. It is easy to assess how much room people take up when eating, and most dining tables are about the same height. But consider the room in which the table will be used – how large or small *can* the table be? What size *should* the table be?

Make use of known ergonomic data.
The **minimum space** is that which gives shared access to seats. It is a system used in fast-food restaurants. The eating space will be small and food may be served from a sideboard or trolley.
The **maximum space** may be far too big for passing food to each other and for holding a good conversation.
The **optimum space** is the best space. Begin with known or discovered ergonomic data regarding place settings and shared areas of access on the table.

Measure the floor space into which the table must fit and calculate the amount of access space available. This floor space has to be shared by the sitting zone and the circulation zone as illustrated. (If only the minimum space is available, then informal meals are likely to be most successful.)

Ideas

Sketches should be made and either discarded or developed until the stage at which a labelled drawing can be produced.
The main consideration will be the support for the table which must be high enough to allow knee room. Apart from the traditional 'leg at each corner' solution, consider:

1. trestles
2. pedestal
3. framework constructions.

Analysis

Analyse the materials available. The table support may use metal bar or tube, but wood, glass or GRP must be considered.

Metal table tops are ideal outdoors but cold and noisy when used inside the house.
Use *wood* for its warmth and interesting grain and colour.
Use *glass* for its transparency – make the table support interesting to look at.
Use GRP for its colour, texture or pattern which can be included in the design.

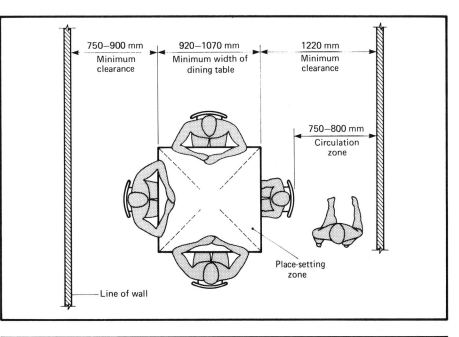

750–900 mm Minimum clearance

920–1070 mm Minimum width of dining table

1220 mm Minimum clearance

750–800 mm Circulation zone

Place-setting zone

Line of wall

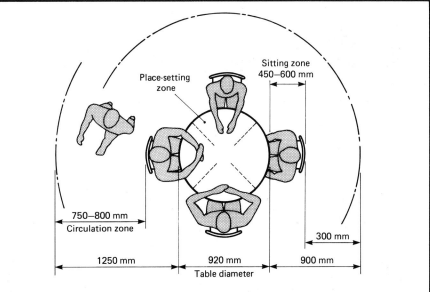

Sitting zone 450–600 mm

Place-setting zone

750–800 mm Circulation zone

300 mm

1250 mm

920 mm Table diameter

900 mm

Design Study 3

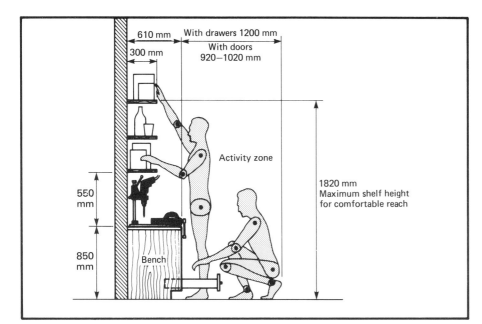

610 mm
300 mm
With drawers 1200 mm
With doors 920–1020 mm

Activity zone

1820 mm
Maximum shelf height for comfortable reach

550 mm

850 mm

Bench

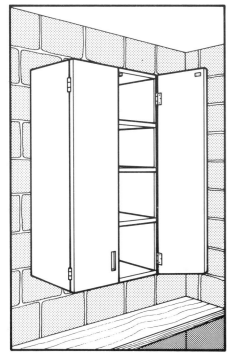

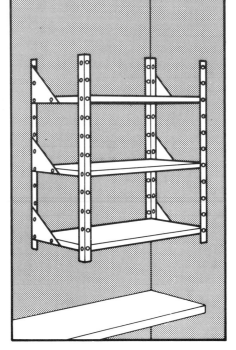

Design a tool container

The container is to hold general metalworking and motor-maintenance tools. It must contain at least one shelf. Devise a method of securing the container to a wall.

Location

Make use of ergonomic data as background information. The illustration is based on data collected for the planning of kitchen spaces, but it can be adapted for use in a workshop or in a garage.

It shows that a workbench fitted with doors uses *less* space than a bench fitted with drawers. The container might be fitted on the wall space above the bench. We have seen how a low fixing will mean that shelves can be reached by the majority of people. But, if the workshop equipment included a pillar drill attachment for a power unit, the bottom shelf would have to be higher (550 mm) than the recommended height (450 mm) above the bench top. An extra allowance of 100 mm may also be needed for a striplight fitted beneath the bottom shelf.

Research

Collect together a selection of common metalworking tools used in the home and the standard tools needed for routine car maintenance.

If these are measured you can calculate the *minimum* size of the container and the *minimum* weight it must be able to bear. You can also get an idea about the shape of the container and decide how much protection the tools need to prevent them from rusting and damage.

Ideas

A conventional approach to the design problem would produce a closed cupboard which would protect the tools. The disadvantage is that an open door at shelf-height could be dangerous. Sliding doors would reduce the effective shelf width.

A more modern approach to the design problem might be to take a materials approach. Open shelving would be the simplest solution. This could be constructed with tough galvanized metal. Holes in the uprights would allow a variety of shelf positions. As such a unit usually rests on the floor, flat metal fillets could be used at the side to give stability to the construction when it is hung from a wall.

Design Study 3 (continued)

Safety

Workshop safety can be increased in different ways. The open-shelf solution shown does not have doors which can be a hazard.

Increase the general light on the working surface by fixing a long fluorescent light beneath the bottom shelf. The light shown is 600 mm long and has a plastic diffuser.
Use one or two clip-on lights to give directional light for specific jobs. The light shown will fix to any part of the shelf unit.

Wall fixing

There are three common types of wall — **solid** (brick or breezeblock), **soft cellular** (building block) and **hollow** (plasterboard on battens).

If the garage or workshop wall is hollow, locate the battens and secure the container unit with woodscrews.
If the wall is of brick or breezeblock, screw into a heavy-duty plastics plug inserted into the brick. Do not plug into the softer mortar.
For the Plasplug shown, bore the hole with a no. 14 masonry drill and insert a no. 10, 12 or 14 steel screw.
If the wall is of a soft cellular building block, use a threaded plastics plug. Insert a locking pin to prevent movement. For the Plasplug shown, bore a hole with a no. 14 masonry drill and insert a no. 8 steel screw.

Prototype

The drawing shows one simple solution to the storage problem. Three manufactured board shelves are fixed to perforated steel sheet sides with woodscrews. The container is screwed to the wall using Plasplugs. The sides are protected by paint and the shelves finished with polyurethane varnish.
Special storage is needed for small items and the tools which could easily be damaged or mislaid on a shelf. This is provided by a plastics-coated wire grid either attached to the wall or clipped to the metal sides.
Straight, curved or ring hooks will hold most items.
A wire basket can also be attached to complete the system.

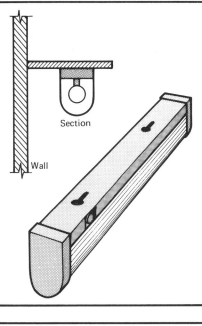

Section

Wall

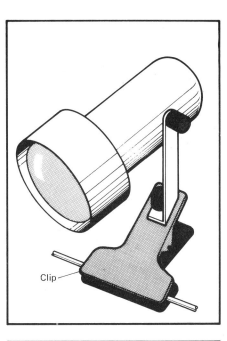

Clip

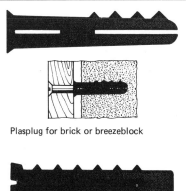

Plasplug for brick or breezeblock

Plasplug for soft cellular building block

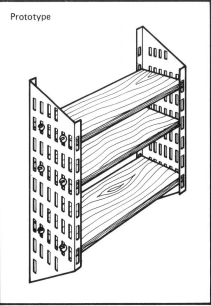

Prototype

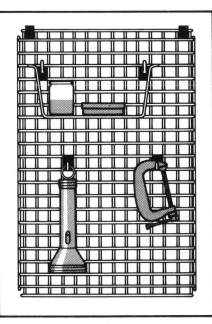

Hooks for use on wire grid

Project Work – An Introduction

Students intending to sit craft examinations with some of the GCE, CSE and GCSE Boards know that they have to produce a project, study or topic. The instructions in the syllabus usually state that the project must be a *personal* study of some part of a craft-based subject which interests the student.

The student is expected to do research, and illustrate the project using drawings or photographs, rather than simply copy information from a textbook.

Choosing a subject

You must first decide on the subject area. From that area choose a topic which interests you and which you would like to study in some detail.

Discuss your choice with your teacher. The teacher may eventually be responsible for marking the work, and his or her advice is well worth taking.

A worthwhile study can be prepared and presented successfully if you:

1. organize yourself to study – the following pages offer advice
2. collect information in the form of facts and opinions
3. add your own judgements and comments to the work to make the study 'personal'.

Here are some typical subject areas from which more detailed studies may be selected:

Surface finishes	Hand tools
Model-making	Adhesives
Musical instruments	Sailing craft
Sports equipment	Village crafts
The furniture industry	Furniture history
A local craftsman	Testing materials
Antiques	Leadwork
Building construction	Heat-treatment
Origins of alloys	Council of Industrial Design

Study outline

Decide on the topic you wish to study and discuss the details with your teacher.

List the possible contents and divide these up into suitable chapters.

Then try to assess the amount of written work and the number of illustrations that will be needed.

The time and effort spent in preparing this outline will be worth while. Such a plan will prevent you from writing too much.

Example

Subject area	– Hand tools
Probable title	– G-cramps
Chapter 1	– Development of holding tools (AD50–1900)
Chapter 2	– Types of G-cramp available
Chapter 3	– Method of manufacture
Chapter 4	– Specific uses of G-cramps

A Plan of Work

A work plan is essential if your study is to be complete before the handing-in date. Work not planned properly is often hurried in the final weeks and days, so that the quality of presentation, if not the content, is below standard.

Allow time to:

1. read books and make notes
2. order books through the library service
3. write to and collect replies from firms and study the information received
4. plan visits to workshops, factories or museums
5. take, develop and print photographs and enlargements
6. prepare line drawings
7. carry out practical tests
8. add page and illustration numbers, title, contents and bibliography pages.

The cost

It is important to assess the **cost** of preparing and presenting your study. If you have more than one study to prepare it may be necessary to limit, for example, the number of photographs you intend to use.
Major items of expenditure can be listed under the following headings:

1. writing and drawing materials
2. photographs
3. travel, telephone and postage.

Letter writing

You may need to write to manufacturing firms for information about their products or to ask if you can visit a factory to see a manufacturing process. It is vital that this letter be properly prepared and, if possible, typewritten. This makes it easy for the firm to read and enables you to have a carbon copy. Many firms are willing to help students with their work and send brochures at their own expense. It is rarely necessary to send a stamped addressed envelope (which would invariably be the wrong size). A letter of thanks for their advice and information is appreciated by them.

Your letter of enquiry must include:

1. your address
2. the date
3. the name of the firm and its address
4. a greeting (e.g. 'Dear Sir')
5. the letter (introduce yourself and state the purpose of your enquiry. Make the enquiry specific.)
6. an ending (e.g. Yours faithfully)
7. your signature and your name.

```
                                        109 Ashby Road
                                        St Albans
                                        Hertfordshire
                                        AL 3 4HB

                                        19 July 1986

The Press Officer
Spear and Jackson (Tools) Limited
Parkhill Works
Bernard Road
SHEFFIELD S2 5BQ

Dear Sir

      As part of my coursework for the CSE examination in Craft
and Design I have decided to make a study of files and filing.

      I use your 'Spearfile' files in the school workshop so I
know that you manufacture several types.

      I would be grateful if you would send me a leaflet describing
the types of file you make and their sizes.

                            Yours faithfully

                            Nicholas Evans

                            (Nicholas Evans)
```

Finding Out

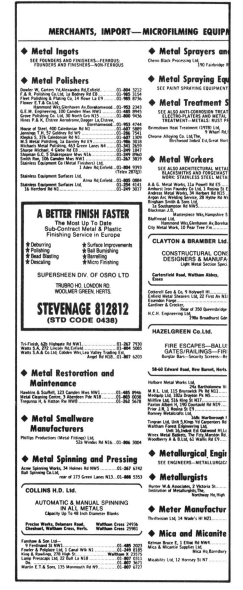

The first problem to be solved when planning a study is how to get enough information to complete it. If you plan your work and do some careful research, the second problem may be to decide what to leave out. You will probably have *too much* material!

A main source of information will be textbooks supplied by a library. A library will stock current periodicals, booklets and leaflets and may keep records and photographs relating to local history and events.

For information on specific products use Trades Directories and the British Telecom Yellow Pages book. These list manufacturers and suppliers in your area. My Yellow Pages show firms under the headings:

Metal Closures, Metal Coating, Metal Finishers, Metal Founders, Metal Hardening, Metal Ingots, Metal Polishers, Metal Restoration, Metal Smallware Manufacturers, Metal Spinning and Pressing, Metal Sprayers and Finishers, Metal Treatment Specialists, and Metal Workers.

Make personal contact with firms, perhaps through sending a letter to arrange visits. Then you may be able to take photographs and obtain samples of materials and products.

If you wish to use a questionnaire, seek advice on its preparation. Interviews must also be carefully prepared so that the right questions can be asked in a logical order. Consider using a cassette tape recorder to help with note-taking.

Using the Library

Do not be confused by the thousands of books you see in a library — only a few of them help you with your study. Every library has the same system to help you to find these books:

The **Subject Index** is a guide to all non-fiction books. It lists subjects alphabetically and gives a class number.

The **Classified Catalogue** contains details of every non-fiction book in the library. The books are arranged according to class number so that details of all the books on your topic will be filed next to each other.

The **Author Index** lists the same details as the classified catalogue, but under the author's name. Use it when you know the author's name.

The cards shown here contain full details of a book. The abbreviations on these examples — C (Central) and CB (Cunningham Branch) — refer to the libraries in my area where the book is stocked. You can order books on special loan from another library.

UPHOLSTERY 645. 5	645. 5 FLITMAN
	FLITMAN, Malcolm Upholstering Batsford 1972. illustrated OVERSIZE BOOK 645. 5 C CB

FLITMAN

FLITMAN, Malcolm

Upholstering

Batsford 1972. illustrated

OVERSIZE BOOK   645. 5   C   CB

Photographs

Photographs can add both meaning and interest to your study. It will be worth getting tips from a teacher of photography, because good photographs taken by yourself will make your study special.

Choose from black and white prints, which you can produce yourself in the school darkroom, or colour prints.

Use colour transparencies *only* if your study is to be presented orally to an examiner.

Choose your subjects with care and then decide how to photograph them.

These photographs of safety goggles illustrate two main methods. One shows a 'studio' shot of the goggles in detail, and the other shows them being worn.

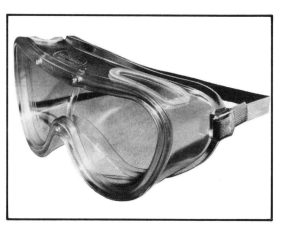

Presentation

The time, thought and expense involved in the preparation of a thorough study deserves a good appearance. To many people, the way in which your work is presented will reflect the care that has been taken with the contents.

The cover need not be elaborate or expensive. A fresh cardboard file with the title in instant lettering and a suitable photograph or drawing is ideal. Do not present your work in a secondhand file made grubby and creased by constant handling.

Typewritten text, instant lettering and good photographs do not ensure good presentation. One example shows care taken with the arrangement of columns, photographs, illustrations, captions and numbering.
The other shows badly trimmed photographs mounted at an angle. It is not obvious which caption relates to which photograph, the heading is poorly spaced and the margin is crooked!

Handwritten studies *must* be neatly written. If you know that the quality of your written work will not be appreciated by the examiner, make an effort to have the text typewritten. In both instances leave good margins on the page, and type with double-spacing on one side of the paper only.

Remember:

1. Insert photographs and drawings close to the appropriate text.
2. When the project is complete, number each page and illustration.
3. Prepare a suitable title page.
4. Add a list of contents or chapter headings at the front of the study.
5. Acknowledge the help given to you by firms and individual people.
6. A page at the back of the book should list the names of the books, their authors and publishers which you have consulted or quoted from.
7. Hand in the study before the limit date.

Nicholas Evans

A HAND CRAFTSMAN

CHANNELING

23

24

17

MACHINING

68

69

25

Examinations

It is likely that you are using this book as part of a course leading to a GCSE examination. The examination may be in a 'one material' subject, metal.
Alternatively, metal and metalworking may be only a part of the study of several materials including, say, wood, plastics and concrete.

The examinations and examination papers have various titles including 'Craft and Design: Metal', 'Technical Studies (Metalwork)', 'Craft, Design and Technology' and 'CDT: Design and Realisation'. They do, however, have one thing in common – a syllabus. You will find that most of the work listed to be studied in each syllabus is in this book, 'Craft and Design in Metal'. You will be able to use this book for studying metalworking theory *and* for your revision. However, you must add to it the extra notes and tips which your teacher will give you throughout the course. You cannot learn workshop skills from a book!

Most of the examinations are designed to find out whether the candidate has sufficient knowledge and understanding of the areas covered in the syllabus to be awarded a certificate. To do this, craft examinations are in several parts. These parts may test practical skills, the ability to solve design problems and an understanding of material and tool technology. Each examinations board has different ways of testing these common skills.

It is quite natural to be nervous about taking an examination, even in a subject which you enjoy and find useful. However, there is no need to be scared of the examination. Most people are frightened of the unknown. Obviously, the more you know about your subject the less frightened you need be.

The syllabus

Most students at school take it for granted that the teacher knows the syllabus and will cover it during the course. However, a teacher may sometimes be working from an outdated syllabus, or may assume that the syllabus will be the same each year. The examinations boards look at each syllabus regularly and make changes. Omitting 'forgework' may not cause much of a problem, but a new section on, say, 'portable electric tools' may mean that there are questions you cannot answer. Ask your teacher for a copy of the syllabus or write to the examinations board for your own copy.

Your teacher may not have enough time to cover all the syllabus. He will have the experience to decide the most important areas for you to study. If you have a syllabus and can find out which areas have been left out, study them on your own if you have time.

CDT: DESIGN AND REALISATION   22/41

CDT: DESIGN AND REALISATION
JOINT O LEVEL/CSE

This syllabus is offered for examination jointly by the East Anglian Examinations Board, the London Regional Examining Board and the University of London University Entrance & School Examinations Council.

The examination papers will carry the names of the three Boards in the London/East Anglian Group.

Candidates will be jointly certificated by their regional CSE Board and by the University of London University Entrance & School Examinations Council.

Candidates from schools in the London Regional Examining Board's region who achieve the required standard will be awarded a GCE 'O' Level certificate at the appropriate grade by the University of London University Entrance & School Examinations Council and a CSE certificate at the appropriate grade by the London Regional Examining Board.

Entries should be made on the normal London Regional Examining Board entry form using the appropriate syllabus number.

Joint O-Level/CSE Examinations will be conducted in accordance with the special regulations for these examinations.

Beginning of a syllabus

Written papers

The most common type of written paper has a selection of questions which require fairly short answers. These questions test how well you have covered the syllabus. They are usually compulsory and are often to be found in a section labelled 'A'. You may then have a choice of questions which demand more time and thought, and longer answers. These test how much you know about a practical process, or whether you can solve a technical problem. These are often to be found in a section labelled 'B'.

Some examination boards mix these two types of question together. Ask your teacher to show you copies of past papers.

From these you can see the layout or format of your written examination. Check the length of the paper and the instructions which tell you how many questions you have to answer. This information can also be found in the syllabus.

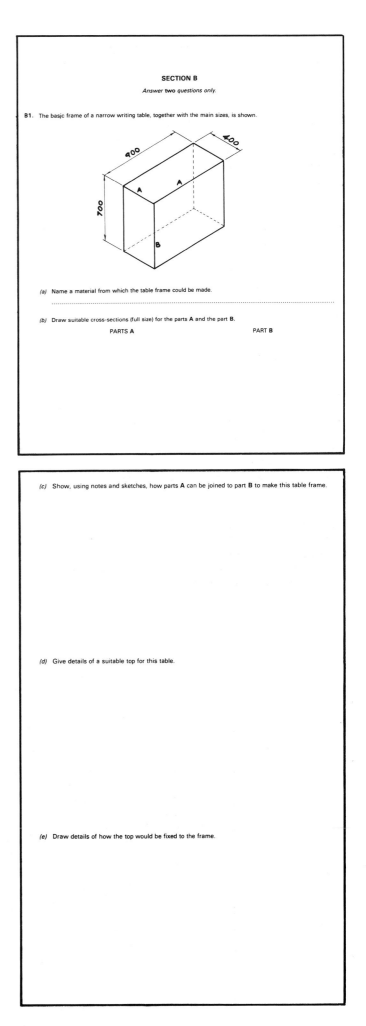

SECTION B

*Answer **two** questions only.*

B1. The basic frame of a narrow writing table, together with the main sizes, is shown.

(a) Name a material from which the table frame could be made.

(b) Draw suitable cross-sections (full size) for the parts **A** and the part **B**.

PARTS **A**   PART **B**

(c) Show, using notes and sketches, how parts **A** can be joined to part **B** to make this table frame.

(d) Give details of a suitable top for this table.

(e) Draw details of how the top would be fixed to the frame.

---

17 From the list of metals given below choose the two used to make Brazing Spelter.

Tin   Zinc   Silver   Lead   Copper   Nickel

1. ....   2. ....

18 Name a suitable flux for brazing and give two reasons for its use.

Name ....

Reasons (a) ....

         (b) ....

19

Name the tool marked with the arrow X.

....

20 What is important about the shape of the tongs chosen for use in forgework?

21 (a) Name the main lathe component shown in the sketch.

     (i)   (ii)   (iii)

     ....

     (b) Give the use of the three parts marked on the sketch.

     (i) ....

     (ii) ....

     (iii) ....

22 Name the process used for hardening the surface of mild steel. ....

23 Name the main material used to make the group of metals called ferrous metals.

4

Sample 'A' questions

Sample 'B' question

Design papers

These papers usually have a choice of design problems. They ask you to find a solution to one of them. Each paper will demand some drawing skills. Find out whether you will need to draw formal projections, or whether sketch solutions will do. This will tell you what to practise.

The syllabus will say whether or not the paper will be given to you before the day of the examination. If it is, you will have a chance to plan your work.

THE ASSOCIATED EXAMINING BOARD
for the General Certificate of Education

June Examination, 1981—Ordinary Level

DESIGN & CRAFTWORK (METAL) 017/2 & 3

Design and Realisation of Design

(a) 017/2—Design is to be held on **Thursday, 4 June, 2.00 p.m. to 4.45 p.m.**

(b) 017/3—Realisation of Design is to be held on a date between **5 June and 26 June** (inclusive).

017/2—DESIGN

2 hours and 45 minutes allowed for the examination

This examination paper contains two design questions. Answer **either** question **1 or** question **2**.

Adequate time will be allowed after the examination for making copies (tracings or photocopies) of the working drawing and the list of materials, fittings and fastenings.

You are advised to use the first 15 minutes of the examination to:

(a) study the questions;

(b) relate the question of your choice to your notes and sketches based on the prior information given to centres, which was:

> Question 1. Chaindrives and related problems.
> Question 2. Display of small cacti.

(c) examine the samples of materials available.

At least the first 45 minutes of the examination time must be spent on preliminary sketches which must be submitted for assessment and for which marks are awarded.

The drawing paper for the working drawing will not be issued until this 45 minute period has elapsed.

NOTE: Any sketches or notes resulting from the prior information may be taken into the Design Examination for reference purposes only but **must not be submitted with your examination scripts.**

[017/2 & 3]   © 1981 AEB   [*Turn over*

First page of a Design paper

Practical papers

Your examination may demand that you make a set piece from a given drawing. More likely it will be in the form of a 'Realisation of Design' or 'Design and Make' examination. In these you have to make a piece you have already designed. For these examinations, make sure you have practised the necessary craft skills and can perform the tasks in the time allowed.

Where to study

The following advice applies to all your subjects. (The same is true of the advice about knowing the syllabus.)

Most of your study will be in the form of homework. It is essential that you have a quiet, well-lit place where you can work undisturbed. This is especially important in your examination year. For all sorts of reasons (usually brothers and sisters!) this may not be easy. Try to arrange a time with the rest of the family when they will let you work undisturbed. If this is impossible, try working in the reference library room of your local library. It may take some time to get used to this, but the effort will be worth it. The room will be warm and well-lit, and reference books will always be at hand.

Of course, work in a library has its disadvantages. For example, it is not possible to listen to the radio or record player! You may miss these, but you cannot work properly with them on. It is better to work hard and then listen while you have a drink and relax. You will then have earned your free time!

Study programme

To do battle with an examination is not unlike planning an attack in war! Candidates with the best plan of campaign will probably do best. Make your plan with the aid of a diary, and perhaps a wallchart.

Begin by listing all the things you do regularly, such as paper rounds, youth clubs and games. Then list all the special events in which you might be involved, such as jumble sales and school 'open' days. Include events which you would like to attend, such as dances and football matches. Do not forget birthday celebrations and holidays! You should then note any regular television or radio programmes which you want to see or hear. These are useful as relaxation.

With luck, the rest of the time is available for study and, later, revision. If that time is not enough then you will have to give up some of your activities. Remember that your examination year is an important one, and you will need to work if you want to do well.

Study time

Research has shown that most people can study really well for only about forty minutes, or an hour at most. They have also discovered that a rested mind works best. A session before breakfast should help you more than the same amount of time at night.

Mealtimes and short periods of television viewing make good relaxation times. Use them to break up your study programme into forty-minute sessions.

Note-taking

Your teacher may give you an exercise book to take notes in. However, it is most helpful to make notes on loose-leaf paper to keep in a hardback file. In this way extra notes and drawings or answers to sample questions can easily be kept together.

Notes are an aid to learning. They are best if they are in your own words rather than simply copied from a book. Some books, such as this one, are written in a way which is like good note-taking. There are short paragraphs of information and labelled drawings. Key words in your notes should be underlined, perhaps in a colour. Drawings should be simplified so that you can use them quickly in an examination question.

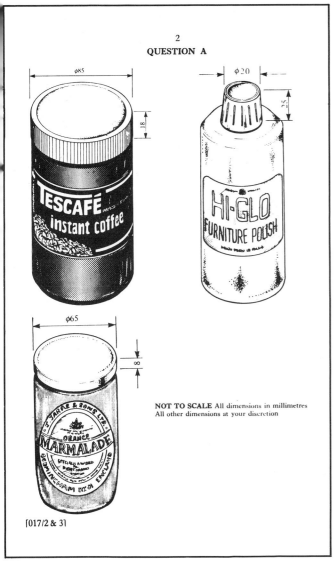

QUESTION A

TESCAFÉ instant coffee

HI-GLO FURNITURE POLISH

ORANGE MARMALADE

NOT TO SCALE All dimensions in millimetres
All other dimensions at your discretion

[017/2 & 3]

QUESTION A

Sauces, jams and preserves are sold in a variety of screw-top glass containers, the tops of which are made from metal or plastics and vary in size from 20 to 90 millimetres in diameter.

At the time of bottling in the factory the use of machinery sometimes results in these tops being screwed so firmly to the glass containers that they are extremely difficult to release, particularly by elderly people and others lacking a strong grip.

Design a device which will ease the task of unscrewing these container tops. The device must be suitable for use with all the containers [**illustrated on page 2**].

Consideration should be given to the requirements of kitchen hygiene.

017/2—DESIGN
QUESTION B

On School prize days awards are made in various subjects of the curriculum to pupils showing excellence in effort and/or achievement.

It has been decided to award a trophy to the boy or girl who is judged to be the best designer–craftsman in your school. The trophy will be held for one year.

Design a trophy for this purpose, which symbolises good design and craftsmanship. The trophy must not exceed 300 millimetres in any overall measurement.

For the chosen question:—

1. You are expected to show by your solution an appreciation of the materials, processes and constructions of the craft.

2. Make preliminary sketches leading up to a final design, together with any explanatory notes. Marks will be awarded for these preliminary sketches and notes showing the development of ideas.

3. Make complete working drawings (assembly and detail parts drawings) of your final design, a cutting list of materials, and indicate the "finish" you intend to use.

4. *Attach all preliminary sketches to your working drawings.*

[017/2 & 3]

Sample Design questions

Vocabulary

Far too many candidates enter a technical examination without knowing some of the words and phrases needed to answer questions accurately. A good candidate will have a 'technical vocabulary' as well as normal writing skills. Modern examination questions rarely ask for the simple labelling of a tool or joint. Nevertheless, this book labels the main parts so that they can be learned. You can refer to them when describing, say, a cutting or maintenance process.

Words which describe processes are often used in a particular sequence. They should be grouped together in your vocabulary pages. An example of this is the four processes required to rivet. These are boring, setting, doming and finishing.

Revision

Revision is a different form of studying. It involves looking at work which has already been studied and *not* at new areas of work. It is important to remember this when you are near examination time. If you have forgotten to study some part of the syllabus, it is best to leave that part and concentrate on revising what you have studied. The conditions you need for revising are the same as for studying. Revise in a quiet, warm, well-lit room when you are feeling fresh. Revise in a systematic way with a fixed finishing time, so that you are not overtired.

Have revision sessions as often as you can and repeat the revision of the most important parts of the syllabus.

Make sure that you fully understand the work you revise. If you do not, ask your teacher to help you.

Testing

Testing is an important way of revision. Ask your teacher for some past papers and use these, as well as questions from books, to test your knowledge and understanding. In this way you will discover which areas of study need to be revised again.

Towards the end of your revision period you should try to answer questions in the actual time you will have in the examination.

Verbal testing is answering a set of questions asked by a friend. It can be useful, and it makes revision more fun. But do not rely on it — remember that you have to write and draw on the day!

Do not revise immediately before an examination. Revise thoroughly beforehand, and use the hours just before the examination to relax.

The examination

Having studied methodically and done your revision thoroughly you have nothing to fear from the examination itself. The problems that remain are concerned with organization. Teachers can recall too many instances of candidates arriving on the wrong day or at the wrong time! It is important to check both the day and the time of each examination.

Collect together all the materials you need. For written examinations, where special equipment is not needed, take two pens, two pencils, a rubber, a ruler, coloured pencils and a watch.

You may be taking an examination during a time of the year when you are not regularly attending school. It would still be foolish to present yourself for examination incorrectly dressed. Find out if your school requires you to wear school uniform and, if it does, wear it. It may not make much sense to you but it would be stupid to get excited about it and lose your concentration, or even be prevented from sitting the examination.

Try to maintain your regular eating and travelling habits. Always eat a meal before the examination (a hungry candidate is inefficient) and make sure that your transport gets you to the examination without hurry or anxiety.

Go to the lavatory. It is inconvenient to go during the examination, it disturbs other candidates and it wastes *your* time.

The examination paper

The front of the examination paper should be familiar to you. Whether or not the paper allows separate 'reading time' you must first read the instructions. Make sure you know how many questions are to be answered and follow any advice about the time to be spent on any particular question or section. It is a waste of time if you answer five questions when only four are needed.

Most examination boards are anxious to assess your skills and allow a reasonable length of time for you to answer questions.

However, you should ensure that you allow yourself enough time to do the work. You will lose marks if you only have time to answer, say, three questions when four are needed.

Obey instructions about where your answer should be put. Short answer questions will usually instruct you to 'underline', 'fill in', 'circle', 'complete', 'list' or 'label'. Obey these instructions.

WELSH JOINT EDUCATION COMMITTEE
Certificate of Secondary Education

CYD-BWYLLGOR ADDYSG CYMRU
Tystysgrif Addysg Uwchradd

CSE 11/1

CRAFT AND DESIGN—METAL (Theory)

(2 Hours) P.M. 18 June 1980

	Leave Blank
Enter below the numbers of the questions you answer in the order in which you answer them. **SECTION A**	
No.	
No.	
No.	
No.	
No.	
No.	
No.	
No.	
No.	
No.	
SECTION B	
No.	
No.	
TOTAL MARKS	

Centre Number ....

Candidate's Name (in full) ....

Candidate's Examination Number ....

Candidates should answer **ten** *questions from Section A, and* **two** *questions from Section B.*

Each question in Section A carries six marks.

Each question in Section B carries twenty marks.

Insert the numbers of the questions you answer, in the order in which you answer them, in the mark grid above.

All sizes are in millimetres unless otherwise stated.

No certificate will be awarded to a candidate detected in any unfair practice during the examination.

10332 [*Turn over*

Front of a Craft and Design—Metal paper

THE SOUTH-EAST REGIONAL EXAMINATIONS BOARD **29/1**

for the Certificate of Secondary Education
(a company limited by guarantee)

METALWORK Paper 1

Tuesday, 13th May, 1980   60 questions. Answer all questions   Time allowed: 1 hour

READ THIS FIRST

Spaces are provided at the top of the answer sheet for your name (surname and initials only) and subject. WHEN YOU ARE TOLD TO DO SO fill these in using block letters.

Your teacher will tell you what to enter in the 8 boxes and the 10 lines. Follow his instructions carefully.

The answer sheet is filled in by joining the mauve coloured marks in the appropriate boxes with a black felt tip pen or an HB pencil like this

Each line you draw between the mauve coloured marks should be BLACK and CLEAR.

If you make a mistake and join the mauve coloured marks in the wrong box, shade the lower half of the box thus

Then join the mauve marks in the correct box. Do not rub out an incorrect line.

The Question Paper

THERE IS ONLY ONE CORRECT ANSWER TO EACH QUESTION

1. Read each question and the answers which follow it.
2. Choose the correct answer.
3. Now turn to the answer sheet.

The Answer Sheet

1. The black numbers refer to the questions and the mauve letters to the answers.
2. Find the number of the question you are answering.
3. Across the letter for the answer you have chosen, draw a line between the mauve marks.
4. Draw only ONE line in answer to each question.
5. If you change your mind, do NOT rub out your first choice, but shade the lower half of the box and then join the mauve marks in the correct box.
6. If you decide later that your first choice was after all correct, ask your teacher what you should do.
7. Here is an example:

QUESTION PAPER

(Question No.) 3. The patron saint of Wales is

A St. Andrew
B St. George
C St. David
D St. Patrick
E St. Christopher

ANSWER SHEET

The correct answer is C, therefore you mark the Answer sheet like this:

3 A B C D E

WHEN YOUR TEACHER TELLS YOU TO START:

8. Begin at Question 1 and work steadily through the paper.
9. If you cannot answer a question, go on to the next.
10. When you have reached the last question, go back and attempt any questions you have left unanswered.

SB 33   1   **Turn over**
© The South East Regional Examinations Board   29/1

Objective tests

The most common failing amongst examination candidates is not answering the question or put another way, not obeying an instruction. Sometimes these key words or instructions are in **bold type** or *italics*, but often they are not. It is pointless to write about milling a surface if the question asks for diagrams to show how it is best done! It is equally pointless to *draw* all the tools you would use for enamelling a brooch if the question asks for a list of them! Mistakes of this kind are frequent, but need never happen.

Other instructions may include, 'Draw in pencil' or, 'Leave this margin blank'. Obey them all.

Above all else *do not panic* and *do* spend time thinking. Think about your choice of questions, and think about the answers, before you start to write or draw. All examiners would agree that time spent thinking is rarely wasted.

Write neatly and label drawings. Information that cannot be read will not gain marks.

The sheets shown (*Different ways of asking for information*) cover different ways of asking a question. Each requires a different kind of answer.

In the examples given in A1 and A2 you have to *read* the question and write the answer on a dotted line.

In A3 you have to *look* at the drawings and write the answer in a box.

In A4 you are asked to state the equipment used to obtain a finish. The answer is written in the boxes under the heading 'Equipment'.

You need to look at the diagram in A5 and then *draw* the answer on the paper.

A6 is divided into three parts (a), (b) and (c) and each has three boxes to be filled in — you need to give nine answers.

A7 has two boxes for each of the three parts. Each box needs two answers, labelled (i) and (ii). You need to give twelve answers in all.

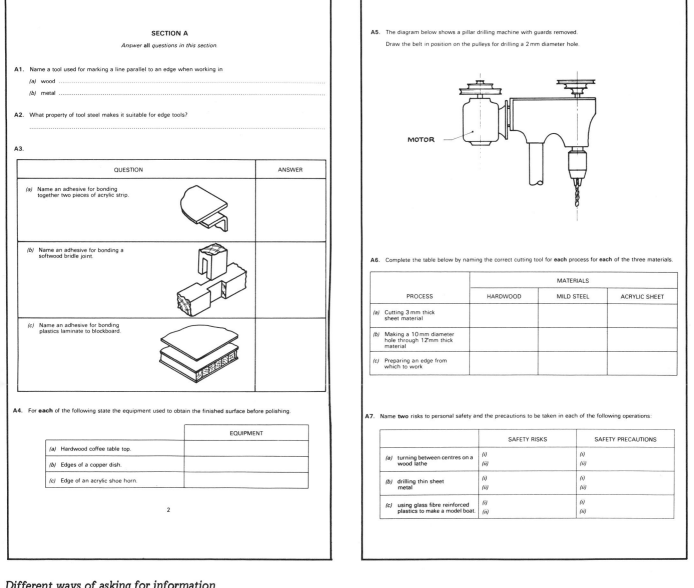

Different ways of asking for information

Marking examination papers

For most people, what happens to examination answer papers is an unimportant mystery. It is true that the work is done, and nothing can be done to improve it. However, it may be worth knowing what happens to your paper. A candidate who fails and who blames the examinations or the examiner, is probably being unfair.

Your script is sent to an Assistant Examiner who will look at several scripts before attending an examiners' meeting. At this meeting the Chief Examiner makes clear the way in which marks will be given for each part of each question. Later, the Assistant Examiner will begin his marking and send some samples of scripts to the Chief Examiner for him to check that the marks are being given correctly. The marks for each paper are added up and put onto a computer sheet. If a mistake is made here it is usually found when the examinations board check each and every script. It is almost certain that your script will have been fairly marked and checked.

Who is a typical Assistant Examiner? He is likely to be an experienced craft teacher, with a family, who does the marking at home both before and after a full working day. He has to work at speed to mark all his scripts before the mark deadline.

It should now be obvious to you why it is to your advantage to obey the instructions given, draw neatly and write clearly! The examiner is only human and, although he will try to be patient, he may lose patience with a badly presented paper.

The results

Each examinations board has its own method of arriving at a final mark. In some, your teacher contributes some of the marks based on your work at school, that is your coursework.

The Chief Examiner and members of a committee meet each year to decide on the grades to be awarded. Your final mark will be changed into a grade.

If you have followed the advice in this book you will probably be delighted with the result. If the grade is well below that which you or your teacher expected then it is possible to ask the examinations board to remark your paper(s). This is expensive, but the cost may be worthwhile if you need a higher grade to secure a job. Do not worry in case the examiner has given you too many marks — your original grade cannot be lowered!

Exercises

Materials

1 From the list given below state the metals which are non-ferrous:
copper, mild steel, wrought iron, zinc, cast iron, carbon steel, brass, aluminium

2 What metals are used to make the following:
nail punch, forged poker, baking tray, hot-water tank, kitchen sink, surface plate, garden rake, car body, leg vice, hacksaw blade

3 Name the two metals used to make each of the following alloys:
brass, soft-solder, gilding metal, hard-solder

4 From the list given below state both the softest and the hardest metals:
gilding metal, copper, carbon steel, lead, aluminium, mild steel

5 From the list of metals given below state which is the 'odd one out':
brass, aluminium, zinc, lead, tin, copper
Give a reason for your choice.

6 List *four* non-ferrous metals.

7 Explain the meaning of the following terms when used to describe the properties of metals.
(a) hardness
(b) toughness
(c) ductility
(d) malleability

8 State three common properties that make aluminium, copper, brass and gilding metal all suitable for art metalwork.

9 Name four cross-sections of metal commonly obtained from the metal workshop store.

10 Explain how ONE of the following metals is produced:
tool steel, mild steel.

11 Select one of the steel-making processes listed below:
(a) electric arc
(b) basic oxygen
(c) open hearth
Describe, using labelled diagrams, the sequence of operations from charging the furnace to the production of the steel.

12 Name the metal that is produced in each of these furnaces:
(a) blast furnace
(b) electric arc
(c) Cupola

13 Describe in detail how you would anneal:
(a) copper sheet
(b) aluminium sheet

14 Four lengths of 19 mm diameter medium-carbon steel bar must be heat-treated to make each of them different. One each has to be:
(a) as hard as possible
(b) as soft as possible
(c) as tough as possible
(d) most suitable for machining
Describe how you would achieve each condition.

15 What causes the tempering colour to form on a tool during heat-treatment?

16 Blue, yellow, straw and purple are colours which can be seen when tempering steel. Starting with the coolest temperature, place the colours in order.

17 Describe the heat-treatment necessary before a cold chisel, formed from octagonal carbon steel, could be used.

18 The jaws of spanners are case-hardened to make them resist wear. Explain the term 'case-hardening' and say how it might be done.

19 Name each heat treatment described below:
(a) A screwdriver tip is heated to blue heat and quenched in water.
(b) A curved steel plate is heated to red heat and cooled in air.
(c) A flat copper sheet is heated to red heat and quenched in water.

20 What do you understand by the following terms:
(a) extruded – when applied to aluminium
(b) drawn – when describing copper wire
(c) hot-rolled – when ordering mild steel strip

21 What is meant by the term 'work-hardening'?

22 Which metal is likely to block up the teeth of a file quickly?

23 Say why an object taken from a pickle bath should be washed and scrubbed.

Handtools

24 Show how you would measure accurately the depth of a blind hole.

25 Use diagrams to show how the following tools are best set to a dimension of 20 mm:
(a) inside calipers
(b) outside calipers
(c) spring dividers

26 Name each of the tools shown below and for each an example of its correct use.

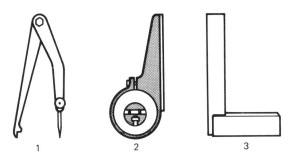

1   2   3

27 What is the purpose of each of the gauges shown below?

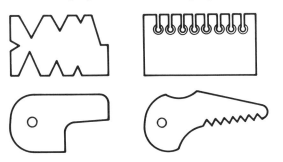

28 Name two tools used to find the centre of a round bar. Use sketches to show clearly how each tool is used.

29 What tools would you use to measure, to an accuracy of 0.01 mm, the inside and outside diameters of the cylinder shown below?

30 The drawing below shows a small clamp. List the tools you would use to mark out the slope marked 'A'. Describe how you would mark out the shape.

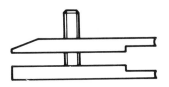

31 The drawing shows the shape of a side plate of a bull-nose woodworking plane to be made from 3 mm thick BDMS. Make a list of all the tools you would need to mark it out.

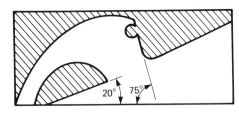

32 The drawing below shows the blade of a sliding bevel made from 3 mm mild steel.
Use notes and/or sketches to show how you would:
  i)   mark out the angle of 60°
  ii) mark out the circular end
  iii) mark out the slot
  iv) cut out the slot
  v)   case-harden the blade

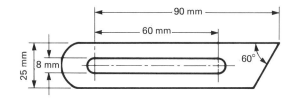

33 What is a surface plate used for? Why is the underside of the plate ribbed?

34 Complete the drawing below to show a micrometer reading of 8.85 mm.

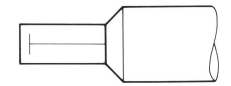

35 What is the reading on the micrometer shown below?

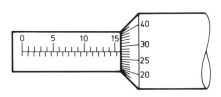

36 Give a use for each of the following measuring instruments and state why it is the most appropriate one to use:
  (a) Vernier caliper gauge
  (b) micrometer depth gauge
  (c) dial gauge

37 How would you check an Engineer's square for accuracy?

38 Name and give the use of the tool shown below.

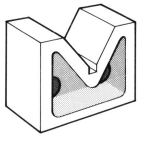

Show two other pieces of equipment commonly used with it.

39 A hand vice is used to grip a small piece of thin metal to be drilled on a power drill. Give reasons why you should *not* hold the metal in your hands.

40 Make simple drawings of the jaws of a machine vice to show how they can hold effectively the three different pieces of metal shown below while the holes are drilled.

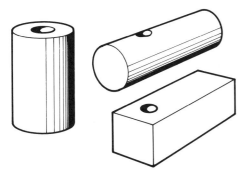

41 Why do the cast steel jaw plates on an Engineer's vice have serrated faces? How can soft metal, such as aluminium, be held in these jaws without being damaged?

42 Make a drawing of a pair of combination pliers. Label the cutting and holding parts of the jaws.

43 Explain briefly why combination pliers must not be used for the following purposes:
(a) tightening a nut
(b) removing work from an acid bath
(c) holding hot metal

44 What type of tinmans snips are used for cutting internal curves in thin sheet metal?

45 (a) A 200 mm deep sawcut is needed parallel with and close to the edge of a metal sheet. How would you adapt the hacksaw to make the cut?
(b) Make a simple sketch to show the set of a hacksaw blade.
(c) When buying a hacksaw blade you must state the length required. Give two other details needed by the shopkeeper.
(d) Give two reasons for a hacksaw blade breaking in use.

46 Hacksaw blades have different numbers of teeth per 25 mm. Why are they made in this way? State the blade you would use (the number of teeth per 25 mm) to cut 25 mm diameter bars of:
(a) aluminium
(b) mild steel
(c) steel tube with a wall thickness of 1.5 mm.

47 The drawing shows three full-size sections through mild steel. For each of them state the number of teeth per 25 mm on a hacksaw blade you would choose to saw through the material.

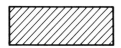

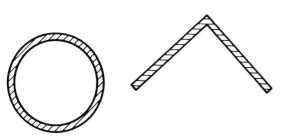

48 The drawings below represent two full-size sections through mild steel. Make a copy of each section in the correct position for cutting with a hacksaw. In each drawing show the position of the hacksaw blade.

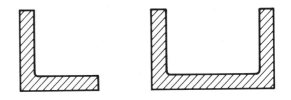

49 The cold chisel shown below has faults which make reconditioning necessary. List these faults and state why they occurred.
Give an account of the processes necessary to restore the cold chisel to good condition.

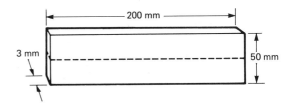

50 The drawing shows a piece of mild steel 200 mm x 50 mm x 3 mm thick which is to be cut along the broken line with a hacksaw.
State why the hacksaw frame will have to be adjusted and show how you would make the adjustment.

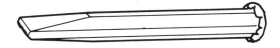

51 How is the blade held in a junior hacksaw frame?

52 State the main feature of a piercing saw blade and show how it is held in the saw frame.

53 Why is a tension saw so called?

54 (a) Files have different grades of cut. Name four of them.
(b) What is the name of the edge of a file which does *not* have cutting teeth?
(c) What can you do to help prevent pinning when filing?
(d) Why should 'pins' not be left on a file?
How might a file handle become dangerous to use?

55 Which files would you use:
(a) To fettle a cast lead fishing weight?
(b) to remove excess silver solder from a piece of jewellery?

56 Name the four file shapes shown below.

57 The drawing shows a piece of 4 mm BDMS.
 (a) Describe how you would roughly cut out the waste marked 'A' and 'B'.
 (b) Draw sections to show the shape of each file used to finish each of the numbered sides or edges.

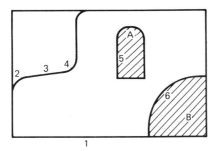

58 Draw the cutting end of a standard twist drill. Name the main parts and show the principal angles.

59 A twist drill has been re-ground so that the cutting edges are unequal in length. Describe the kind of hole this drill would produce.

60 Use diagrams to show the correct use of:
 (a) a countersunk hole
 (b) a counterbored hole

61 What is meant by the terms:
 (a) clearance-size drill?
 (b) tapping-size drill?
 (c) blind hole?

62 Make a labelled sketch of a drift and explain its use.

63 Which of the metals aluminium, brass, high-carbon steel and tool steel:
 (a) is drilled at the slowest speed?
 (b) is drilled at the fastest speed?
 (c) does not need a coolant or lubricant?

64 A bar of BDMS must have a hole drilled to accommodate a bolt. Explain how this would be cut on a pillar drill.

65 What cutting fluid, if any, should be used when drilling: mild steel, aluminium, brass, cast iron?

66 You have to drill a 22 mm diameter hole into an aluminium casting which will not fit into the machine vice.
 (a) Describe how you would securely fasten the casting.
 (b) Explain the method you would use to drill the hole.

67 You have to drill a 6 mm hole through the diameter of a 19 mm bar. Assume that its position has been marked with a centre punch. Use sketches to show how you would hold the bar in position and ensure that the hole is diametric.

68 You have to drill a 4 mm diameter hole down the axis of a 25 mm bar held in the lathe. Name and draw the drill you would use *first*.

69 (a) Name the tool shown below.
 (b) What is it used for?
 (c) The top of the tool has a square head. Give the name of the tool you would use to turn it.

70 Draw a pulley arrangement for a 5-speed pillar drill. On it show the position for the belt to run at its fastest speed.

71 Use drawings to show the difference between an open-ended spanner and a cranked ring spanner. Explain one situation when you would use each of these spanners in preference to the other.

72 Name the tool used to tighten each of the following:
 (a) the chuck of a pillar drill
 (b) a recessed nut with an hexagonal head
 (c) a nut with an hexagonal head
 (d) a screw with a cross-slotted head

73 What is the name given to the tool in which a tap is held? In what way is the length of the tool important?

74 Explain the similarities and differences between a pair of round-nose pliers and a pair of flat-nose pliers.

75 A normal slotted head screwdriver has several 'faults'. Illustrate three of these 'faults' and show how the use of a 'Supadriv' slot would avoid each of them.

76 What is an Allen key?

Jointing

77 Draw and name three types of rivet. State three materials from which they could be made.

78 Make a series of drawings to show how you would rivet together two pieces of 6 mm mild steel plate with a snap-head rivet closed by countersinking.

79 Explain, step by step, how you would rivet together the bright drawn mild steel plates which will form the stock of a sliding bevel. The positions of the three rivets are indicated.

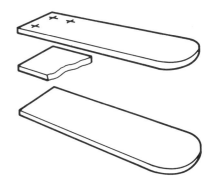

80 Explain the advantages of using a pop rivet.

81 Suggest two methods of allowing a riveted joint to turn freely.

82 Use drawings and notes to describe how you would join together the two pieces of mild steel shown below:
 (a) using rivets finished flush with both outside surfaces
 (b) using snap-rivets projecting from both sides.

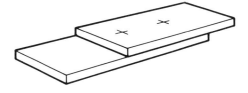

83 Before forming the second head on a rivet the plates to be joined are set. What does this setting do? Sketch a rivet set.

84 Make drawings to show two methods of locking a nut on to a bolt.

85 Use notes and line drawings to explain:
(a) pitch
(b) clearance size
(c) die nut
(d) tee-bolt
(e) drunken thread

86 What do you understand by the term 'drunken thread', and how might such a fault be avoided?

87 Make a drawing of a bolt with an hexagonal head. On it show four details you would have to specify when buying such a bolt.

88 Draw a socket-head grub screw and name the tool used to turn it.

89 The diagram below indicates a screw thread. Name the diameters labelled 'A' and 'B'.

90 Explain the difference between a machine screw and a bolt.

91 Name the screw that has an hexagonal socket in its head. Draw the tool used to loosen or tighten such a screw.

92 A 9 mm diameter brass rod is to be threaded at one end. Use notes and sketches to explain how you would cut the screw thread using hand methods. Use the following sub-headings:
(a) Preparing the rod
(b) Preparing the die and die stock
(c) Adjusting the die
(d) Testing the thread size

93 (a) What is a die nut?
(b) Describe two situations when you would use a die nut instead of a die and die stock.
(c) Name the tool used to turn a die nut.

94 The drawing below shows a circular split die. Explain the use of the two screws labelled 'A' and the centre screw labelled 'B'.

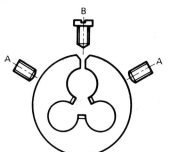

95 You are to write an instruction sheet for Second Year metalworkers, explaining how to cut an M10 internal screw thread. Write out step-by-step instructions in the correct order.

96 When cutting a screw thread, why is it best to cut the internal nut thread before cutting the external bolt thread?

97 Fittings can be bought which enable materials to be joined together without being permanently fixed. Describe an example of an appropriate use of one such fitting.

98 Make simple drawings to show both a straight soldering iron and a hatchet soldering iron in use.

99 Explain how you would prepare a new soldering iron for use.

100 Which solder would be most suitable for joining:
(a) the tubes of a mild steel bicycle frame
(b) the corners of a tinplate tray
(c) two wires in a radio set which must not corrode

101 Draw a piece of work which uses two grades of silver solder. Clearly mark the two grades and briefly explain why the two grades were necessary.

102 Explain the term 'sweating' or 'sweat soldering'.

103 (a) Fluxes are described as either passive or active. What does this mean?
(b) Name a flux suitable for use on tinplate. State whether it is an active flux or a passive flux.

104 Describe a suitable use for an epoxy resin adhesive. Name the materials and say how the surfaces should be prepared.

105 Make a drawing of a small copper cylinder to be silver-soldered along the seam. Show how you would wire up the cylinder. State the type of wire you would use.

106 A tube has to be joined to a flat baseplate. What would be the strongest method if the tube was made of copper and the baseplate of brass?

107 Two pieces of mild steel are to be brazed together in the position shown in the drawing below.
(a) Sketch a suitable joint.
(b) Describe how you would prepare the metal for brazing.
(c) What material would you use to join them?
(d) State the type of flux you would use.
(e) How would you know that the joint had reached the correct brazing temperature?

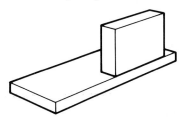

108 Brazing spelter is an alloy of two metals. Name them.

109 You are to weld together the two pieces of angle-iron shown below. Describe fully how you would make the joint, from preparation to cleaning up.

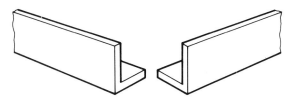

110 Make diagrams to show the principle of arc welding.

111 Describe two different types of flame used when gas welding. Name the processes for which each is suitable.

Shaping

112 The drawing shows a simple tin tray.
(a) Sketch its development.
(b) Explain the process of soft-soldering the corner joints.
(c) Draw an edge finish to the tray which would improve its appearance and make it safer to handle.

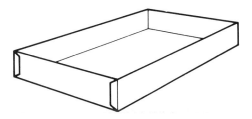

113 Make a drawing and explain the use of each of the following:
(a) folding bars
(b) hatchet stake
(c) groover
(d) creasing iron

114 The drawing shows a flour scoop made from tin plate. Describe:
(a) how you would bend this shape
(b) the best way to form the grooved seam marked 'A'
(c) how you would make the handle

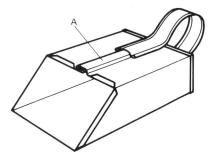

115 (a) Give an example of work in which a piece of bright drawn mild steel had to be annealed. Why was it necessary to anneal the steel?
(b) Describe in detail how the BDMS was annealed.

116 Explain the differences between the processes of raising and hollowing. Make a sketch of an example of a piece of work made by each process.

117 What is meant by the term work-hardening?

118 As sheet aluminium is worked it hardens and becomes difficult to shape.
(a) Explain why this happens.
(b) Name and describe the process by which the metal can be made soft again and easier to shape.

119 Explain the process of planishing. What state must the stake be in and why?

120 Beginning with a copper disc, describe and name the proceeses by which it is made into a symmetrical shallow bowl. List all the tools you would need to use. How would you test the accuracy of the shape?

121 The drawing is of a dish made from gilding metal.
(a) Show how you would choose the size of the blank.
(b) Make simple drawings and notes to show how you would prepare a disc for hollowing from a square piece of metal.
Name the tools and materials used.
(c) Use drawings to show in detail how you would planish the dish after hollowing it.
Name the tools used and label your drawings.

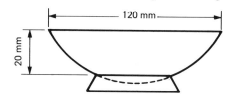

122 Make a sketch of the following hammers and explain their uses:
(a) raising
(b) planishing
(c) repoussé

123 The drawing below shows a flared beaker. Make a sketch to show its shape *before* flaring. Describe, using an annotated drawing, how the beaker would be flared. Name the tools used.

124 (a) What is repoussé work?
(b) What material is the supporting block usually made from, and how is it prepared for use?
(c) Sketch a chasing tool used for incising the outline of a design on the metal sheet.

125 Describe the stages in making a napkin ring from 18 gauge gilding metal. Show *two* alternative ways of decorating the surface of the ring. Describe *one* of the processes.

126 (a) Why is softened copper pickled?
(b) Which acid is used, and at what strength?
(c) Draw a pair of pickling tongs and state the material from which they are made.
(d) Give reasons why hot metal must not be put into a pickle bath.
(e) How is the pickled metal treated before it can be worked again?

127 The drawings below show three common faults in the making of beaten metalwork. Explain how each of the faults could be avoided.
   (a) Solder from the seam of a cylinder has run out when the base was being soldered in position.
   (b) Binding wire became soldered to the seam of a cylinder when the seam was being made.
   (c) A shallow dish has developed hollows and bumps in the surface as it was being planished.

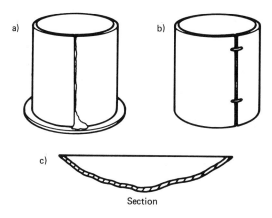

128 Name the parts of the anvil marked 'A' and 'B' on the drawing below. Give an example of forgework carried out on both parts.
   Draw a tool which fits into the hole marked 'C'.

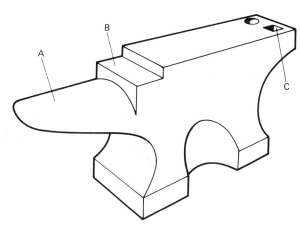

129 Use annotated sketches to explain the use of the following:
   (a) swages
   (b) flatters
   (c) hot and cold sets
   (d) fullers

130 Make simple line drawings of each of the following tongs.
   (a) open mouth
   (b) closed mouth
   (c) hollow bit
   Explain one use for each of them.

131 What is the difference between drifting and punching? Use drawings to show why holes formed by this process in wrought iron are preferred to drilled holes.

132 Explain three of the following forgework terms:
   upsetting, flaring, clinker, burning, piping

133 The drawing below shows a gate hook.
   (a) Describe forging the eye.
   (b) Describe drawing-down and forming the hook.
   (c) Describe in detail forming the twist, beginning with marking out. List the tools used and indicate working temperatures.

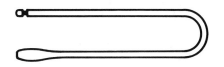

134 The drawing shows part of a cycle lock made from 8 mm diameter mild steel — a groove has been turned in one end of a lathe.
   (a) Explain how you would bend the rod to a 20 mm radius.
   (b) Show how you would flare one end.
   In each case, name the tools you would use.

135 You are to make the scroll shown below from 9 mm square black mild steel.
   (a) From your design how would you work out the length of metal needed to make the scroll?
   (b) Assume that the metal has been drawn-down. Describe how you would bend the scroll. List the tools you would use.

136 The drawings below show four forging processes.
   (a) Name each of them.
   (b) Sketch the tools used and briefly describe each process.
   (c) Explain why careful heating is essential to processes C and D.

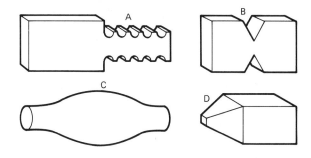

Casting

137 Use brief notes and simple sketches to explain four of the following foundry terms:
   (a) core print
   (b) blow hole
   (c) cope
   (d) parting powder
   (e) rapping
   (f) fettling

138 Explain in detail how you would make a pattern from wood. State how you would ensure that it will be the required size when cast and how it will release from the sand.

139 (a) Describe how you would decide whether or not moulding sand was too damp to use.
(b) Explain the use of the following foundrywork tools:
i) de-gassing plunger
ii) heart and gate tool
iii) bellows
iv) combined wedge and flat rammer

140 (a) List three requirements of successful moulding sand.
(b) Explain the term 'green sand moulding'.
(c) What is 'facing sand' and how is it used?

141 The simple wood pattern shown below is painted red and yellow. What do these colours show?
What is the purpose of the filler on the pattern?
Draw a section through a moulding flask with this pattern removed, ready for pouring. On it clearly show and label the runner, cope, gate and riser.

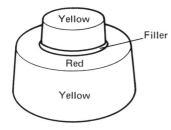

142 (a) If moulding sand is rammed too hard, what problem may be caused?
(b) Sketch and name two types of moulding trowels and explain their uses.

143 Show how you would make a simple sand core.

144 When casting:
(a) State what might happen if the pouring temperature of the metal is too low.
(b) State two probable causes of unwanted holes which appear in castings.

145 List three safety precautions that should be taken to ensure safe pouring of molten metal. Sketch a foundry worker and label the safety clothes he wears.

146 (a) The drawing below shows a split pattern for a hacksaw handle. Why are split patterns necessary?
(b) How are the halves of the pattern aligned and held together?
(c) The casting is to be made from aluminium. What kind would you use and why?

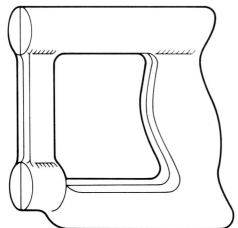

Machine tools

147 You are to machine the fitting shown below from 32 mm brass bar. Describe the stages in making the fitting. List the tools used and state the spindle speeds selected for each part of the turning process.

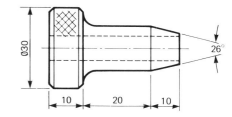

148 (a) Use sketches and brief notes to describe two different methods of adjusting a lathe tool bit to the correct cutting height.
(b) Name two problems which may occur when a tool bit is set above centre height.
(c) What is the likely cause of chatter with a lathe tool?
(d) Name and draw lathe tools which will produce the shoulder shapes shown on the drawings below.

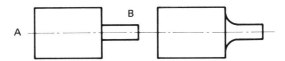

149 The drawing shows a handle made from hexagonal aluminium bar.
(a) State the name of the lathe chuck you would use to hold the bar.
(b) Give step by step instructions for setting up the compound slide for taper turning and producing the taper shown. The included angle is $30°$
(c) Draw a top view showing the lathe set up for parting off the handle.
Label the workpiece, chuck, tool post and cutting tool.

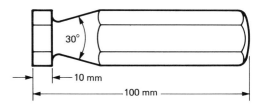

150 Suggest one possible cause of each of the following faults which may occur. In each case explain how the fault could be corrected.
(a) When turning, the metal near the dead centre turns blue.
(b) Work which should be parallel has a slight taper.
(c) The surface of the work has a poor finish.

151 Each three-jaw self-centring chuck is provided with two sets of jaws.
(a) Make line drawings to show the differences between the two sets.
(b) Explain a use for each set of jaws.
(c) Write down the procedure for changing from one set of jaws to the other.

152 You are to bore a 38 mm diameter hole 25 mm deep in the end of a 63 mm diameter mild steel bar. Describe the process using the following headings:
(a) Setting up work on the lathe
(b) Starting boring
(c) Checking internal diameter
(d) Checking depth of hole
(e) Ensuring a flat base to the hole

153 Drawing A shows part of a drill ground for general use. Explain why a drill would be reground as shown in drawing B.

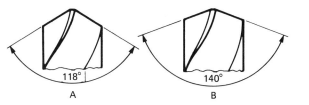

154 State two reasons why it may be necessary to change the speed of a pillar drill.

155 The drawing below shows four different sections through mild steel bar. For each of them, name the chuck you would use to hold a short piece centrally for turning.

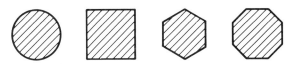

156 The drawings below show lathe tools with different top rake angles. Name the metal best cut with each one.

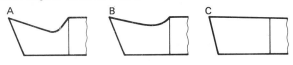

157 Draw *four* different shapes of lathe tool and name each one.

158 Name the types of knurling shown on the drawing below.
Make a sketch of a knurling tool.

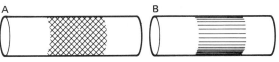

159 Draw a simple plan view of a lathe set up to cut a long taper.
Name three important and relevant features.

160 The section below shows an iron casting which has to be secured on to a machine table. Use sketches to show how this could best be done:
(a) making use of the tee slots
(b) without using the tee slots

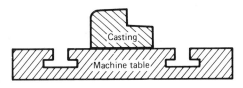

161 Name the three milling cutters shown below and give a correct use for each of them.

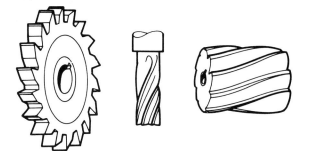

162 List, in the correct order, the stages of marking out the plate shown below in BDMS bar.
How would you machine the 18 mm projection? Give a step-by-step account, including the method of holding the bar being machined.

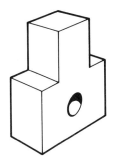

163 (a) Give one of the functions of a clapper box.
(b) Use a drawing to show why a clapper box is sometimes 'set over' on the shaper.
(c) What is the quick-return mechanism on a shaper? Why is it so useful?
(d) After setting up work in the shaper, why must you 'pull the machine over' by hand before switching on the power?

164 The drawing shows two faults in the way in which a lathe tool has been set up.
(a) State each fault and describe the effect of each fault on the turning process.
(b) Make a drawing to show the correct setting-up.

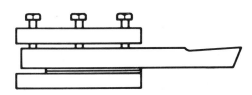

165 The drawing below shows a mild steel workpiece being turned on a lathe.
Name and draw the lathe tools which would be used to make the cuts labelled A, B, C and D.

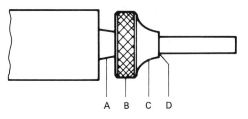

Machine tools — Safety

166 The drawing shows a 3-pin plug of the type which is commonly fitted to portable power tools.
 (a) From what material should the casing be made?
 (b) For each of the terminals L, N and E, state the sheathing colour of the wire that should be connected to it.
 (c) Why is a 13-amp fuse fitted in preference to a 5-amp fuse?
 (d) What is the function of the part marked 'X'?

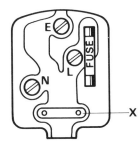

167 A friend has borrowed your portable power drill to bore holes in plasterboard. Make a list of the safety checks you would make when the drill is returned to you.

168 You have just finished using a centre lathe. What safety precautions would you take before leaving it?

169 There are many causes of accidents in the workshop. Under each of the following headings, write down *two* things that might cause accidents. Explain why each might be dangerous.
 (a) the workshop floor
 (b) unsuitable clothing
 (c) work not held securely
 (d) the pillar drill

170 In a sentence, explain the circumstances in which each of the following should be used.
 (a) goggles or safety glasses
 (b) hairnet or cap
 (c) face mask or respirator
 (d) barrier cream
 (e) leather gloves

Workshop safety

171 Explain the safety precautions you should observe when:
 (a) cleaning copper sheet in acid
 (b) annealing copper sheet on a brazing hearth
 (c) drilling a hole in copper sheet on a drilling machine
 (d) cutting copper sheet with a bench shear or guillotine
 (e) polishing a copper dish on a spindle polishing machine

172 List four metalworking tasks for which goggles or protective spectacles *must* be worn.

173 Describe the safety clothing which must be worn when pouring molten metal in the foundry.

174 Explain two safety precautions you would take when working with glass-reinforced-plastics materials.

Finishing

175 What is galvanizing?

176 Give two reasons why metals are given a chromium plating. Name two other metals used for plating metals.

177 Name suitable surface finishes for the following:
 (a) aluminium dishes
 (b) bicycle frames
 (c) watering cans
 (d) garden gates
 (e) sheet steel litter bins

178 Name two abrasive materials suitable for polishing non-ferrous metals.

179 Give a clear but brief description of two of the typical finishes for mild steel listed below. Name the tools and materials used.
 (a) clean and bright
 (b) blued
 (c) gloss paint
 (d) polythene coated

Plastics

180 Give a brief explanation of the following terms applied to plastics:
 (a) fillers
 (b) inhibitors and accelerators
 (c) release agents
 (d) pinholing

181 Explain the differences between:
 (a) gel and gelcoat
 (b) pot life and shelf life
 (c) thermosetting and thermoplastic
 (d) chopped strand mat and woven glass-fibre

182 You are to embed the working parts of an old alarm clock in resin to make a paperweight. Describe your method of working and state clearly the precautions you would take to ensure a perfect finish.

183 Three simple tests are often applied to plastics — cutting, gentle heating and burning. For each of the materials listed, state what happens in each test:
acrylic, polystyrene, polythene, PVC

184 Describe the laying-up of a glass-fibre tray with a decorative layer. List all the materials you would use. Suggested headings are:
 (a) Mould preparation
 (b) Laying-up techniques
 (c) Finishing and cleaning up
 (d) Safety precautions
 (e) Faults to avoid

185 Draw a simple section to explain how a vacuum-forming machine works. Name two common items which could be produced using this process.

186 For the articles listed below select the most suitable plastics material. Give one good reason for each choice:
yoghurt carton, floor tile, car rear-light covers, liquid-soap bottle, garden hose, dustbin, deep-freeze storage box, TV-cable covering, corrugated roof, beachball, curtain rail

Enamelling and jewellery

187 A 75 mm diameter jewellery casket is made of gilding metal and is to have an enamelled lid as the main decorative feature. Design the structure of the lid. Choose one method of enamelling and explain, in order of procedure, how you would complete the work.

188 When you begin to use enamel faults commonly occur. List three of these common mistakes and explain how each process should have been carried out.

189 The lid of a 75 mm square copper box may be decorated by piercing, punching or etching. Describe *two* of these techniques to produce a simple design.

190 Briefly explain the use of each of the following materials when making a copper dress decoration.
(a) Water of Ayr stone
(b) dilute sulphuric acid
(c) jeweller's rouge
(d) polyurethane lacquer

191 The drawing below shows a full-size belt buckle made from copper. Use sketches and brief notes to explain how you would cut the slots. Name the tools used.

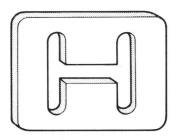

192 The silver pendant shown below is to be decorated by filling the holes with transparent coloured polyester resin. Explain how you would fill the holes. Include a description of preparing the resin.

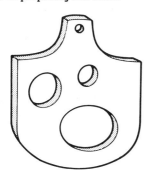

Upholstery

193 What kind of filler would you use for the following jobs? State your reasons.
(a) a kitchen-stool top
(b) a padded headboard for a bed
(c) a lounge chair

194 You have to choose a cover for:
(a) a child's mattress
(b) a seat for an elderly person
List all the considerations you would take into account to help you in your choice.

Design

195 Design a toasting fork to toast teacakes on an open fire.
(a) List the design requirements and make exploratory sketches.
(b) Mock-up the prongs and explain the results of tests made with it.
(c) Make a formal drawing of the revised design.

196 Design a forged bracket to support a double-sided shop sign measuring 600 × 450 mm made from 16 mm marine plywood. On your finished sketch indicate the types and sizes of materials and a suitable finish. How would you secure the bracket to a brick wall?

197 Design a stand to hold three 30 mm diameter cricket stumps in the sports-hall nets. The stumps must move when struck by the ball, and then return to their upright position.

198 Design a house number plate which will be visible from the pavement 10 metres away. It is to be fixed to a brick wall.
Take into consideration appearance, construction, size and finish. Annotate your finished sketch.

199 Choose an article you have designed and made during the last year. State the brief, and indicate the stages you went through to solve the problem.
Write an evaluation of the finished product. How could faults have been avoided during the problem-solving stage of the design?

200 Assume that a ladder is set at 30° to the house when used to reach upstairs windows. Design a tray to hold a one-litre paint tin in an accessible position near the top of the ladder. Consider the ease of fitting and removing the tray.

201 Make sketches of preliminary design ideas for one of the following:
wall rack to hold box spanners, fixed shoe-scrapers, motor trophy from spare parts, paint mixer for use in a power unit, cycle lock, golf trolley, gardening tidy, hose-reel dispenser, sledge, table-tennis table supports, library stools

202 Design an indoor watering can to hold not less than one pint of water. The final design should not drip or spill water where it is not wanted.

203 It is often difficult to draw-file or polish the face of thin material.
Design a device which will fit into an Engineer's vice and hold 3 mm thick sheet metal not more than 38 mm wide. Your final design should be produced as a labelled isometric drawing.

204 Design a jig to make a corner joint of 12 mm square tube brazed together at right-angles to each other. The jig must not interfere with the brazing operation. On your final design drawing show details of the construction, including specifications of screw threads.

205 Analyse the design requirements for a camper's cutlery set consisting of a knife, fork and spoon.

206 Design a holding device for use as a mitre clamp when picture framing.

207 Design an easel to support a painter's canvas. The easel must be stable and easy to adjust, as lightweight as possible and have a means of holding materials such as paint and paint-brushes.

208 The drawing below shows a nutcracker made from cast-iron.
(a) Use notes and simple drawings to explain the principle by which it works.
(b) Show one other principle on which a nutcracker design might be based.
(c) State which method you prefer and give reasons for your choice.

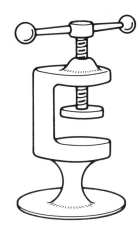

209 Design a sledge to be made from 19 mm diameter mild steel tube. Show how joints would be made and how a seat or platform would be attached to the frame.

210 On an A3 sheet of drawing paper develop your ideas for making one of the following:
   paper punch, vegetable rack, microphone stand, flowerpot display, shoe rack.

211 Develop ideas for making a line winder for a box kite. On your sheet show any mechanism or joints in full-size detail. Name the materials and suggest an appropriate surface finish for each part.

212 Design a toy suitable for a child at nursery school. The design should consist basically of a container which could be used to transport small objects or sand and should be shaped to encourage a child's imaginative play. Specify sizes, materials and finish, and provide a cutting list.

213 Design and make a centre-piece for a dining table which will support a vegetable dish. The design must incorporate safely two 'night light' candles as a source of heat.

214 Design and make a fitting which will diffuse the light from a standard 60 W bulb and, at the same time, demonstrate the qualities of the chosen material. The fitting may be wall mounted or free standing.

Wood

215 (a) Using simple sketches to illustrate your answer, show two methods of producing veneers.
(b) Name two methods of laying veneers and describe on these methods.
(c) What is the advantage of using wild-grained timber as veneer rather than in its solid state?
(d) Use sketches to show what is meant by: (i) stringing, (ii) cross-banding.

216 The door of a small hardwood cabinet is to be made from 12 mm blockboard.
Use sketches and notes to show how you would:
(a) lip the edges of the door
(b) veneer the door with a straight-grained veneer
Would you veneer one or both faces? Give reasons for your answer.

217 Distinguish between and give the main characteristics of:
(a) ash and oak
(b) hardboard and plywood
(c) blockboard and chipboard
Give an appropriate use of each of these six materials.

218 Which joint would be strongest in preventing the rail A be pulled from the leg B?

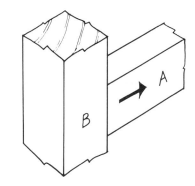

219 When nailing thin pieces of wood together, what can to do the nail to prevent the wood from splitting?

220 State the *four* details you would need to give when buying box of 100 wood screws.

221 The sketch shows a length of dowel prepared for use in a dowelled joint. Explain the groove and the chamfers.

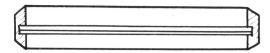

222 What is meant by the term 'impact' adhesive?

223 What grade of glasspaper would you use to:
  (a) rub down the paintwork on an old door
  (b) finish the surface of a hardwood coffee table before polishing it?

224 Why is it usual to apply a brush polish or other sealer to a piece of wood before polishing it with wax polish?

225 Using notes and sketches, show clearly how each of the following *pairs* differ in use and construction.
  (a) a raised head woodscrew and a countersunk woodscrew
  (b) a butt hinge and a tee hinge
  (c) a box lock and a cupboard lock

226 Name the saws most suitable to make each of the cuts shown on the drawing.

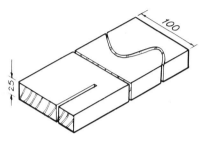

227 The drawings show parts of three different joints in which a chisel is used to remove the waste wood.
  (a) Name the three joints.
  (b) Name the chisels you would use on each joint to remove the waste wood. Use notes and sketches to illustrate your choice.
  (c) Choose *one* of the joints and explain, with sketches, how you would overcome the problems of removing the waste wood cleanly.

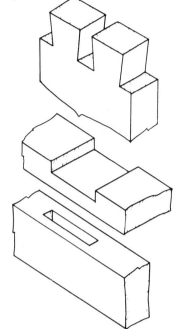

Acknowledgements

I am very grateful for the help given in compiling this book by the following organizations, firms and individuals — many of whom supplied photographs:

Alias (UK)   Aluminium Federation   Ambig   Antocks Lairn
Assay Office   Bahco Record Tools   Barlow-Whitney
E.P. Barrus   Black and Decker   Boxford Machine Tools
Bostik   British Pewter Service   British Railways Board
British Standards Institution   Burgess Power Tools
Cabachon Furniture   W. Canning Materials
Carborundum Abrasives   Carron   Carver   Ceka
Ciba Geigy (UK)   Jonathan Clarke   Colchester Lathes
John Coleman   Concrete Utilities   Cooper Group
Charles Cooper (Hatton Garden)   Clamcleat
Copper Development Association   Crayonne   Cubestore
Alan Dawson   Deltaflow   Denford Machine Tools   Devcon
Dexicon   Durham Chemicals Distributors   Nigel Edmondson
Elementer   Emmerich   English Sewing   Ergonom
Alan Evans   Evode   Falcon Bicycles   Fidor   Flamefast
Formica   Frith Brown Tools   Gabro Engineering
Sir Frederick Gibberd   GKN Screws and Fasteners
Glasgow Museums and Art Galleries   Glasgow School of Art
Glynwed Appliances   John Hall Tools
Harmsworth Townley   Jack Hart   Kenneth Hartwell
Haut-fourneau et Fonderies de Cousances
David Hilton Cutlery   Herzim   Hille
Holcroft Castings and Forgings   W.J. Hooker
Hunterian Art Gallery   ICI   Petrochemicals and Plastics
International Tin Research   Interspace   Kee Klamps
Lead Development Association   Letraset   A. Levermore
B. Lilly and Sons   Isaac Lord   Lune Spinners   3M (UK)
Macreadys   Martindale Protection   Sir Henry Moore
Multicore Solders   Murex Welding Products   Neill Tools
Nike International   OMK Design   Paramo Tools Group
Pel   Pirelli   Plasplugs   Plastic Padding   Pratt Bernard
Prestige Group   Presto   Probus Kitchencraft   Pulsafe
Qualcast   Race Furniture   Rawlplug   Ronson   Rustins
Saltwater   Sandrik   Seid International   Sony
Spear and Jackson   Spectra Automotive Products   Spectrum
Stanley Tools   L.S. Starrett   Startrite Machine Tools
Frankie Stephens   Charles Taylor
John Taylor (Bellfounders)   Tebrax   Tefal Holloware
Herbert Terry and Sons   Thor Hammer   TMT Design
Tritrade   Trylon   TI Raleigh   Vaughans Foundry Tools
Velcro   Victor Castware   Victoria and Albert Museum
Vise-Grip   Vono   John H. Wickersham   Wilkhahm Products
Gavin M. Willacy   Yale Security Products

ESSENTIAL SPORTS

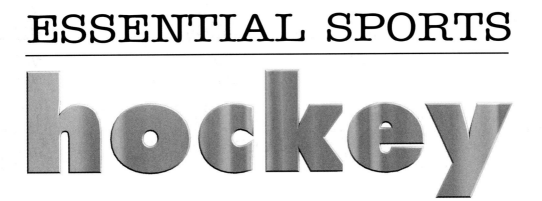

ESSENTIAL SPORTS – HOCKEY
was produced by

David West Children's Books
7 Princeton Court
55 Felsham Road
London SW15 1AZ

Designer: Rob Shone
Editor: James Pickering
Picture Research: Carlotta Cooper

First published in Great Britain by Heinemann Library, Halley Court, Jordan Hill, Oxford OX2 8EJ, part of Harcourt Education. Heinemann is a registered trademark of Harcourt Education Ltd.

07 06 05 04 03
10 9 8 7 6 5 4 3 2 1

ISBN 0 431 17374 5 (HB)
ISBN 0 431 17381 8 (PB)

British Library Cataloguing in Publication Data

Smith, Andy
Hockey. - (Essential Sports)
1. Field Hockey - Juvenile literature
I. Title
796.3'55

Printed and bound in Italy

PHOTO CREDITS :
Abbreviations: t-top, m-middle, b-bottom, r-right, l-left, c-centre.

Front cover - Alex Livesey - Getty Images. Pages 3, 4-5m, 14t, 22t (Scott Barbour), 5, 8tr & br, 26r, 28r (Simon Bruty), 7b, 10 both, 10-11, 14m, 15b, 17m, 18 both, 19l, 20 all, 24t, 25l, 30 (Stanley Chou), 11, 29t (Mike Powell), 12, 22b, 28l (Alex Livesey), 12-13, 16t, 24b (Jack Atley), 17t, 19r, 23b, 25r (Adam Pretty), 21 (Nick Laham), 23t (Al Bello), 26l (Ezra Shaw), 26-27 (Elsa Hasch), 29b (Mike Hewitt), 4-5t, 6 both, 6-7, 7m, 8tl, 15m, 16b, 27 - Getty Images. 8ml & m - Wisden advertisement is reproduced by kind permission of John Wisden & Co. Ltd. 8bl, 9 all - DITA International B.V. (Netherlands) / DITA Field Hockey, LLC (USA).

An explanation of difficult words can be found in the glossary on page 31.

ESSENTIAL SPORTS

hockey

Andy Smith

Heinemann
LIBRARY

Contents

Alex Lupton of the 'Hockeyroos' – Australia's women's team, and the 2000 Olympic champions

Morris Brown College stadium in Atlanta, USA – one of the venues at the 1996 Olympics

Hockey sticks are always in demand in India.

Introduction

Hockey is derived from a number of ancient stick and ball games, although it was not known as hockey until the late 18th century. In its modern form, it is reckoned to be the fastest team game in the world, and it has become even quicker since the 1980s with the widespread use of artificial pitches. The stronghold of the game is in India and Pakistan, though it is widely played in South Africa, Australia, Germany, the Netherlands (the 2000 Olympic men's champions) and in Great Britain, where the club game is flourishing. The EHL Men's Premier League contains clubs from Doncaster in the north to Canterbury in the south east, while the EHL Women's Premier League is concentrated in the Midlands and the south.

History of the game

How did hockey begin? Probably when one of our ancestors picked up a stick and hit a stone down a track.

Shinty evolved in Scotland from a game said to have been played by Celtic legends. Apparently, King Alexander of Scotland was a good player in the 12th century.

WILD BEGINNINGS

Drawings on ancient tombs in the Nile Valley depict two men holding sticks with curved ends, with a ball in between them. As the tombs were built around 2,000 BC, it is assumed that the game has been around for about 4,000 years. Therefore hockey is the forerunner of all sports played with an implement, such as cricket, golf and polo. Hockey has similarities with the Irish sport of hurling, which dates back to 1,300 BC. The Romans played a game called paganica, in which a ball, filled with feathers, was propelled with a club.

By the 1920s, hockey was regarded all around the world to be a women's game.

THE FORMATIVE YEARS

Hockey was played in English public schools in Victorian times, while the first club, Blackheath in south east London, was formed around 1861. It was a rough game, played in a massive area of 247 metres by 64. A national association was set up in 1886, and the first international, Wales against Ireland, was played in 1895. Early forms of hockey were considered too barbaric for women to play, but the first women's club, Moseley Ladies in west London, was founded in 1887.

In the 20th century, hockey became a favourite sport for girls at school.

COMPETITION

Olympic hockey was first played in 1908 in London, when Britain won gold, but the sport was not included in 1924, as it did not have an international ruling body. The International Federation was formed immediately, though the British Hockey Association did not join until 1970. Until recently, hockey was one of the few remaining amateur sports. Today, coaches and players may be paid.

A GAME OF TWO HALVES ...

British women's hockey remained separate from the men's association until 1997, over 100 years after the first women's club was formed. Progress of the women's game was hampered by the idea that the game should not be played for prizes or rewards – an attitude which persisted until the 1960s – and concerns about the clothing worn on the field.

Germany won the 2002 World Cup, after beating Australia 2-1 in March of that year.

At the 1952 Olympics, the Netherlands and West Germany used old-fashioned English sticks.

INDIAN STICKS

India's first hockey clubs were started in the 1880s. As a measure of how quickly the game rose in popularity there, India won Olympic gold for the first time in 1928, and went on to win at the next five Olympic Games! In the 1950s, Indian hockey stick makers introduced a stick with a short toe which gave better control. It soon came into general use, replacing the longer and heavier English stick.

Kit

Like most sports, hockey has developed over the years, not least in the quality of the kit available.

Hockey kit in the 1920s borrowed from other sports – especially cricket and soccer.

KIT DEVELOPMENT

Little is known about the kit used in early forms of hockey until 1867, when boys at Tonbridge School in Kent are said to have made their own sticks from branches, cut from nearby woods and bent into shape. Early women players had to wear skirts that reached within 25 mm of the ground, and straw hats!

The Indian national team in their dressing room cluttered with kit

A 1930s advert for Wisden hockey kit

The outdoor stick weighs up to 800 g.

Indoor stick

Goalkeeper's stick

Hockey sticks being made in India, 1996

STICKS

Most woods have been used to make hockey sticks – even oak in the early days. Holly and maple were tried until the 1920s when the standard stick was ash with a cane handle. By the 1950s, Indian stick manufacturers were using mulberry, which can be easily shaped. Today, some sticks have a polyurethane plastic finish. Others are stiffened with fibreglass.

THE BALL

Different balls are used on different surfaces. Leather balls are best on grass, while dimpled plastic balls are used on artificial turf. In senior games the ball weighs about 155 g, and 100 g in youngsters' hockey.

Balls used in indoor hockey are usually white or yellow.

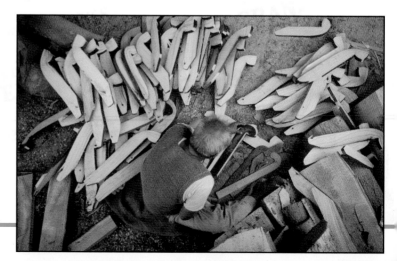

TECH TIPS – PLAYER PROTECTION

As hockey is such a fast game, played with a hard ball, every player must be adequately protected from injury. Gum shields and shin guards are essential. Shin guards can vary from pads covering the lower shin, to prosthetic guards covering the ankle and the whole shin bone.

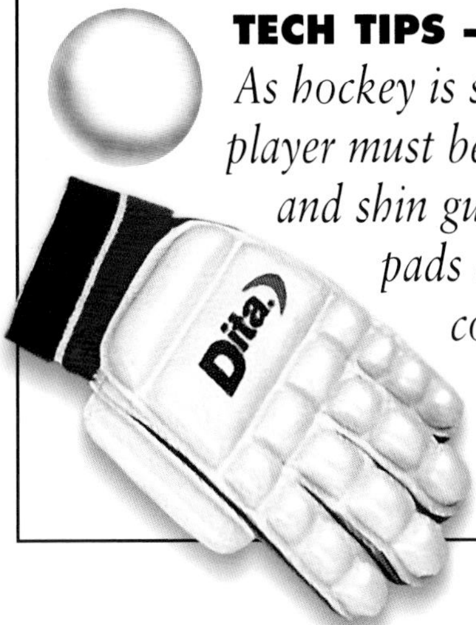

The development of protective equipment has been extensive in the modern game.

BOOTS

You should choose boots that feel the most comfortable, with plenty of support for the foot and heel. Use long studs in wet conditions, short studs where it's firmer. On artificial turf, wear pimpled soles. For comfort, some players choose boots that are half a size too big and wear an extra pair of socks.

Today, hockey boots are smart, durable and comfortable.

GOALKEEPER'S KIT

This specialized position requires special kit. Wearing a helmet takes some getting used to, and it is no use having one that does not fit properly and obscures your view in any direction. Right and left gloves differ. The right, or the stick holding hand, has padding on the outside, while the left is padded on the inside to prevent bruising when stopping shots with the hand.

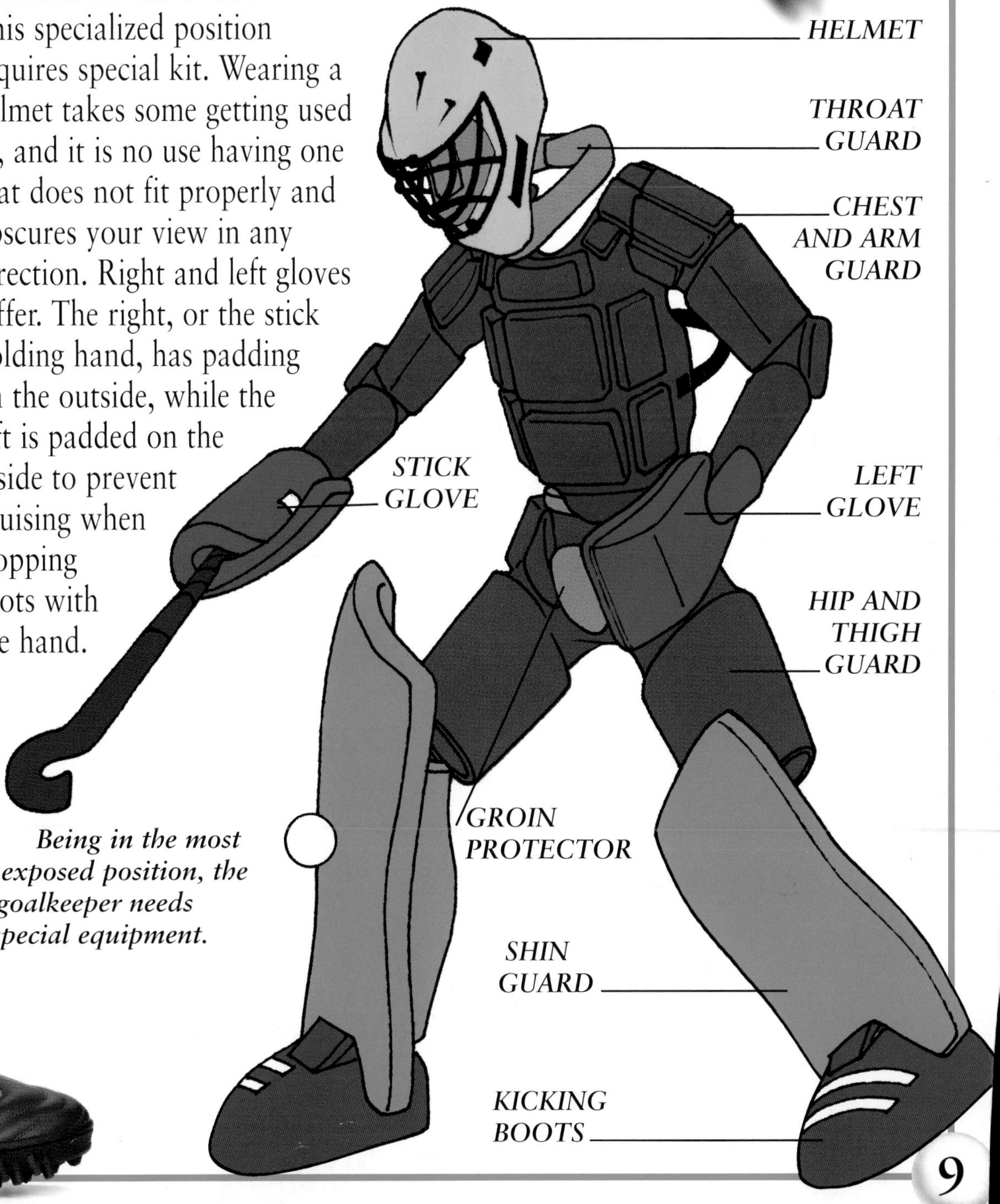

Being in the most exposed position, the goalkeeper needs special equipment.

HELMET

THROAT GUARD

CHEST AND ARM GUARD

STICK GLOVE

LEFT GLOVE

HIP AND THIGH GUARD

GROIN PROTECTOR

SHIN GUARD

KICKING BOOTS

Rules of the game

For a game in which the ball frequently moves at speeds up to 160 km/h – it's no surprise that two umpires are needed.

Foul! No player may trip, push, strike or handle another player.

The card system for rough play – green is a warning; yellow means at least five minutes off the field; red sends a player off for the rest of the match.

GAME AIMS

Simply, the main aim of the game is to score more goals than the opposition, and so win the match. The goals are twelve feet wide and seven feet high. These are smaller than football goals, but nobody is allowed to shoot from outside a 16-yard area. So, you often see a defensive line-up with all the players from one team lined up in a wall, blocking the route to goal.

A penalty stroke penalises foul play in the 16-yard area, or a foul anywhere on the field that prevents a probable goal.

RULES

As in football, offside is a feature of hockey, though only inside the 25-yard line. An attacker is offside if there are fewer than two of the opposition between him and the goal line. Obstruction is also a foul, though uniquely in hockey, this is when the player in possession shields the ball from the opposition. The penalty awarded by the umpire for unfair play could be a free hit, penalty corner or penalty stroke, depending on where the foul occurred.

OFFICIALS

The umpires, in conjunction with a timekeeper, keep control of the game. The umpires take one half of the pitch each, operating from opposite sidelines. In the early days, an umpire could only give a decision after an appeal had been made by one of the sides. In the early 1900s that changed, so that the umpires had complete charge.

TECH TIPS – UMPIRES' AREAS OF RESPONSIBILITY

Pitch measurements were drawn up when imperial units (inches, feet and yards) were used instead of metric units. One yard equals 0.914 metres. Standing on opposite sidelines, umpires are responsible for the whole area inside one 25-yard line and for half the area between the two 25-yard lines. Here, umpires deal with fouls coming towards them. The diagram below shows how this works.

The umpire is well positioned to see Australia's goal against Spain in the 1996 Olympics.

Pitch and positions

Legend has it that Native American tribes played a form of hockey lasting several hours, with the goals kilometres apart and about 1,000 players on each side. Times have changed!

Games on synthetic pitches are rarely called off, even in heavy rain.

THE PITCH

Top class games are played on full-sized pitches. The field should be 100 yards long by 60 yards wide. This gives internationals and top class players room to move, and pass accurately and quickly. Less experienced players are better suited to a smaller pitch, perhaps 60 yards long and 45 yards wide. Synthetic surfaces are rapidly taking over from natural grass.

MARKINGS

These are 3 inches wide. The centre line divides the pitch into two halves. The side lines and back lines indicate when the ball is out of play. A penalty corner can be awarded for a foul within the 25-yard lines. Goals may be scored within the shooting circles, and penalties must be taken from the penalty spot.

A full-sized pitch marked out for a game

100 yds (92.5 m)

BACK LINE

5 yds (4.5 m)

7 yds (6.5 m)

SIDE LINE

SHOOTING CIRCLE
The goalkeeper cannot kick the ball outside the shooting circle. The ball cannot be lofted deliberately into this area from a distance away.

PENALTY SPOT

10 yds (9 m)

16 yds (14.5 m)

10-YARD MARK

60 yds (55.5 m)

Utrecht, Holland, venue of the 1998 World Cup Final

TECH TIPS – ZONES

The most important task when attacking is to keep possession of the ball. When defending, your aim is to regain the ball. Each side should use every area, or zone, of the field to gain an advantage over the opposition, whether they are attacking or defending (right).

Attacking zone – *using speed and thought, create goal-scoring chances.*

Midfield zone – *keep possession, look to attack.*

Defensive zone – *mark, challenge and prevent shooting chances.*

If the attacking side knocks the ball over the back line, the defence restarts the game with a 16-yard hit-out.

CENTRE LINE

25-YARD LINE
All players except the goalkeeper and penalty taker must be beyond this line during penalty strokes. Penalties are awarded for fouls committed inside the shooting circle.

If the defending side accidentally knocks the ball over the back line, the attacking side restarts the game with a hit or push from the 5-yard mark.

A ball deliberately knocked over the back line by the defending side gives the attacking side a penalty corner from the 10-yard mark.

When the ball goes over the side line, the game is restarted with a push or hit. The side touching the ball last gives away possession.

16-YARD MARK

5-YARD MARK

5 yds
(4.5 m)

16 yds
(14.5 m)

25 yds
(23 m)

3 in (7.5 cm)

2 in (5 cm)

7 feet
(2.1 m)

18 in (46 cm)

GOAL LINE

4 yds
(3.7 m)

SURFACES
Hockey was almost always played on natural grass until about 25 years ago – it was called 'field hockey' in the USA to separate it from 'ice hockey'. The game is much faster on synthetic surfaces, and they require much less attention than grass fields. The last major tournament on grass was the 1982 World Cup.

TECH TIPS – THE PLAYERS
The usual formation, especially in schools, is the 1-2-3-5 line-up (below). Sometimes, the inside forwards are withdrawn towards midfield, making a 1-2-3-2-3 formation.

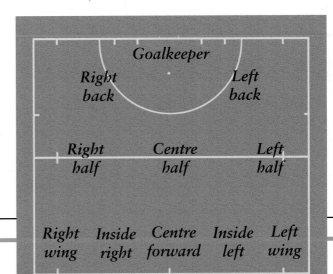

Goalkeeper

Right back   Left back

Right half   Centre half   Left half

Right wing   Inside right   Centre forward   Inside left   Left wing

13

Goalkeeping

Artificial pitches and the development of protective equipment have radically changed goalkeeping. But the goalkeeper's essential skills never change – confidence and bravery.

HANDLING THE BALL

Peter Mills, the England goalkeeper in the 1970s, was the first to stop high balls with his left hand. This is more difficult than it sounds, because it is against the rules to hold the ball or propel it forwards. Keepers can deflect the ball wide of the goal, or if the shot is coming straight at them, use the flat of the hand to drop the ball downwards but not forwards. Modern gloves make this a less painful exercise than in Mills's day.

Move off the line to confront the attacker and narrow the angle.

POSITIONING

In general, the goalkeeper stands between the ball and the centre of the goal to narrow the angle available to the attacker. As the player moves into the circle, the keeper advances a stride or two off the line. If the ball is passed, the keeper must move to a new position to cover the new angle of attack.

TECH TIPS – ANGLES

A goalkeeper should be adjusting position at all times according to the whereabouts of the ball. When facing a lone attacker, the keeper should force the attacker to go to the keeper's open or stronger side.

Attack from the front – the keeper comes out to narrow angles.

Attack from the side – keeper stays back and guards goalpost, leaving narrow shooting angle on one side.

SKILL DRILL – SHOT STOPPING

This is an exercise that improves skills and sharpens up reactions. The keeper starts on the knees, and the feeder hits the ball to either side. The keeper dives to save, then immediately gets back on to the knees to stop the next shot.

Practise diving with your legs together to form a solid barrier.

Practise with a team mate using light training balls or tennis balls.

Try the same routine from a squatting, then a standing position. Other players can be used to hit rebounds.

USING THE STICK

It is not always possible to use the pads or the left glove to save every shot. The goalkeeper should be prepared to use the stick for shots that are out of normal reach. The keeper should be balanced, weight slightly forwards, eyes on the ball. React to the ball and aim to use the left hand. But if this is impossible, when the ball is high and wide of the keeper, use the length of the right arm and the stick to stop the shot.

When the ball is out of reach of the left hand, use the stick.

Eyes on the ball, weight forwards, use the pads to block the shot.

KICKING

A goalkeeper should use his pads to stop low, straight shots. Stay poised, leaning forwards so your weight will provide momentum, and keep your eyes on the ball. As the shot comes in, thrust the pad forwards with your head over the knee, and block it. The ball should then be pushed away with the stick or kicked to the sidelines, not back into the danger area in the middle of the circle.

Defence

The defence's main task is to prevent a goal being scored against their team, but they are also expected to gain possession, to set up attacks.

One-on-one marking. Between the opponent and the goal, stay close, eyes on the ball.

DEFENSIVE AWARENESS

Defenders must mark attackers to prevent passes between them, to intercept passes or to force an error. The three main methods of marking are one-on-one, zonal marking or a combination of the two. In one-on-one, the marker should be positioned between the opponent and the goal, eyes on the ball. Zonal marking is where each defender takes charge of a particular area and any opponents who come into that area. In combination marking, it is one-on-one around the ball with the covering defenders in zones.

DEFENDING SET PIECES

Only four players plus the goalkeeper are allowed to defend at penalty corners. The keeper is equipped to deal with shots on goal. One player advances from the line to obstruct the striker. Another is behind and left of the first defender, to cover passes to other attackers. The two other defenders cover the goal either side of the keeper.

Defending a penalty corner. The goalkeeper organises the defence. It is important for defenders to practise the drill used at set pieces, such as penalties and free hits.

A reverse stick block, expertly performed

TECH TIPS – GRIP

In the open grip, the left hand is at the top of the stick, with the right hand half way down. In the reverse position, the stick is turned by the left hand, and supported loosely by the right.

Open stick grip

Reverse stick grip

A UNITED FRONT

The defence is a team within a team. Wherever possible, the defence should work on tactics and strategy together in training sessions. Use attack versus defence drills, where the attackers outnumber defenders.

BLOCK AND TACKLE

Tackles should ideally see the defender gaining possession and setting up his or her team's attack. It is important to watch the ball and time the intervention correctly. Jockey for position and try to force your opponent on to the reverse stick side (the defender's open stick side).

Daniel Sproule of Australia tackles the Indian defence in Kuala Lumpur, 2001.

TECH TIPS – TACKLING

Tackling opponents is a matter of timing and concentration. Stay balanced, don't dive in too soon, wait for the chance to strike.

1 Open stick block – attacker is guided to defender's right, weight moves to left leg with stick held close to ground, forming barrier.
2 Reverse stick block – defender uses reverse stick if attacker moves to defender's left.
3 Jab tackle – head of stick is pushed towards ball, right leg providing force. Ball is struck at its base to move it up and away.

1

2

3

Midfield

Being in the engine room of the team requires skill and stamina.

PLAYING THROUGH THE MIDDLE

No team can score a goal without having possession of the ball. The centre midfield is the route through which the defence can channel an attack. The midfielder also has a defensive role – winning the ball from the opposition.

Once the ball is under control, be aware of the options. Which team mate is in the best position to receive a pass?

RECEIVING THE BALL

Players who can take a pass and instantly control it are invaluable. The open or reverse stick methods can be used for receiving a pass, before the player dribbles or shoots. Players should practise stopping the ball, before moving it on, as well as controlling the pass on the move.

A player with good control wins extra space and time.

SKILL DRILL – PASSING

Practise your passing and receiving skills with a team mate. Run parallel to each other, passing the ball between yourselves. Control the pass, dribble a few yards and pass it back. This is a simple, but invaluable skill.

Path taken by ball

Left player uses reverse stick to receive and pass ball.

Aim pass in front of receiver, so they can run on to it without stopping or slowing down.

Right player uses open stick to receive and pass ball.

1 THE PUSH – *Hands apart, the body stays low, weight transfers from the right to left foot. As the right arm pushes forward, the left hand pulls back, giving power to the stroke.*

2 THE REVERSE PUSH – *For left-to-right passes, the stick is reversed and the ball struck using a short downswing.*

3 THE SCOOP – *Hands apart, right foot placed to the side of the ball, left leg pushes weight forward, stick head gets under the ball which is lifted into the air.*

4 RECEIVING – *Stay upright and balanced, keep your eyes and stick in line with the ball, keep the stick still and cushion the ball on impact.*

PASSING THE BALL

Knowing when to pass and when to hold the ball can only be learned through practice. Three types of pass are shown above. Others are the 'hit', used for passing the ball quickly over longer distances; the 'slap' is similar to the push but harder over a long distance; the 'flick' is used to lift the ball into the air. For passing to be effective in match situations, the passer must know which team mate is in the best position to receive a pass, and be in control of the ball.

A congested midfield, as Australia play South Africa.

MIDFIELD BATTLES

Some coaches ban the term 'midfield', because they believe it creates a defensive attitude in players' minds. Nevertheless, the defensive element of the midfielder's game is every bit as important as attack.

Craig Parnham plays a push pass for England against Japan in the 2002 World Cup.

If you keep the ball under close control, your opponent has less chance of making a successful tackle.

Attack

Attacking play in hockey means much more than simply blasting shots towards the goal.

CLOSE CONTROL

Keeping possession of the ball is essential. Surrendering the ball too easily to the opposition results in the loss of the game. If you practise keeping possession of the ball, you will soon build up the confidence to keep defenders at bay.

DRIBBLING

While hockey is essentially a passing game, there will be times when a pass is not possible. For example, if the opposition successfully marks you, dribbling the ball or running with it under control of the stick might be necessary. Once a player has learned how to dribble, he or she should practise dummying or dodging to outwit any opponents.

TECH TIPS – DRIBBLING

When dribbling at speed, it is important to keep the ball in a position where the legs move at a natural stride, not too close or too far ahead.

Basic open stick dribble – The ball is ahead and to the right of the feet. The head is held up, making passes easier to spot.

*Indian dribble –
1 The ball is moved forwards from right to left.
2 The stick is reversed ...
3 ... and the ball is moved from left to right.*

1

2

3

Having beaten the opponent, look for the passing options.

Keeping your eyes on the ball is the key to success in any ball game.

TECH TIPS – DODGING

Dodging means outwitting and beating an opponent in a one-on-one situation. It is important that the ball is under tight control – if it is too far ahead, the opponent can easily make the tackle. No defender can make contact with an attacker's body or stick when making a tackle, so the advantage is with the dribbler.

1

2

3

Right to left feint –
1 Move to your right side (defender's left).
2 With the defender leaning to the right, sharply drag the ball left.
3 Use reverse stick to bring the ball under control.

DODGING

When dodging, you should give your opponent the false impression that you are about to move one way. As your opponent commits to covering that move, and leans one way, you should quickly change direction and sweep past him or her on the other side.

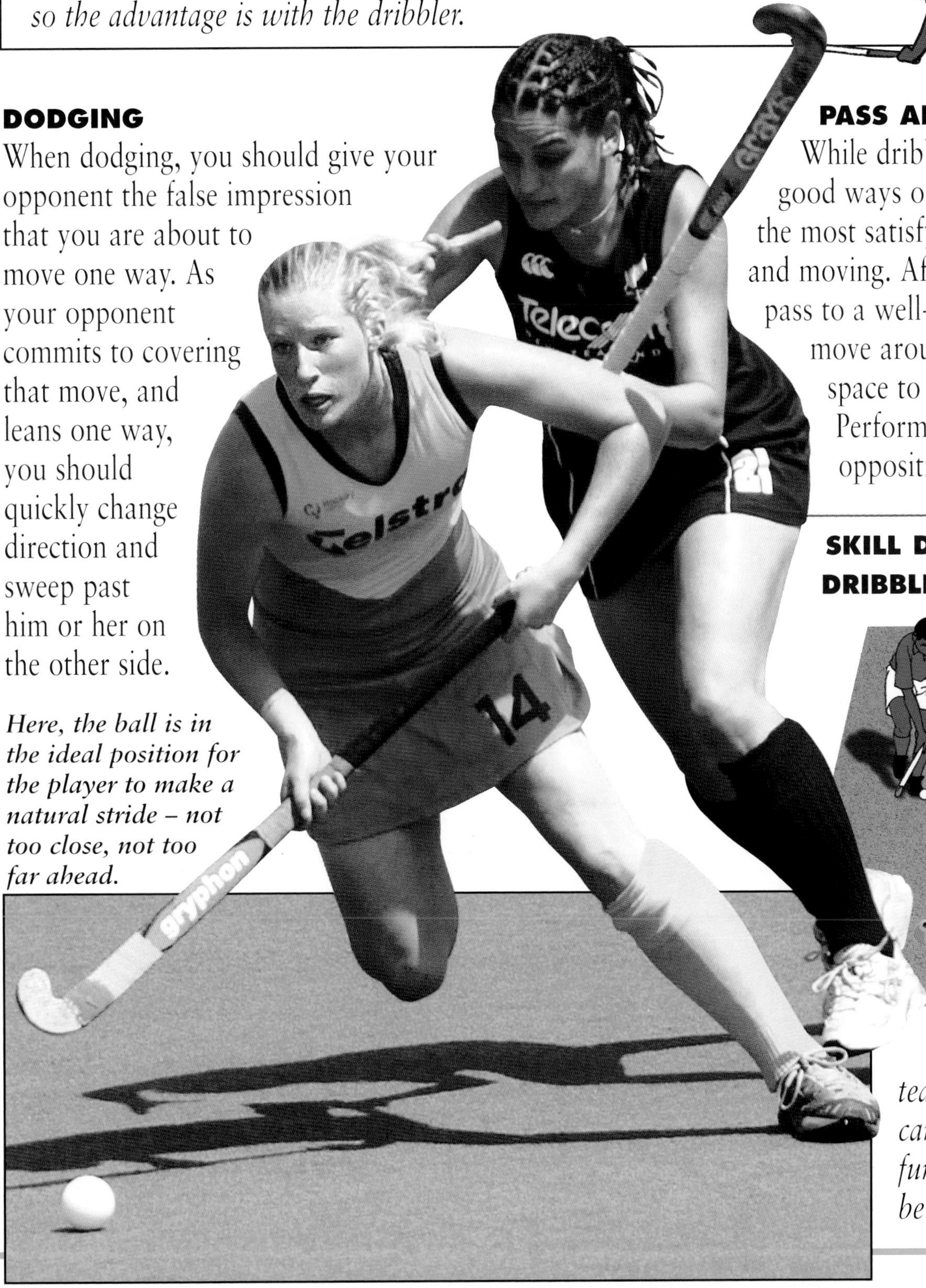

Here, the ball is in the ideal position for the player to make a natural stride – not too close, not too far ahead.

PASS AND MOVE

While dribbling and dodging are good ways of beating an opponent, the most satisfying way is by passing and moving. After controlling the ball, pass to a well-placed team mate and move around the opposition into space to receive the return pass. Performed at speed, this has the opposition chasing shadows!

SKILL DRILL – DRIBBLE RACING

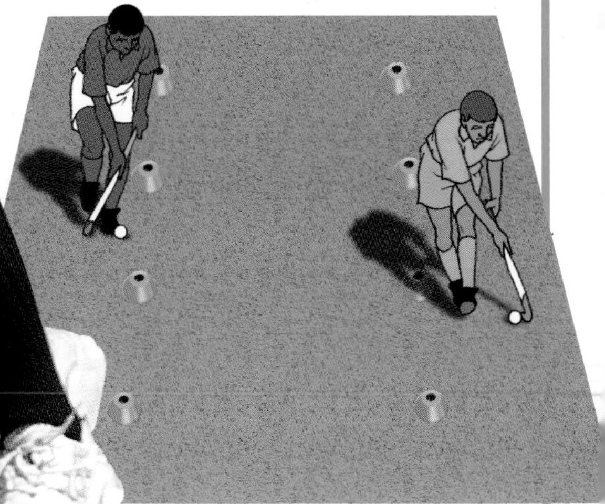

Competing against a team mate in a dribble race can make the drill more fun. Vary the distance between the cones.

21

Teamwork

No player, no matter how skilful, can win a match alone. Communication within the team is essential.

ATTACKING AS A TEAM

To create openings in the opposition's defence, your team needs to be able to change the point of attack, to pass the ball out to the wings to stretch the defence, and pull players out of position by constant movement off the ball. Consequently, every player in the attacking team has a part to play.

Attack as a team, supporting your team mates all the way.

Team talks harness team spirit. Encouragement is essential, and being aware of the game plan is vital.

DEFENDING AS A TEAM

When the opposition has the ball, the defenders must adopt their positions quickly, otherwise the attack will reach the goal. They must defend as soon as possession is lost. In the opposition's circle, forwards should try to delay the ball being cleared, to allow their own defenders to take up position.

Defenders

Defensive triangle

Attack

Attack aims to disrupt defensive shape and create space.

Defence aims to maintain shape and cover attackers.

SKILL DRILL – ATTACK AND DEFENCE

This is a useful exercise at training sessions. Match your team's attack and defence against each other. Concentrate on special parts of the game, such as attacking down the flanks, so that the defence can become accustomed to using the sideline as a barrier for the opposition.

Defending a penalty corner – do the job you've been assigned.

SET PIECES

Set pieces occur when the referee blows for an infringement or when the ball goes out of play. The eight set pieces are penalty corners, penalty strokes, corners, free hits, 16-yard hits, hit- or push-ins, the push back and the bully. The attack and defence should both practise moves to master their set pieces.

TECH TIPS – PENALTY CORNERS

Defending sides can only use four players plus the goalkeeper within the circle. The rest must be beyond the half-way line. Attacking players may be anywhere on the field except in the circle, except of course the player putting the ball into play.

Defenders have to be ready to combat the attacking side's tricks.

Attackers attempt to deceive the defence with decoy runners and strikers.

Australia's Jenny Morris takes a shot.

TECH TIPS – FORMATIONS

Your team should make use of the special abilities available from each player. This may mean altering formation to accommodate a sweeper or an extra midfielder.

1-2-3-5 – the basic attacking formation

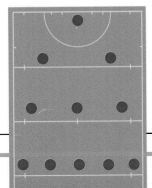

1-1-3-2-4 – sweeper strengthens defence.

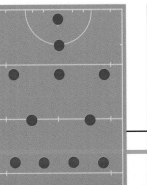

1-1-3-3-3 – midfield gives team flexibility.

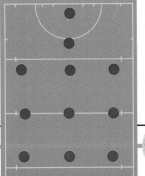

Going for goal

It's a simple idea – the team that scores the largest number of goals wins. But putting the ball into the net is more difficult than it seems.

HITTING THE TARGET

Most goals in hockey, apart from direct shots after penalty corners, are scored from within a 10-metre radius of the goal. Even from that distance, accuracy cannot be guaranteed. You can improve your chances by staying balanced. Good strikers are strong in the legs, so even at an awkward angle, they have a stable base for the shot.

STRENGTH AND SPEED

Obviously, the harder a player can hit a shot and the quicker the ball travels towards the goal, the more chance it has of eluding the goalkeeper and finding the back of the net. But hard shots are not just a matter of how strong a player is – timing is a key factor, and taking your eyes off the ball could easily result in a scuffed shot.

Even a goalkeeper wearing full kit can't protect every part of the goal.

The slap hit is a low-body position, with the right hand down the stick with, as ever, eyes on the ball.

SKILL DRILL – ACCURATE SHOOTING

This drill helps shooting and balance. On a signal, the keeper runs to the five-yard mark and back. At the same time, the striker dribbles the ball around a cone placed five yards from the top of the D, returns and shoots at goal.

Repeat drill with cone to left of goal.

Adjust cone distance, so that shot coincides with keeper getting back in position.

TECH TIPS – SHOOTING

A good goal-scorer never has to think about which shot to use – it is just a natural reaction. But you can only develop this level of instinct by practising hard. Try to add as many shooting techniques to your repertoire as you can.

1 THE HIT – Hands together at the top of the stick, the left foot moves alongside the ball. Your weight shifts to the left leg, as your arms swing down. Straighten your wrists as the ball is struck. The stick follows the direction of the ball.

2 THE SLAP – Similar to the hit shot, but the right hand is further down the stick and the body is lower. The right arm gives the ball speed.

3 THE FLICK – With hands apart, the weight shifts to the left leg as the stick head lifts the ball. Hold the ball for as long as possible before flicking it away.

POISE AND BALANCE

As soon as the ball has been controlled in the circle, the attacker should shoot as quickly as possible, to prevent the goalkeeper moving into a covering position. Ideally, the striker should be well balanced with a good body position.

Following through helps direct the shot on target.

It is not always possible to remain balanced at speed.

STAYING SHARP

Regular goal-scorers should be prepared to shoot at any time. The successful striker should leave the opposition off-balance. Your chances of shooting and scoring, whether by speed or by stealth, can be increased with practice. Strikers who regularly find the net always boost the morale of their team.

25

Hockey variations

Stick and ball games are common throughout the world. New styles are always being added to this range of sports.

The matches between Kilkenny and Tipperary, in the All Ireland Hurling tournament, are always a sell-out at Croke Park in Dublin.

HURLING

Like hockey, hurling is renowned as one of the fastest team games in the world. It is a national sport in Ireland, administered by the Gaelic Athletic Association. A 15-a-side game, the object is to drive the 4.5 oz (127 g) ball through goalposts 21 feet high and 21 feet apart. As in rugby, there is a crossbar, eight feet from the ground. Three points are scored when the ball goes under the bar, one point when it goes over. In Scotland, shinty is closely related to hurling and hockey.

LACROSSE

Lacrosse is a ten-a-side game. You score by throwing the 5 oz (142 g) rubber ball into a six foot square goal. The lacrosse racquet, or crosse, is shaped like a hockey stick with a triangular net at the end for catching and holding the ball.

Unlike in hockey, personal contact, such as shoulder charging, is allowed in Lacrosse.

Russia met Canada in the World Junior Ice Hockey Championship in Manitoba, in 1999.

MINI HOCKEY

Mini hockey was developed to provide an introduction to the game, and a basic grounding for young players. Learning the skills of hockey with a small stick and smaller, lighter balls has encouraged many eight- to ten-year-olds to progress to the full game when they are older.

ICE HOCKEY

Ice hockey in its modern form dates back to the 1860s, when the game was played on the frozen Kingston Harbour in Ontario. Canada remains a stronghold of the game, with teams playing in the National Hockey League (NHL) in the USA – the foremost professional league in the world. In the UK, there have been various attempts to popularize the sport since the 1920s. Currently, the Superleague involves teams from all over the country, including the Belfast Giants from Northern Ireland.

ODD HOCKEY

Ever heard of octopush? This strange development of the game is played underwater! Another adaptation, taking in elements of both hockey and ice hockey, is roller hockey. Hockey on rollerskates became an international sport in 1910, when an inter-club tournament was held in Paris. The first European Championships were staged in England in 1926.

Octopush – not for the faint-hearted. Only decent swimmers need apply.

27

The world of hockey

Hockey was once a strictly amateur game, and winning cups and medals was frowned upon. Today, it has a more professional image.

HOCKEY TODAY

The game is now played in almost 100 countries on six continents. It is a major sport in India and Pakistan, widely played throughout Europe and also in South Africa and Australia. In South America, Argentina is now a major force, especially in the women's game.

THE WORLD CUP

Hockey grew enormously in popularity between 1970 and 1980. The European Cup was inaugurated in 1970. A year later, the first World Cup was held and won, not surprisingly, by Pakistan who have taken the men's world title on four occasions. The women's World Cup was established in 1974, and women's hockey was first played at the Olympics in Moscow in 1980. Argentina built on the promise of their Olympic silver in 2000, by winning the World title in 2002.

The top hockey nations compete for the World Cup. There have been ten men's tournaments so far. After Pakistan, the most successful men's teams have come from the Netherlands, who have won three times.

In India, children are encouraged to play hockey from an early age.

WORLD CUP WINNERS

Surprisingly, India has only won the World Cup once.

MEN	WOMEN
1 Pakistan (1971, 1978, 1982, 1994)	1 Netherlands (1974, 1978, 1983, 1986, 1990)
2 Netherlands (1973, 1990, 1998)	2 West Germany (1976, 1981)
3 India (1975)	3 Australia (1994, 1998)
4 Australia (1986)	
5 Germany (2002)	4 Argentina (2002)

THE OLYMPICS

Men's hockey was included in the Olympics for the first time in London, in 1908. Four of the six teams involved were from Britain, and the England team took the gold. India dominated the Olympics from 1928 to 1956, winning all six gold medals without losing a single game. More recently, the gold medals have gone to Europe – Britain (1988), Germany (1992), the Netherlands (1996 and 2000). The women's gold medallists in 1980 were Zimbabwe. Since then, Australia have won three times (1988, 1996 and 2000) while the Netherlands (1984), and Spain (1992) have also taken gold.

Hertfordshire and Manchester contested the BAA Millennium Youth Games Grand Final in August 2000.

Against the odds, Spain beat Australia 2-1 in the Olympic semi-finals in 1996.

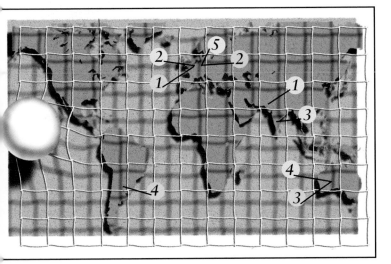

TOURNAMENTS

International tournaments now abound in hockey. As well as the Olympics, the World Cup and the European Cup, the Asian Games began in 1958, and have been dominated by India and Pakistan. The Pan-American Games started in 1967, the first winners being Argentina. Elsewhere, Oceania, Australia and New Zealand compete annually for the Manning Cup. The East African Championship features Kenya and Zimbabwe as its strongest participants.

Staying fit

Fitness is essential if you're to last the pace for 70 minutes.

To enjoy the game to the full, you need to stay fit. Training helps you to prepare for matches, prevents injuries and speeds up recovery.

HEALTHY EATING

Players who do not stick to a healthy, balanced diet are soon found out at top level. Eat foods from the basic groups – dairy products, meat, fish and chicken, fruit, vegetables and cereals – and you should absorb enough vitamins and energy. On training or match days, eat a couple of hours before the start, then drink liquids – plain water is best – to prevent dehydration.

EXERCISE

Use the pre-season period to build up stamina and strength. A full game lasts 70 minutes, during which you will be expected to sprint, run and turn without tiring. Mix sprint drills with longer distance running, time your runs and aim to improve each time. Gym work can improve your strength. During the season, work on flexibility. As well as team training to improve understanding and skills, try the circuit drill carrying a hockey stick. Running, jumping and turning with the stick will become second nature – a useful asset on the field. And don't forget to warm up before each match.

TECH TIPS – KEEPING THE TANK FULL

On match days, eat breakfast about six hours before the start, with foods that are easily digestible. Sip liquids through the morning. Lunch should also be easily digestible. Beware of drinking too many heavy liquids during the match. In the evening, replace all that lost energy!

Timetable for match day. Try to stick to the same routine each time. You might feel like eating a huge lunch, but you'll feel better if you don't!

12pm,
Light lunch –
Pasta or jacket
potato with beans
or cottage cheese   Liquids
Liquids
8am, Breakfast –
fruit juice, cereal   3pm, The match –
or porridge, fruit,   liquids during
yoghurt, toast with   game, banana at
jam or honey   half-time
7pm, Dinner – meal rich
in carbohydrates and
proteins, isotonic drink   Liquids

SKILL DRILL – FEELING THE BURN

Circuit training in the gym is an ideal way to keep fit. Set up four or five different exercise areas. One might be for bench steps, another for press-ups, a third for skipping. Rest for 45 seconds after each circuit.

20 m

1 Dribble around cones.
2 Jog. 3 Do ten sit-ups.
4 Sprint. 5 Jog.
6 Do ten press-ups.

Glossary

DEHYDRATION loss of fluids in the body, resulting in energy loss

DRIBBLING running with the ball under close control

DUMMYING making to go one way, then confusing the opponent by darting the other

FEINT first move when dummying

MARK being close enough to an opponent to tackle or intercept a pass

OFFSIDE an attacker is offside inside the 25-yard line if there are fewer than two defenders between him and the goal

ONE-ON-ONE when one defender marks one attacker

OPEN STICK normal stick position with the toe outwards

PROSTHETIC artificial, usually plastic, referring to protective kit

REVERSE STICK stick position with the toe inwards

SET PIECE methods of restarting the game, such as penalty corners and free hits, after the ball has gone out of play or infringements

SYNTHETIC artificial, referring to playing surfaces other than natural grass

ZONAL MARKING when players mark areas, not opponents

Further information

Sports Council
16 Upper Woburn Place,
London,
WC1

The Hockey Association
Norfolk House,
102 Saxon Gate West,
Milton Keynes,
MK9 2EP

The All England Women's Hockey Association
51 High Street,
Shrewsbury,
SY1 1ST

International Federation of Women's Hockey
Associations
44a Westminster Palace Gardens,
London,
SW1

Federation Internationale de Hockey
Boulevard du Regent 55,
1000 Brussels,
Belgium

Hockey Australia
Level 1, 433–435 South Road,
Bentleigh,
Vic 3204
www.hockey.org.au

International Olympic Committee
Chateau de Vidy,
Case Postale 356,
CH-1007 Lausanne,
Switzerland

Index